"Getting History Right"

"Getting History Right"

East and West German Collective Memories of the Holocaust and War

Mark A. Wolfgram

Lewisburg
Bucknell University Press

Published by Bucknell University Press
Co-published with the Rowman & Littlefield Publishing Group, Inc.
4501 Forbes Boulevard, Suite 200, Lanham, Maryland 20706
www.rlpgbooks.com

Estover Road, Ploymouth PL6 7PY, United Kingdom

British Library Cataloguing in Publicaton Information Available

Library of Congress Cataloging-in-Publication Data
Wolfgram, Mark, 1970–
Getting history right : East and West German collective memories of the Holocaust and war / Mark A. Wolfgram.
p. cm.
Includes bibliographical references and index.
ISBN 978-1-61148-006-1 (cloth) — ISBN 978-1-61148-007-8 (electronic)
1. Holocaust, Jewish (1939–1945)—Public opinion. 2. World War, 1939–1945—Public opinion. 3. Collective memory—Germany. 4. War and society—Germany. 5. Collective memory—Germany (East) 6. Collective memory—Germany (West) 7. Popular culture—Germany (East) 8. Popular culture—Germany (East) 9. Politics and culture—Germany (East) 10. Politics and culture—Germany (West) I. Title.

D804.45.G47W65 2010
940.53′18—dc22

2010002896

⊗™ The paper used in this publication meets the minimum requirements of the American National Standard for Information Sciences—Permanence of Paper for Printed Library Materials, ANSI/NISO Z39.48-1992.

Printed in the United States of America

Contents

Acknowledgments

I HAVE BEEN FORTUNATE TO DRAW UPON NUMEROUS SOURCES OF funding for this project across many years. My budding interest in Germany was given a great lift when I was able to spend a fully funded exchange year at the Free University of Berlin with support from my undergraduate institution, Western Michigan University. There are many wonderful faculty members at Western, who took extra time and encouraged me as a young student of the social sciences, but Jim Butterfield deserves special mention for his encouragement and support. While my fascination with Germany, and in particular Berlin, was well anchored after that exchange year, it took several more years for me to turn to Germany's Nazi past. When I decided on graduate school, I did not see what else could or needed to be said about Germany's Nazi past. While at the University of Toronto, I settled on a rather conventional study of German foreign policy, but it quickly became obvious to me that the Nazi legacy was frequently playing a role in framing modern day German politics. I was becoming more fascinated with how perceptions of the past played a role in current political life. But I still needed to find the right theoretical framework.

I then moved on to the University of Wisconsin-Madison to finish my PhD. The ideas for the project began to take clearer form in two critical seminars during my graduate studies there. Michael Schatzberg's graduate seminars on qualitative research methods and especially his course Politics and Culture in Comparative Perspective were formative. I began to appreciate new possibilities of what one might study within the discipline of political science. I was able to play further with these ideas during a special summer seminar entitled The New Germany and the New Europe at the University of California-Berkeley, supported by the German Academic Exchange Service (DAAD) and run by Rob Holub. I was able to attend the Berkeley seminar thanks to the generous support of the DAAD, which I will have multiple opportunities to thank. While at Berkeley, I met Andy Markovits, who was one of the seminar's special faculty participants. He had some advance sections of his then soon to be published book *The German Predicament* with him, which he shared with me. Andy was from the first instance very generous with his time, insight, and advice. We shared our first coffees together in Berkeley and have shared many others since. Creative scholarship requires a special place and time for reflection and engagement with others. Madison and Berkeley were these places for me.

The Friedrich-Ebert Foundation gave me a six-month predissertation fellowship in 1997, which was critical for establishing a clearer vision of what I could do with a longer stay in Germany. I still have my massive newspaper clipping files from that stay, which impressed on me further the way narratives about the Nazi past influenced German politics today. In 1999–2000, a year of field research in Germany was supported again by the DAAD, the Vilas Graduate Fellowship at the University of Wisconsin-Madison, and the Joan Shorenstein Center on the Press, Politics and Public Policy at Harvard University. Professor Hans-Peter Müller at the Humboldt University was my host and *Doktorvater* for the stay. He played a critical role in helping me gain access to some of the archival material. I also want to thank Jürgen Mackert, Steffen Sigmund, and Ilse Scholz for their collegial friendship and helpfulness while I was at the Humboldt University.

During my stay in Germany, there were many institutions and employees who were not only open, helpful, and enthusiastic, but also simply friendly to a guy with a funny accent (I was particularly proud when some thought I was Dutch) and probably too many questions. The Federal Film Archive in Berlin was more than generous with its time, facilities, and staff as they permitted me to view almost thirty films. My viewing of some of this material was very labor intensive for the institute, as some of the rarely viewed films had not been transferred to videotape. In such cases, an employee had to change role after role (I never knew how many roles a full-length film included!) for me at an editing table. I wish to thank Mr. Schmidt, Mrs. Buchholz, Mrs. Kuschke, and Mr. Foitzik. At the *German Radio Archive-Berlin [Deutsches Rundfunkarchiv-Berlin]* I am deeply indebted to Mrs. Langguth, Mrs. Kreft, Mrs. Ulrich, and Mr. Fischer. It was Mr. Fischer who called to my attention the existence of television viewer surveys in East Germany, a resource that has yet to be fully exploited by scholars. I was very happy to work again with Mr. Fischer at the archive's new home in Babelsberg in August 2004, to complete some additional field research. At the *Picture Archive for Berlin [Landesbildstelle Berlin]*, I wish to thank Mrs. Köhn and Mr. Fischer.

Doing research on television and using television programs in research entail a difficult process. Even public television stations often expect large sums of money for the use of their programs by others, and their facilities are often not designed to accommodate researchers, as editors and programmers race to meet deadlines. These circumstances are most unfortunate, as television has played a critical role in our cultural and political lives. Fortunately, a number of Germany's public broadcasters made all or some of their archives available to me. I had little or nothing to offer in kind to these very busy institutions, and their support is most gratefully acknowledged. At the Bayerischer Rundfunk (BR), I would like to thank Mr. Fischer, Mr. Josef Fedeli and his assistants, and thank Mr. Fedeli again for the rides to the subway station. At the Norddeutscher Rundfunk (NDR), I would like to thank Mrs. Helga Wildauer, Mr. Kröger, Mrs. Helms, Mrs. Kunde, and Mr. Hahn-Ebert for their very generous support in terms of time and use of their facilities. At the Zweites Deutsches Fernsehen (ZDF) I would like to thank Dr. Schmitt and Mr. Scheller for their very helpful support and guidance in the use of the archive. Mr. Scheller went out of his way to make my work at the ZDF both productive and pleasurable, while also giving me a "behind-the-scenes" tour of the facilities. I would also like to thank the Süddeutscher Rundfunk (SDR) for mailing several programs to me in Berlin, thus saving me an expensive trip.

The University of Wisconsin-Madison was a wonderful intellectual home for my entire graduate education. The support I received from the faculty and my graduate student cohort is something for which I will long be thankful. I especially want to thank the members of my dissertation committee, Richard Merelman, Michael Schatzberg, and Graham Wilson, who allowed me to carry out a research project that was far from the disciplinary norm. Professor Rudy Koshar provided additional guidance as an external adviser.

The Charlotte W. Newcombe Foundation provided much-needed financial support for a year of writing the dissertation, and my first employer, Carleton University, awarded me a generous set of research funds to spend on an additional month working at archives in Berlin in August 2004. A Summer Research Grant from the College of Arts and Sciences at Oklahoma State University gave me a month of additional support to work on revisions of the book manuscript.

I have also benefited from presentations and discussions of my work with students and faculty members in many different forums including Western Michigan University, Cornell University, Princeton University, University of Oklahoma, Carleton University, and the Humboldt University, Berlin, Germany. The following friends and colleagues read parts of the manuscript and offered very helpful advice: John TeVelda, Jason Maloy, Mike Darroch, and Jenny Wüstenberg. Many thanks also to the anonymous reviewer, Greg Clingham of Bucknell University Press, and Julien Yoseloff and Christine Retz, both of Associated

University Presses for their very helpful, constructive, and encouraging comments.

Charles Gilbride encouraged my love for learning from an early age as my favorite high school teacher. But the love of learning, discovery, and asking questions began even earlier at home with my parents and the rest of my family. For my wife, Vesna, thank you for your love, support, and encouragement. Thanks to all of you.

Parts of this manuscript have previously appeared in print. I thank each of these journals for allowing me to republish parts of those articles here.

"Gendered Border Crossings: Germany's Films of Division." *Symploke* 15, nos. 1–2 (2007): 152–69.

"Blood and Redemption: German Collective Memory of Elite Resistance against the Nazis." *Journal of Political and Military Sociology* 35, no. 1 (Summer 2007): 63–84.

"The Holocaust through the Prism of East German Television: Collective Memory and Audience Perceptions." *Holocaust and Genocide Studies* 20, no. 1 (Spring 2006): 57–79.

"Rediscovering Narratives of German Resistance: Opposing the Nazi 'Terror-State.'" *Rethinking History* 10, no. 2 (June 2006): 201–19.

"West German and Unified German Cinema's Difficult Encounter with the Holocaust." *Film and History* 32, no. 2 (2002): 24–37.

"Getting History Right"

1

Collective Memory, Politics, and Culture

WHY DOES THE PAST MATTER SO MUCH TO US? WHY DO WE EXPEND political and material resources on getting history right, on getting the interpretation of the past correct? We are passionately and emotionally tied to our personal pasts as well as the pasts of our national communities and other groups. We cannot leave the past alone; we have to get the meaning right. Quite often, as will become clear in this study, we feel that we owe a special debt to our ancestors, especially those who died in our all too frequent wars.

Elites, civic groups, and individuals struggle to maintain or change the representations of the past over time. The perpetual struggle for mastery of a nation's historic narrative is a competition for a scarce resource as real as any economic good. It is a struggle for legitimacy, for the speaker or ruler to be seen as right and just, and therefore possessing authority. It is, therefore, a political struggle. All of this leads us back to questions of identity, identity formation, legitimacy, and the links between identity and memory at both the individual and the social level. It is also a struggle for meaning in the face of human mortality and for the living to bear witness for the dead and justify their present exercise of power over others. These questions are at the center of this book and the growing interdisciplinary scholarship of social and collective memories. To answer these questions scholars need to engage in a vigorous study of culture and politics, meaning and symbols.

The present volume highlights the political struggles over the multiple meanings of the past in the context of three German societies: the postwar societies of East and West Germany from 1945 to 1990, and the society of reunified Germany in its first decade, from 1990 to 2000. By reflecting on the struggle for meaning, this book touches upon many of the basic dilemmas of human existence. Once the human consciousness fixates upon the mortality of the individual and the potential meaninglessness of death, there is a struggle in life to create meaning and order through creative symbolic activity. By focusing on meaning, this book places culture and symbols at the center of its analysis and by so doing falls outside mainstream political science. This is a work in culture and politics,[1] not political culture.[2] Rather than a traditional work in political culture, where individual attitudes are aggregated into populations, this book is a study of culture and politics, of shared beliefs and values, and the struggle over their meaning. To examine this relationship between culture and politics, I will look at a comparison of East and West German societies and their respective encounters with the difficult history of National Socialism, the Second World War, and the Holocaust. This is also a study of contrasts, of how and why the collective memories of these traumatic events in an authoritarian and in a democratic society changed over time. It is a study that shows how the changing boundaries of the collective memories and the cultural matrix molded political events, making some more likely and others less likely over time.

Consider the following questions: Why was the Ludwigsburg Central Office for the Investigation of National Socialist Crimes only established in 1958, thirteen years after the war, with a staff of twenty and a mandate only to investigate crimes that occurred outside Germany? How could a former Gestapo officer sue in a West German court in the 1950s for his full pension and a bonus, in respect of the rank he received while deporting Jews, and win? Why in July 1979 did the Bundestag, the West German Parliament, barely vote in favor of eliminating the statute of limitations for crimes of murder and genocide, when at the beginning of that year it was perfectly clear that the Bundestag was going to refuse to extend the same statute of limitations? Why could Hans Globke, a person intimately involved in the writing of the Nuremberg Laws, which legalized discrimination against Jews, serve as a close adviser to West Germany's first chancellor, Adenauer, in the 1950s and 1960s? Why was Hans Filbinger, another prominent Christian Democratic politician with a checkered past during the National Socialist years, only brought down by scandal in the late 1970s? Why did the East German government at first demonize and ridicule the July 20, 1944, plot to assassinate Hitler and then in the 1960s turn Claus von Stauffenberg, one of the chief plotters, into a hero? Why was there renewed interest in Jews and Jewish history in East Germany in 1988? Why did a discussion of the crimes of the Wehrmacht only erupt in the 1990s, after Germany's reunification? Why was it only in the 1990s that the Hamburg Institute for Social Research began to collect photographs from the families of former soldiers and then create a highly controversial exhibit known as the "Crimes of the Wehrmacht Exhibit"? Why did it take forty-five years after the war to begin exploring the narrative of "German" rather than only "Nazi" perpetrators, as if Germans and Nazis were separate analytic categories?

To understand these essential political events and many more in the postwar histories of East and West Germany, one needs to grasp the importance of collective memories, which are shared and contested in every society. For example, if one wants to understand why Jews have a vastly more important public role and more political power in Germany today than in 1946, one needs to understand Germany's cultural matrix and the changing nature of Germany's collective memories. Jews living in Germany today have more *legitimacy* to speak in public than Jews in the past because the collective German interpretation and understanding of the past have fundamentally changed, especially since the 1980s. Their democratic citizenship, their right to participate in social discourse, their greater inclusion in contentious politics, have all changed because the collective social interpretation of the past has changed. Getting history right matters.

This observation, supported by the research presented here, demonstrates the fundamental and underappreciated importance of including collective memory studies in our study of political life. Our ability to understand and explain the success and failure of democratization as well as the relative power of different individuals, groups, and institutions in a society may well depend upon our scholarly ability to chart the changing nature of the cultural matrix. As Anthony Cohen, David Lan, Mary Douglas, and of course Claude Lévi-Strauss along with numerous other anthropologists have demonstrated time and again, the past offers a powerful source of legitimacy, which actors can try to mobilize in the present. What political scientists need to realize is that this is just as true for our so-called modern people as the so-called primitives of anthropological interest. There is a greater unity of inquiry among these disciplines than is often readily acknowledged. As Mary Douglas once lamented, "So little has been done to extend the analysis across modern and primitive cultures that there is still no common vocabulary. Sacraments are one thing, magic another; taboos one thing, sin another. The first thing is to break through the spiky verbal hedges that arbitrarily insulate one set of human experiences (ours) from another set (theirs)."[3] In this study, I combine "their" mythology with "our" collective memories and emphasize humanity's common concerns with the legitimate exercise of power and reconciliation between individuals and groups for past wrongs.

Collective Memory Studies and Political Analysis

There is a rapidly growing interdisciplinary literature in memory, collective memory, public memory, and historical memory studies, terms that some scholars use interchangeably. Scholarship in this field, however, is primarily that of historians, anthropologists, sociologists, and philosophers.[4] There are, in comparison, relatively few works from political scientists.[5] One reason for this is that collective memory studies, by their very nature, demand a rich diversity of qualitative methodologies including content analysis, ethnographic field research, oral history, and interviews.[6] There is a culturalist orientation in the field of comparative politics, but this field of research is one of the least populated in the discipline.[7] In short, political scientists tend not to work with cultural data and the interpretive traditions in the social sciences. I will return to an explanation and a defense of the culturalist perspective later.

The research presented here provides one of the few sustained comparisons of East and West German reflections on the Holocaust and World War II.[8] Furthermore, along with Kansteiner and Art, I have sought to bring to light how ordinary Germans reacted to and made sense of elite debates and representations of the past in popular culture.[9] A good deal of the scholarship on collective memory has dealt, in some manner, with Germany and the Holocaust, although most of these studies have focused on West Germany. As with other books that deal with the National Socialist past and the German encounter with that past, the Holocaust is central here as well. But to understand the Holocaust narrative in Germany, one must see it in relation to other German narratives of heroism, sacrifice, victimhood, and resistance. This study looks at how these narrative threads, often studied in semi-isolation, collided and interacted with one another. I have made every attempt to avoid any misunderstanding on this delicate point. One cannot understand National Socialism without placing the Holocaust and anti-Semitism at the core of Hitler's political project. Yet West German society basically rejected this interpretation for about three decades, and prior to 1989, East German society never really confronted the Holocaust.[10] This has led to a general misperception that a collective German silence vis-à-vis the Nazi past prevailed, when in fact Germans, East and West, discussed the Nazi past intensely. They even referred to the Holocaust, if obliquely, from the very beginning. Ever since the end of World War II, Germans, Jews, and others have been struggling to get this history right.

Popular perceptions and the general tone in much of the scholarly literature argue as follows: while Germans had once repressed the Nazi past, they now fully embrace the consequences of that past in their public and private lives. This is Daniel Goldhagen's conclusion in his much-discussed *Hitler's Willing Executioners.*[11] In another recent book on the Holocaust in American life, Peter Novick commented, "The air-ing of the series [*Holocaust*], in January 1979, became the turning point in Germany's long-delayed confrontation with the Holocaust. . . . It was an American 'soap opera' that shattered thirty years of German silence on their wartime crimes."[12] Novick is not primarily concerned with the German example in his book, but his assumption that the silence was only broken in 1979 because of the showing of *Holocaust*, while widely held, begs for further analysis.

The evidence presented here challenges this widely held perception of a German silence toward the Nazi period and its crimes. Rather than a past that was wholly repressed, I provide evidence that shows an almost compulsive need for Germans to talk about the Third Reich, but from a uniquely German perspective. It has always been a matter of "getting the history right," and this has led to a number of intense political struggles over the proper interpretation of the past. Other scholars have also begun to point to the ways in which German society has sought to make the Nazi legacy "a usable past," one in which the German nation is defended and justified before history.[13]

Rationality and Instrumentalism versus a Comparative Culturalist Approach

The culturalist argument put forward in this book argues against viewing humans as purely rational actors who simply manipulate culture and cultural products to serve rational interests. This is the rational choice or intentionalist school of thought. The field of collective memory studies includes works that tend to view human action as largely rational, conscious, and intentional, implying that the past is manipulated to serve present political interests. Hobsbawm and Ranger take a top-down perspective, in which the focus is on the ability of elites and the state to manipulate cultural symbols to direct the masses, whereas others argue for a bottom-up resistance to elite attempts to define the past.[14] The culturalist perspective does not dismiss the existence of such intentional manipulations by both the powerful and the weak, but it does argue that such analysis is incomplete. The rational choice, instrumentalist position cannot tell us where the rational actor interests originated and quite often risk falling into the tautological position of arguing that actors do what they do because it is in their interest to do so.

"Why do actors view their interests and their world as they do?" the culturalist scholar is wont to ask. Marc Howard Ross writes, "What they [rational choice and instrumental arguments] lack is thoughtful consideration of where interests come from in the first place, how interests get defined in specific cultural contests, and the ways that culture structures appropriate ways to pursue them. The theories and language of interest and institutional analysis that are the bases for most political analyses make too little space for identity and culture and pay too little attention to how they directly affect conflict."[15] Writing three decades earlier, Abner Cohen expressed a similar lament for much of political science, "Above all, they suffer from an implicit assumption that political symbols are consciously intended symbols and when some of them write of 'political socialisation' their accounts are mechanical and unidimensional."[16] Instead, Cohen argues, we need to consider a two-dimensional humanity that takes into consideration both "symbolic action" and "power relationships."[17] Symbolic action is tied to struggle over meaning, while political and economic power relationships deal with physical coercion and material wealth.[18] The culturalist perspective in comparative politics argues for the study of Cohen's two dimensions, the material and the ideal, the political and symbolic, politics and culture. The point is not to displace completely the study of the material roots of power in society, but rather to argue for the inclusion of meaning, culture, ritual, and symbol, while not making culture wholly dependent on material political power. In the words of Jeffrey Alexander and those working in the field of cultural sociology, scholars need to view culture as having a relative autonomy from social structure, or Cohen's power relationships.[19] Alexander writes, "When described in the folk idiom of positivism, one could say that the more traditional sociology of culture approach treats culture as a dependent variable, whereas in cultural sociology it is an 'independent variable' that possesses a relative autonomy in shaping actions and institutions, providing inputs every bit as vital as more material or instrumental forces."[20] As David Kertzer summarizes, "But this image of 'political man' as a rational actor who carefully weighs his or her objective circumstances and decides on a course of action based on an instrumental calculation of self-interest leaves out culture and all that makes us human."[21] Although the language and disciplines of each of these authors differs there is a unity in their argument for dealing explicitly with meaning and culture as something not merely derived from political power. Meaning and culture are not epiphenomenal; they are not merely extensions of political power, which the puppet masters manipulate in a rational manner to control the masses. Rather, political power is itself constituted and rooted in culture, in shared meanings, and in the perceived correctness of a leader's actions. We need to engage humanity, as Cohen has argued, along two dimensions: culture and politics.

While those working in the collective memory field of scholarship have largely embraced a culturalist approach, much of the literature has remained focused on elites and elite culture. While these studies are certainly of value, and my research is also engaged with elites and this prior scholarship, collective memory scholars also need to take popular culture seriously. In terms of a dialogue with the national past, people engage this history through the mass media, and through socialization in families and other social groups. In modern technological societies, the tradition of oral history has been weakened by the dominance of images on television and the Internet, and perhaps by the demands of both the marketplace and state ideology. Research into collective memories requires looking at pictures as well as texts and how the two interact.[22] Working on collective memory in political science means that the scholar must overcome some tendencies within the discipline toward quantitative analysis, which discourages this kind of culturally and interpretively oriented work.

Anne Norton's suggestion of thinking about culture as a matrix is a useful point from which to begin, for it emphasizes the relational nature of the meanings attached to both material objects, such as a film, and ideal objects, such as the nation.[23] We need to see actors operating in a cultural matrix, within which they attempt to define themselves, their interests, and their behavior. At the same time, other actors within the same matrix will be either collaborating with or resisting these attempts to create meaning and define interests. As we will see, the cultural matrix enables and constrains actors. As the boundaries of the matrix change over time, the relative power of the different actors may shift. For example, when a discourse about the Holocaust developed within the cultural matrix of the 1980s in West Germany, Jews found themselves in a very different power relationship to the rest of German society. Whereas West German society had, by and large, marginalized or ignored their voices for three decades, Jews in the 1980s had a new legitimacy to be heard in public and new power to resist and challenge German narratives about National Socialism. This is an excellent example of Cohen's two dimensions of power interacting with each other. The rationalist or intentionalist scholar is at a loss to explain why Jewish voices gained new legitimacy and symbolic power in the 1980s.

For many political scientists, this instability in the historical narrative is a nuisance and a problem to be overcome, rather than a point for scholarly inquiry. Traditionally, they have only been interested in history because of clear material, rather than symbolic, outcomes flowing from path-dependent developments, historical switches, or structural and institutional analysis. The assumption is that one needs only to find the authors who "got history right" and then use their data. When there are differences of opinion about the proper interpretation of history, then the researcher must set out to do the best he can or "sample," in a statistical sense.[24] Collective memory research does not seek to resolve this problem created by a widespread loss of faith in historical positivism.[25] Instead, it extracts from the academy these debates about getting history right and looks at how various social actors seek to reshape the cultural matrix and are at the same time shaped by that matrix. Rather than seeing endogeneity or feedback as a problem of model specification,[26] I view intersubjectivity as a fact of all human social life and part of all research into the cultural matrix and collective memory, in which agents shape structure and structure shapes agents.[27]

Core Research Findings

Let us now take a look at some of the core findings of this research. First, I point to two postwar myths that are in some ways specific to the German cases. Then I draw four more general conclusions that may be applicable to other cases of how societies deal with their difficult histories.

Postwar Mythology

Two core mythologies of the postwar era were either firmly in place, which was more or less true up into the 1970s, or falling apart, as during the 1980s. The myths are basically the same in East and West Germany, but their collapse was more pronounced in the West. First, Germans constructed a thick rhetorical barrier that made Germans and Nazis separate analytic categories. This mythical barrier faced its most serious challenges in the 1990s, as I show later in the public's reaction to the Wehrmacht exhibit. Some Germans have now begun to grant the perpetrators a human form and history, perhaps even growing to recognize the role family members had played in the fascist state. The second core postwar myth is that of the Nazi terror state, on which I elaborate later. In brief, while there was certainly a terror state, it did not function in the manner that the historiography and popular culture popularized in the postwar years. Rather than a general terror apparatus, the Nazi terror was directed at specific groups, such as the communists, socialists, and Jews, often with the willing assistance of ordinary Germans.[28] In the postwar mythology, both German societies used the mythology of a general terror state as a popular exculpatory tool for explaining the weakness of the German resistance.

Four Generalizations

Let me at this point suggest several expectations and generalizations, which scholars can take from my comparison of the two German cases.

First, we can expect democratic societies to show more dynamism and organic social development with regard to reinterpreting their past than authoritarian societies. Second, the various media through which individuals encounter the past, such as film, newspaper stories, novels, television programs, are shaped by the cultural matrix and dominant social ideologies. There is a basic *memory-market dictum*, which scholars can apply to other cases: memory makers need access to "capital" to take their products to market, and the more capital intensive a product is, the more sensitive the producer will be to prevailing attitudes either in the population at large (democratic regime) or in state ideology (authoritarian regime). Third, generational turnover may prove critical to freeing up social space and offering more opportunities for discussing the past from different perspectives. Last, the ethnocentrism of death will often, if not always, mute empathy and identification with members of other groups. Paradoxically, this can act as a barrier to recognizing crimes committed by members of one's own group, even if an individual has suffered greatly at the hands of the regime.

Let me offer some elaboration on each of these points. First, I have constructed a comparison of a liberal democratic state with an authoritarian state. The quality of the comparison is enhanced by the fact that I can observe the implications of the regime type while holding culture and the past constant. One could reasonably expect at the outset that the democratic and pluralistic West German state would allow for more memory and potentially more justice for the victims of National Socialism than the authoritarian East German state. Although this was largely true by 1989, the West German pathway toward more memory was fraught with fierce battles over the proper representation and meaning of the Nazi past. The breakthrough did not occur until the 1980s.

The West German case should perhaps serve as a warning of what our expectations should be with regard to various attempts to engineer truth and reconciliation in more recent cases of democratization after authoritarian rule. The fact of the matter is that the vast majority of the criminals never see themselves as perpetrators. In the German case, even those one would probably classify as "Nazis," such as former SS officers, saw themselves as having served Germany or perhaps as having defended Western civilization against Bolshevism and Eastern barbarism. Many other Germans, whom one would not classify easily as perpetrators even though they became bound up with the Nazi regime, saw themselves primarily as victims of National Socialism, not unlike the Jews. German society only broadly began to recognize the uniqueness of the Holocaust and Jewish victims in the 1980s. From that point forward, different social groups fought fierce battles over the labels *victim* and *perpetrator*.

In the case of the authoritarian East, the state's overwhelming domination of the public communicative space severely limited the voice of victims, except those whom the state officially sanctioned. Indeed, the state sought to destroy those who argued on behalf of the Jewish victims of National Socialism. While Jeffrey Herf has already written a masterful history of these developments from an elite discourse perspective, the present work seeks to illuminate more of the popular discussions.[29] In sum, democratic pluralism offers the potential for more memory and justice, but as the West German case demonstrates, formal democratic institutions embedded in a deeply embittered and resentful cultural matrix may well yield minimal results for decades.

Second, one needs to consider the *memory-market dictum*, that is, how different types of media that exist in a society depend upon state and market ideologies. As an extension of the first generalization, it is worth noting how different media in the West German case dealt with the Nazi past. For example, films were much less likely to serve as a forum for asking difficult questions than West German public television, which dominated the television market into the 1980s. Although West German television producers rarely risked open confrontation with their audiences, they did show more courage, from time to time, in presenting programming that challenged the two central postwar mythologies. These challenges were by far the exception until the cultural shift in the 1980s. By the 1990s, even public broadcasters had to be more sensitive to the market forces as more private broadcasters entered the competition for viewers.

The following general proposition should hold true in other cases: the more capital intensive a given medium, producing a film compared to writing a book, and the more dependent it is on market success, the less challenging the material produced. This will, of course, differ from case to case, depending upon the size of potential minority populations and thus niche markets. The general point, however, is that market forces can have their own censoring effect upon the process of collective memory formation. Market-based societies are not free of ideological constraints. Now that the Internet has driven many of these costs toward zero, we may be entering a new period in collective memory formation, but the consequences of this are beyond the realm of this study and the period covered.

A third expectation, linked to the first two, is that one may well have to wait for significant numbers of one generation to pass from the scene before fundamental changes in the collective memory process will be possible. Generational turnover is one mechanism that permits new interpretations of the past, as those with direct involvement and high emotional stakes in certain versions of the past lose power. The discussion of generations along with all collectivities requires great care, and I beg the reader not to misconstrue the category of "generation" as a condemnation of all members of an entire generation or "Germans" in general. Nothing written here should be misconstrued as a charge of "collective guilt."

Nonetheless, the fact must be recognized that the vast majority of those who experienced National Socialism firsthand remained, by and large, highly resentful of Jewish narratives and in general resisted a wholesale condemnation of National Socialism as a criminal project. Until members of this generation began to leave positions of power, not only as elected politicians but also as editors, producers, authors, and heads of households, German discussions of the Holocaust, public and private, were severely muted.[30] The importance of this generational factor will differ significantly from case to case and depend upon the population size of those still tied emotionally to the previous regime. Their position in key institutions will also play a critical role. For example, how many of the sympathizers with the previous regime find themselves in the bureaucracy, the military, or the judiciary? In the German case, the extent of collaboration and open identification with the regime was so widespread that a massive generational turnover by the 1970s was necessary before serious cracks began to emerge in the core postwar mythologies (see chart 2). Again, the East-West comparison is useful, in that it demonstrates that generational turnover alone is not enough to spur discursive change, for the same demographic changes in the East failed to shake significantly the state's hold on the past and its public interpretation.

A final generalization is the ethnocentrism of death, which tends to reinforce in-group loyalties regardless of attitudes toward the leadership of a regime. There is a basic human need to mourn death and to assign it meaning, to escape the potential meaninglessness of death.[31] In this manner, the survivors become trapped in a certain allegiance to the goodness of the group, even if the leadership is thrown into disrepute. For example, it is relatively easier for one to give meaning to the loss of a son on the eastern front if he died for Germany rather than Hitler. Here, we can again see a reason why Germans constructed a rhetorical barrier between Germany and Hitler, between Germans and Nazis. If Hitler's fascist state was essentially an evil enterprise, for which the sacrifice of German life was not justified, then one faces a serious dilemma. For reconciliation with those harmed by Hitler's Germany, one has to recognize this fact and therefore also recognize the perhaps complete senselessness of one's own sacrifice. Otherwise, one has to cut Hitler off from Germany and divide the two concepts. If one wished to separate Hitler from Germany, one then needed to identify with the "other Germany," or the German resistance. While there was certainly German resistance worthy of praise in a new democratic Germany, such as those Germans who saved Jewish lives, the early focus was on an elite resistance, which was problematic in its constitution and goals. I return to this in much greater detail in the chapter on collaboration and resistance. Thus, to sum up this point, the massive loss of life for one's own group, of which one must maintain an essentially positive view or simply exit, tends to create another layer of resistance to dealing with the past and opening the way to reconciliation with the victims. Information that challenges the essentially good nature of one's own group generates cognitive dissonance[32] and quite often a rejection or relativization of the uncomfortable information. One of the core reasons we struggle over the meaning of the past, especially regarding mass death in war, is to save the dead from a meaningless death.[33]

Methodological Solutions for Studying the Process of Collective Memory Formation

I set out to answer three core questions within the context of the two distinct German cases: (1) do representations of the past change over time? (2) what political consequences, if any, flow from these changing representations of the past? and (3) what impact does a pluralistic democracy or an authoritarian regime have on the first two questions?

Most importantly, this work seeks to link the macrolevel discussions and representations of the past in political speeches, newspaper articles, television, and cinema with the memories or perceptions of individuals at the microlevel, who interact with the macrolevel and with other individuals on a daily basis.[34] Each of us learns the history of our nation in three ways: (1) through immediate personal experience, either mediated or unmediated; (2) through intergenerational dialogue, largely in the family; and (3) through macrolevel generated narratives about the past as seen for example in film, television, schools, and other locations of public socialization.[35] Like much of our experience of the world, our connection to the past is largely mediated through other individuals and social institutions. One of the goals of this work is to link the changes between the macro and micro, for too often studies of memory or collective memory have only highlighted macrolevel discussions and assumed that these must have some impact upon individual perceptions.[36] As we will see, the East German government had mixed results in shaping its population's views of the past despite their almost exclusive control of all macrolevel representations in the society.

Collective Memory and Individual Memory: The Macro- and Microlinkages

To analyze this social encounter with the past, I work with the theoretical concept of collective memory, but let us first begin with the individual and individual memory and then look at the position of the individual in society. The identity of any individual is intimately bound up with his or her memories of the past, for it is memory that provides a continuity of character over time for any individual. This is not to suggest that memories are static in nature; in fact we regularly remember and forget parts of our past, and we may even create complete fictions, which eventually become part of our memories or self-narratives. Thus, it is useful to view memory as a process of remembering and forgetting, which all individuals experience, and to recognize that identity and memory are intimately linked.

Psychology focuses upon this process of remembering, forgetting, and the constant restructuring of memory in individuals, and cognitive psychology has indeed taught us a great deal about the way in which the mind functions.[37] But humans live with others in complex cultural and institutional contexts. Maurice Halbwachs, a French sociologist of the early twentieth century, suggested that even something as intimate to the identity of the individual as memory must also have some social dimension.[38] To express this individual process of remembering and forgetting in a social context, Halbwachs proposed to study the collective memory of groups.

At this point, one often encounters a great deal of confusion about what exactly collective memory is, where it can be found, and how it might be studied. In proposing the study of collective memory, Halbwachs was not proposing some sort of collective consciousness, which somehow linked the individuals in a group. Rather, he wanted to suggest that while memory only existed at the level of the individual, there was a fundamental social component to the process of remembering and forgetting. People remember and restructure their memories by communicating with others and by confronting the artifacts of material culture, such as photographs.

Let us consider the example of a family and its collective memories. It is Christmastime, and the grown children have returned to the home of their parents with their own children. They spend part of the time in the evenings reflecting on the previous holidays spent together, and the parents take particular pleasure in reflecting upon the earliest years with their own children, who are now grown. The family exchanges stories of what they did in the past, and the mother may even produce a photograph album to offer further evidence of what the children had worn and where the parents had placed the tree in a given year. Through these discussions, perhaps prompted by the photographs, the family is recreating and restructuring its collective memories or shared understandings of the family Christmases. They are also reconfirming their social bonds through the ritual celebration of the holiday. Individual members are structuring these group discussions and are also at the same time reevaluating their own memories and narratives vis-à-vis those of the group. A further role for this intergenerational dialogue is revealed as the family seeks to integrate and socialize the grandchildren into the group through the retelling of these stories. In this way, they become attached to a past they never experienced directly. None of this should imply complete harmony among the family members or a single collective memory, and indeed they probably struggle over the past, its meaning, and its legitimacy. Control over these traditions and their enactment is reflected in the power relationships within the family.

As memories are malleable and unstable, the photographs in the album become an important point of reference for all the members of the family, but the photographs do not embody any fixed meaning. Meaning is generated through the interaction of individuals with each other and their physical environment. They tell and retell stories until they develop their own mythology and narratives of the past. The photographs are imperfect, for they offer only bits and pieces of the past.[39] Perhaps a single photographer had taken most of the pictures, thus making her perspective more salient than others. As we will see throughout this book, the links between images and memory are important, and photographs of the past have the power to shape memories in the future.

I find it most useful to think about the *process* of collective memory formation, rather than trying to measure, find, and describe *the* collective memory of a group. In fact, we probably should always use the plural, *memories*. The process focuses on the following triangular relationship: An individual encounters a representation of the past (film, photograph, dance, theater, museum exhibit, oral history) in a given social context (cultural matrix). Meaning is generated out of this three-way interaction—we should *not* try to locate a fixed meaning in any object. The meanings will be multiple, the cultural matrix will change over time, and individuals will reach different conclusions and interpretations as they interact with each other.

The analogy of the family is useful, for it helps to illustrate a number of important points about the nature of memories and collective memories within even extremely large social organizations such as that of the nation. As has the family, the tribe or nation also has its narratives, mythologies, and collective memories of the past. And like the family, the nation is not a homogeneous social organization, as different members and factions are likely to have very different memories and connections to the past. A further important parallel between the family and the nation is the socialization of different generations into a larger group through the retelling of stories, narratives, and myths of the past. Although the grandchildren never experienced the Christmases of their parents, they will incorporate the stories of those earlier years into their own lives and memories. The grandchildren may decide to hold on to certain family traditions, such as lighting the lights of the tree on Christmas Eve, because this adds to their sense of belonging to the family and the generations that preceded them.

Nations also seek to integrate each successive generation into the traditions of the collective, its mythologies and historical narratives. These traditions seek to define the cultural and physical borders of the nation and to highlight its positive characteristics, for in helping to define the community, the traditions must explain why the community is good and worth sustaining. These rituals help to establish the cultural boundaries of the community.[40] In this manner, the nation-family is constantly regenerating itself and grounding its legitimacy in the past. None of this should imply harmony, however. Although the reasons why any family or nation splits apart are incredibly complex, one component of that division will in all likelihood be the group's inability to agree about the past and to reconcile past differences or conflicts.

While nations and families strive to create positive narratives of their existence as communities of the good, the histories and collective memories of nations and families can be very troubled by past crimes and abuses. Families, tribes, and nations try to create myths about past transgressions so as to maintain the essential goodness of the collectivity, even if certain members transgress fundamental laws. Neither a nation nor a family can sustain itself on a legacy of crimes and inhumanity. As such, transgressions run counter to the a priori goodness of the community; they need to be resolved and explained through a dialogue between those living in the present and their connection with the past. This is the purpose and source of many myths. There may also need to be an extended process of reconciliation and forgiveness, for this past to be laid to rest. A failure to maintain a fairly unified narrative of the past and how to include or exclude past transgressions can threaten the integrity of the family or the nation.[41]

The exclusion of Jewish narratives from both German societies, until relatively recently, has harmed this process of reconciliation. Now that the perpetrators are largely dead, the process of reconciliation and forgiveness falls largely to a new generation, wholly innocent of past crimes, but not relieved of the burden that has been passed to them. We may be witnessing the birth of a new Germany, which can mourn honestly the loss of its Jews not simply as an imposed burden of shame but as a regrettable act of self-mutilation. The building of the new Jewish museum in Berlin with its brilliant architectural voids, empty spaces, and unused exhibit spaces emphasizes the absence, the loss, while also providing powerful narratives of Jewish life in Germany.

This universal human experience of feeling bound to or building upon the past stands at the center of this book and makes some of its findings of greater general interest. Why do we feel any need at all to be grounded in the past? Here again, the powerful parallels between so-called ancient and primitive societies and us moderns are fascinating to ponder. There is no question that modern industrialized society has changed many aspects of human society and ways we relate to each other in our daily lives. But many of the fundamental problems and questions of human community remain with us. Who should rule and why? What is the basis of legitimacy? What is social justice? How does one deal with transgression and reconciliation? How do we deal with death and the threat of meaninglessness?

On the question of legitimacy, there are powerful and telling parallels between the ancients and today's modern societies. The legitimate exercise of political power remains today rooted in the ruler's connecting in a symbolically meaningful way with the ancestors. It is for this reason that the past matters so much. The fundamental roots of any society are found in the past and pass to us through the past. Each Mayan ruler of Copán built his extension to the central temple upon the foundation of the previous ruler and his tomb.[42] In the Rhodesian civil war, religious figures acted as mediums between local chiefs and the ancestors, through whom the chiefs received their legitimacy.[43] In modern American society, there is an unending stream of books dealing with the founding fathers of American democracy and the Constitution, which they created. Their intentions are constantly debated, as the Constitution and the writings of the founding fathers are the voices of the ancestors for American society.[44] The fact that this process appears to be largely embedded in an apparently rational process of legal deliberation should not disguise the importance of the past, for what is a common law tradition without the principle of *stare decisis*, although even here a new cultural matrix may lead to groundbreaking reinterpretations of past law, as with *Brown v. Board of Education.*

Just as ancient civilizations struggled to maintain the legitimacy of the community and its rulers through traditions and rituals turned back upon the past, modern nations continue to define themselves in terms of a national history. But the meaning of that national history is always open to multiple interpretations, and therefore history as a narrative and collection of myths becomes an area for intense political struggle. Getting history right matters a great deal to us in modern society as well, for we are seeking a communication with the ancestors of the nation. If we fail to get the narrative right and reconcile expansive differences of interpretation, the very survival of the group may be in jeopardy. Without a shared sense of the past and its meaning, there can be no shared future.

Discursive Field Analysis: Diachronic Research into Collective Memories

Any single group's history is so vast, complex, and contradictory that one first needs to restrict the field of inquiry. For this study, I have selected four events that have proven to be highly contentious in the postwar German history of this century. West German society, and to a lesser degree East German society, commemorated these events on an annual basis, thus making the study of their representation with time series analysis more feasible. They are (1) November 9, 1938, the Nazi burning of synagogues and the imprisonment of thousands of Jews; (2) July 20, 1944, the failed attempt to assassinate Hitler; (3) June 17, 1953, the uprising in East Berlin; and (4) May 8, 1945, the German surrender to the allies. To study German memories of the Nazi era across time in a reliable and valid manner, I had to find a way to divide "the Nazi past" into measurable units. I did this by selecting the four historical events listed. As each event had a specific temporal reference point, I could then look in my various data sources, in particular television and newspapers, around the date of commemoration throughout the postwar years and find relevant material. For film, commemorative dates were less important, as there were simply fewer of them. Although they were still substantial in number, I was able to use filmographies with short synopses and secondary literature to find films related to these same events.

In each case, I was less interested in the specific representation of these events than the themes associated with them. To capture these themes, I used a qualitatively oriented content analysis methodology to capture the latent content and deep structural meaning in each newspaper article, television program, film, or archived interview. I also recorded the manifest content such as the length of programs, the length of the newspaper articles, the number of films shown in a given year, audience size, and so forth. Much of this manifest content is presented in the charts in the appendix. I used an open coding process, with the discursive themes as an initial guide.[45] From this process, I was able to identify the two core mythologies of postwar German society, mythologies I did not initially expect to find.

Each of the four historical events is linked to the thematic tensions, discursive fields, or narrative topics, whose evolution I wanted to observe over time. I was not interested in writing a history of the historical events themselves, but rather a history of how Germans had memorialized these events over time: November 9, 1938, and Kristallnacht[46] helped to outline the discursive field of victims and perpetrators. Who persecuted whom and why? The attempted assassination of Hitler on July 20, 1944, became a focal point for the discursive field of collaboration and resistance in the postwar years. This became a usable piece of history that ordinary Germans and public figures employed to defend themselves against perceived charges of collective guilt, especially in the early postwar years. The date June 17, 1953, highlighted the thematic tension of the unity and division of the German nation after the loss of national sovereignty and the division of the state. Finally, the discursive field around May 8, 1945, showed the polarization of the discussion into either liberation or defeat. Why did the new, postwar, democratic West German society view the end of the war as a defeat when the very end of the war paved the way for a new democratic society?

These discursive fields of collaboration-resistance, perpetrator-victim, unity-division, and liberation-defeat are in no way unique to each historical event. For example, there is a great deal of discussion in the popular culture about Germans as victims in debates about the war and the ending of the war. The chapters of this book are organized around the historical events so as to aid the analysis and organization of information, but I will discuss each of the discursive fields as they cut across the events themselves.

The rest of the book will proceed as follows: Chapters 2 and 3 deal with the representation of the Holocaust and the discursive field of victims and perpetrators in, respectively, East and West Germany. The other chapters combine the East-West comparison. Chapter 4 examines the discursive field of collaboration and resistance through the portrayal of July 20, 1944, attempted assassination of Hitler. Chapter 5 explores the various meanings given to the division of the country and the discursive field of unity and division. Chapter 6 closes the empirical work with an examination of the discursive field of liberation and defeat in relationship to the representations of May 8, 1945, and the end of the war. Finally, chapter 7 offers some concluding observations and pulls together a number of important observations based upon the comparative nature of this research and further advances the main argument of this study that our present encounters with the past have a powerful effect on our political life.

The past and its contours in our societies today are but parts of the much larger cultural matrix. My argument is not that scholars should engage the past and collective memories at every possible corner, but rather that political scientists must reengage culture and culturally based research more than they have in the recent past. Our ability to understand the societies, institutions, and states we study will remain truncated and impoverished to the extent that our scholarship remains removed and distanced from our neighboring disciplines in the social sciences and the humanities. Collective memory studies are one of many possible meeting points for improving our understanding of how we struggle to reconcile ourselves to past injustices.

2

Victims and Perpetrators: The View from the East

EACH OF THE NEXT TWO CHAPTERS IS DIVIDED INTO TWO SECtions, which outline the macrolevel trends of how East and West German society represented the persecution of the Jews between 1945 and 1998. Each section begins with a brief institutional overview of how each society organized its broadcast media and film industry and how these institutional structures influenced the type of images produced. I introduce these institutional arrangements here, as they have implications for each of the following chapters. I also draw comparisons of how each state shaped the political, economic, and social spheres. The relationship between the regime type, either authoritarian or democratic, and the structuring of public representations is also explored. After I have presented the Holocaust empirical data for the East in chapter 2 and the West in chapter 3, I draw some basic conclusions at the end of chapter 3 on how and why these representations of Jewish persecution changed in the two societies. I also suggest how we can begin to conceptualize the linkage between the micro- and macrolevels of representations in terms of causation.

The central theme of these two chapters is that of the victim and perpetrator. As we will see, one common narrative from the German perspective is that the Jews were victims much like themselves. For example, Germans dedicated their earliest memorials to the nonspecific "Victims of National Socialism" or the "Victims of Tyranny." We will also see examples of the two postwar myths discussed in the introduction. First, the cultural products discussed in these two chapters clearly show the construction of a mythical wall between the good Germans and the evil Nazis. Second, the terror state myth reappears regularly in cultural products to explain the perceived passivity of the population while elites and others provide an exculpatory interpretation of that passivity in their narratives. These German narratives clash with the Jewish interpretation of this same "passivity."

Calling the terror of the Nazi state a myth is certainly going to raise some eyebrows, but let me emphasize once again that a myth is not necessarily untrue, but rather a specific narrative about the past invested with symbolic power. One key symbol of the Nazi terror is that of the Gestapo, and as will be seen in much of the film, television, and newspaper material, the existence of an omniscient and omnipresent *Terrorstaat*, or "terror state," is taken as a given and used to explain German mass behavior. Time and again, no sooner has someone issued a verbal statement against the *Führer*, National Socialism, or the chance of victory than the Gestapo agents in the black leather overcoats enter the room and haul away the offending citizen, who is never to be seen again.

For many living in Germany after the war, the existence of the so-called Nazi terror state became an exculpatory tool for both leaders and individuals to explain away the lack of German resistance to the Nazi regime. This indeed was not only the popular sentiment at the end of the war, but also the original position of scholars in the 1950s. This early scholarship supported the strong institutional view of the Gestapo and also assumed that the entire German population was terrorized equally.[1]

Scholars have only more recently begun to question the nature of this terror state, and Eric Johnson's work on this point is very important. Stated briefly, Johnson's work reveals the mythical nature of the terror state in many German narratives by showing the following: (1) the Gestapo was institutionally too weak to carry out massive investigations and instead depended upon widespread and popular collaboration; (2) only specific groups, such as Communists, socialists, and Jews, were targeted;[2] (3) the vast majority of Germans, 75 percent according to Johnson's interviews, regularly broke laws that carried the most draconian punishments without fear of punishment, such as listening to foreign radio broadcasts.[3] The Nazi terror state did exist, and the violence did increase toward the end of the war,[4] but in the postwar period, it became an exculpatory narrative and a myth of generalized terror of the state against the society, rather than of society working with the state to marginalize or remove undesired social groups, or of individuals settling other personal scores. In the postwar period, the popularity of the regime for most of its existence is forgotten,[5] in the context of this myth, and terror is used to explain German compliance and "passivity."

For most of the postwar period, East and West Germans ignored the victimization of the Jews or subsumed it under a universalized view of everyone's having suffered at the hands of the Nazis. The later discovery of the Holocaust as public knowledge in the 1970s eventually opened a challenge to these postwar mythologies.

COLLECTIVE MEMORIES OF THE HOLOCAUST IN THE EAST

The Structure of the GDR Mass Media

Following the principle of democratic centralism, state control over the mass mediums of print, radio, and television all originated with the Politburo of the Socialist Unity Party (SED) [Sozialistische Einheitspartei Deutschlands]. The Politburo directly controlled the Press Office of the Council of Ministers, and this body in turn oversaw the State Radio Committee and the State Television Committee. The latter ran two television stations, DFF1 and DFF2. DFF1 began very limited broadcasts in 1952, and DFF2 was added later as more of a cultural channel.[6]

The Press Office of the Council of Ministers regulated the press sector, which granted licenses to a restricted number of political and functional groups. The SED ran the national daily *Neues Deutschland*, which had a circulation of 1,100,000 in 1988. There were also 14 daily SED district newspapers or *Bezirkszeitungen*, and 219 other local editions, which were particularly popular. The bloc parties, which were not independent parties but rather satellite parties of the SED, also had their own newspapers.

The ADN [Allgemeiner Deutscher Nachrichtendienst] was the single state news agency, which provided officially sanctioned versions of the news for both the print and broadcast media. The party line was defined by the Department of Agitation and Propaganda of the SED Central Committee, and local editors and directors implemented the central decisions. Most of them had received their education in the ways of party controlled media through their studies in the department of journalism at the Karl-Marx-University in Leipzig. Because of this high level of centralization, I limited my newspaper research to a single publication, *Neues Deutschland*, which was the primary party newspaper.

Despite a highly centralized system, which was very effective at controlling the flow of internally generated information, the citizens of the GDR did have access to Western media sources largely through the broadcast media of West Germany. Only the most remote areas of northeastern Mecklenburg close to the border with Poland and the so-called valley of the clueless [*Tal der Ahnungslosen*] around the city of Dresden were unable to receive West German broadcasts because of geographical location. Access to the Western print media was effectively cut with the building of the Berlin wall in August 1961, but the borders had already become progressively less open in the years leading up to the final closure. The end result was that the GDR government never had a monopoly on the flow of information. Although the

Walter Ulbricht government, East Germany's first government, attempted to block private reception of Western broadcasts and threatened those who did receive Western broadcasts with prosecution, Erich Honecker relaxed these restrictions after 1973. It was during this time that the state focused more intensively on its youth, particularly through television, to try to win them over to the party's socialist ideals. It was also during the early 1970s that the state turned to television viewer surveys in the hope of making its message, increasingly packaged as entertainment, more effective.[7]

Like the leaders of other modern states, the East German leadership was anxious to know what its population was thinking about the issues of the day. However, unlike open democratic systems, which regularly report on public opinion, the East German state kept very tight control over its findings. In 1964, the SED Politburo established the Institute for Opinion Research and gave the television service its own division for viewership research.[8] While the general polling data are of limited use, the television survey data are of much greater interest.

The East German television service was also interested in what its viewers thought of its programming, and I have used this as a proxy data set for the limited public opinion polling in an attempt to understand mass attitudes and perceptions better. Obviously, one must be very scrupulous in using polling data collected in such regimes, and I will return to this point later. Although since the 1970s around 90 percent of East Germans regularly watched West German television,[9] GDR citizens never wholly ignored the domestic television service. And thanks to archival records of television viewer surveys, which were conducted sporadically beginning in 1964 and then systematically in 1968, we also know a good deal about what East Germans were watching, how many were watching, and also quite often their views and opinions of the programs and related subjects. At a minimum, the surviving archival records tell us the *Sehbeteiligung*, or viewership percentage, for almost all programs beginning in 1968. One of the broadcaster's primary concerns was to maintain as much market share vis-à-vis the West as possible, so the viewership percentages took into account the number of televisions directed toward the West. This information was never made public in the GDR.

Equipped with this information, the East German programmers were able to place their strongest programs, such as the youth programming and the crime dramas, in key time slots. For example, the crime dramas *Polizeiruf 110* and *Der Staatsanwalt hat das Wort* often captured around 50 percent of the market.[10] These were, however, the exception. Still, despite the high level of viewership directed toward West Germany, between 1985 and 1989 there were 313 premieres on DFF1 with 192 of them gaining 20 percent or more of the market. Therefore, a rating of 20 percent can be used as a benchmark for success, in terms of a GDR television program's reaching a significant share of the population. The data on viewership trends over time are sketchy, but from what is available one can conclude that viewership peaked during the 8:00 p.m. prime time slot, and viewership remained relatively constant for this slot from 1970 to 1989 at around 40 percent with a downward trend from 1986 to 1989 to 32 percent.[11] Viewers rated programs on a 5-point scale with 1 being the best. Between 1971 and 1977, the average rating for all programs ranged between a high of 2.84 and a low of 3.08, with entertainment and sport consistently rated above average and journalistic programs slightly below average.[12]

What is the reliability of the data?[13] This question needs to be answered from two sides. First, did the state's agents cook the numbers to produce an overly optimistic picture? Although the narratives accompanying the data in the internal weekly reports often tried to put a positive spin on what were in fact quite low viewership numbers, the often bleak picture that emerged from the numbers adds to one's confidence in the hard data. If the viewership was basically zero, then the internal weekly report faithfully shows this.

The second and more problematic question that naturally arises is whether or not one can trust the responses of the interviewees. This problem clearly exists in more open societies as well,[14] but the pressures of living in an authoritarian state could easily push the respondents to give even more misleading answers.[15] Fortunately, those responsible for designing and administering the interviews were well aware of this fact. In their jargon this was known as avoiding *politischer Erklärungsnot*, or "political need to explain."[16] This meant that the interviewers designed the questions so that ideally the interviewee would not feel compelled to explain why he or she had not seen a particular program. Furthermore, the interviewer had to show identification and was also legally required to guarantee the anonymity of the interviewee. The questionnaire forms were designed to guarantee that anonymity. Whether or not this was believed in all cases is certainly doubtful, but again one should remember that the full extent of state surveillance was only revealed after 1990. Moreover, segments of the viewing population were not sheepish or slavish yes-men for the interviewers. Members of the intelligentsia as well as party members often hated the kitsch entertainment programs and gave them very low ratings. In short, there is ample evidence of a critical viewership that was willing to voice its complaints. This hardly means that the data are flawless, but it does suggest that the numbers hold some level of validity and reliability.[17]

By the 1970s, the state was significantly more relaxed about the viewing of West German television, perhaps in part recognizing that entertainment, whatever its source, was a useful form of propaganda. In an otherwise very useful history of GDR viewing habits, Michael Meyen underestimates the potential propaganda effect of entertainment by suggesting that most viewers simply were not interested in the political content of the shows.[18] Rather than making them indifferent to the state's propaganda, this made them a better target. Popular police shows, such as *Polizeiruf 110*, helped to demonstrate the legitimacy of state authority in maintaining order. The viewing of West German television also sometimes helped to reinforce East German identity, as some East Germans felt insulted by the way West German television portrayed them.[19] And we should not forget the popularity of sporting programs, which the state used to reinforce a sense of competition and accomplishment vis-à-vis the West. Furthermore, Meyen's interviews with East Germans after 1989 show an East German population that was skeptical of the objectivity of both East and West news broadcasts, preferring to believe that the truth was probably somewhere in between.[20] This created just enough of an opening for the East German state to have its say as well and have some influence over its population's perceptions. The East German journalists were at their propagandistic best when they simply portrayed the "reality and truth" of life in the West by focusing on the closing of hospitals, unemployment, homelessness, and drug abuse. Such factual programs helped to increase the East Germans' own sense of security in socialism, whatever its flaws.

East Germans were able to follow broadcasts through newspaper listings as well as specialized broadcast magazines. *Unser Rundfunk* [Our Radio] existed before the beginning of television broadcasts and slowly began to integrate television material into its format. As the television content continued to grow, the publication then became *Funk und Fernsehen der DDR* [Radio and Television of the GDR] in 1960 and finally *FF Dabei* in 1970, which ended publication after reunification sometime around the end of 1995.

Victims and Perpetrators in GDR Newspapers and Television

The first postwar five-year anniversary for Kristallnacht fell on November 9, 1948. At the time, the semisovereign states of the FRG and the GDR had not yet been founded, but the division of Berlin and the country was already well under way. The complexities of the 1945–49 transition are not captured in this research as I am concerned with the *longe durée*. When looking at the following data, one needs to keep in mind that the public discussion in the GDR was almost exclusively state sanctioned and did not necessarily reflect popular attitudes, so it is critical not to conflate the public with the private.[21]

The first mention of Kristallnacht appeared in a small advertisement under the heading "Memorial Services in the Synagogues"[22] giving notice that there would be services in the synagogues in memory of the tenth anniversary of the Kristallnacht. The notice appeared at the end of the newspaper under the heading "The Latest Berlin Activities." Directly above this one could read, "Free Surplus for Retirees and Homemakers." Those who qualified could receive ten kilos of potatoes and vegetables with the presentation of the proper identification papers. The juxtaposition of the two notices symbolized the mood of 1948, in which the pause for reflection competed with daily survival. But for the Jews who had decided to stay in Berlin or were not yet able to leave, November 9, 1948, was also a time to reflect on the precarious position of their community in the land of the perpetrators.

Just to the right of the notice for the free potatoes and the Kristallnacht memorial services, the heading reads, "Your Party Calls You!" with a list of festivities dedicated to the 1918 November Revolution. Portraying a more open time in the city of Berlin, the notice listed districts in both East and West Berlin. The juxtaposition of these three announcements symbolizes the location of Kristallnacht in official GDR memory for the next thirty-five years. For almost the entire history of the GDR, the celebrations of the November Revolution would displace any recognition given to the Holocaust or Kristallnacht, with one exception. In 1988, the GDR leadership would try to outdo their Western counterparts in commemorating the fiftieth anniversary (see chart 6).

On the following day, *Neues Deutschland* ran an excerpt from *Das Dritte Reich und Sein Ende* [The Third Reich and its end] by Paul Merker, who was a leading member of the Communist Party up to the beginning of 1949, when he began to find himself in trouble for his wartime writings, which had called for the recognition of Jewish suffering at the hands of the Nazis. Merker and Leo Zuckermann's work along with that of a few other German Communist émigrés during the war represented the only time that Jewish suffering moved from the periphery to the center of Communist antifascism.[23] In 1948, Merker continued to be an advocate of restitution to Jewish survivors and advocated Communist support for the new state of Israel. Within a year's time, however, Stalin and leading East German Communists turned against the idea of restitution and support for the new state of Israel.[24] Merker and Zuckermann both became victims of the anticosmopolitan purges, a new wave of anti-Semitism and anti-Zionism sweeping the East under the direction of Moscow. This article probably represents some of

Merker's last words in public on the matter, but their publication shows the fluidity of the situation in 1948.

In the excerpt, Merker used the Communist instrumentalist argument that capitalists employed anti-Semitism as a tool to distract the working class from attacking the capitalist system as a whole. In this instrumentalist theory, the Jew was a symbol and scapegoat for the negative sides of capitalism. Merker also located anti-Semitism at the center of the Nazi movement, although still in an instrumentalist manner. "In reality, however, the Nazi racial hatred did not spring up from irrationality but rather a cold contemplativeness. The stepwise increase of the terror until mass murder, in agreement with the realization of specific political goals proves this."[25]

The instrumentalist perspective placed the entire blame for the anti-Semitic campaign at the door of capitalism, fascism, and the Nazi leadership. This economic reductionism in the Marxist interpretation of Jewish persecution had no reason to analyze German and Christian cultural traditions of anti-Semitism stretching back well before the development of modern capitalism and class conflict.[26] This instrumentalist theory also painted a very passive picture of the German population, thus invoking the Communist version of the terror state myth, while also drawing a clear distinction between the Nazi puppeteers and the hapless masses. The role of propaganda as having "put the conscious of the populace to sleep," as one television program characterized it, appeared to relieve the ordinary German of any need to account for his or her own behavior. It was also a message that was easy for the population to accept, for it relieved them of any direct responsibility. Kurt Pätzold, one of the GDR's leading historians of anti-Semitism, further anchored the instrumentalist perspective in his doctoral dissertation "Antisemitismus und Judenverfolgung" [Anti-Semitism and the Persecution of the Jews] in 1973, although in his later writings he also moved some distance from this economic reductionism.[27] As we will see, his commentaries in *Neues Deutschland*, while addressing the Holocaust again after two decades of relative silence, returned to the instrumentalism outlined by Merker in 1948.

Considering the impact of the cosmopolitan purges, which continued through the early 1950s, it is not surprising to find that there was not a single article commemorating Kristallnacht in 1953 or 1958. In terms of what this meant for the public commemoration of Jewish suffering and the Holocaust in the GDR, the winter purges of 1952–53 permanently placed both on the periphery of public memory until the 1980s.[28]

When the GDR leaders did turn their attention to the past, they were interested in remembering the heroes of the antifascist resistance. At the time that the SED leadership turned the former concentration camps of Buchenwald and Sachsenhausen, the latter located just outside Berlin, into national memorials in 1958 and 1961, they were woven into the narrative of the antifascist tradition. In 1994, when I first visited the Sachsenhausen camp, one could still see some of the original GDR exhibits. A discussion of the Jewish prisoners was almost completely absent from the exhibit. While never primarily a camp for Jews, Sachsenhausen had held Jewish inmates in a separate segregated part of the camp.[29] The antifascist liturgy of the GDR needed active Communist heroes, not "passive Jewish victims." I will return to the inaccuracy of the concept of Jewish passivity in the next chapter; it is a biased view of Jewish behavior, which was common to both East and West German portrayals of Jews.

In 1963 and 1968, there were only a couple of brief articles addressing Kristallnacht. Heinz Schenk, the chairman of the Jewish Community for Greater-Berlin (East Berlin), commented in his article, "In contrast to West Germany, our brethren in the GDR, a state of humanism and humanity, can live in peace and quiet."[30] The state used such laudatory comments from Jewish leaders on a regular basis to bolster the image of the GDR as being an antifascist state that had overcome Hitler's fascism in all its forms.

The first piece of television material my research uncovered dealing with Jews and the Holocaust was *Die Bilder des Zeugen Schattmann* [The Pictures of the Witness Schattmann][31] first broadcast in four parts beginning on May 23, 1972. The four-part television film was produced by the DEFA studios and directed by Kurt Jung-Alsen, a prominent DEFA film director. The novel of the same title by Peter Edel (1921–83) forms the basis for the script.[32]

The archival and public relations materials demonstrate that the program's creators clearly viewed *Schattmann* as part of a series celebrating antifascist heroes. Nonetheless, the Jewish identity of the main character is central to the narrative, and the persecution and murder of the Jews are dealt with in an explicit manner. East German television rebroadcast *Schattmann* in January 1979 during the day for school classes, and then again in November 1982 as a feature film in prime time. By 1982, the film's Jewish and Holocaust content had been pushed to the forefront of the presentation. Peter Edel, a Jew, worked on the production of the film, and the crew filmed parts of the drama on location in Auschwitz. Edel was a Jewish victim of the Nazis and had worked as a forced laborer and spent time in several different concentration camps including Auschwitz. His novel is largely autobiographical in nature and reflects his commitment to the GDR and the state's antifascism. This also meant that he was a strident anti-Zionist. In an essay for *FF*

Dabei that accompanied the 1982 presentation of the film, he compared the black smoke over Beirut after Israel's invasion of Lebanon in the same year to that of the crematoriums during the Holocaust.[33]

The film's narrative is told to us as evidence being presented in an East German court by Frank Schattmann, the main character, in a trial against Hans Globke, who was being tried in absentia for crimes against humanity. Such a trial actually did take place in the GDR. Earlier in his career, Hans Globke had worked as a legal councilor in the Weimar Republic. During the Nazi years, he helped to formulate the Nuremberg Laws (1935), which legalized and rationalized the Nazi racial segregation policies toward the Jews. After the war, he worked for West Germany's first chancellor, Konrad Adenauer. Although the object of frequent criticism not only from the GDR but from other countries as well, Chancellor Adenauer vigorously defended Globke, who claimed he had worked to prevent greater evil. While also a representation of the Holocaust, *Schattmann* was part of a long series of polemical attacks that the GDR launched against the Bonn Republic, charging that many functionaries with problematic Nazi pasts continued to work in the West. Rather than mere polemics, though, the GDR's charges were often true, particularly with regard to the legal profession.[34]

The testimony by Frank the witness referred to in the title of the film, is the basis for the film's narrative, and the rest of the first episode is told as a flashback. The frequent use of flashbacks in narratives about the Holocaust in German cinema creates a distancing effect, which limits the immediacy of the historical events for the audience. At the same time, their use permits the presentation of the present in which the characters have learned from the past. Examination of this didactic element is central to understanding the Holocaust genre in East and West German cinema, for these films represent attempts by Germans to recreate the moral community of good Germans or "the other Germany," in contrast to the polluted Nazis.[35]

The first segment is entitled "Der Freitagabend" [The Friday Evening], and Frank's narrative takes us back to October 1942. We see Frank leave a Siemens' factory, where Peter Edel had worked as a forced laborer, and follow him as he goes to meet his wife, Esther. He has something important to say to her, but he will tell her later. Most of the evening is spent around the dinner table for the Sabbath, and we are introduced to the various Jewish characters. The passivity and resignation of the group become unbearable for Frank, and he finally erupts screaming, "What are you waiting for, a miracle? The Messiah?" The portrayal of Jews as passive victims is a leitmotif of German cinema; it is a representation that also suggests the victim's complacency in his own suffering. We observe Frank looking at a slip of paper several times with the word *Tomorrow* written on it, and we can begin to guess that he does not intend to go down without a fight. The somber Sabbath is finished, and the guests begin to return to their homes. Frank rips the yellow stars from his coat and that of his wife. Esther is shocked: "What are you doing?" she asks, to which Frank replies, "What we have to do." The first episode closes with Frank and Esther beginning their lives as Jews in hiding.

"Der Entschluss" [The Decision], the second part, accompanies Frank as he follows the instructions implied by the word *Tomorrow*. He has contact with the Communist resistance, represented in the no-nonsense, tough-talking working-class figure of Helmut Wall. Wall recounts the events surrounding Kristallnacht, stating, "There isn't any racial question. That's class conflict in the street, not race conflict." Frank and Esther decide to join Wall in the Communist resistance, and we see the three of them plastering antiwar posters on the walls around Bebelsplatz in Berlin. In a quick series of events, Frank is rounded up with other Jews but is released because of his status as a Gestattungsjude, or "tolerated Jew," a Nazi category for Jews of mixed marriages. Upon returning to his apartment he discovers a note from Esther stating that she is leaving him. Frank's mother dies as well. With his ties to the more passive female characters severed, Frank is even more determined to continue his risky resistance work. He returns to his apartment, smashes the illegal radio, burns papers, and prepares to leave his past behind. But he has already been denounced, and the men of few words and leather coats arrive to take him away. The Gestapo has arrested him.

The third part of the series, entitled "Wiederkehr" [Return], offers a critique of West Germany as the land of former Nazis, another leitmotif in GDR popular culture. We learn more about Frank's capture, interrogation, and torture at the hands of Mr. Koberschulte, who now lives in the West. Of greater interest is the final episode, "Die Vorladlung" [The Summons], part of which was filmed on location at Auschwitz. In the present, Frank has a new girlfriend, Andrea Wohlfahrt, and they return to Auschwitz in the hope of setting Frank free of his past. We see them at Auschwitz with the icon of the iron gate, which marks the camp's entrance. Frank walks into one of the crematoriums, which is now nothing more than the outlines of a foundation and some bricks. While standing there, Frank reflects upon the fate of all those who had been at that final Sabbath celebration in October 1942. The scenes from the camp life are the starkest moments in the entire series, and one of the very rare examples of German film narratives taking the viewer inside one of the death camps.

Masses of disoriented prisoners are moved in this direction and that direction. Frank sees an old Communist friend, but then he is swept away. He is handed a bar of soap that he believes has been made from the fat of Jews burned in the crematorium and told to shower.[36] He is then forced to stand in the freezing cold with others as water is sprayed on them. The Kapos are shown helping the SS guards. There are medical selections. Some are sent to one side to live for another day; others are sent to the other side to be killed immediately. Then we finally reach the most traumatic moment that Frank has come to face as we learn the fate of his wife, Esther. Apparently they have not seen each other since being separated during Koberschulte's interrogation. One day he sees her again in the camp as she is thrown into the back of a truck to be taken away and murdered. Returning to the present, Frank places some flowers in front of building number 10 where he last saw his wife.

After leaving the camp, they visit the house of Chopin, which is filled again with people of different races, suggesting the international unity of the Communist movement. The music, the white rooms, and the peacefulness of the scene suggest the final transcendence of hate between different races and cultures. The two have entered a kind of heaven after leaving the ruins of Auschwitz. Frank is finally able to place the murder of his wife behind him and seals his future with Andrea with a kiss, love's redemption. He is then heard giving his final words to the court calling for a world without hatred between people.

How did the East German television audience respond to the film? The average viewership for the four parts was 28.6 percent with an approval rating of 2.88.[37] The preparer of the report compared these results with those of other contemporary films, which fell under the heading of "Struggle against Fascism." Compared to the other antifascist films in the series, this film attracted a below-average audience. The members of the SED, however, were much more frequent and enthusiastic viewers. The average SED viewership for the four parts was 38.4 percent, a full 10 percent more than for the average. Their evaluation of the entire series was also more positive, as SED members gave an overall rating of 2.59 compared to 2.88 for all viewers. Members of the intelligentsia were particularly impressed with the second episode, giving it a 1.38 rating. This episode showed Frank and Esther entering the resistance with the Communists.

What else can we learn about East German views toward Jews, the Holocaust, and Jewish resistance during the war? Most unfortunately, the interviewers asked the more detailed qualitative questions after the presentation of the first three episodes, and they made no similar report in the following week's report for part four. Thus, the audience had not yet viewed the most dramatic and difficult scenes from the Holocaust shot on location in Auschwitz. Nonetheless, there are a couple of clues to suggest that the Jewish subject matter of the film was of particular importance for the viewers. When asked about their mood after having viewed at least one of the first three episodes, 46 percent of the viewers expressed feeling depressed or defeated, a full 10 percent more than was the case after having viewed "Arthur Becker," another installment in the heroes of antifascism series. A greater percentage of the viewers also felt emotionally disturbed after viewing the fate of the hero, 67.4 percent compared to 59.0 percent for *Die Verschworenen* [The Conspirators], another antifascist film.

Finally, when asked the open-ended question "What was most interesting in this film?" most of the viewers simply gave no answer (46.5 percent), but of those who did give some response, almost half (23.7 percent) found the Jewish themes in the film the most interesting.[38] The last piece of evidence shows at least a minimal interest in the fate of the Jews during the Third Reich, and the slightly more negative mood of the viewers after viewing the film at least suggests a greater than average feeling of the burden of the past. Frank's dual identity as both a Communist resister and a Jew makes him easier to identify with than perhaps a "pure Jewish figure." Still, his character type is rather rare in both East and West German cinema. First, he represents one of the few central Jewish characters to appear in German cinema since the end of World War II. More importantly, he is a Jew who offers resistance, although not violent resistance.

The fact that Peter Edel was able to have his autobiographical work published in 1969 and that DEFA dedicated substantial resources to the filming of the novel in 1971 demonstrates a significant change in the official commemorative culture of the GDR toward Jewish issues. While still stridently anti-Zionist for geopolitical reasons, *Schattmann* marked the beginning of a new willingness to discuss the Holocaust and to address the issue of anti-Semitism. Obviously the strictures of an official instrumentalist interpretation of anti-Semitism were still firmly in place, but nonetheless the fate of the Jews was beginning to reenter narratives about the past in the East as well as in the West. Indeed, they were never wholly absent, as we will see later in discussing East German cinema.

In terms of newspaper reports, there was nothing about the Holocaust or Kristallnacht in 1973, as with the preceding years. In contrast, in 1978, there was a spike in activity just as there was in West Germany toward the end of the 1970s. *Neues Deutschland* published a number of short articles noting state efforts to preserve the memory of Germany's Jews through the maintenance of physical artifacts. One article noted that since 1976, the state had donated 150,000 DM for the maintenance of the three Jewish cemeteries in East Berlin, including the one in Weißensee, which is the largest Jewish cemetery in Europe.[39] A special exhibit entitled "Vergeßt es nie" [Never Forget] was opened,[40] and the state was renovating the synagogue in the Rykestraße in the East Berlin district of Prenzlauer Berg for the Jewish community. While the Oranienburger Street synagogue was being maintained as "a memorial," this designation can be viewed somewhat cynically as simply neglect. Ten years later, the state celebrated the maintenance and restoration of the same landmark. Judging from the lack of repair and the poor state of many buildings in the East, there were many such "memorials" to the war.

The only substantive article to appear in 1978, entitled "Der Pogrom, der Profit und der Weg in den Tod" [The Pogrom, the Profit and the Way into Death],[41] was written by Professor Kurt Pätzold. The article is significant, for it clearly outlined a class rather than a cultural interpretation of anti-Semitism, which was the theoretical position accepted by the SED. This was the same implicit theoretical basis for *Schattmann*, as well as Merker's writing in 1948. According to Pätzold, Kristallnacht was just one more step of brutalizing the population and preparing them for the slaughter of war. The common German was portrayed in a passive role vis-à-vis the demonic forces of fascism that were driven by the capitalist need for greater and greater wealth. "The pogrom was a diabolical act in a whole chain of actions that were directed at the total fascist and racist incitement of the people and finally toward the training of the cannon fodder for the politics of world domination of the German Imperialism and its brown hordes." This theory maintained implicit anti-Semitic stereotypes. He continued, "In the concentration camps, the newly arrived Jewish prisoners got to know the representatives of the other Germany, those whom they had ignored because of their bourgeois upbringing and social station, indeed they had viewed them as the enemy. Communists and other resistance fighters proved through their behavior, through their words of comfort, a lively sympathy and solidarity with all the victims of fascism." As Herf has demonstrated with his detailed study of official public commemoration, once the GDR quashed the issue of reparations at the beginning of the 1950s, the Jewish issue disappeared from public discussions. When it did begin to reappear in the 1970s, it was marked by an instrumentalist theory of anti-Semitism, which largely removed the question of guilt and responsibility. Rather than helping East German society to deal with its past, this theory helped to bury a past that apparently had no bearing upon modern society except to say that real existing socialism had already destroyed anti-Semitism. Rather than denial, these trends created a strong sense of dissociation for East Germans vis-à-vis the persecution of the Jews.

One can observe this instrumentalist theory in the mass culture of the time. In 1982, GDR television presented a brief thirty-minute documentary entitled *Die Nacht der Pogrome* [The Night of the Pogroms].[42] The subtitle reads, *To the Memory of the 'Kristallnacht' 1938.* But what appears to be billed as a documentary about Kristallnacht, has little or nothing to say about the actual events or the need to remember the suffering of the Jews. In the opening, the Holocaust is represented by the familiar iconography of corpses piled on top of each other. But the author, Kurt Goldstein, immediately retreats to abstractions and vague references. He claims that 1938 was just another in a series of acts of arson similar to 1933 and 1939. At the same time, he reduced the racial theories of the Nazis to the issue of class. Again, the unique position of the persecution of the Jews during the Third Reich is obliterated. He even goes so far as to issue the standard West German conservative line by describing the Holocaust as "these crimes committed in the name of Germany." Peter Edel's commentary adds nothing in terms of historical analysis. He is only concerned to justify the GDR's geopolitical opposition to Israel and Zionism. After the documentary shows images labeled as being from the Warsaw Ghetto and general scenes of wartime destruction, we are given the visual link to the present as we are told of Israel's invasion of Lebanon and the suffering of the Arabs. The visual montage tries to draw parallels between the Holocaust and the Second World War, on the one hand, and the Israeli invasion of Lebanon in 1982. Edel closes the documentary by calling for a Palestinian homeland and a different Israel.

In 1983, there were no television programs directly related to the fate of the Jews, but the old DEFA film *Ehe im Schatten* was shown late on the evening of November 9. I will return to this material in the film section later. Its inclusion in the evening's programming does show some sensitivity of the programmers as to the importance of the day. But in a curious twist, the write-up for the film in *FF Dabei* denies this connection, noting that the film was only being broadcast on the fortieth anniversary of the death of Joachim Gottschalk, whose life is portrayed in the film. While his Jewish wife is mentioned, there is no other mention of Kristallnacht or the Holocaust. The Nazis' persecution of the Jewish wife is central to the story, because the dramatic tension of the film's narrative turns on whether or not the husband will remain true to his wedding vows under such extreme conditions. Together, they choose suicide rather than personal betrayal.

The year 1988 marked the final five-year anniversary of Kristallnacht in the GDR. It was also the fiftieth anniversary. Since the late 1970s, there had been a growing public interest in the fate of Germany's and Europe's Jews during World War II in West Germany, and official state ceremony had grown more elaborate to reflect this. The antifascist state that claimed to have destroyed anti-Semitism at its roots was not going to be outdone by its dubious neighbor in placing the fate of Germany's Jews at center stage.

GDR television offered its viewers a full hour documentary in prime time on the evening of November 8. *Als die Synagogen brannten* [When the Synagogues Burned][43] is far superior to its 1982 predecessor as the camera actually turns in the direction of 1938 and does not push contemporary geopolitics to the forefront. However, the core theoretical perspective remains unaltered, as Professor Pätzold worked as a consultant. In this documentary, the viewer learns about Kristallnacht and the Holocaust. Eyewitnesses actually tell what they saw on the evening of Kristallnacht, and photographs show the burning synagogues. Still, the show contrasts the passivity of the Jewish capitalist scapegoats with the active resistance of the Communists. Even less satisfying are the explanations given for the behavior of the common Germans during Kristallnacht and the Holocaust. They are simply excused by noting that the population had been paralyzed by fascism; ordinary Germans had become a slave to fascism through the all-powerful propaganda of the Nazis. What could they have done? The documentary closes with a statement from Siegmund Rotstein, a prominent Jewish leader in the GDR, who reaffirms that socialism has destroyed anti-Semitism at its roots. Thus, the film offers the cathartic experience of allowing the viewer, once again, to feel freed from the past.

The documentary reached a relatively small audience of only 13.3 percent, which was typical for historical documentary work in both Germanys. The viewership was higher among members of the SED and the *Intelligenz*, 19.5 percent and 21.4 percent, respectively. Of greater interest was the lack of knowledge about the Holocaust and Kristallnacht among those under the age of twenty-five. Of youth between the ages of fourteen and twenty-five, 60 percent claimed to have learned something new from the documentary, while 100 percent of those between the age of fourteen and seventeen made a similar claim. Finally, the use of eyewitnesses appears to have been a very effective measure to reach out to the audience, with 97 percent admitting that they were emotionally moved by their testimonies.[44] Unfortunately, the report on the program is very brief and does not give us any clues as to what this new information might have been. The numbers do suggest, however, a general lack of information about the Holocaust in East German society. It also suggests that the growing awareness of the Holocaust in the West during the 1980s was not crossing into the East. Although Lutz Niethammer has claimed that easy East German access to West German television led to a shared virtual community,[45] this piece of evidence and others presented here suggest that this was not the case for the discussions relating to the Holocaust.

The state inundated the print media with information about Kristallnacht and the Holocaust as the state sought to increase its symbolic legitimacy (see chart 6). The ceremonies were primarily for international and not domestic consumption. One of the most important Western figures to appear at the ceremonies was Heinz Galinski, the president of the Jewish Community in West Berlin. Galinski's comments were obviously heavily edited, for an interview with him is reported without the use of a single direct quote, although his call for the support of Israel's right to exist was printed in *Neues Deutschland*, signaling again the potential for a shift in GDR policy toward Israel.[46] More typically the articles were directed toward the official ceremonies and speeches, which the SED had prepared for the occasion. Honecker was almost always at center stage as he greeted guests from around the world. One can only read an article entitled "Erich Honecker's Moving Meeting with Jewish Personalities in the Staatsrat" with great cynicism.[47] Honecker's speech offered little in the way of remembering the Jewish victims of "Hitler-fascism" and instead sang the praises of the socialist state as finally having overcome the roots of anti-Semitism.[48]

One year later, the geopolitical changes sweeping Eastern Europe hit the GDR as well. Honecker stepped down in fall 1989, and November 9, his successor declared the German-German border open. On October 3, 1990, Germany was reunified under the leadership of Chancellor Kohl, whose Christian Democratic Party had won a resounding victory in the first free East German elections, held earlier that spring.

For our story here, the most important impact of reunification was the loss of a unique East German public voice in the mass media. The federal government created the Treuhandanstalt, a holding company for all of East Germany's socialized industries. The Treuhand executives then set about privatizing the economy as quickly as possible in a process that became known as "shock therapy." The details of the fierce debates that have surrounded the process of transforming socialist states into market-based democracies need not concern us in great detail here.[49] However, some of the outcomes are relevant. One result of economic shock therapy has been that an East German entrepreneurial class has probably failed to take shape.[50] Ownership of all the East German newspapers, with the exception of *Neues Deutschland*, quickly passed into the hands of West German publishers. In his comprehensive study of German media, Peter Humphreys concluded, "In sum, Unification has been a West German take-over. . . . The characterisation of the former GDR as a 'media colony', or some such term, is a description that one comes across frequently."[51] The same West-led takeover occurred in the broadcast sectors, where West Germans supervised the transfer of the broadcast rights and all senior positions went to West Germans.[52] Two new public corporations were added to the public ARD network, the Mitteldeutscher Rundfunk (MDR) and Ostdeutscher Rundfunk Brandenburg (ORB). Both of the stations have maintained some of the old and popular DFF entertainment programs, especially the crime dramas such as *Polizeiruf 110* and some children's programming. They also regularly show some old DEFA films and produce programs of local interest, as do the other ARD members. MDR and ORB have become forums within which East German perspectives and concerns can find a public. The ZDF was also granted some old DFF broadcast frequencies and can be seen anywhere in the East. In summary, the public space of Eastern Germany in the unified Germany was quickly void of unique East German voices, except for the PDS, the successor party to the SED, and its paper *Neues Deutschland*, and the MDR and ORB public broadcasters.

For this reason, *Neues Deutschland* continued to offer a uniquely East German perspective, if from a rather narrow political perspective. One concern, which appeared in a *Neues Deutschland* editorial and the West German press as well, was whether or not celebrations for the "fall of the wall" might displace the public memory of 1938.[53] Most articles were more concerned with the present than the past. For example, they addressed issues such as anti-Semitism, the planned inscription for the Neue Wache memorial,[54] the failure to provide adequate compensation for the Roma and Sinti,[55] the shift to the right in popular politics and further restrictions on asylum seekers,[56] and a comparison of 1938 with the anti-asylum riots in Rostock in 1992, during which a house for asylum seekers was firebombed to cheering crowds.[57] Taken as a whole, the articles continued to echo parts of the antifascist traditions that had been central to GDR nationalism. While the claim that socialism has solved the problem of hatred toward foreigners and Jews was now gone, a critique of current problems with 1938 as a backdrop again raised the question of fascist elements still present in the society. At the same time, similar critiques could be found in the West German mainstream center-Left papers.

The articles for 1998 were even more subdued. There were journalistic reports on the speeches given by the federal president, Roman Herzog, and by Chancellor Schröder, and Ignatz Bubis, the then-leader of Germany's Jewish community.[58] Bubis claimed that there was a new culture of "turning away" in Germany, and he launched a strong criticism against comments made by Martin Walser, a well-known German author. I will return to this debate in the section on West Germany. Rather than suggesting the arrival of the Fourth Reich, the editorial merely questioned whether or not the political speeches reflected Sunday sermons of good intentions rather than true commitments to removing anti-Semitism from German society.[59]

The Historical Development of DEFA Cinema

As with the East German print and broadcast media, the state centralized the film industry.[60] The origin of DEFA in Berlin was based upon the Soviet seizure of the extensive facilities in Potsdam-Babelsberg, which had previously been the heart of the Ufa [Universum-Film AG] film empire. The Soviet Military Administration (SMAD) granted the original license in May 1946.[61] In 1950, all of the shares went to the new GDR state, and in 1952 DEFA was nationalized. As with the rest of the nationalized industries, DEFA was put into the hands of the Treuhandanstalt in July 1990 and sold to the French conglomerate CGE in December 1992.

The primary reason for the centralization in 1952 was to try to guarantee the state a monopoly over the reeducation process. Those returning from exile in Moscow had been impressed by what they saw as the success of Nazi propaganda, and the KPD made plans for the reeducation of the German population.[62] These attempts to place the sphere of culture under state control led to a series of problems for DEFA, as the company had to shelve numerous completed and nearly completed films to conform to the ever changing ideological environment. In the end, artistic creativity often suffered, but not for the lack of artistic vision, as many talented filmmakers tried to make a career in the East, although some such as Wolfgang Staudte eventually left for the West.

Party membership was more heterogeneous in the early years as members filtered back into Germany from their many different places in exile, such as Paul Merker's in Mexico. However, the party soon set about a process of Stalinization, and the party leadership quickly fell almost exclusively into the hands of those who had served their time in exile in the Soviet Union. Prior to the Stalinization and purges of the early 1950s, there was a rather open environment for artistic creativity. Kurt Maetzig, one of the most productive East German filmmakers, had the following to say about the early years and the director's ability to address issues forcefully, "But I have to say that this only really holds true for the first period, which today I still think was a wonderful period—the years from 1945 until say 1949—and then a lot changed."[63] In 1950, the party was making preparations for show trials and a new purge of party members. Within the arts, state officials attacked "formalism," which was seen as an element of Western individualism seeping into the cultural fabric of the new Communist state. These restrictions had a negative impact upon the ability of DEFA to produce films, and in 1952 filmmakers were able to use only one third of DEFA's production capacity.[64]

After the building of the Berlin wall in August 1961, there was again renewed hope that the SED leadership would feel more secure and therefore permit some opening of the social sphere to address problems. As Kurt Maetzig put it, "After the closing of the frontier we thought it was now a good moment to deal with the internal problems of the GDR because, before, we were always being told 'it is a very difficult and dangerous situation at present, you must act in a disciplined manner, it's not the moment to criticise everything.' "[65] Scholars also agree that the Eleventh Plenum of the Central Committee of the SED in December 1965 marked a new period of extreme coercion by the state. After 1965, a number of filmmakers never worked for DEFA again, and others were temporarily removed to less prestigious posts. The party banned eleven films in 1965 and 1966.[66] Although production figures for DEFA stabilized for the remainder of its existence, except for the period of transition and eventual sale in 1992, there remained points of extreme friction between cultural producers and the state (see chart 7).

Despite all of the ups and downs of trying to create art in a state where art was considered part of a continuing social revolution, talented artists did decide to remain in the East. One cannot easily make use of terms such as *self-censorship*, for there were many artists who were interested in building this new society. Wolfgang Kohlhaase, another prominent East German director, commented that the relationship between the artists and the state was not a wholly adversarial one, especially in the 1950s. In a 1990s interview, Kohlhaase said, "Despite huge differences of opinions, there was, for many years, a kind of solidarity between art and politics. This applied to the film industry as well."[67] He continued, "And we weren't constantly at war with the authorities. There were times when we had a good laugh."[68]

Recognizing that the years between 1946 and 1949 were unique, I still classify the films made in this period as belonging to the East as they have a political message distinct from those being made in the West at the same time. Clearly both sides wish to claim the recognized masterpieces of Wolfgang Staudte, *Die Mörder sind unter uns* and *Rotation*, but I will classify them here as belonging to a more Eastern tradition of film production.

The Holocaust in East German Cinema

Cinema represents the most lavish and resource-rich narrative of the past that modern societies have thus far produced. A point of inspiration for combining the study of film with collective memory research arose from similar work that Henry Rousso conducted in his research on French representations of Vichy France.[69] Rousso sorted these postwar films in different periods. I wanted to see whether the appearance of Jewish themes in DEFA film could also be placed into distinct periods. This requires a broad reading of the narrative surrounding November 9, to include Jews in Germany, the persecution of Jews, and the Holocaust. I began with the following questions in mind: Are there interesting patterns in the number of films produced and the date of their release? What can we learn from the film narratives in terms of the discursive field of victims and perpetrators? What kinds of patterns emerge from a qualitatively based content analysis of the material?

One quantitative measurement was to count how often Jews, the persecution of the Jews, and the Holocaust appeared in East German cinema. The common scholarly perception is that both German societies were generally silent on the Nazi past and questions surrounding the Holocaust for much of their history. As I have suggested in the introduction, this is not a totally misconceived observation. Still, it is a particular kind of silence about the past that openly embraces parts of the past for a time but then discards them.

As chart 7 shows, compared to the total output each year, very few films addressed questions relating to the persecution of the Jews and the Holocaust. Of interest are the production of three such films before the founding of the GDR in October 1949 and the gap that exists until the middle of the 1950s. Using the chart as a type of seismograph, we can see how the relative openness that Kurt Maetzig referred to during these early years within DEFA is transformed into a narrative silence created by the anticosmopolitan purges beginning around 1950. Then there is a string of films made between 1956 and 1967. We need to view these films as a unique series. After 1967, there are just a few additional films.

What do the individual films have to say about the persecution of the Jews and the Holocaust? One of the most studied German films of the postwar era in either the East or the West is Wolfgang Staudte's *Die Mörder sind unter uns* [The Murderers Are among Us] (1946),[70] which was also DEFA's first film. Staudte had taken his script to the French and the Americans as well, but they had refused to grant a license for the script. One of the most striking features of the film is the portrayal of the regular German military's brutality rather than simply that of the SS or special Einsatzgruppen. In this very early film, the narrative barrier between Nazis and Germans is much less distinct.

The film centers on three main characters: Mertens, the cynical doctor troubled by his memories of the war; Susanna, a beautiful young woman who has recently been released from a concentration camp but with hope for the future; and Brückner, a former military officer who murdered women and children in a Polish village on Christmas Eve 1942 in retaliation for partisan activities. Mertens witnessed the results of Brückner's order. In a truly gripping scene, the German soldiers herd together the women and children of the Polish village and gun them down in cold blood.

There are several fairly unique aspects to the scene. First, the killing is not merely carried out "off camera," as is more frequently the case in later films. The scene also eschews the postwar mythology of the "clean Wehrmacht." Rather than marking the perpetrators clearly as SS, which soon becomes standard fare in films from both the East and the West, the massacre is carried out by regular army soldiers. The fact that the German military regularly participated in such atrocities is hidden in almost all East and West postwar cinema.[71] In later years, almost all cultural products reinforced rather than challenged the rhetorical barrier between good Germans and evil Nazis.

Even though the victims shown in this case are not clearly identified as Jews, I have included the film within this section because it clearly represents violence against innocent victims by German perpetrators. Staudte attempts to make a reference to the Jews when we see Brückner unwrapping his lunch, which is wrapped in newspaper. Before the wrapping is tossed aside, the headline "2,000,000 People Gassed" is clearly visible. Also, at the end of the film we see Mertens crushing a star in his hand, which he had meant to place on a Christmas tree. There are two visual associations being drawn here, first between the Jews and the star, and second the Christmas tree and the murder of the Polish villagers in 1942. By leaving the reference to the Jews open ended, Staudte was able to encourage German audiences to engage his film and its questions. The extremely defensive and anti-Semitic reactions that the film *Lang ist der Weg* (discussed in chapter 3) drew appear to justify his choice. Whether the audience made the connection themselves is indeed questionable, but the director's intentions are clear. The film enjoyed wide popularity and had attracted an audience of 5 million by 1951.[72] To put that number in perspective, though, an estimated 14 million would go to see *Grün ist die Heide* [Green Is the Heath] (1952), one of the most successful *Heimat* films in West Germany.[73]

Kurt Maetzig's first film, *Ehe im Schatten* [Marriage in the Shadows] (1947), also addresses the persecution of the Jews but in a more direct fashion.[74] The film is based on the true story of a German actor who poisons his Jewish wife and then himself rather then allow the Nazis to force them to separate. In an interesting twist on the film and the story, none of the secondary literature mentions the name of the real-life Jewish wife although the actor Joachim Gottschalk is named regularly. The Jewish wife remains even more in the shadows. Unlike in *Die Mörder sind unter uns*, there is no ambiguity about the identity of the victims, but our attention is drawn more to the German actor than to his wife. The dramatic tension has little to do with the question of whether or not the Nazis will murder her or both of them. They want him to leave her, to renounce his vow to her. Instead, his primary challenge is to remain true to his wife in the face of such extreme adversity. As was the case for many other films dealing with the Nazi years, the Jew is inserted into the story to pose a moral dilemma, which a good German usually resolves successfully. Will the German actor remain true to his marriage vows despite the collapse of the world around him? The film was extremely popular and opened in all sectors of occupied Berlin, reaching an audience of more than 10 million.[75] Two years after its premiere, the film was still showing in Berlin and was ranked ninety-first in terms of success by the cinema owners.[76] The film was also awarded a "Bambi," which was for a time the German equivalent of an Oscar for the most artistically valuable film. The award was run by the Burda publishing house and based upon a survey of film critics. The fact that the award was given to a DEFA production reflects the fluidity of these early years, when it was far from clear that the division of Germany would become fixed for the next fifty years. The film clearly shows that at least some segments of the German public, including important film critics, were willing to engage the issue of Jewish persecution. But as the rejection of *Lang ist der Weg* demonstrates in the next chapter, popular audiences and elites also set limits on what the society could discuss and show within the cultural matrix.

Erich Engel, who worked closely with Bertolt Brecht at the Berliner Ensemble for much of his career, directed the next DEFA success, *Die Affäre Blum* [The Blum Affair] (1948).[77] Using a setting in the Weimar Republic and not Nazi Germany, Engel is able to examine the roots of anti-Semitism and political violence, which eventually led to the Nazi ascendancy in the 1930s. The success of this political and crime drama can be traced in part to its fast-moving pace and popular crime genre. Even a year after its 1948 release, the film was ranked sixteenth in terms of success at the Berlin box office and was given an "especially valuable" film rating.[78] In the story, Jakob Blum, a Jewish industrialist, is wrongly accused of a murder for clear anti-Semitic and political reasons. The police capture the true murderer and, despite the evidence against this individual, encourage him to testify against Blum. Although Blum's identity as a Jew is clearly portrayed as one of the reasons he is falsely accused, the film encourages the audience to identify with the more sympathetic and honest German detective, who works hard to uncover the truth. Once again, the Jewish character poses a moral dilemma for a good German.

For the next eight years, the DEFA film studios did not produce a single film that dealt at any significant length with Jews, anti-Semitism, or the Holocaust. One can clearly see the chilling impact of the anti-cosmopolitan purges.

The next string of films dealing with Jewish subject matter can be put into two categories, those that attack the continued existence of anti-Semitism in West Germany and those that return to the historical years of German fascism to examine the struggle for survival. Of the remaining eleven DEFA films, three fall into the previous category, *Zwischenfall in Benderath* [Incident in Benderath] (1956), *Der Prozeß wird vertagt* [The Case Will Be Postponed] (1958), and *Chronik eines Mordes* [Chronicle of a Murder] (1965).[79] Each of the films picks up the antifascist theme that capitalism is responsible for both fascism and anti-Semitism and therefore must exist in West Germany, although the films also portray sympathetic West Germans, who help the Jewish characters. In each of the films, a Jewish character must confront either former Nazis or racial hatred from his or her fellow citizens. In *Chronik eines Mordes* a Jewish woman must deal with her past and the past of the village when she recognizes the mayor as a former Nazi. When the West German government offers her money rather than justice, she kills the mayor and herself.[80]

The rest of the films are set in the time of the fascist dictatorship. Four of the films are not well known and generally do not appear in the literature. *Lebende Ware* [Living Goods] (1966) deals with Kurt Andreas Becher, who was the SS officer responsible for numerous war crimes in Poland and eventually the deportation of the Jews from Budapest in 1944. After the war, he went on to become a successful businessman in the West, using the wealth he had stolen from Budapest's Jews.[81] *Das Tal der sieben Monde* [The Valley of the Seven Moons] (1967) falls within the genre of antifascist resistance during the war and focuses upon German and Polish partisans fighting the fascists.[82] Within this setting, a love affair develops between a German resistance fighter and a Polish Jew, illustrating that love can overcome ethnic differences. *Stielke, Heinz, Fünfzehn* [Stielke, Heinz, 15] (1987) looks at fascism through the eyes of a fifteen-year-old youth, who then discovers that he is a Mischling, of mixed German-Jewish blood.[83] The film is rather unique in that it invites the audience to view fascism through the eyes of a Jew. Jewish characters almost without exception are not central characters, or when they are central to the story, it is because they permit others to help them and thus prove their own humanity. *Die Schauspielerin* [The Actress] (1988) also gives the audience a chance to view fascism through the eyes of a Jewish woman, although this time the actress and "Jewess" of the title is only playing the part of a Jew.[84] In a gender reversal of *Ehe im Schatten*, the German woman takes on grave risks to remain close to a Jewish colleague, whom she loves.

The remaining four films have been widely discussed in the literature. Two of the films, *Sterne* [Stars] (1959) and *Professor Mamlock* (1961), are from Konrad Wolf, who until his death in 1982 was the best known and respected DEFA director.[85] Another veteran DEFA director, Frank Beyer, filmed the other two movies, *Nackt unter Wölfen* [Naked among Wolves] (1963) and *Jakob der Lügner* [Jakob the Liar] (1975).[86] In *Sterne*, a German soldier, the main character, proves his humanity through his love for a Greek Jewish woman. In 1943, a group of Greek Jews are waiting in Bulgaria to be transported to their death in Auschwitz. His encounter with her and the love he develops for her allow him to transcend his fascist upbringing, and he finally recognizes the crimes of his country. He decides to join the partisans, although not in time to save the Jewish woman. The closing shot is of her train heading for Auschwitz.

Professor Mamlock is based upon the play of the same title from 1933 by the director's father, Friedrich Wolf. In the play and Konrad's adaptation, Professor Mamlock is an assimilated Jew and a political liberal who believes in the strength of the constitutional state. His faith in the legal system blinds him to the true intentions of the Nazis. He realizes his mistake too late and shoots himself after a series of humiliations. In the play, the suicide is successful, but the film version only leaves him wounded.[87] The main characters' failure to realize the true nature of the Nazi state in time supports implicitly the Communist claim to have been the opposition of the first instance. This theme of "resistance too late by non-Communists" is a leitmotif that runs through much of GDR culture.

Frank Beyer's fifth film, *Nackt unter Wölfen*, is often credited as the first German film to deal with life inside a concentration camp, and it would have appeared first as a film if the SED leadership had not blocked its production in 1955.[88] As a result, the story appeared first as a novel of the same title by Bruno Apitz. It was first filmed for television and broadcast on April 10, 1960.[89] The story would play much the same role as *The Diary of Anne Frank* in West Germany in providing students a literary window on Germany's fascist past. The story takes place in the concentration camp of Buchenwald; thus while the action takes place in a camp, it is not a death camp for the Jews. Buchenwald was a camp primarily for Communists and other political prisoners. The oath to destroy fascism that the inmates at the camp swore to each other became legendary in the GDR, as did the "self-liberation" of the camp celebrated in the history books, which ignored the role that the approaching American military forces played in the liberation.[90]

The effect of this writing of history can be seen in East German memories of the war. When asked which nation played the central role in defeating the fascists in 1995, 87 percent of East Germans named Russia compared to only 24 percent of West Germans.[91]

The action of the film is focused upon the struggle of the Communists within the camp to organize into an effective resistance force in preparation for the liberation. These plans are potentially jeopardized when a young Jewish boy, often referred to simply as "the Polish child," is smuggled into the camp. Again, as has been the case in many of the other films, the Jew is primarily present to allow the German figures in the film to validate their own humanity. As for the perpetrators, they are again carefully marked as members of the SS and therefore polluted and outside the moral community of the Communist resistance.

Beyer's second film on the same theme was *Jakob der Lügner.* It is the only East German film ever to be nominated for an Oscar. Rather than looking for sympathetic German characters who are helping Jews in some manner and thus restore our faith in humanity, *Jakob* is centrally focused upon its Jewish characters and enters their world of the ghetto. There is no escape, rescue, or survival. There are no good Germans with whom the audience can comfortably identify. If the audience is to find any hope in this film and for the characters, they will have to believe in Jakob's lies as well and hope despite his lies that what he says is in fact true. Perhaps the Russians are not far away; perhaps the ghetto will soon be liberated. Jakob begins to tell lies to others in the ghetto at first to dissuade a fellow inmate from trying to escape, since the guards clearly would have shot him. When he discovers that his words give hope, he continues to lie. Most touchingly, his lies give life and sustain a little girl's hope as well.

But the reality of the Holocaust rushes back into the ghetto, and the Germans clear it street by street taking everyone to the waiting cattle cars. Hope has prevented nothing, and the normality that the Jews had slowly tried to reconstruct around themselves is again shattered. Unlike many other scenes that take place in the cattle car, there are relative calm and enough space to sit. There is resignation rather than terror.[92] There is even a window, and the little girl wants to look out the window. We follow her eyes to a view of the outside world filled with clouds and a blue sky, which is a visual reference to the fairy tale Jakob had told her during his imagined "radio broadcast" that he had created for her. The film then cuts sharply to black, but the film has not ended, and we hear the high-pitched whistle of the steam train as if it has entered a tunnel. But it is a tunnel from which we do not emerge.

There are important parallels between *Jakob* and the much more recent film *Life Is Beautiful* (1997).[93] Both films involve father figures, only figuratively in *Jakob*, who try to maintain the illusion of innocence and wonder for their child. There are also some important differences, for *Jakob* never actually enters the concentration camp, as the film ends on the train, whereas in *Life Is Beautiful* the father must work hardest in the camp to maintain the illusion of normality for his son. Although the father dies, his son and wife survive and provide hope for the future. In contrast, *Jakob* is a much darker film, for the beautiful life of time before the ghetto is only shown in flashback, and there are no survivors. The liberation never happens and the film ends with the shrill pitch of the train whistle and blackness.

As we will see in the following chapter, the East German films have a similar pattern to the West German films in establishing and maintaining the postwar myths of the terror state and the division between Germans and Nazis. Although the newspapers, television programs, and films celebrate the partisan and Communist resistance to fascism and therefore obviously differ from the West German films, it is only the identity of the resistance figures that differs, not the resistance itself nor the form it takes. That is to say, German-on-German violence is clearly avoided, and the good German characters demonstrate their humanity through their relationships, sometimes love relationships, with Jews. As the material in this chapter demonstrates, the Holocaust narrative was never wholly absent from the macrolevel discourse in the East, but its presence remained more muted when compared with that in the West, especially when compared to the period 1975–89 (see charts 4 and 7). One can still see the traces of this discursive pattern today, in that East Germans are significantly less likely than West Germans to identify the Holocaust with the Nazi period.[94]

3

Victims and Perpetrators: The View from the West

THIS CHAPTER FOLLOWS THE SAME FORMAT AS THE PREVIOUS. FIRST, I explain the basic structures of the media in West Germany. Then I look at how West German newspapers, television, and film discussed the discursive field of victims and perpetrators over time. At the end of the chapter, I draw some general conclusions for chapters 2 and 3.

THE INSTITUTIONAL STRUCTURES IN THE FEDERAL REPUBLIC

In the absence of German sovereignty in the occupation zones, the occupation commanders strictly controlled the media. They controlled the radio stations and film production and issued the licenses necessary for starting a newspaper. After the founding of the Federal Republic on May 23, 1949, Konrad Adenauer, the first chancellor, and his economics minister Erhard pursued a free market economy with limited state intervention, in contrast to the process of nationalizing industries in the East. The Americans were particularly interested in making sure that antitrust legislation was adopted to prevent the concentration of capital in monopolistic industrial concerns, which they viewed as having contributed to the rise of fascism in Germany.[1] This market orientation held true for the print media, but public radio and television broadcasters dominated the broadcast market until the early 1990s. The political factions from the Left and the Right sought to influence each of these markets, and these political struggles took place within a federalized political system.

The federal system devolves cultural policy to the *Länder*, the individual provinces and three city-states. Therefore, control over the public radio and television stations falls to the individual *Land* governments for establishing a television council and administrative council. In principle, these councils represent "socially significant groups," but politicians also exercise influence over the political balance of the councils. Thus, party politics has always had a role in the structure and the content of the public broadcasting services in Germany. All of the *Land* level service providers then joined together to form the Arbeitsgemeinschaft der Rundfunkanstalten Deutschlands, or ARD. The goal of the occupying powers was to allow for public ownership while preventing strong centralization. Konrad Adenauer's Christian Democratic Union/Christian Social Union government rejected this settlement and tried to recentralize control. Adenauer was particularly determined to weaken or destroy *Land* control over broadcasting and attacked the "Red" Nordwestdeutscher Rundfunk, which later was split into the Westdeutscher Rundfunk and Norddeutscher Rundfunk. The 1950s were marked by many legal battles between the federal and provincial levels of government.[2] In the end, Adenauer was blocked from forming a separate national channel by the Federal Constitutional Court, which recognized the federalized role of the *Länder* in cultural affairs. After blocking Adenauer's initiative, the members of the ARD set up a second national station, the Zweites Deutsches Fernsehen [Second German Television], or the ZDF, in 1961.[3]

The print media have operated with greater freedom from direct government or party political influence. But as in other capitalist systems, independence from direct government control does not mean independence from politics. Although many German workers have the right of participating in management decisions, what is known as *Mitbestimmung*, or codetermination, journalists struggled for this right in the 1950s and lost. The Works Constitution Law of 1952 rejected the codetermination rights of journalists and placed owners clearly in control of determining the *Tendenz*, or political direction, of their publications.[4] Thus, unlike in the East German case, it was necessary here to consider several different newspaper publications to cover for potential ideological differences. My sample included the right of center *Frankfurter Allgemeine Zeitung* (FAZ), which is read nationally, the prestigious left of center weekly *Die Zeit* and finally *Der Tagesspiegel* for coverage of Berlin, and which lacks the strong partisanship reflected in the other two papers. In terms of mass circulation, the tabloid *Bild* has a greater circulation than all these papers combined, but previous studies have already given attention to the popular press.[5] There was no need to replicate that research here. Rather, I chose to focus on television, another popular mass medium, which scholars have not studied as widely.

In the early postwar years, the film industry faced a confusing network of regulations with many different local standards.[6] Numerous social and political actors struggled to gain control of censorship rights over the film industry, but the end result was the creation of the Freiwillige Selbstkontrolle der Filmwirtschaft (FSK), which was first proposed in May 1948. Once the various parties had agreed that there should be a single national regulatory body, the following debates and struggles were between different social actors, primarily the Catholic Church and the industry, over the final composition of the regulatory board. In the end, the FSK board was composed of fifteen members, eight from the industry and seven representing collectively the state, religious organizations, and youth offices.[7]

Rather than a mere censorship board, the FSK was to have a role in shaping the actual ideological content of films made in the 1950s. In 1951, the German *Länder* created the Filmbewertungsstelle der Länder (FBS), which later became the Filmbewertungsstelle Wiesbaden (FBW). Although the FBS and then the FBW did not rate the films, they could grant tax breaks to film companies that produced *wertvoll* [valuable] or *besonders wertvoll* [especially valuable] films. The FBS/FBW was dominated by government officials, and thus a clear ideological variable was thrown into the calculations, which film companies had to consider when producing films.[8] The end results were a lack of experimentation, an avoidance of controversial portrayals of the past, and a high level of provincialism. It was during this era that the *Heimat* films, literally "homeland films," became particularly popular, with over three hundred made in the 1950s. The genre included highly idealized themes of German tradition and life, almost always set in folksy villages and natural settings.[9] This was the system that many young directors rebelled against at the Oberhausen Film Festival in 1962. The result was a New German Cinema dedicated to heightening the aesthetic tastes of the mass public, although they in turn also demanded state subsidies.

In brief, the three media used to represent the macrolevel cultural matrix about the past in West Germany are, by and large, much freer of direct state control, but not wholly uninfluenced. The state's control is less hegemonic, but it is not absent. German federalism did not remove politics from television broadcasting; it merely moved it down one layer in the multilevel governance structures.

One must also consider the impact of the market on West German productions.[10] Whereas the state dominated in the East, the market dominated in the West. The demands and tolerance of that market for controversial confrontations with the past were anything but unbounded. This market influence, in contrast to an ideological state, allows us to draw greater inferences about the thoughts, ideas, and beliefs of the German public as a whole. If films with certain similar characteristics were more popular than others, then we can assume that the

German viewing public found them nonthreatening and comforting in some manner.[11] One must keep in mind that the three media outlets, film, television, and newspapers, had different levels of exposure to the market over time. Film has always been the most exposed to mass market pressures. To generate profits, films had to appeal to the broadest possible audience. Newspapers are also highly dependent upon mass markets, but these can be smaller and more partisan in nature. In contrast, the noncommercial public broadcasters, which were largely insulated from market pressures, dominated German broadcast television until the beginning of the 1990s.[12] This analysis helps us to understand why some German television broadcasters in certain instances could take chances in broadcasting controversial programs, which the programmers must have known would anger many of their viewers. These observations help to demonstrate the *memory-market dictum* outlined in the introduction.

The Print Media in West Germany and Holocaust Memory

Der Tagesspiegel published two articles in 1948 (see chart 5). One of the articles was about the 1918 November Revolution while the other looked specifically at the tenth anniversary of Kristallnacht.[13] The latter article was a brief report about a memorial service involving a Catholic and a Protestant priest as well as a rabbi. The newspaper report did not identify the perpetrators in any manner, and there was not a broader discussion of the persecution of the Jews. The religious setting as the memorial location without a clear presence of the state characterizes the typical ceremony in the earliest years. One reason why this earliest report occurred in Berlin was that after the war, Berlin had Germany's largest Jewish population.

In 1953, both the Frankfurt and Berlin papers ran very short articles marking the anniversary. Again religious groups organized the ceremonies, although the Berlin senator for culture spoke at one of the ceremonies. The Society for Christian-Jewish Cooperation [Gesellschaft für christlich-jüdische Zusammenarbeit] promoted one memorial service. At the Steinplatz in Charlottenburg, which is located in the heart of West Berlin, the Federation of the Persecuted of the Fascist Regime [Bund der Verfolgten des Naziregimes] unveiled a memorial marker. The memorial was constructed from the stones of the old synagogue, which had stood in the Fasanenstraße. In 1959, the new Jewish Community Center was opened on the same street. The *Frankfurter Allgemeine* report, only fifty-six words in length, merely noted the events that had taken place in Berlin the previous day. As in 1948, one can see the importance of civic organizations in structuring the earliest public acts of memory for Germany's disappeared and murdered Jews and in carrying out acts of collective remembrance.[14] In the earliest years, the initiative for creating public acts of remembrance about the Holocaust was primarily from the side of the society rather than the state.

The twentieth anniversary of Kristallnacht saw a significant increase in the level of activity within the society and greater participation by the state. Although they did not take part in the ceremonies, Chancellor Adenauer and Federal President Heuss both wrote letters to the Central Committee of the Jews in Germany. Little was reported on the contents of the letters except to note that Federal President Heuss identified with the Jews through the destruction of the synagogues. Once again the perpetrators remained invisible and even the victims were reduced to their houses of worship.

The Berlin *Tagesspiegel* began to offer images of the perpetrators by running two photographs with their historical report "Three Times the 9th of November"; the other two cases were the 1918 abdication by the kaiser and the attempted putsch of 1923.[15] One photograph showed SA men marching with a poster supporting the boycott of Jewish shops. While the photograph of the SA men does clearly suggest anti-Jewish action, it appears to have been limited to crimes against property. The date of the image is not shown, but it is probably from the first boycott against Jewish businesses in April 1933. This article falls into a subgenre of reporting on Kristallnacht that shows a particular fascination with the multiple meanings of the date in German history. The media would continue these discussions later when the Berlin wall fell on November 9, 1989. The author of the article granted one third of his story to Kristallnacht and did make direct reference to Auschwitz and what he called "the mass murder."

The center of the ceremonial activity was again Berlin with its relatively large Jewish population. Within the city districts of Berlin, there were ceremonies on slightly different themes. In the district of Kreuzberg, District Mayor Kressmann remembered the resistance fighters. The Steinplatz in Charlottenburg was used again as a meeting point for a brief ceremony in which District Mayor Bruhn placed a wreath at the memorial first created in 1953.

The highest level of state involvement revolved around speeches given by Berlin's mayor, Willy Brandt, a future federal chancellor. He spoke along with Heinz Galinski, the chairman of the Jewish Community of Berlin. Very little was actually reported on what was said, but we know that Mayor Brandt and Chairman Galinski both spoke at a founding ceremony for the new Jewish Community Center for Berlin, which was to open for the Jewish New Year in September 1959. The Jewish Community Center remains an important center of Jewish community life in Berlin and is still located in the Fasanenstraße, where the old synagogue used to stand. Galinski addressed two different audiences. First, he tried to assuage lingering German fears that the Jews had returned as avengers of the dead. He also directed his comments to the Jewish community living outside Germany, which had at times been critical of those Jews who had decided to remain. He claimed that this was a new Germany. Galinski said, "This building is not only a document of the Jewish assertiveness [*Behauptungswillen*] and evidence of loyalty in a civil homeland, but also gives shining witness to the will of the new German democracy."[16]

The reporting in the *Frankfurter Allgemeine* was sparse but did place a brief notice on the front page stating that Chancellor Adenauer had sent a letter to the Central Council of Jews in Germany [Zentralrat der Juden in Deutschland]. The contents of the letter promised reparations for material damages. However, the perpetrators of these crimes remained hidden behind the abstraction of National Socialism. For example, the compensation was directed at "the suffering which National Socialism had brought to the people of Jewish faith."[17] Another article in the same paper also avoids clearly identifying the perpetrators by slipping into the passive voice, "everywhere in Germany synagogues were burnt down and Jewish shops and apartments were destroyed."[18] The same theme of crime against property rather than persons is shown in *Die Zeit*'s first article addressing Kristallnacht. Significantly, the author, Hans J. Robinsohn, was Jewish and able to report on his experiences in Hamburg in the 1930s.[19]

Berlin remained the center of memorial ceremonies in 1963, although it should be remembered, as shown in the work of Y. Bodemann,[20] that Jewish communities around Germany regularly held ceremonies marking November 9. Berlin was filled with various ceremonies and acts of commemoration in 1963. Many of the districts held their own small public commemorations. In Neukölln, the ceremonies became a multimedia event with the showing of the film *Deveti Krug* [The Ninth Circle] (1960).[21] The Yugoslav film portrays the attempts of a Yugoslav family to save a young Jewish woman by having her marry their son. The rescue fails and the woman is sent to a concentration camp. Although we know little about the actual content of the ceremonies, the memorials that civic and state groups created around this time tended to blur the line between victims and perpetrators. Two of the memorials have the inscriptions *Mahnmal für die Opfer des Nationalsozialismus* [Memorial for the Victims of National Socialism] and *Für die Opfer der Gewalt* [For the Victims of Violence]. It is worth noting these two inscriptions, for they are the very words that reappeared on Chancellor Kohl's *Neue Wache* memorial in 1993. The German public at the time found these statements uncontroversial, as they were able to read their own suffering into them. The unique status of Jewish victims remained obscured. At the beginning of the 1990s, German and Jewish commentators would criticize the same sort of inscriptions, which fail to distinguish between different victim groups, thus demonstrating how the boundaries of the cultural matrix had shifted over the thirty-year period.

Galinski was present at the unveiling of a new memorial in Schöneberg, which marked the spot where a synagogue had stood previously.[22] He directed his words less at the past than the present, in which former Gestapo officials and members of the SS continued to work in positions of public administration in West Germany. It was during this time that there was a growing list of scandals of former Nazis serving in the judiciary and legal professions. Galinski's outrage was Jewish outrage, which found little echo in the rest of the society at the time. The article contrasts his "Jewish" demands for vengeance and justice with the "Christian" call to forgive one another and to seek reconciliation with God during a memorial service held in the Sühnekirche [Church of Atonement] in the concentration camp of Dachau. The Sühnekirche was the Protestant counterpart to the previously constructed Catholic Todesangst-Christi-Kapelle already present in Dachau.[23] Christians invited Jews to join in the Christian services. The service, again like the inscriptions on the memorials, was to the memory of "all the victims of National Socialism." The unique nature of Jewish suffering was again subsumed within the Christian Church, which demanded reconciliation with God, rather than earthly justice. When the Danish rabbi Melchior spoke during the service at Dachau, he was careful to differentiate between the Germans of the day and the previous Nazi regime,[24] although 42 percent of those living in Germany in 1963 belonged to the Nazi generation.[25] Such comments could not present more clearly the subservient role of "the Jew" in such services, for clearly "the previous regime" had been manned and supported by "today's Germans." Galinski's outrage was hardly the dominant voice.

But we can already note a change in the tone of Galinski's presentation compared to that in the 1950s. The boundaries of the cultural matrix were changing, and a growing fringe of intellectuals and critical journalists decided to challenge Chancellor Adenauer's reintegration of former Nazis into the public life of the republic. The challengers were clearly in the minority, but a countermemory movement was well under way. One important resource for this group was the growing symbolic legitimacy of their claims.

The *Frankfurter Allgemeine* also ran a couple of brief stories covering religious memorial ceremonies. There was a call for remembering "the victims of National Socialism" and the forgiveness of sins.[26] The *Frankfurter* also published its first major essay on the topic of Kristallnacht, which ran for a full page in the special section of the newspaper called "Bild und Zeiten" [Picture and Times]. The photographs included with the article again show damage to property, but the human victims are nowhere to be seen.[27] The tone of the article, while giving a full and accurate recounting of the events, is also archetypal for the conservative perspective: "[The crimes] which were committed in the name of Germany through German deeds . . . were so harmful . . .that we, in order to shake off an almost unbearable weight upon our national feeling, . . . sometimes wish we had the ability to wander out of our history."[28] This inability to empathize with the Jewish perspective is almost a universal problem for all German attempts to commemorate the Holocaust. The author continued: "The world stared at the time in disbelief at this wounding of fundamental human civilized behavior which was ordered by the National Socialist leadership. Likewise dazed and outraged was the overwhelming majority of the German population, even if they could give no audible expression of their feelings, and from the Party itself were expressions of . . . embarrassment and indignation to be heard."[29] If this majority was silent, how can we possibly measure this hidden sentiment? Graml was projecting his own wishes onto the silent masses. His defense of even Nazi Party members, however, becomes even more troubling and certainly speaks to the times in which he lived. The essay eschewed any attempt to characterize Kristallnacht as a Jewish tragedy by constantly returning to the theme that this was now a burdensome history for the German nation. Rather then seeking out the perpetrators, the essay helps Germans feel sorry for themselves. Although he mentioned the legal basis for much of the discrimination, he never attempted to examine the role of the courts, the bureaucracy, and many ordinary Germans in the persecution of the Jews.

As one can see in chart 5, the overall coverage of Kristallnacht for 1968 was down from 1963, as can in part be explained by the absence of the Frankfurt Auschwitz trials. The trials had gained a good deal of coverage on the radio (see chart 4) and other media, but the stories of the trial proceedings did not lead to a sustained discussion of the Holocaust in German society. The relative lack of coverage or interest in Kristallnacht shows that the lack of Holocaust commemoration was not one of the primary targets of the student movement.[30] *Die Zeit* in fact lent all of its 1968 coverage to the student movement and the 1918 revolution without any reference to Kristallnacht. The *Frankfurter Allgemeine* only reported a silent march in Cologne by those wishing to warn against neo-Nazi tendencies in German society. There was only a passing comment about the historical damage to Jewish property without identifying the human suffering or drawing any linkage with Auschwitz. Public figures again placed wreaths "at the graves of the victims of fascism."[31]

The fortieth anniversary of Kristallnacht in 1978 saw the first committed entrance of the federal government into the ceremonies of commemoration and a displacement of society-based initiatives. The spheres of politics, economics, and society joined at the end of the 1970s to create a sustained narrative about the Holocaust and the persecution of the Jews. For example, see charts 3 and 4 for the level of discussion in the cinema and on the radio. There was a new social willingness to engage the topic within the broader society outside those civic groups that had always been committed to the memory of the Holocaust. This was due in large part to the passing of the Nazi generation from each of the political, economic, and social spheres (see chart 2).

In Berlin, civic demonstrations in memory of Kristallnacht continued to be organized. Around five thousand took part in a silent march organized to mark the anniversary. There was also a protest outside the home of a Mr. Lischka, a former SS leader, who had been responsible for deporting the Jews from France in 1940–43.[32] The *Frankfurter* also had a longer list of civic activities than in the past, including some specifically Jewish activities, rather than acts of memory directed at the more anonymous "victims of National Socialism." For example, there were to be a silent march to the Jewish cemetery and prayer at the site where Germans had forced Jews together and humiliated them in public.[33] Although memorial services involving the Christian Church were still common, Jewish-specific activities began to move the unique suffering of the Jews to the center of civic commemorative activities as well. The balance of narrative power was shifting within the cultural matrix.

It is important to note that the heightened public discussions preceded the showing of the American television drama *Holocaust* in January 1979, which scholars often identify as the main cause of breaking the "silence" of the Holocaust in Germany. Rather than providing a dramatic shift, *Holocaust* landed in a cultural context dramatically more open to its narrative than at any previous moment in West German history. It was able to build upon and became part of a larger momentum for change.

Unlike in the past, some of the speakers did not try to skirt the issue of Jewish suffering. Federal President Scheel clearly portrayed Jewish suffering in this speech and went beyond the destruction of property.

"Millions of Germans had seen [the arrest and deportation 30,000 Jews to the concentration camps], and they had done nothing against it, or could not do anything."[34] In contrast, more conservative speakers like the CDU leader Helmut Kohl and the CSU Bavarian interior minister Tandler used the occasion to compare fascism with Marxism and to make general proclamations about the need for human rights.[35] As in the past, church leaders organized a number of special services to mark the anniversary including a service in the Sophienkirche, which is located in East Berlin.[36]

Also occurring at the time was a fairly public debate about whether or not the Bundestag, the federal parliament, should extend again the statute of limitations for crimes of genocide. The scheduled expiration of the statute of limitations for such crimes had already been extended twice, in 1965 and 1969, and was again set to run out in 1979. In each of these *Verjährungsdebatten*, the conservative opposition to extending the statute of limitations had grown stronger. This time the CDU leader Helmut Kohl spoke against the extension along with the FDP leadership, which had also opposed the previous extensions. When the Bundestag finally voted again in 1979, it was determined that there was no expiration date for such crimes against humanity, but the vote was the closest in history at 253 for and 228 opposed; if 38 members from the CDU/CSU faction had not defected, the vote would have failed.[37]

The most symbolically powerful and public moment of 1978 was Chancellor Schmidt's speech in the synagogue of Cologne, which had been rebuilt in 1959. Here was the chancellor of Germany entering a synagogue and asking the Jews for reconciliation. Prior to 1978, the majority of ceremonies involving Germans had been located in churches. Schmidt was careful to set aside the question of guilt and collective guilt by noting that individuals living today were almost all innocent.[38] He then went on to link the possibility that there were still guilty members in German society to the need to discuss openly the possible extension of the statute of limitations. The shifting boundaries of the cultural matrix created a new context within which civic and state leaders waged political battles over symbolic issues. The changing boundaries of the cultural matrix gave new legitimacy to those arguing for the abolishment of the statute of limitations for genocide.

Conservatives, on the other hand, were not at all pleased with the current tone of the debates about Germany's history. Joachim Fest, a prominent conservative historian and journalist, saw little need for Germany's chancellor to be prostrating himself before the Jewish community and the world. In an essay published in the *Frankfurter Allgemeine*, Fest recognized the need to deal with one's own history, but in a language typical of conservatives, referred to fascism and the Holocaust as a series of "accidents" or "tragedies" as if fate alone had been responsible for the outcome.[39] Similarly to Graml's 1963 essay in the *Frankfurter*, Fest focused upon the careful planning of the top Nazi officials in orchestrating the 1938 attacks. This clearly was not an act of popular anti-Semitism. Like other conservatives, he was willing to read the passivity of the Germans in a kinder light than the Jews who witnessed 1938. The fact remains that the individual reactions of Germans to the events of 1938 were certainly varied, but conservative commentators mark the passivity as indifference mixed with empathy, fear, and shame. Jewish commentators who actually experienced the attacks were less kind in their reading of this passivity. But this passivity, Fest noted, was common for all of Europe, and in fact the world at the time. Why had Jews who attempted to flee by ship been turned back by the other democracies? Why did the allies fail to bomb the camps in the east? These were also acts of indifference and passivity, Fest argued. He then closed his essay with a thinly veiled reference to the "avenging Jew" demanding compensation by stating, "The millions of murdered Poles and Russians have found few lawyers."

Die Zeit published several long essays related to the Holocaust, and the editorial line was clearly in support of extending the statute of limitations.[40] In one article, the author followed a small group of former SS comrades on a "nostalgic tour" of Czechoslovakia. They wanted to remember the good times during the war, including their work at the concentration camp of Theresienstadt. When asked whether they felt any shame or guilt, one of them responded, of course not. "We were Europe's soldiers and did our duty like all soldiers."[41] This concept of "Europe's soldier" is a popular reference to a long-standing revisionist version of World War II that focuses upon the so-called defensive war against the eastern barbarism of the Soviet Union. This and doing one's duty are archetypal themes, which appear in many German war films. We will return to these themes in the chapter on May 8. Although the *Historikerstreit*, or "historians' conflict," attracted a great deal of attention among intellectuals in the mid-1980s,[42] these same revisionist tendencies had been present since the 1950s. Again, it was the changed cultural matrix of the 1980s that made these arguments so explosive.

The national political scene shifted to the right with Helmut Kohl's leadership of a new CDU/CSU and FDP coalition beginning in 1982. As a source of data, the newspapers were always the most sensitive to the here and now of politics, and there simply was nothing to report in 1983. The only speaking engagement listed in any of the three papers was that of West Berlin's mayor Richard von Weizsäcker and Heinz Galinski at the Fasanenstraße Jewish Community Center in Berlin. In terms of the broader public, the speeches might as well not have been given, for there was no reporting on their content. There were also no reports of independent civic groups' taking any actions. As with the other five-year anniversary dates, the coverage was quite sparse (see chart 5).

All of this was to change again in 1988 when West and East Germany competed with each other to demonstrate their respective commitment to commemorating Kristallnacht. Unlike the East's generation of pure political spectacle, there was a fair amount of substance in the West along with a political scandal. The single most impressive display of memory work was put together by *Der Tagesspiegel*, which published a special twelve-page insert entitled "In Front of All Eyes" [*Vor Aller Augen*]. This was also the title of a special exhibit at the Academy of the Arts sponsored by the paper and others. The complete title of the exhibit was "In Front of All Eyes: Persecution, Expulsion and Destruction of Jews in Germany."

Der Tagesspiegel made a significant effort to report not only the history of 1938 and the persecution of the Jews to all Berliners, but also the roots of anti-Semitism in Germany. While the instrumentalist theory of anti-Semitism had deadened research into cultural anti-Semitism in the East, the West had also been very reluctant to search for the roots of anti-Semitism outside the Nazi Party. In contrast, these *Tagesspiegel* reports were extensive and unflinching in their criticism and analysis. Rather than a history of the Third Reich and the few guilty leaders, the articles probed the role of the press, the church, photographers, and Jewish community leaders during the Nazi years. There were also discussions about anti-Semitism in contemporary Germany.[43] The editors included photographs not only of destroyed synagogues, but also of Germans forcing Jews to march in front of their fellow Berliners through the streets in broad daylight to deportation centers. Regular police officers, not regular army or SS troops, guarded the marching columns of Jews.[44] One photograph shows the piles of bodies in Buchenwald, while another shows the deportations taking place in Hanover in 1942.[45]

An article by Günter Beukert, an Associated Press (AP) photographer working in Berlin in November 1938, reminds the reader of why the visual history from the Nazi period needs to be handled with care.[46] The Nazi propaganda officials allowed photojournalists to operate in Germany, but the propaganda ministry had to clear all photographs before they could be sent out for publication. Thus, the images we have of Kristallnacht are exactly the ones that the Nazis wanted released. We see and therefore we *remember* the synagogues that the Nazis set on fire but the human costs remained hidden, although they too were photographed. One photograph that Beukert did not even bother to submit to the censors showed a shop owner trying to defend his store against the SA. The SA men then beat him. With this one image, the passive Jew, whom the Nazis wanted to portray, is erased and the "night of broken glass" is replaced with a man being beaten by a group of SA men. But since this image cannot be seen, the memory of the event is lost, except for Beukert's retelling of the story. The texts about Kristallnacht had thus far tended to follow the visual story of the photographs the Nazis allowed to be released.

Journalists began to seek out and report more of the Jewish perspective and their views of German "passivity." Shimon Sachs had the following to say about the passive German society: "I have asked myself again and again, what sort of thoughts the people around us had at the time, those who behaved inhumanly and brutally at the time, and others still gloating. They all had closed their hearts and doors before the outlaws, the branded, before other people, to whom death was devoted."[47] He continued, "This changing behavior of the fellow citizens, their look towards us, first appraising, later rejecting, often with hate and malicious joy [Schadenfreude], never to forget is the feeling of powerlessness because of fear and abandonment." Such articles began to explore the cultural roots of anti-Semitism with greater intensity.[48]

The reporting in the *Frankfurter Allgemeine*, *Die Zeit*, and *Der Spiegel* had less to do with memory work and more to do with political scandal. Their collective reporting was almost solely focused upon the speech by the president of the Bundestag Phillipp Jenninger, the political fallout from the speech, and his eventual resignation two days later. Eventually almost everyone agreed that Jenninger was a decent fellow and certainly not a Nazi sympathizer, but in his speech he had quoted Nazi officials at length without distancing himself properly from what he was reading. The atmosphere within which the speech was held almost overdetermined his failure according to Ian Buruma. "Perhaps neither the setting of his speech nor the words entirely explain the debacle. It also had something to do with the climate of suspicion in Germany. Greens, liberals, and leftists suspected conservatives of using every opportunity to whitewash the war and conservatives suspected Greens, liberals, and leftists of rubbing German noses in Auschwitz."[49] As the editorial in the *Frankfurter Allgemeine* read the following day, "That the hour of remembrance in the Bundestag would be vacated by the Greens is fairly normal."[50]

Chancellor Kohl also held a speech in the west-end synagogue of Frankfurt, and his invitation to speak at the Jewish ceremony was questioned by some because of his support for the Bitburg ceremony held with President Reagan in 1985. There was some heckling from the audience calling him a liar. Kohl again emphasized that the Nazis had organized the anti-Jewish actions, reinforcing the German-Nazi division. Therefore, the shame of the day lay in the passivity of the Germans rather than their active participation. Although the chancellor was willing to name the crimes against the Jews, he did not clearly identify the perpetrators. The Jews appeared to have been primarily victims of an abstraction, National Socialism.[51] In an editorial, the *Frankfurter* reminded the younger generation that when confronting the older generation they should remember the terror of the time, which prevented action against the state or in support of the Jews.[52] The editorial invoked the terror state thesis to excuse inaction and passivity. According to Kohl and the *Frankfurter*, only the Nazi generation could judge itself, and it had found itself by and large innocent of all crimes.

One essayist in *Die Zeit* tried to explain the German passivity at the time but also referred to the "rule of terror." In stark contrast to the Jewish memories of Galinski and Sachs reported earlier, Leicht tried to give the same passive glances of the Germans a different meaning. "Many looked away cowardly in silent rage, but nonetheless there were many acts of private sympathy and a few acts of public solidarity with the maltreated."[53] Jewish and German memories of that passive glance that the Germans gave to the Jewish victims could not be more different! In highlighting this discussion about German passivity, the goal is not to prove one or the other more historically accurate. This is probably an impossible task. Rather, I want to highlight the divisions in interpretation that existed between Germans and Jews about *the meaning* of that passivity. These articles, television programs, and films engage in a struggle over meaning within the cultural matrix. It is a struggle in which material factors play a role, as I have tried to emphasize in talking about the political economy of image production and the memory-market dictum, but it is also to a very large extent a symbolic struggle in which symbols are the tools of action.

After the reunification of the country on October 3, 1990, many international observers and German intellectuals anxiously watched to see how the Holocaust would be remembered in the new German state. The antiforeigner violence that swept Germany in 1992 and the reckless recognition of an independent and nationalistic Croatia and Slovenia in 1991, thus feeding the extreme nationalistic movements in Yugoslavia, left many with the impression that a new, more assertive German nationalism was on the rise. The question that was on the mind of many observers was whether or not a unified Germany would continue to take responsibility for its past. The conservative-nationalists had always seen the memorialization of the past as a barrier to building a normal German nation, a nation like other nations.[54] Essayists and editorialists in all three papers noted the multiple meanings of the day for Germans.[55] After the cultural shift of the 1980s, Chancellor Kohl found it difficult to revive the memorial tradition of the 1950s and 1960s at the *Neue Wache* memorial with its generic epitaph, *To the Victims of Tyranny*.[56] The new cultural matrix offered Jews an ever-greater public forum within which to project their own interpretations of the past.[57]

Despite all of the concern, relations between Germans and Jews had, perhaps, begun to develop in a new direction. Perhaps for the first time, some of the articles and programs began to express a *sense of loss*. Rather than the day's being only a burden because of the shame and guilt associated with it, it was also a moment to reflect upon what had been lost. Throughout all of the reports up to 1998, a sense of mourning had always been missing. Previously, commentators had attempted to try to explain the behavior of ordinary Germans, or political elites had admonished the younger generation not to be too judgmental, for they had never experienced life in a terror state. Although the commemorations had eventually given Jewish suffering a central place in the ceremonies, and Germans began to enter synagogues rather than rabbis' entering a church, the ceremonies and the reporting were almost always marked primarily by discussions about guilt (and rejecting it), shame, and responsibility.

By 1998, the tone appeared to have shifted to one more of mourning and a sense of loss. It is too much to claim that the division of the Holocaust, the division between Germans and Jews, has been overcome, but there were hints of a new point of view that saw the Holocaust as something that had been done to *us* and *ourselves* as a German society and community rather than just to *them*. Nonetheless, the *by us* narrative and the identity of the perpetrators remained weak. This was not the self-pity of earlier years in which Germans sought to cast themselves as victims alongside Jews, but rather a perspective in which some German authors began to regret the loss of Germany's Jews, not because of the resultant shame and charges of guilt, but because of their valuable role in German society.

For example, in a report about the rebuilding of a synagogue in Dresden that the National Socialists had destroyed the author maintained the division between Germans and Nazis, but there was more of a celebratory tone to the article. With the rebuilding of the Dresden synagogue, the author saw Germans and Jews' reclaiming their joint history. Other synagogues had been rebuilt, but this one would be rebuilt with the aid of the Saxon government to the tune of 20 million DM. Furthermore, not only was the rebuilding project mentioned, but the author gave details about the Jewish community that used to live in Dresden. We learn that of the 6,000 Jews who lived in Dresden before the war, only 174 had survived, including Victor Klemperer, whose diaries have given us an inside view of the Nazi regime.[58] Moreover, there were details of what the Jews had done historically for the city, how they had helped to make Dresden one of the cultural and scientific centers of Europe. The article showed the reader a map of the Old City of Dresden and the centrality of the synagogue to the layout of the inner city. Not only was the most important Jewish building in the city located at its heart, but it was designed and built in 1840 by Gottfried Semper, the city's most prominent architect. German and Jewish histories were intertwined again, as they always had been, in the rebuilding of the synagogue.[59]

Another article went beyond "the Nazis" and looked at how the Nazi state had co-opted so many different sectors of the society. There was a long article looking at the history of volunteer fire departments at the time and their willingness to cooperate with the SA during the burning of the synagogues. We know that the fire departments in large cities such as Berlin and Dresden all the way down to the small localities were present for the burning of the synagogues because their presence was necessary to assure that neighboring "Aryan" buildings were not damaged. Despite an evening filled with thousands of arsonist acts, there was apparently only one act of resistance when some firemen attempted to extinguish the flames despite orders not to do so. In Berlin, witnesses have claimed that the firemen stood around joking with the SA members as the synagogue in the Fasanenstraße burned.[60] Such reports brought new perspectives on German "passivity" to light.

In another article, an example of German activism for the defense of Jewish property was given in the story about Wilhelm Krützfeld, a Berlin police officer, who sought to fend off a mob at the Oranienburger Straße synagogue in Berlin.[61] Although he was demoted and pensioned by the Nazis, he was not shot on sight, thus offering another insight into the nature of the terror state mythology. Such local histories and other commemorative initiatives were becoming more commonplace. In Potsdam, students had put together an exhibit along with their professors to give witness to the fate of the Jews of their city.[62] In Berlin, the twelfth annual Jewish Cultural Days opened with a wide range of activities, which in this year focused on the links between Vienna and Berlin.[63]

The year 1998 was not without intellectual and political bickering. A very public debate erupted between Ignatz Bubis, the president of the Central Council of the Jews in Germany, and Martin Walser, one of Germany's best known postwar authors. In its simplest form, the debate was about how to remember the Holocaust, and whether Germany was now "normal." The discussion became wide ranging as many other commentators weighed in on the subject of remembering Auschwitz, and *Der Spiegel* ran a cover story on the debate.[64] The debate even began to attract international attention, and Roger Cohen ran a story in the *New York Times*.[65] One beneficial outcome of the debate was that some of the ritualized behavior between Germans and Jews had been upset and overturned so that members of each community could criticize members of the other community without immediately being labeled as deviant. Jews and Germans set aside some of the ritualized "niceness" toward the other, and they created a new discursive space within which, perhaps, more open debates could be held in the future.[66]

West German Television and the Holocaust

In 1953, the first full year of television broadcasting, the ARD presented a fifteen-minute program entitled *Schicksalstag 9. November* [Day of Fate 9th of November].[67] Although there are no other details about the program, it probably followed the same format as we have seen in the newspapers, in which the program discussed the multiple events on this "fateful day."[68] In 1958, the ARD offered a similar program, entitled *Schicksalstag des deutschen Volkes* [Fateful day for the German Nation].[69] Denoting the role of fate suggests a distancing of human responsibility for the events linked with the ninth while also marking it as a day of fate solely for "the German Nation." In his extensive analysis of German television between 1955 and 1965, Classen notes that prior to 1960, November 9 was not used as a symbolic date to discuss anti-Semitism on television.[70]

Thus, it is surprising to find that the BR presented the French documentary film from Alain Resnais, *Night and Fog* (1955), at Easter in 1957.[71] The fact that the BR showed the film at such an early date is surprising. In 1956 the German Foreign Ministry worked to influence the French Foreign Ministry to block the premiere of the film at the Cannes Film Festival.[72] After protest from some French intellectuals and press coverage in *Le Monde*, the film was shown at Cannes but outside the competition. The German government's official defense of this move was that the film threatened to give new life to hatred against the Germans. This was not the only time the Foreign Ministry worked to block a film premiere at Cannes.[73] At the same time, the film certainly had its German supporters. It was shown at around this time at the Berlin Film Festival in the presence of Willy Brandt, then the president of the Berlin Parliament. An edited version of the film was also shown to school classes in Germany. Some copies removed Hanns Eisler's musical soundtrack for the pictures from Westernbork, a Dutch transit camp to the death camps in the east, when *Das Deutschlandslied*, the national anthem, was played in the background of the original.[74] I will return to the public reception of Resnais's masterpiece later, when the ZDF showed it in 1978.[75]

Waldhausstr. 20 was unlike many television dramas produced at the time.[76] Rather than the usual sparse theaterlike stage settings, this television film strove for a higher level of realism and probably was better received by the public. Reflecting the close work between the church and Jews in trying to create a brotherhood of faith, which was reflected in the early joint efforts at memorial services reported in the newspapers, the film helps to support the image of a Christian Church that took great risks to save Jews. This was a common theme of the time in television dramas. The ZDF had a series entitled *Menschen helfen Menschen* [People Help People], which dealt occasionally with the theme of Christians' helping Jews.[77]

In this way, such films and television dramas were able to help reinforce social beliefs and faith in a good Christian community, which had maintained its faith in the face of Nazi barbarity. These films are an excellent example of how cultural products can work to strengthen and legitimize existing social institutions. The church was an essential institution in the lives of many Germans after the war, as it was one of the few social institutions that emerged from the Nazi period with its legitimacy comparatively intact. However, it would be a mistake to view culture in a purely functionalist manner.[78] Culture and cultural products are not merely stabilizing or equilibrium seeking, but also potentially the main vehicle for social disruption and revolution. The playwright Roth Hochhuth was able to use his play *Der Stellvertreter* [The Deputy] (1963) to attack these very sensibilities and to try to disrupt this highly biased view of church activities during the Nazi years. Film directors launched such criticisms against the role of the church during the fascist years on a more regular basis in later years, as, for example, in the films *Das schreckliche Mädchen* [The Nasty Girl] (1990) and *Leni* (1994).[79] We will return to these films in the next section.

Waldhausstr. 20 was completely in tune with its times when it portrayed the passionate dedication and self-sacrifice of Pastor Tornqvist, a Swedish pastor, in his attempt to save Jewish lives in wartime Berlin. When he first discovers a group of Jews and a German deserter hiding in the basement of his church, he is upset. This will jeopardize the position of the church's mission in Berlin! But then he begins to realize that this indeed is the church's mission. After a series of escapes and near-captures, in which Pastor Tornqvist puts himself in harm's way, he arrives too late at the meeting point but sees that the others have safely boarded the ship to Sweden and are sailing away. The closing shots show him watching in satisfaction as the ship steams away, as we hear the dogs of the SS in the background. He is trapped, but he turns to face his pursuers and walks toward his martyr's cross.

The Christian symbolism of self-sacrifice and martyrdom is unmistakable at the end of the film. These same images of a redeeming martyr recur in various forms in many postwar narratives. This is especially clear in the narratives surrounding the July 20 assassination plot discussed in chapter 4, so we will return to this point later. In this TV drama, there is no attempt to explain or examine the roots of anti-Semitism, as this would obviously require an examination of the church's own anti-Jewish theology.[80] The SS officers are evil but pragmatic. All of this tends to lead one to the conclusion that the anti-Semitism in the film can only be accounted for by an insane Nazi leadership. Their implied insanity places them outside the history of the German community.

During its first full year of broadcasting in 1963, the ZDF presented two programs related to the ninth, although there is only archival material for one of them, *Bilanz eines Verlustes* [Balance of a Loss],[81] with the subtitle "Jewish Fellow Citizens in Germany—Yesterday and Today." The forty-five-minute film hosted by Joseph Müller-Marein, the chief editor of *Die Zeit*, and Karl Marx, chief editor of the *Wochenzeitschrift der Juden in Deutschland* [Weekly Newspaper for the Jews in Germany], was based upon interviews with Jews still living in Germany. The film dealt explicitly with the persecution of the Jews during the Nazi regime and did not shy away from the Holocaust. Although the producers tried to talk to Jews still living in Germany, they spoke almost exclusively with official representatives who carefully avoided any sensitive issues.[82] The program demonstrates an early attempt to address the theme of loss, rather than just shame or redemption, and reminds us that the discursive development of different themes is not linear or exclusive to specific periods. Instead, one can find bits and pieces of the different themes at many different points in time, as demonstrated by the film *Long Is the Way*.

Bilanz eines Verlustes attracted a fairly small audience of only 12 percent despite being shown in prime time after a popular entertainment program. Those who did view the program were also quite negative in their reaction. Although the program as given a +3 rating, about half of the viewers rejected the program, stating clearly, "One should leave the past in peace, I do not want to hear or see anymore."[83] In terms of the audience surveys that I used in this research, for almost every program dealing with National Socialism and the Jews between 10 percent and 20 percent of its viewership expressed such sentiments. The 50 percent reported for this program is certainly well outside this estimated norm. One reason for this might be the explicitly Jewish perspective of the film. When films or television programs included Jews saved by Germans, this could be comforting for the audience. When Jews talked explicitly about their suffering without the theme of redemption, represented by the good German saving a Jewish life, the subject was more likely to stir up feelings of guilt and resentment.

At the same time, the other half of the viewers were somewhat enthusiastic in their support of the program. Some commented that there should be more such programming on television, and others thought such programming particularly important for the younger generation so that they could learn from the past and prevent such events from recurring. Such data help to offer a more differentiated view of German society as wholly supporting neither silence nor disclosure, and the program itself shows an attempt by public television to engage in difficult questions about the past. The polarized reactions should also remind us that the meaning of a given social artifact is not *in* the artifact but created in practice and social interaction.

Broadcast as part of a Week of Brotherhood, *Die Verschlossene Tür* [The Locked Door][84] again has a good German going to the rescue of a Jew. At the beginning of World War II, Baron von Kedell is given some new land in Poland as compensation for the loss of his estate in the Baltic. He learns that he will be given the estate of a Polish family with the name of *Redzinski*, but they too are not the true owners of the land. To his surprise, Kedell discovers the true owner of the estate deadly ill in one of the rooms, a Jewish banker named Dr. Levi. His own brother had died in an accident during the resettlement of the family from the Baltic, and he hopes to use this false identity to save the life of Dr. Levi. The baroness is able to nurse Dr. Levi back to health, but the chance of discovery is always hanging over the household. Eventually Kedell's son and wife abandon him and Dr. Levi when it becomes clear that he is willing to sacrifice the well-being of the family to save Levi's life. Shortly before the end of the war, Dr. Levi's true identity is discovered, but a breakthrough on the eastern front allows the Russians and Poles to arrive before the Nazi officials. But now the Polish mob wants to kill all of the Germans. Baron Kendell is able to flee in time through the warning of a friend, but Dr. Levi remains, believing that he is safe. However, he is mistaken for his "brother" by the fanatical Polish crowd and shot.

Die Verschlossene Tür has a number of similarities to *Waldhausstr. 20.* The narrative inserts Jews into the story as a way for the main protagonist to prove his humanity in difficult times. The madness that is seeking to kill all of the Jews is external and abstract in both stories. In the qualitative evaluation of the program for the audience survey, the analyst noted that the narrative was effective in subverting traditional German defensiveness in handling Jewish themes. This is apparently the reason why the film was well received with a +5 rating and a fair share of the market with 24 percent.[85] The good German is twice dispossessed of his estate by the fateful turn of world events beyond his control, and he is threatened, in the end, by a racist Polish mob. The German audience did not appear to question his being compensated with "Polish" property, which had been made possible because of German occupation of that country. As in most narratives where Germans are shown in occupied territory, their presence is tolerated or even welcomed by some locals. The Polish mob allowed the German audience to view themselves as victims at the end of the film on equal footing with the Jew, who is sacrificed to the Polish mob as a "German," because of his mistaken identity. Despite this very soft handling of "the Jewish question," 14 percent of the viewers still complained, "Always these Jew-films."

During the same Week of Brotherhood, the WDR presented a film from Kurt Hoffmann, who had been unsuccessful in finding a film distributor for his work *Das Haus in der Karpfengasse* [The House in the Karpfengasse].[86] After the WDR broadcast, the small Gondel film distributor in Hamburg picked up the film for distribution. Hoffmann was probably surprised by his original difficulties in finding a distributor for his newest film, for he was a well-known German director of light entertainment with three previous "best director awards" to his credit.[87] This included his 1959 production *Wir Wunderkinder* [Aren't We Wonderful], which was an attempt to deal with the Nazi period through comedy and a cabaret style of humor.[88]

Hoffmann based *Karpfengasse* on M. Y. Ben-Gaviel's 1957 novel of the same title.[89] The author had sent a copy of his book to Hoffmann, who was an old school friend, and the director was so moved by the story that he had a script prepared by 1959. Since the story takes place in Prague, Hoffmann thought it best to film on location in the city. This immediately drew a harsh reaction and protests from German refugee groups, which were extremely hostile to any interaction or "collaboration" with the Communist regimes in the East. As a result, the film distributors began to withdraw their support. The *Neue Zürcher Zeitung* criticized his choice of filming venue, noting, "How honest can this film be against tyranny when the tyrants want to help make it?"[90] Only the small "neue filmform" distributor was prepared to release the film, but they were unable to find any movie houses interested in showing it.[91] Thus, the finished film project was dead until the WDR picked it up for television. This is a good example of the memory-market dictum, where the capitalist's fear of public rejection could work as a very powerful censor, and as an indicator of perceived public attitudes. German public television could take a risk that the film industry shied away from.

The film was also to have been shown at the Cannes Film Festival, but the organizers withdrew the film. At the time, news reports said the festival directors had rejected the film because of "technical-aesthetic" considerations.[92] However, it now is fairly clear that the film was pulled under direct pressure from the German Foreign Ministry. The German ambassador in Paris apparently was responding to domestic political pressure organized by the Bundestag CDU member Gustav Adolf Gedat.[93] Hoffmann also had to deal with very negative and aggressive public charges that he was a Communist sympathizer, for having made the film in Prague, and of being a *Nestbeschmutzer*,[94] the dirtier of one's own nest.

In the end, the film received numerous German film awards. Hoffmann was awarded the Deutschen Filmpreis as best director, and the film was given first place in the "best film" category.[95] The Protestant and Catholic Churches also awarded the film special recognition in their respective film publications. But without the backing of a large German distributor, the film never reached the German public except for its original television premiere. At the end of 1965, it was not even ranked among the top 190 films for the year.[96] Part of this resistance to the film might also have been orchestrated by local film control boards, which were also responsible for giving film recommendations. The Filmgutachtungskommission für Jugend und Schule [The Film Expert Commission for Youth and Schools] in Berlin voted 5:2 against recommending the film, again because of its "artistic shortcomings."[97]

What was then so controversial about the content of this film? If it had been produced in another country by a different director in a different time, there would be little to get excited about. The film opens with the camera surveying the mystical rooftops of Prague as the narrator tells us about the Jews and their history in the city.[98] What follow are four short narratives about different characters who live at 115 Karpfengasse at the beginning of the German occupation. Unlike in previous television films where the audience is given the opportunity to identify primarily with good Germans helping Jews, they are asked to identify directly with Jewish characters without German intermediaries. Moreover, the Germans in the film, rather than strictly Nazis or SS, are responsible for the suffering of the Jewish characters. It was another thirteen years before German audiences would have a domestic film production dedicated to a Jewish point of view with *David* (1978).

In 1966, there was a short film production at the BR called, *Denn ihrer war die Hölle* [Because It Was Hell to Them] based upon a book from Inge Deutschkron.[99] According to the BR's own archival records, the film was never broadcast.[100] The film was produced as part of the BR Student Program and shows without subterfuge the humiliation and brutality to which the Germans subjugated the Jews. It is all the more shocking in its portrayal of life in the Jewish ghettos and concentration camps for the images have been drawn by children. The publication of the drawings in the book and the filming by the BR challenge the claims by many scholars and intellectuals that the Holocaust defies representation. The children's drawings are all the more shocking because they present the Holocaust in all its cruelty and barbarity without reservation and in simple drawings. They do not feel bound by intellectual discussions about "the limits of representation"; they need only to express what they have witnessed.

One of the earliest dramatic representations of concentration camp life in West German cinema or television is Egon Monk's *Ein Tag* [A Day].[101] Although there is a stark portrayal of life in a concentration camp in 1939, this is before the creation of the death camps in the east. Nonetheless, the portrayal is realistic and harsh and does directly address the persecution of the Jews. Most significantly, the audience is introduced to the Communist resistance. As will be shown in chapter 4 on July 20, narratives about Communist resistance are almost wholly absent in West Germany. Not only do we learn about the resistance of the Communists outside the camp, but we also learn about their organization within the camp and their attempts to control the brutality of some of the criminal inmates while also trying to help the Jews. The final scenes in the drama provide a shattering contrast with the reality of camp life as we witness life back in the city. We see dance contests, people going to the theater, and life continuing much as normal for most of Germany society. By juxtaposing the camp life with the everyday normality outside the camp, Monk was leveling a powerful critique against the terror state thesis. We follow the camp commander into a restaurant, and he glides without moral hesitation back into normal society. Monk then blends in the sounds of the camp over this image of normality, and the two worlds collide in aural and visual dissonance.

Ein Tag is a remarkable film for its day. It not only directly confronts the unique persecution of the Jews in the camps but also allows Communists to be respectable members of "the other Germany." In contrast to *Lang ist der Weg* and *Denn ihrer war die Hölle*, *Ein Tag* demonstrates that it was possible not only to create subversive cultural products but also to have them reach mass audiences. After the showing of the American television series *Holocaust* in 1979, some critics made blanket condemnations of the German cultural production since the war, asking why Germany had never produced such a work. The truth is that there were earlier examples, but some of them such as *Lang ist der Weg* simply did not find an audience because distributors refused to touch them. In the early postwar years, there was no television outlet, which later saved Hoffmann's *Das Haus in der Karpfengasse* from oblivion. Hoffmann's film offers many of the sentimental messages that made *Holocaust* such an emotional and popular package, but his film was playing to the Germany of 1965, not the Germany of 1979.

The earlier ZDF presentation of *Bilanz eines Verlustes*, and its search for Jews in Germany, found many echoes in the following decades. A similar hour-long program was presented on the BR in 1972, *Juden in München (Münchner Juden)* [Jews in Munich/Munich Jews].[102] The program is based upon a series of interviews with Jews about their childhood in Munich, their experiences with the persecution of Jews, and their decision to return to the city. Almost a decade after the ZDF *Bilanz eines Verlustes*, the willingness to confront the past, to engage Jews living in Germany, and to ask them about their experiences had become much greater. This includes a willingness to go through the gate of the concentration camp and to begin to explore what happened inside. The political sphere and state had yet to engage the memory of the Holocaust fully, and many victims were still reluctant to speak about their experiences.

All of this was to change dramatically in 1978, but the roots for the social upheaval that followed had been developing ever since the end of the war. The year 1978 became a well-defined turning point in West Germany in no small part because this year marked the fortieth anniversary of Kristallnacht, which had since the end of the war been a day for remembering the Holocaust at the more local level, as the newspaper reports from Berlin have demonstrated. The federal government had begun to recognize the day as well with Chancellor Adenauer's first letter to the Jewish community in 1958.

This revolution in public commemoration was not limited to Germany by any means. Henry Rousso has marked 1974 as the beginning of a French obsession with Jewish memory and current manifestations of anti-Semitism.[103] Rousso identified a 1940s revival in the cinema, with some films beginning to pose questions about French fascism and collaboration with the Germans in deporting the Jews.[104] Two films in particular shook French society, Marcel Ophuls's documentary *The Sorrow and the Pity* (1971) and Louis Malle's *Lacombe Lucien* (1974).[105] It was within this charged atmosphere of new cultural possibilities that Claude Lanzmann began a ten-year project to interview as many Holocaust survivors as possible along with some of the perpetrators for his documentary *Shoah* (1985).[106] Unlike Alain Resnais's 1955 *Nuit et brouillard*, which was a cause for scandal and political manipulation at the

Cannes Film Festival, these films found a resonance within French society and became part of a wide-ranging public debate about Vichy, collaboration, and the resistance. Peter Novick has also noted that the 1970s were the turning point for discussions of the Holocaust in American society.[107] These broader cross-national patterns deserve further investigation and should remind us that discursive change is not constrained by territory and the sovereign state. Perhaps the scholarship on Holocaust memory is reaching a point at which such a cross-national synthesis can be attempted, but this remains outside the boundary of this current study. In a limited manner, this study demonstrates exactly this fact by looking at how the East and West German states and societies generated differentiated views of the past, and how the competing memories and countermemories clashed.

The ZDF dedicated two evenings to Kristallnacht's commemoration. The premise for *Das letzte Ghetto* [The Last Ghetto][108] was promising although its execution left almost all critics disappointed. Arno Rattay, the documentary's director, went to a Jewish hotel in Luxembourg to conduct interviews with German Jews close to Germany but not in Germany. Many found it very difficult to discuss the past.[109] One prescient reviewer in the *Frankfurter Rundschau* noted that it was all well and good to talk with the victims, but at some point Germans would have to turn the cameras on the perpetrators as well, and thus on themselves.[110] As we see later, this also began to happen, but the challenge remained to identify the perpetrators as something other than Nazi abstractions of evil, as in *Waldhausstr. 20.*

The following evening the ZDF presented two further programs. Immediately after the 9:00 p.m. news broadcast, Alain Resnais's 1955 documentary *Nuit et brouillard* [Night and Fog] was shown, followed by a talk show program called *Die Bonner Runde* [The Bonn Round], which was hosted by Johannes Gross, a German Jew.[111] Resnais's work is an oft-cited visual work on the Holocaust because as does Lanzmann in *Shoah* he avoids the use of the perpetrator's camera in showing the victims of the Holocaust. The narration for the film was written by the French poet Jean Cayrol, who was himself a prisoner at the Mauthausen concentration camp. The German translation of Cayrol's text was done by the poet Paul Celan, who also was a survivor of the Holocaust. As did many other survivors, such as Primo Levi, Celan was not able to accept life after his experiences and eventually committed suicide in 1970.

The quality of the television survey data is much more limited after the late 1960s, as many of the qualitative comments are dropped, and one is left only with the viewership percentage. This gap can be partly filled by the systematic recording of telephone calls placed to the ZDF in response to its broadcasts. Obviously such data do not allow one to deduce what percentage of viewers held the views of those who called, since there is a great deal of self-selection. In general, those who place telephone calls tend to make negative comments. Nonetheless, the data are useful in gauging how strong a reaction a program elicited, compared to other similar programs, and what range of negative comments could be found in the general population.

Das letzte Ghetto drew almost solely negative comments. Of the 56 calls placed that day about the program (146 calls were placed because of signal problems) only 3 were positive. The types of negative defensive reactions that the program elicited were wide-ranging. One caller complained that the suffering of the Germans was never shown. Another caller felt threatened again by accusations of collective guilt. There were even three personal threats made against the director Rattay. Earlier on the evening of the eighth, the *ZDF-Magazin*, a current affairs program, had dedicated part of its programming to Kristallnacht. This program also drew five critical calls with at least one caller again arguing against the collective guilt of the Germans.

The following evening the number of calls almost tripled to 139, although slightly fewer viewers saw Resnais's *Night and Fog* and the *Bonner Runde* than *Das letzte Ghetto*. Once again most of the calls were very critical. Viewers complained that they were "overfed" with Jewish material the past two days, while others again complained that such material was designed to pass on the collective guilt to the next generation. There were numerous other defensive reactions: Hitler was Austrian, not German; concentration camps were invented by the English; the documentary was nothing more than a French propaganda film; where are the reports about German suffering in the Russian prison camps; where are the reports about the guilt of other countries? Notice how the collective guilt thesis is easily turned on others. The log for the day also reported a couple of positive calls, or at least calls during which the viewer began to cry. One caller tried to explain through tears that "we did not know about these horrors." One can only imagine the reaction that the BR may have received after its first broadcast of the same documentary in 1957.

On the tenth, the ARD broadcast the NDR production *Als sie in Deutschland mit Steinen nach uns warfen* [When They Threw Stones at Us in Germany].[112] The critics had responded very positively to the documentary and often compared it to Rattay's *Das letzte Ghetto*, which many considered a failure. The simple documentary is composed of interviews with three German Jews, who successfully fled to England before the war. The narrator tries to draw a parallel between the biblical deliverance of the Jews out of Egypt and their flight from Germany.

Significantly, none of them had returned to their former homeland to live, but only Hans Fuchs clearly states his refusal ever to return to Germany. He says that it would be impossible for him to meet Germans and not to know how they had behaved at the time. Except for Fuchs's comment, the three interviewees avoid any specific critique of Germany or Germans then or now. Although all the German newspaper reviews I read praised the documentary, I was left with the impression that the director wanted to present Jewish witnesses to his German audience, but that he had been very careful in the material he decided to present. For example, the only female interviewed is hardly even "Jewish" in that she arrived in England as a child of German Jews but was raised by Christians and sees herself today as Christian. She is used as an example of Christian forgiveness, which contrasts in a rather unfortunate way with Fuchs's reservations. The juxtaposition of the two interviews reinforces the prejudice of Jews' being vengeful and resentful, in contrast to the Christian community based on forgiveness.

The impact of all these programs paled in comparison to what was coming. In April 1978, the American television network NBC broadcast a television series entitled *Holocaust.*[113] The miniseries was a financial success: 120 million Americans watched some portion of the show. In America, there was a debate about the merits and dangers of turning the systematic extermination of Europe's Jews into a commercial and dramatic product. For many European cultural critics, the fact that the product was from America's Hollywood was particularly distasteful.

In May 1978, *Der Spiegel* ran a story about the political ins and outs of putting *Holocaust* on German television.[114] The article even had to define the term *Holocaust* as "mass murder," as the word *Holocaust* was hardly in wide circulation at the time in Europe or North America.[115] The television series introduced the term into the German everyday vocabulary for the first time, as it did in the United States as well. The WDR already had plans to purchase the program, but for the show to be broadcast outside the regional net of the WDR and over the entire ARD network there needed to be a simple majority of support from the various regional program directors. In the end, *Holocaust* was broadcast over the entire ARD network at the end of January 1979. The public reaction was overwhelming, and a wide-ranging public debate developed about Germany's past, the overcoming of the past, the meaning of the past for the present, the lack of information in school textbooks, and so forth. *Holocaust* was on the cover of *Der Spiegel* the following week and was immediately followed by another cover story on Auschwitz and a multipart series about Auschwitz and the Holocaust.[116]

There are entire books dedicated to the reception of *Holocaust*, so I will be brief in my comments here.[117] The social phenomenon of *Holocaust* demonstrates that the making, meaning, and reception of a particular work of art are heavily dependent upon the time within which it lands. In many ways, *Holocaust* was already embodied in *Lang ist der Weg*, and if it had been created at the earlier date would probably also have failed to find a distributor. Even in 1979, some of the ARD directors had shown resistance to broadcasting the series. Furthermore, the medium of television shaped the reception of *Holocaust* by significantly condensing the impact of the product into a narrow frame of time. If it had been released as a film in the cinemas, there would not have been the follow-up discussions after an episode or the ability to call in to the various talk shows that were dedicated to the program. By appearing on television, *Holocaust* became the topic of discussion at the microlevel the following day and created an interactive environment between the viewer and the television stations. In contrast, the temporal impact of cinema is often much more diffused and usually lacks the same opportunities for interaction.

In terms of the public reaction to the series, it is interesting to note that the number of viewers who did not wish to engage the material at all because "one should forget this past" (22 percent), or had viewed the film and found that "the Germans should not be disparaged in such a manner" (10 percent), are roughly the same as what was seen in the television surveys of the 1960s. The hard-core segment of the society that had resisted engagement with the history of Jewish persecution in the past had remained relatively unchanged.

For those who were willing to engage the material, their opinions about what should have constituted ethical behavior at the time had changed. Before viewing *Holocaust*, only 45 percent of the respondents felt that Germans had a moral duty to make reparations with the victims. After viewing *Holocaust*, the number jumped to 54 percent. Before viewing the film, only 49 percent of the respondents thought the assassination attempt against Hitler had been justified, but afterward 63 percent found the plotters morally justified in their action![118] While the political and policy implications implied by the changes in attitude from a single film are difficult to measure, it is reasonable to propose that a very different piece of reparation legislation could have been created in 1978 than in the 1950s. The fact that a single film was able to shift this to a majority position, at least for the short term, clearly shows that perceptions of history can have direct and significant impact upon the political sphere by changing the boundaries of the cultural matrix. *Holocaust* also demonstrates that cultural products are not merely system sustaining or functional, but also engines for value, opinion, and cultural change.

Culture as a Matrix

In terms of formulating public policy, political leaders are always constrained and enabled by the culture within which they live, for culture outlines the realm of the politically possible and acceptable. Political scientists often make a mistake when they view politicians as pure rational actors, somehow exterior to the culture within which they live, as if they were completely void of any emotional sentiments. Political and social elites may certainly try to functionalize or instrumentalize history to suit their own "rational goals," but they may also fail, and the social dynamics can spin out of their control.[119] Furthermore, how is one even to define this rationality as disembodied from the culture? Can one realistically and seriously claim that German politicians are completely void or even primarily void of any sentiments, passions, or emotions vis-à-vis the nation's history? If the burden of proof to show that culture matters politically would be to have *Holocaust* spark a social movement for reparation payments to slave workers, then I think critics of a cultural and symbolic approach will never be convinced of the evidence that those interested in culture and symbolism in politics can provide.

One probably should avoid altogether discussions of variables and cause-effect relationships when discussing culture and cultural products.[120] It is probably more useful to think of changing cultural boundaries, which make some actions more likely while limiting others. For example, the growing prevalence of Jewish voices in German society is not the result of growing Jewish power measured in any material sense. Rather, their growing influence and ability to speak and be heard in public forums such as television, newspapers, and films are a result of a symbolic shift that grants greater value to what they have to say and their perspectives on German society. There can be no doubt that the cultural space vis-à-vis the persecution of the Jews and the Holocaust opened dramatically in the late 1970s. What followed was a sustained discussion about Jews and the Holocaust on West German radio (see chart 4), in films (see chart 3), and on television and in newspapers.

Mourning Loss

Die Verschwindenen Stetl [The Disappearing Shtetl] is one such search for the lost Jewish communities of Bavaria.[121] In the documentary, the director searches for the vanishing traces of previous Jewish shtetls or communities, in Bavarian villages. Before the war there were about thirty-five thousand Jews in Bavaria; now basically none is left. Those who survived have left forever. There is a true sense of loss and mourning in the documentary, which is something new and unique to the productions of the 1980s and 1990s and similar to the trend in some newspaper reports noted earlier. The *Burgermeister*, mayor, in one of the villages had the old synagogue restored in 1980 because he wanted to restore some of the earlier village life and to educate the youth. But in other villages, the synagogues' former lives are all but forgotten as they are used as a garage for a tractor, or a stall for animals or turned into apartments. There are only tiny hints, which the trained eye can spot, of their earlier uses as houses of worship. As the Jewish architecture collapses or is transformed and the older villagers die, the memory of a shared German and Jewish life in Bavaria is disappearing. In the documentary, these facts are met with a sense of mourning and loss. It does not yet lead to a search for the perpetrators, but such narratives can begin to weaken the "otherness" of the Jew for a German audience. The documentary seeks to remind the audience of a common life, once shared.

Ten years after the watershed events of 1978, there was a new openness in some of the documentaries about Kristallnacht. In *Reichskristallnacht: Die November-Pogrome 1938* victims are allowed to express their anger, rage, and disappointment, and the perpetrators are sought out and asked to account for their behavior.[122] The ZDF presented a new documentary *Als die Synagogen brannten . . .* [When the Synagogues Burned . . .].[123] The ZDF also presented its five-part television series *Die Bertinis* [The Bertinis], which followed the history of a Jewish family in Hamburg.[124] Jews were no longer the moral stand-in needed to prove the moral action of some Germans. They had become a subject worthy of their own story.

The BR *Reichskristallnacht* documentary has a much sharper edge than the documentaries from 1978. The perspective of the victims is less vague and deferential toward the German audience. Dr. Bernard Horn's eyewitness testimony from his experience in Frankfurt am Main is unambiguous. He saw some SA men beating a woman so severely that he was sure she probably had died of her injuries. The following day, the Germans forced him and others into the street to clean up the broken glass and smashed furniture. He recalls, "We were observed like animals in the Zoo." His fellow citizens of Frankfurt mocked him as he labored. One is left asking, "Where is all of the empathy, all of the silent rage to which so many German commentators have pointed?" The other Jews interviewed for the documentary also do not recall any "empathy" or silent support emanating from the Germans around them.

In an attempt to capture part of the perpetrator perspective, the directors interviewed Walter Käflein, whose father had been a police officer at the time. Walter was thirteen at the time of the anti-Jewish actions, and he recalls how his father was visited by local party supporters and told to do nothing that evening. Unlike Dr. Horn, Käflein can remember the outpouring of empathy that the Jews received from those standing in the street. Never have the memories of the victims and the perpetrators been shown to be so divided! Rather than the SS, the icon of Nazi evil in the cinema, he recalls how his father and other civilian police officers "had to" (*mußte*) seek out their own Jewish family to take to the deportation center. Obviously recalling what his father had told him, Käflein is proud to recall how dedicated his father was to his duty. The elderly Jewish women whom he had gone to deport offered him money if he would let them run away. He refused, the son proudly reports. The deportation itself was anything but a secret. People had gathered who were "curious," in the eyes of Käflein, and that might explain why he was there. He recalls some people cursing the Jews, and the narrator asks him, "What did they say?" "Oh, for example, 'You dirty Jewish pig. Now you're going where you belong.' "

Whereas the perpetrators had been wholly absent previously, German directors now began to turn the camera upon their own society. Rather than asking the viewers to empathize only with the victims, directors began to show the perpetrators. Rather than the abstraction of National Socialism, viewers began to learn more about ordinary German perpetrators. For example, Dr. Horn reports on how the leather coats that his mother had bought for the family store for the Christmas season appeared hanging in the display windows of the neighboring stores after their store had been plundered. Käflein tells us of his morally upright father who did his duty and did not allow the "clever old Jewesses" to escape. Ingelore Winter tells us of how she tried to play with a Jewish classmate, "who looked Jewish or what I thought a Jew should look like." German crimes and German prejudices were finally placed before a German audience.

Finally, the film introduces us to Dr. Fritz Hippler, who used to work in the film section of the Ministry of Propaganda. Perhaps this information might have put some viewers on edge. But then, after all, there had been good people in all parts of the Nazi bureaucracy, some might have reasoned. He then tells of how he went through the streets on the ninth and tried to stop a group of thugs from threatening a family in their apartment by identifying himself as an officer. An off-camera voice asks him, "What kind of ID was it?" The audience learns that Hippler was an SS-Obersturmsführer, or first lieutenant. Well, one might still try to defend him; "Not all members of the SS were criminals. Look at Chancellor Kohl at Bitburg in 1985." And then the directors splice in some scenes from the 1940 anti-Jewish film *Der Ewige*

Jüde [The Eternal Jew], one of the most notorious anti-Semitic films, which graphically compares rats and Jews in spreading disease and preying upon the German population. The audience then learns that Dr. Hippler directed the film. In trying to justify himself, Hippler notes that he believed in the good aspects of National Socialism and was willing to put up with the "crazy Nazi stuff against the Jews" in order to achieve the higher ideals of the party. Revealing the perpetrators did not guarantee any particular reaction from the audience. In 1978, roughly 30 percent of Germans probably still sympathized with Dr. Hippler's position, for they too believed that National Socialism had been a good idea that was poorly implemented.[125] As did many former "good Nazis," Hippler found the postwar era accommodating and was still able to work in the film industry.[126]

West German Cinema and the Holocaust

West German cinema's engagement with Jewish themes follows a similar pattern to what has been seen in the other data sources.[127] As can be seen in chart 3, the appearance of Jewish characters and themes remains relatively flat up to the middle of the 1970s and then explodes over the next fifteen years. This cultural buildup occurred largely independently of the political sphere, which only became heavily engaged in late 1978. At the same time, the cultural reach of film was decreasing, except when it was recycled on television. Whereas there were nearly 800 million individual visits to the cinema in 1957, this had quickly collapsed to 200 million by 1967 and has stabilized around 100 million since. Of these 100 million, only 10–20 percent viewed domestic productions.[128]

The qualitative trends follow a similar path of development to those in television dramas. The earlier films use Jews to provide a moral dilemma, which is often successfully resolved through the German protagonist's helping the Jew. The role of the church is never seriously questioned in the early films, while it is regularly criticized in the later films. The later films also provide examples of Jews who exist in their own right and independently of any German need to prove the moral worth of "the other Germany" in the face of National Socialism.

In the following section, I will outline these changing moral narratives across time by citing some films as examples. In doing so, I have tried to include films that have not received much attention to date. The numbers tell only part of the story, for it would be a misperception to say that German society had turned its back on the Holocaust after 1990 as over 6 million Germans went to see Steven Spielberg's

Schindler's List in 1994, which also contains a good German narrative.[129] At the same time, a domestic product from Michael Verhoeven, *Mutters Courage* [Mother's courage], hardly attracted even a handful of viewers in 1996. There is no doubt, however, that Jews disappeared rapidly from domestic German products after 1990. The reasons for this are unclear but are probably linked to the sudden reunification of the country in 1990 and a new cinematic fad of using this as material for exploring the wild and untamed east.

In 1948, *Lang ist der Weg* [Long Is the Way][130] was the first West German film to confront the Holocaust from a Jewish perspective, violent Jewish resistance, the deportations, and the death camps. Because of its explosive content, its initial social impact was limited to a handful of Berliners who saw the premiere in the Marmorhaus film theater. The film never found a German distributor and to this day remains one of the most important and unknown German films of the postwar years. Occasionally the film was shown at private film clubs around Germany, but it never has reached a wide audience.[131] The Jewish community has only very recently rediscovered the film, and the National Center for Jewish Film at Brandeis University made a restored copy with new English subtitles available. The film was shown at the 1996 Jewish Film Festival in New York and was also awarded the Spirit of Freedom Award at the 1996 Jerusalem Film Festival. But for fifty years, the film disappeared into the archives.

Completed in 1947, the film opened at the West Berlin Marmorhaus on the Kurfürstendamm at the beginning of September 1948. The film also opened in Paris, Vienna, and New York in December 1948. The Marmorhaus was the first Berlin movie house to reopen after the war and was a premier location to attract public attention to a new film.[132] Although the film was later well received in New York, segments of the German public were very hostile it. In October 1948, a poll was conducted of those attending the film at the Marmorhaus. One of the questions the audience was asked was whether or not they thought the film could have a conciliatory effect. Thirty-three percent said no because they believed a large share of the mass public was still inflexible in their prejudices.[133] The article on the film hesitates to state against whom the prejudice was directed, but there is no question that the Jewish main characters did not have the sympathy of some in the audience. Herbert B. Fredersdorf, one of the film's two directors, told the Berlin *Der Kurier* reporter that it was difficult to find any theaters willing to show their film. Fredersdorf noted at the time that this was hardly surprising, when "the Auschwitz crematorium is greeted with applause and cat-calls of 'There weren't enough that went in!' " Although DEFA partisans and East German authorities later pointed to *Die Mörder Sind*

Unter Uns and *Ehe Im Schatten* as examples of their willingness to deal with the Nazi past, in contrast to the West's, *Lang ist der Weg* was not given a warm reception in the East Berlin press. With the anti-Semitic and anti-Zionist purges gathering steam in East Berlin, the *Berliner Zeitung* attacked the film's pro-Zionist message.[134]

Greeted with a reticent and sometimes open anti-Semitism in the West, the film failed to attract the capital interests necessary for its distribution. Confronted by official anticosmopolitan purges in the East, the film had no chance there. It soon disappeared from the mass media landscape of German society and has since been neglected by most film scholars as well. Yet the very existence of the film confronts the widely held belief that German society was all but wholly silent on the matter of the Holocaust until the late 1970s. I will turn to the narrative of the film in a moment, but first I want to set up some other examples for a point of contrast and deal with some other themes so that one can understand this hostile reaction to the film.

As the evidence of this chapter shows, there was a growing social awareness of the Holocaust that had begun before 1978 and was then accelerated by the political events marking the fortieth anniversary of Kristallnacht. The period before this accelerated discursive activity cannot be misconstrued as a hotbed of activity, but neither is it an absolute silence. It is a peculiar kind of silence in which the persecution of the Jews is often acknowledged in a very brief manner. For example, in Frank Wisbar's *Nacht fiel über Gotenhafen* [Night Fell over Gotenhafen] (1959) there is a brief scene at a party when a Jew (an old man with a long beard and a star of David marking him) literally pops out of a closet and is hauled away by the SS. A clean-cut and dashing German naval officer comments, "We heroes stood here and let this happen."[135] In this instance, the military is shown as having "let it happen," although not participating. A similar passing reference is made in *Haie und kleine Fische* [Sharks and Small Fish] (1957) when Teichmann, the main character, learns that his friend's father has just died in a concentration camp. His friend comments tersely before shooting himself, "And my father had a criminal background, his grandparents were Jewish." While these examples certainly are not what many of us have in mind when we talk about *Vergangenheitsbewältigung*, the overcoming of the past, nor is it total silence. It is a peculiar kind of silence. If, on the other hand, the persecution is more central to the story, as in the television drama *Waldhausstr. 20*, then the victims are shown, but the perpetrators remain largely masked, abstracted, or demonized through the SS or the Nazis. We will return to the portrayal of the military in the chapters dealing with May 8 and July 20.

The most significant trait of *Lang ist der Weg* is that it takes a Jew's perspective, something that was not seen in German cinema for another thirty years, until *David* (1978). Significantly, both films were written and directed by Jews. Although there would occasionally be East and West German films between 1948 and 1978 that did include central Jewish characters, the German point of view was rarely, if ever, abandoned. Notable exceptions are *Jakob der Lügner* and *Karpfengasse*, the latter only gaining an audience through television. Jews were almost always objects for the German camera and audience.

West German authors did attempt to imagine Jewish characters, but as the literary scholar Ernestine Schlant has observed, these attempts were almost always failures. Thus, it should not be a surprise that German directors struggled to put Jewish perspectives on the screen. This is not to say that this was impossible or that "true" portraits are those of people only who know the ghetto, but German portrayals of Jews often quickly fell back on stereotypes. Ruth Klüger, who survived her deportation to Theresienstadt and Auschwitz in her youth, made the following observation of German attempts to create fictional Jewish characters: "[These characters] are derived not so much from observation or a study of Jewish history as from two sources, the tradition of anti-Semitism on the one hand and unresolved guilt feelings about the Holocaust on the other. The two trends seem to be opposite, but they are really two sides of the same coin, as brutality is often the flip side of sentimentality. And they can both serve the same function of self-gratification by providing a sense of superiority towards those who are presumed to be weak or morally deficient."[136]

As my analysis of the newspaper reports and television programs has shown, by the end of the 1980s and during the 1990s a modest process of mourning for the victims had begun; it was only possible because sections of German society began to empathize with the victims as victims unique and distinct from them, yet related to them. Unlike the ceremonies of the 1950s and 1960s dedicated to "the victims of fascism," Jewish victims became a separate category. This required the construction of new social categories, ceremonies, and rituals to separate Jewish and German victimhood. One part of this separation was represented by moving memorial ceremonies out of churches and into synagogues. The building of the new Jewish Museum in Berlin is another institutional response to this sense of loss.

As Schlant notes, this was far from the norm throughout most of Germany's postwar history. "This [empathy for the other as other] is a radically different position from the one adopted by perpetrators who have tried to identify with the victims because they see themselves, too, as having been 'victimized' by the Nazi apparatus; instead of grieving for the other, they feel sorry for themselves."[137] This feeling sorry for oneself, as a German, can be seen over and over again through the films of the 1950s until the present day. Although the persecution of the Jews eventually found a place in German cinema, the history presented by German cinema is one dominated by German suffering and piles of German corpses at the hands of the Nazis, the Gestapo, and the terror state.

The problem of how to grieve for the loss of the soldier-father on the eastern front and for the Jew at the same time has yet to be resolved. To grieve for the father, one must find meaning in his sacrifice and death. To make his death moral and noble, it must be separated from Hitler's fascist state and connected to the concept of *das Vaterland*, the true Germany, and the community of the good. The war must become a defensive war directed against the oriental barbarism from the east, and the military must be separated from the SS and the Holocaust. The strength of these myths, however inconsistent and illogical, should not be underestimated. They remain "true" and continue to provide a strong emotional attachment to the past for German politicians, social elites, and ordinary Germans.

Lang ist der Weg is a semiautobiographical account written by the film's lead Jewish actor, Israel Becker, who plays the lead character of David Jedin in the film. The film opens in Warsaw with daily life continuing as normal in the streets until the German planes fly overhead and the bombing begins. The scene is important because the beginning of the war is rarely shown in German films. Rather, Germany's defensive war against the east is portrayed more often. We are then taken inside the apartment of an elderly couple when a knock falls upon their door. Their faces are filled with tension, which is only relieved once their son, David, fills the frame of the doorway. He says only one word, "Ghetto." A line is drawn on a map, and we witness the Jews' moving into the ghetto. A long line of dispossessed Jews is framed by the camera, the buildings, and the street.

The horrors of ghetto life are clearly shown and the narrator reminds us of the thousands who died in the ghetto through disease and hunger even before the deportations. And the deportations arrive as well. The Jedin family is shown being transported to some unknown location. David is determined to do something, anything, and jumps from the train. It appears that he might have been shot by the guards. The soldiers on the train are portrayed as regular military rather than the SS.

David has survived his jump from the train and tries to seek assistance from two Polish farmers. The first attempts to betray him; the second helps him. In a highly symbolic scene, he takes his leave of the helpful farmer to join the partisans in front of a large crucifix in a field. The Polish farmer prays at the cross, and the camera uses the thorns on Christ's head as a visual transition to the barbed wire fence that surrounds the camp where David's parents have been sent. In the concentration camp, David's father is sent immediately to the crematorium, and his face is superimposed over the image of smoke rising into the sky as he prays.

David has reached the Polish partisans, but he has to capture his own weapon and prove his worth by killing a German guard. One of the partisans gives him a pistol, and there is a great deal of hesitation on David's part. He questions his willingness to fight. The partisan reminds him of those who have been sent to the camps, "For them, we must fight." To soften his transition into a resistance fighter, David kills or subdues the guard, but outside the camera's frame. The rest of his resistance activities are not shown. This was very explosive material. One must remember that even the attempted military coup of July 20, 1944, was never widely accepted as a morally justified act. Therefore, to have a Polish Jewish partisan (!) shoot and kill a German soldier was nothing short of high treason. In German war films, German-on-German violence is almost wholly absent; in other words, such violence is at the very periphery of the cultural matrix, that which can barely be conceived. Only when a German has been marked symbolically as a Nazi, and therefore insane, can he be killed. Remember that just before the showing of *Holocaust* on television in 1979, only 49 percent of Germans saw the attempt on Hitler's life as justified.

Images of fighting are spliced in with nonspecific scenes of partisan fighting. The war ends, and the long way home begins. Uncertain of the fate of his parents, David begins his long search for them. He returns to Warsaw to discover their apartment in the hands of someone who purchased it "legally" once they had been evicted. Most of the rest of the film is spent in a camp for displaced persons, DPs, where he meets Dora and discovers with her a new hope for the future. They struggle to make themselves feel useful during the long months and years in the DP camp. Eventually he discovers that his father was murdered in Auschwitz, but that his mother may still be alive.

Unsuccessful in finding his mother, David returns to the camp and asks Dora to marry him. She rejects his proposal at first. "Things happened in the camp," she says without being able to put her feelings and memories into words. Importantly, it is David, the Jew, who now imposes a silence on the Holocaust by telling her, "You have to forget all of that." The scene reminds us that the perpetrators were not the only ones who wanted to forget and remain silent about the Holocaust. In the end, she agrees to marry him. The film ends with David's finally finding his mother and looking forward to a possible future in Palestine. The final shot is of two men working a field with an ox and plow followed by the words "Long is the way indeed."

Although the film would never play to mass audiences in Germany, independent film clubs continued to show it throughout at least the 1950s: the Hamburg Film-Club in April 1952, the Hagen Film-Club in September 1952, the Essen Filmclub in January 1953, the Dortmund Filmclub in January 1955, the Club of Film Journalists in February 1959, and certainly many others.[138] Yet, even with its powerful presentation of Jewish persecution, resistance, and willingness to rebuild after the war, the film could not escape its own time or the moral narrative of the 1950s. One need only reflect again upon Schlant's observation about empathy and self-pity when reading the following from a 1952 newspaper article introducing the film: "The presentation of the Jewish fate grips us deeply. But let us not overlook: the Second World War, which in the end became a war of extermination, was advanced not only in the darkness of inhumanity portrayed in the film. The war did that also in the atrocious realm of all air raids against the civilian population, no matter from which side the attacks were led."[139]

Although the 1950s are commonly held to be a period of silence, there are a number of films that address Jewish persecution. In *Ich weiß, wofür ich lebe* [I Know What I'm Living For] (1955),[140] we learn of how a Red Cross nurse saved two Jewish boys during the war. In the present, however, the loving and caring mother must struggle with the courts to maintain custody of the children.[141] In *Friedericke von Barring* (1956), a German woman falls in love with a Jewish director and goes with him to America but returns to Germany after his death.[142] *Ein Lied geht um die Welt (Die Joseph-Schmidt-Story)* [Song around the World] (1958) is a biographical film about the tenor Joseph Schmidt, who was forced to emigrate from Germany because of his Jewish heritage.[143] *Liebling der Götter* [Favorite of the Gods] (1960) follows the story line of *Ehe im Schatten*, except that in this case the German film actress Renate Müller suffers because of her love for a persecuted Jew, once again putting German and Jewish suffering on the same plane.[144] The persecution of the Jews is recognized without broaching the true extent of the horrors organized by the Nazi regime.

The wartime persecution of the Jews, Auschwitz, and the Holocaust first begin to appear in the 1960s. If the 1950s were marked by a partial silence, the 1960s opened with new investigations, trials, and public knowledge. First, in 1961 the well-publicized capture and trial of Adolf Eichmann in Jerusalem raised public awareness of the process by which the mass execution of Jews had taken place.[145] Then from December 1963 to August 1965, the horrors of the Holocaust were presented before a German court. The Frankfurt Auschwitz trials not only generated media attention (see chart 4), but also sparked new and more challenging works of art. The trials were the first high-profile German attempt to deal with their own war criminals.

Even prior to the Frankfurt Auschwitz Trials, Wolfgang Staudte, now working in the West, sought to draw attention to the continued presence of former Nazi lawyers and judges in the West German legal system in his film *Rosen für den Staatsanwalt* (1959).[146] Later, Peter Weiss used the trials and transcripts as the basis for his play *The Investigation* (1965). In the same year, the film *Zeugin aus der Hölle* [Witness from Hell] sought to push the viewer even closer to a confrontation with Auschwitz.[147] The now-forgotten film was produced by Artur Brauner, who is himself a Holocaust survivor and responsible for the production of many films dealing with the Nazi past through his CCC production company. The story parallels the reality of the Frankfurt trials. Lea Weiss, a survivor, is asked to give testimony by a state prosecutor from Ludwigsburg in an upcoming trial against a former concentration camp doctor who participated in human experiments. The film focuses upon the psychological trauma that the witness must relive in trying to provide testimony to the court. Although Lea originally agrees to provide testimony to reveal the whole truth about the camps, she is pursued by her own fears and nightmares and eventually commits suicide before the trial begins.[148]

The 1960s were also marked by an aesthetic revolution in German cinema, which became known as the Young or New German Cinema.[149] The birthplace of this idealistic movement of filmmakers wanting to break with the traditions of the 1950s, and by implication the Nazi years, was the city of Oberhausen in 1962. The filmmakers stated their goals in the Oberhausen Manifesto, the key point of unity their opposition to "Papa's" cinema. Although the New German Cinema movement produced a number of award-winning films, and some of the films, especially by Rainer Werner Fassbinder, became the darlings of international film festivals, its attention to Germany's Nazi past was occasional at best. The filmmakers were on an aesthetic quest, which occasionally led them back into the past, but this was not the primary goal or critique.

The rescue of Jews from the Nazi Holocaust became a popular theme in the following years. Stories of near-escape, hiding, and self-sacrifice became common narrative themes in the films dealing with Jews. The much more common fate of mass murder and gas chambers remains offscreen, for there is no redemptive theme, no sign of hope in such places. *Wie ein Hirschberger dänisch lernte* [How a Hirschberger Learned Danish] (1968)[150] gives an account of how some Danes worked to save the Jews in their country during the occupation. In *Stern ohne Himmel* [A Star without a Sky] (1980), a group of German youth find a Jewish child who has escaped from a concentration camp as the end of the war is drawing near.[151] Jews also go into hiding with Christian help in *Blutiger Schnee (Zu Freiwild verdammt)* [Ruth] (1983),[152] *Bittere Ernte* [Bitter Harvest] (1984),[153] and *Versteckt* [Hidden (Forbidden)] (1984).[154] *Versteckt* is based upon the true story of how Gräfin Maria von Maltzahn saved the life of a Jewish publisher and author with whom she was in love.

If one simply were to look at many German film narratives about the persecution of Jews during the Nazi regime without any outside knowledge, it would be very difficult to piece together what was actually going on. The threat of death is certainly pervasive, but the true scope and scale of mass murder as well as how it functioned would remain largely a mystery. Perhaps the most effective dramatization of the Holocaust at its roots within the National Socialist movement is Heinz Schirk's *Die Wannseekonferenz* [The Wannsee Conference] (1984),[155] which attempts to recreate the January 1942 meeting at the Wannsee Villa in Berlin among top government officials and their planning of the Jewish genocide. The conversations and dialogue are fictionalized, as no verbatim transcript of the meeting exists, but the historical recreation is effective and legitimate, for it places the Holocaust at the center of the National Socialist program and not at its fringe, where some revisionist historians have tried to place it. The main theme brought across by the film is the bureaucratic nature of the genocide. During the meeting, one of the officials present questions the rationality of the anti-Jewish measures and the deportations, which will only add to the burden on the rail network and the ability of the army to move its troops. Reinhard Heydrich's response is central to the message of the film: "It is not a question of priorities. The steps toward a Final Solution are as important as all other war efforts. . . . Whenever we fight the Jews, we're fighting for the Reich."[156] The final shot of the film shows a soldier playing with his dog. The image is frozen along with a single note on a piano to underline the normality that could exist alongside mass murder.

The end of the 1970s and the beginning of the 1980s also saw the return of Jewish voices and Jewish perspectives to German cinema. Although he had been making critically recognized films for almost a decade, Peter Lilienthal in *David* finally restored a Jewish perspective of Jewish persecution.[157] Lilienthal, a German Jew, had fled to Uruguay with his mother in 1939 at the age of ten and had only returned to Germany in 1956. Based upon the autobiographical novel *David: Story of a Survivor* by Joel König, the film keeps its attention focused upon its central Jewish character as he experiences Nazi-led violence until his eventual emigration to Palestine. Not since *Lang ist der Weg* had a German film been able to empathize with a central Jewish character, and this time with some mass audience appeal. The film won the Golden Bear award at the 1979 Berlin Film Festival and reached a wider audience as a result.[158]

The return of Jewish memories to the German filmmaking process also meant the return of a Jewish perspective, which had been lost since the production of *Lang ist der Weg* immediately after the war. This was also the case for many documentaries, which were created by the children of survivors beginning in the 1980s. As children of survivors, they primarily experienced growing up Jewish outside Germany with parents who did not talk about the past. The personal documentary became a vehicle for many talented second-generation Jews to explore the roots of their own identity, which their parents often refused to discuss. Those born after the war were just reaching the age when they could take this personal quest to a wider audience through documentary film.[159] One such personal quest begins when Irene Lilienheim Angelico's father gives her the copy of a manuscript he wrote in 1947 about his experiences in the Dachau concentration camp and living in Germany after the war before his immigration to Canada. Her documentary, *Dark Lullabies*, explores the question that so many have already posed, "Why?"[160]

The personal documentaries of the second generation are a perfect example of how microlevel memories are transferred or not transferred within families. In some cases, the domestic silence pushed creative individuals from the second generation into public spaces to explore their Jewishness and their family's past. In this manner, the macrolevel discussions about the past are constantly being fed by the microlevel experiences of many different individuals. The two levels are constantly in interaction with each other. This, in part, helps to explain the late 1970s turning point not only in Germany but in other countries as well. Israeli society also experienced an extended period of ambivalence and silence toward the Holocaust as it did not fit within the Zionist national framework of heroism and action. Yael Zerubavel locates the critical Israeli turning point around the trauma of the 1973 Yom Kippur War, which made it easier for those dedicated to an active Zionist nationalism to identify with the vulnerability of the victims of the Holocaust.[161] The lack of a clear triumphant military victory helped Israelis to identify with past Jewish victims outside the state of Israel.

Obviously, there are many other films that one could discuss from the 1980s, but I want to close this chapter by focusing on three films, which address Jewish themes and were made after 1990. They have not generated much discussion thus far in the secondary literature because of their recent appearance, and only one of the films, *Aimée und Jaguar*, has recently had a major North American release. These films are of particular interest because many feared that a reunified Germany would become more nationalistic and begin to turn its back on the Nazi past.

The same year as the release of *Schindler's List*, two much smaller German productions returned to Jewish themes as well, and both played to much smaller audiences. *Auf Wiedersehen Amerika* had an audience of just over fifty thousand, while *Leni* only reached just over twenty-seven thousand viewers, after the filmmaker failed to find a distributor. With such small audiences, it no longer makes sense to view such films for their social impact, but rather to view them as examples of new cultural possibilities within the cultural matrix. They did not attract mass audiences, but the society had changed to such an extent that such films could be produced in the 1990s, while there is nothing to compare them to in the 1950s.

What did the postunification films have to say? *Auf Wiedersehen Amerika* [Goodbye America] (1993)[162] is a film about two Polish immigrants in America who have been living there for at least the past thirty years and have now decided to return to Poland. The character of Isaak is rather unique in German cinema, for he represents a Jew who refuses to embrace warmly even the newest incarnation of a democratic Germany. As he bluntly puts it, "I don't want anything to do with the Germans!" In general, Jewish characters in German cinema have often returned to Germany to find a new democratic land that they could warmly embrace, but this has often reflected more of a German wish rather than a Jewish reality.

In contrast, Jewish authors have often expressed deep reservations about returning to Germany or the former sites of their persecution at the hands of the Germans and others. In his autobiography, Peter Gay closes with thoughts about his difficult and partial reconciliation with his former fatherland.[163] When she returns to Germany for the first time, Irene Lilienheim Angelico uses a scene at a train station filled with drunken football fans and guards with large dogs visually to reinforce her unease at returning to the land of her father's persecutors. In a moving and powerful documentary that travels among Poland, the United States, and Israel, Marian Marzynski tells viewers about his own survival as a Jew in Poland. He tried to return to his shtetl once in 1969 but simply found it impossible to confront the remaining villagers with the questions he had.[164] The Israeli scholar Dan Bar-On had to return to Germany to pursue his research on the children of the perpetrators and spent many uneasy moments traveling the land of his family's persecutors.[165]

The national normalcy that so many young Germans crave because they rightly see themselves as innocent of the crimes of their parents and grandparents appears to them to be withheld by some Jews living inside and outside Germany. This often leads to resentment, for they mistake these reservations vis-à-vis Germany as a personal indictment. The cycle of resentment and self-pity can only be broken through a process of true mourning for the loss of Germany's and Europe's Jews and an empathetic identification with the victims, the survivors, and the children of the survivors.

For those seeking an answer to the question of "why," *Leni* (1994) may perhaps be the most fully realized story of the Holocaust ever made.[166] The story is powerful because it shows how the Nazi state worked even without terror and black-clad Gestapo agents. The movie opens in a small German village with the birth of a Jewish child in a church or monastery. The child, Leni, is baptized, and Sister Ludowiga takes the baby to an old couple, Johann and Alwina Aibele, and asks them whether they will raise her. They agree and become very attached to their little Leni. Everything continues as in any other childhood until the mayor discovers that "something does not make sense with the descent." Rumors begin to spread through the village that Leni might be Jewish, and the other children begin to tease her. The village priest, who has made anti-Jewish comments, is confronted by a socialist teacher about his anti-Jewish positions. "Were not Mary and Joseph Jewish?" he asks.

The scenes of village life and at the Aibele farm are far away from major world events. Rather than an apology for ignorance or an attempt to exculpate the characters in the upcoming murder of Leni, the apparent innocence of the village life is haunted by the fact that without direct threats from the Nazi bureaucracy, the villagers are willing to comply with the orders of the state. Unlike Edgar Reitz in his use of village life to create a separate other Germany in *Heimat* (1984), the director Leo Hiemer is willing to allow his main characters to disappoint the audience because of their collaboration.[167]

At Christmas Johann receives a letter from the mayor stating that the child must be sent away. There are a series of confrontations between the mayor and the family during which he tries to make clear to them that as an Aryan couple they cannot take care of a Jewish child. Johann's first reaction is to ignore the demands of the state, represented by the mayor, and he goes to the priest hoping that Leni will be allowed to attend school with the other children. But the priest turns him away, and Johann's family becomes more isolated from the life of the village. It is this everyday anti-Semitism and the closing off of social contacts that left the Jews isolated and vulnerable not only in the village, but also in the city.

Johann and Alwina continue to receive letters demanding that they send Leni to Munich. The socialist teacher advises them against it and recommends that they try to hide the child. But the elderly couple feels that it would be better to send her to Munich and carefully pack a suitcase for their little girl. A nun is even at the train station to greet them and to travel to Munich with Leni. The couple is sad to see her go, but this appears to be the only option. Then, Leni's suitcase is returned to them. Johann and the teacher set off to Munich to find out what has actually happened. They break into the Catholic center and discover that all of the children are gone. A worker at the center answers their questions in a matter-of-fact manner: "This has been going on for years. Every 6–8 weeks they arrive and collect the children. Sometimes a sister goes with them." Johann finds Leni's mittens, her hat, and the doll with which she always traveled, abandoned in one of the rooms.

The power of the story lies in portraying the implications of the villagers' behavior toward Leni and the family. Even if they did not personally put her on the train, the behavior of the villagers makes it necessary for her to be sent away. There is no question that had Leni been welcomed into the village life, Johann and his wife would never have sent her to Munich. The role of the church is also quietly exposed through the priest who appears to have encouraged the villagers to isolate Leni's family. Unlike *Heimat*, which appears to keep the villagers protected from the evils of a faraway Nazi state, *Leni* shows how those politics and the influence of the state were able to penetrate everyday life and draw upon already existing anti-Jewish prejudices. This distance does not protect the villagers from their moral responsibility vis-à-vis Leni, who is their neighbor. Rather than being the mythical silent masses that were frozen by fear in the terror state, the villagers use simple prejudice to contribute to the little girl's death. The complete innocence of the child makes the Holocaust all the more incomprehensible.

The film is based upon a true story from the Allgäu and was carefully researched by the director, Leo Hiemer. The setting in an idyllic village goes beyond the mere recreation of reality as Hiemer clearly intends to create an inversion of the typical *Heimatfilme*, which were extremely popular in the 1950s. Hiemer had the following to say about the use of this setting for the story: "If it is true that the Heimatfilm is the highest form of expression of the German longings for suppression, then there is no more disturbing setting for a Holocaust story than our home."[168]

The final postunification film to deal with Jewish persecution is the commercially successful *Aimée und Jaguar* (1998).[169] The film had attracted over 1 million viewers in 1999, something that German films rarely achieve in their own domestic market. The film still deals with the persecution of Jews in wartime Berlin, but the central focus is upon a love affair between a Jewish lesbian, Felice Schragenheim, and the proud Aryan mother, Lilly Wust. The film was based upon a best-selling novel by Erica Fischer of the same title. The intense and doubly forbidden love affair, which develops between the two women after Felice decides to seduce Lilly, certainly is the strongest attraction of the film, which is conventional in its storytelling. Although we do learn a bit about Felice's work in the Berlin underground, the war quickly falls into the background as the lovers discover their passions together. Felice begins the love affair without telling Lilly her true Jewish identity, and this revelation to a dedicated Nazi mother is almost too much. But the relationship endures until Felice is finally captured and deported.

Conclusion

In contrast with the state-dominated model presented by East Germany, West German newspapers, television, and cinema offered the occasional subversive piece of cultural work, but in general the capital interests needed to produce television programs and films reflected conservative popular sentiments. Without a broader social interest or social resonance, subversive works could rarely find the funding necessary to take them to a larger audience. The possibility of a breakthrough during the Frankfurt trails of 1963–65 was met by a general apathy or hostility in the broader society. For example, polls conducted immediately before and after the trials, which the German media widely reported, saw only a 2 percent decline, from 54 percent to 52 percent of those who thought a line should be drawn under the past, while there was a 4 percent shift in favor of continued prosecutions from 34 percent to 38 percent. In a separate poll from January 1965 a full 60 percent of Germans were opposed to extending the statute of limitations for war crimes.[170]

One of the central questions that this research tries to address is the political impact of changing macrolevel narratives about the past. If one sets aside a simple cause-effect relationship and instead treats culture as a matrix, which opens and closes the probability for different forms of political action, one can see the opening of a new social space within which to discuss the Nazi past. Chart 1 helps to demonstrate this growing openness, reflected in the cultural data discussed. One can see that public attitudes toward the Nazi era were in rapid transition from 1975 forward. Although the lines represent responses to two different questions, both basically ask, "What is your general view of the Nazi era, more positive or negative?" The divergence of the top two lines and bottom two lines after 1975 suggests a greater willingness to critique the Nazi years. This was not a linear progression from 1955 forward, as between roughly 1968 and 1975 more and more people were willing to recognize Hitler's "achievements" as balancing off the negative side of the war. Yet, as the public space and cultural matrix became more permissive of critical discussions of the Nazi era, the possibilities for macrolevel discussions vis-à-vis the Holocaust increased.

This was also a period of important demographic developments and generational change. Defining generations can be a rather arbitrary exercise upon which one can project all sorts of supposed traits, attitudes, values, and trends. This is particularly true for so-called generations that are not defined by any dramatically significant social event of the scope and scale of a war or other massive social upheaval. But the study of generations shaped by massive social upheaval caused by wars is recognized as a legitimate part of sociological investigations dating back to the work of Karl Mannheim. One can safely argue that there is a World War II generation or Nazi generation, which has had a lasting impact upon postwar German society. To define such a generation is not to assign any homogeneous trait to them other than that they shared experiences during a particular time. Their evaluation of that experience varied significantly, as the earliest data in chart 1 suggest. Although we lose the ability to track age and attitudes in the data, what is clear is that the dominant discourse of the 1950s was not the same as that of the 1980s. As those with living memories of the Nazi era passed from employment into retirement, the cultural matrix for critical discussion opened further (see chart 2). By 1980, they accounted for only 19 percent of the total population and 7 percent of the potential labor force.[171] Although their proportion of the potential labor market was all but gone in 1980, members of this generation had dominated leadership and management positions through the mid-1970s. The passing of this generation removed a major point of potential social resistance to a critical evaluation of the Nazi past. Their declining political, economic, and social influence created new cultural space for reevaluating the past within the macrolevel. This does not mean that noncritical attitudes toward the Nazi era were not passed on to a new generation. In 1997, of those who consider themselves as the political Right, 35 percent believed Hitler would have been one of Germany's greatest statesmen except for the war, and 20 percent believed one could not say the National Socialist state was an unjust state.[172] The cultural values that were central to many in the Nazi generation have now been passed on to a new generation of Germans, albeit a significant minority.

Macrolevel Representations: An East-West Comparison

The separate societies created by the division of Germany have created a unique social scientific laboratory within which to conduct some controlled experiments. Using this naturally occurring controlled experiment we can ask the following: Was demographic change alone sufficient to cause a growing social awareness of the Holocaust? If demographic change alone can account for the changing public awareness of the Holocaust, then public awareness of the Holocaust should be relatively the same in both East and West German populations. The evidence refutes this hypothesis. When East and West Germans were asked in 1989/90 and 1996 whether there was something exceptional in Germany's history, there was a clear East-West division. In 1989/90 in the West, 13 percent of the respondents identified the crimes against the Jews compared to only 1 percent in the East. By 1996, this percentage had risen to 20 percent in the West and 4 percent in the East. In contrast, in 1989/90 East Germans were much more likely to mention the Berlin wall (36 percent) compared to West Germans (11 percent).[173] Thus, demographic change was a necessary but not sufficient condition for West German society to begin coming to terms with the Holocaust. The increase in macrolevel Holocaust narratives after 1975 clearly had an impact upon public attitudes toward the National Socialist past. A democratic political sphere, an open civil society in the social sphere, and a capitalist economic sphere sensitive to public tastes were also necessary components of the equation.

4

Collaboration and Resistance: Blood and Redemption

THIS CHAPTER IS ABOUT THE POLITICAL STRUGGLES TO ESTABLISH a mythology of resistance in both East and West Germany. Both regimes sought to use the discourse of resistance to the Nazis as a cornerstone of their postwar legitimacy. According to the liturgy of the West German tradition, even during this time of national insanity and the Nazi occupation, there were those who maintained the light of the true Germany or "the other Germany." In the East, "the other Germany" was the antifascist resistance spearheaded by the Communists. Both states sought to free the nation from difficult questions and investigations into the indigenous roots of anti-Semitism and National Socialism through their frequent reference to the terror state myth, which explained the lack of greater resistance. While the content of the national myths of resistance varied considerably between East and West, there was also similarity in the basic structural form. In writing about these narratives as mythologies, I do not mean to suggest the pure fabrication of historical events, but rather the telling of historical narratives based in fact but imbued with a specific ideological content. Myths are moral tales of ethical behavior from which members of the society are expected to learn the lessons of history.

In both cases, each society and state fashioned its myth's form from the cultural symbols and language readily recognized in a Christian society. The concept of redemption and the cleansing of guilt through blood sacrifices were easily understood by the general German population. In both national mythologies of "the resistance," those who had fought and died in their struggle against the demonic Nazis had enacted a noble sacrifice that then redeemed the whole nation. The claim that these acts of resistance actually lead to redemption for those living in the present is something of mythical proportions and demonstrates the importance of locating discussions of politics within a cultural framework. Only in a society where redemption exists as a possibility can such a discourse have any social meaning or political value.

The redemption of all humankind's sins through the death of Jesus Christ on the cross is at the core of Christian theology, but the symbolism has its roots within the Old Testament, the Torah, and Judaism. In ancient Judaism, a blood sacrifice is able to wash away sin, for "the life of every thing is in the blood, and that is why the LORD has commanded that all blood be poured out on the altar to take away the people's sins. Blood which is life, takes away sins."[1] The ancient Israelites believed that they were able to wash away their sins through the sacrifice of life through a ritual killing. The power of blood or life to redeem the sinful is reaffirmed in the New Testament: "Indeed, according to the Law almost everything is purified by blood, and sins are forgiven only if blood is poured out."[2] Thus, one can see the Judaic symbolism in the Last Supper during which Christ is said to have shared with his disciples his blood represented by wine and his body represented by bread.

Modernity supposedly introduced a secularization of Western democracies and officially atheistic Communism. Nonetheless, the symbolic themes of Christianity continue to infuse many aspects of Western societies. The Christian's faith in redemption and redemptive powers can be found in many aspects of our Western secular societies. Whereas the love of Christ redeems the Christian, secular romantic love is shown as a redemptive force in Western culture. In both the operas of Wagner and many postwar German films, female love redeems or attempts to redeem the wayward male lost in either a mighty storm upon a ghost ship as in *The Flying Dutchman* or a snowstorm in the film *Stalingrad* (1993).[3] Modern democratic and Communist societies are not without their own martyrs and saints.

The fact that a theme of redemption became so important suggests that there must have been some form of guilt, or perceived guilt, that needed to be purged from the German nation. While German leaders rejected the charge of collective guilt at every possible opportunity, collective national innocence was readily accepted or proved through the acts of resistance that elites and the popular culture celebrated. It is only within a culture grounded in Christian faith that the actions of a few resistance members could redeem an entire nation. Nonetheless, many rejected the would-be redeemers as traitors or claimed only their own individual innocence. The celebration of resistance entails great risks, for the destabilization of a resistance mythology can lead to significant social upheaval. The stormy reception of Marcel Ophuls's *The Sorrow and the Pity* in France showed exactly what could happen when national myths were placed under pressure.[4] The celebration of resistance risks throwing into moral doubt the behavior of the supposedly passive masses. To celebrate the resistance is to risk revealing the disunity of the nation, to highlight its bitter divisions and often bloody oppositions and conflicts.

Theater and class help to explain why July 20 became the focus of resistance memory after the war. First, it was the single most dramatic act of resistance attempted by an organized group. The narrative has a central hero, Claus von Stauffenberg, and begins with hope, possibility, tension, and danger. After a clear climax in which the hero has placed the bomb and believes in his success, the narrative ends with betrayal, coincidences guided by the hand of fate, tragedy, failure, and ultimately the death of the hero. The narrative becomes a struggle between the good Germany and the evil embodied in Hitler alone. The failure of the coup plot is told and retold in postwar society as a traditional tragic tale. Second, the heroes of the twentieth also were from the German bourgeois elite. After the war, members of this class within the state, social, and capitalist spheres were in a unique position to trumpet their special status in Germany society and to offer a redemptive message to the masses to help reforge a new social contract.

Eventually, July 20 became a general day for reflecting upon other segments of the resistance. Although the East favored the Communists and the West the bourgeois elites, the two began to mix in the 1960s. By 1994, the ritual liturgy of the twentieth had exploded, and the very idea of what had constituted resistance during the Nazi era was open to broad reinterpretation. For example, in the cultural matrix of the 1990s, those on the political Left were successful in having the criminal records of those who had deserted the army expunged. However, one arm of resistance that was never incorporated into the twentieth was that of Jewish resistance.[5]

The 1944 Coup Plot

The conspirators were composed basically of conservatives and military officers, who were not wholly unified in their plans as to what should follow, if the coup d'état were successful. Some wanted to try to maintain some of Germany's territorial gains, which the war had yielded up to that point, while others wanted to try to make peace with the Western allies and then continue the war against the Soviet Union. In the end, the only objective that united all of them was their opposition to the National Socialist regime. They hoped that removing Hitler would be a fatal blow for the regime and that they then could seize power in the confusion based upon the pretext of finding the coup's plotters.

On July 20, Colonel Count Claus von Stauffenberg entered Hitler's eastern headquarters, known as the Wolf's Lair or Wolfsschanze, which is now in Poland, and placed a timed bomb in a meeting room filled with other top military officials. The bomb was originally placed close to Hitler, but it was moved by pure accident behind a thick wooden leg, which in the end shielded Hitler from the deadly blast. After placing the bomb, Stauffenberg left the room just minutes before the explosion. He then flew back to Berlin to lead the coup attempt, but the coup plotters failed to put their plans into action either through miscommunication or a loss of nerve. Hitler survived the assassination attempt. By the evening, troops loyal to Hitler had executed Stauffenberg and others in the courtyard of the Bendlerblock in Berlin. The Nazis burned their bodies and scattered their ashes. In the weeks and months that followed, the National Socialist regime quickly captured and executed almost all of the conspirators. The Nazis put some on trial in the Volksgerichtshof, and part of the trial was filmed for future use as propaganda material.

Perceived popular support for the Nazi regime remained high enough in 1944 that this was a pressing concern for the conspirators.[6] It was clear to them that the removal of Hitler alone would not be enough to topple the regime. Their plan was to accuse top Nazi officials of the assassination attempt and have them arrested. Their only hope lay in trying to create confusion. Since the war, many German commentators have been much too optimistic about the possible outcome had Hitler actually been killed by the bomb. The National Socialist movement did have a popular mass base, and after the war millions of Germans viewed the coup plotters as traitors. Rather than a quick peace, there was a very good chance that civil war would have resulted. The plotters themselves foresaw such a possibility.

East Germany and the Antifascist Resistance

Antifascism and July 20 in East German Newspapers and Television

From the very beginning, the East German regime sought to celebrate the antifascist movement as the resistance of the first hour, begun in 1933 immediately after the Nazi seizure of power.[7] In terms of memorial festivities marking the antifascist movement, May 8 became the focal point. The East German regime celebrated the end of the war as their joint victory with the Soviet Union. Theirs was not a restoration government of old fascists and the bourgeois elite, but rather a new social revolution founded upon the victory of the progressive antifascist forces. We will return to the portrayal of the antifascist struggle in chapter 6 and remain focused in this chapter upon the construction of a distinct East German countermemory for July 20. As chart 8 shows, the editors at *Neues Deutschland* before 1990 dedicated at least as much coverage to July 20 as at least one of the West German papers in every year except 1964.

One of the first articles to appear in *Neues Deutschland* argued that the conspirators merely sought to save German imperialism from certain defeat after their loss at Stalingrad in January 1943.[8] At first, the East German government did all it could to discredit the conspirators. Not only did they act too late, but they did so in a dilettante fashion and without true resolve. Five years later in 1959, the tone changed dramatically in large part as a result of new historical research, which showed that at least Stauffenberg had been willing to seek contacts with the Communist and socialist resistance.[9] Now their error became one of not working closely enough with the Communists. Stauffenberg quickly became from this point forward a true patriot within the East German tradition. At the same time, the East German countermemory continued to criticize severely the national conservatives around Carl Goerdeler. The Goerdeler group was in fact very conservative and had the restoration of the traditional German aristocracy as one of their primary goals. In one constitution drafted by members of the group, a strong executive was favored over an indirectly appointed national parliament.[10] In these early *Neues Deutschland* articles, the Stauffenberg story was often paired with a profile of a Communist resistance fighter. These individualized portraits of the heroes of the antifascist resistance appeared regularly in the East German press.[11]

By 1964, the discussion of the bourgeois resistance had widened even further as historians uncovered further documentation. The so-called progressives now included such figures as Count Helmut von Moltke and his Kreisauer Circle, Yorck von Wartenburg and Adam von Trott zu Solz.[12] Along with the groups around Stauffenberg and Goerdeler, Moltke's Kreisauer Circle was the third most important resistance group. Moltke had used his Silesian estate as a meeting point for like-minded individuals interested in debating what should follow the collapse of the Nazi regime. Adam von Trott zu Solz had used his position in the Foreign Office and the Abwehr to maintain contacts with resistance figures living in exile before the war, and during the war he tried to keep the allies informed about the activities of the resistance within Nazi Germany.

In 1964, East German television produced its first major program on July 20, *Revolution am Telefon* [Revolution on the Telephone].[13] There was a special article on the program in the East German television guide, and it was shown in prime time on a Sunday evening, thus guaranteeing the largest possible audience. The program was a mixture of dramatic reenactments, documentary footage, and commentary by Dr. Kurt Finker, East Germany's chief historian of the coup. Much of the film has little to do directly with the resistance and simply blends together other Nazi documentary material of Hitler, the Nazi leadership, and the costs of the total war. The never-before-used Nazi propaganda film material of the trial of some of the plotters, possibly filmed by Hans-Joachim Otto,[14] is also included in the documentary. Goerdeler is portrayed in a ridiculous manner while Stauffenberg is shown as an exceptional individual who was willing to renounce his own class background as he was in the process of making a conversion to the Communist point of view when the coup attempt failed. Most importantly, he had been willing to seek contact with the true resistance movement represented by the Communists and supported by the National Committee for Free Germany (NKFD), which had given the conspirators the courage to act. The NKFD was composed of military officers and enlisted soldiers, who were held as prisoners of war (POWs) in the Soviet Union and had banded together to fight the Nazis in July 1943. The documentary closes by showing the national memorials at the Sachsenhausen and Buchenwald concentration camps, which the government by that time had turned into central sites of official memory in the GDR for the suffering of the antifascist resistance fighters.

By 1964 the basic narrative and the countermemory of the East German regime were well established; it did not change in any marked fashion until reunification in 1990. As with the special anniversary ceremonies in the West, the fortieth anniversary celebrations in the East in 1984 were significantly expanded, although the narrative message remained much the same. In both the East and the West, the national-conservative figure of Carl Goerdeler receded further into the background. Stauffenberg remained the center of attention, and the GDR narrative of this hero appeared to lose many of its ideological chains. The Communist resistance was still emphasized more than in the West, but not excessively so. In an extended essay about the coup plot, Prof. Dr. Kurt Finker wrote not only about Stauffenberg, but also about Helmuth von Moltke, Adolf Reichwein, Alfred Delp, and Henning von Tresckow.[15] In fact, considering the almost complete absence of Communists in the West German narratives, Finker's essay approached a greater level of balance than much of the West's commentary. The convergence had gone so far that in July 1989 an essayist in the conservative *Frankfurter Allgemeine*[16] praised both of the 1984 GDR documentaries, *Das Attentat auf Hitler* [The Assassination against Hitler][17] and *Wir haben nichts zu bereuen* [We Regret Nothing],[18] and a third one from 1989, *Stauffenberg: 13 Bilder über einen Täter* [Stauffenberg: 13 Pictures of a Perpetrator], which emphasized his well-cultured background and humanism.[19]

In addition to the two documentaries that were shown in 1984, there was a roundtable discussion among historians about the meaning of the twentieth and a dramatic film, *Der Leutnant Yorck von Wartenburg* [Lieutenant Yorck von Wartenburg][20] based upon a novel from the East German novelist Stephan Hermlin. Within the discursive field of resistance and collaboration, the film again emphasizes the class nature of the resistance to Hitler and specifically the failure of the upper classes. Wartenburg was an actual historical figure and a member of the Kreisauer Circle. Although shown in prime time, the film only attracted a small audience of 6.9 percent and was received as an average film with a rating of 2.62.[21] The film's flashbacks and dream sequences focus upon his bourgeois life and offer the standard criticism that he failed to join the Communist resistance in time. In the end, he is captured and executed by the Nazis.

Das Attentat auf Hitler opens with the same dramatic presentation that opened *Revolution am Telefon* in 1964. Stauffenberg's planting of the bomb is again shown along with the bomb's being moved behind the heavy wooden table leg after he had left, thus having fate once again save Hitler's life. Unlike the previous 1964 documentary, which mocked Carl Goerdeler and the national conservatives, this documentary provided a broad portrayal of the resistance. While the Communists are credited as having begun their resistance efforts in 1933 and having paid the highest price, they are not the sole focus of the film. Stauffenberg, the White Rose student group, the Kreisauer Circle, social democrats, and Christians are all mentioned as having participated in the resistance. However, there is no attention given to any form of Jewish resistance; nor is the Holocaust mentioned as a possible motive for the various resistance efforts. Unlike in the West, where the Holocaust and resistance narratives became interwoven, these two narrative threads remained separated in the East, in large part because the Holocaust narrative was never very well developed.

As do many other documentaries, this one also gives a very ambiguous portrayal of the German public. Within the discursive field of resistance and collaboration, the behavior of the masses remained a problem for both East and West German attempts to create a foundational myth of resistance for the postwar society. The support of the general public for the Nazi regime is handled in an ambiguous manner. According to the narrative of the film, it slowly begins to dawn upon the common man during the war that Hitler is leading the country toward ruin, and only the Communists are able to provide the proper ideological guidance to lead many toward a successful socialist revolution. As in many other documentaries and films, this one also avoids any in-depth analysis of public support for the regime. The film closes with the common question, "How much could have been saved if Hitler had been destroyed?" But what could have been saved is reduced to the suffering of the Germans, and National Socialism is reduced to the figure of Hitler. These are traits common to the Western narratives as well. The documentary received a larger audience than *Wartenburg* with 16.4 percent for the general population and one third of the educated classes, and an overall evaluation rating of 2.86.[22]

Wir haben nichts zu bereuen was by far the greatest surprise of 1984 because of the almost complete absence of party partisanship. In this case, the filmmaker focused upon the basic struggle to find a space within which to organize resistance. The narrative of the documentary is provided by interviews with three widows of members of the Kreisauer Circle, Freya von Moltke, Marion von Wartenburg, and Rosemarie Reichwein, whose husbands had been executed by the Nazis.[23] As Frau Moltke put it, the first act of resistance was simply to meet with other like-minded individuals.

Television programs were not the only media to reflect a convergence between East and West. Between 1983 and 1989, Peter Steinbach had worked to create a more inclusive exhibit of the German resistance in the Bendlerblock, the site of Stauffenberg's execution and the coup plotters' headquarters, in West Berlin. The Bendlerblock had been the location for exhibits and memorial services in the past, but by the early 1980s the material had become dated. Steinbach's job was to create a more comprehensive and permanent exhibit for the memorial site. In 1989, the exhibit finally opened, although not everyone was pleased with the final results. The major controversy erupted, in the West, over the inclusion of Walter Ulbricht, Wilhelm Pieck, the NKFD, and the Communist resistance. The editors at *Neues Deutschland* obviously welcomed the first real embrace by the West of the Communist resistance and reported favorably on the exhibit.[24]

The best way to understand these points of convergence between East and West German narratives of the German resistance is to view them within the context of improving East-West German relations during the 1980s, a situation that had been fostered by Brandt's *Ostpolitik*. This is not to say that the cold war tensions had passed, as the North Atlantic Treaty Organization's (NATO's) and the then-U.S.-president Reagan's two-track plan to deploy new nuclear weapons in West Germany before bargaining with the Soviets from a position of strength in the early 1980s certainly increased such tensions. But overall, the intensity of the ideological battles within the civil society had subsided when compared with their levels in the 1950s during the growing division and the 1960s with the building of the Berlin wall. In the West, the Communist resistance, and in particular its leadership, was often blamed for the division of the country, the unhealed wound from the war. Once that division had been overcome in 1990, the cultural spaces and opportunities for reevaluating the role of the Communist resistance in the cultural matrix had grown even greater.

After the reunification of the country in 1994, *Neues Deutschland* was fairly free of the old antifascist messages, although it did engage in the ideological newspaper battles of that year. The debate about the position of the Communists in the German resistance had only really begun in 1989 with the Steinbach exhibit in the Bendlerblock. By 1994, the position of the Communists and the ever-expanding understanding of what actually had constituted an act of resistance were heavily debated in the Western press. Chancellor Kohl's adherence to the well-established traditions of public memory for the twentieth sparked much of the controversy. This led some leftist radicals to occupy the exhibit in the Bendlerblock early in the morning, and other protesters tried to disrupt the ceremonies in the Bendlerblock courtyard. Dr. Kurt Finker continued to write in *Neues Deutschland*, thus showing how the paper had become a forum for former East German intellectuals, who were largely shut out of the Western media.[25] He criticized both the antifascist historiography of the GDR and the anti-Communist historiography of the Federal Republic. Of greater importance, he sided with those who were now throwing the entire legacy of the twenieth into disarray with the open admission that while they deserved to be recognized for their sacrifice, one had to recognize that almost all of the conspirators had been willing to work with Hitler up to a certain point.

Antifascism in GDR Film

The twentieth always remained somewhat on the fringes of GDR state-led nationalism, as the foundational myth for the East was May 8. *Neues Deutschland* was always filled for weeks with articles about the end of the war and the victory of the antifascists around the eighth. The antifascist message was pervasive in East German life and within the discursive field of resistance and collaboration. The continuous *Antifaschismus* campaign run by the state was an attempt to enlist East Germans in the socialist cause. For the party, it was part of a struggle to create the new socialist man, to win the people over not only to acquiesce and comply outwardly, but to internalize a new system of values based on human compassion.

The eastern model of redemption required that one save oneself through good works within a strict social order directed by the party. This inner struggle is portrayed over and over again and became the single most important leitmotif of East German culture.[26] Conversion to the socialist worldview is always shown as a process of personal enlightenment throughout East German cinema and literature, whether it takes place during the Nazi period and leads to resistance or occurs after the war in the period of rebuilding. This process of enlightenment and conversion is not without its own religious undertones, as it reflects St. Paul's conversion to Christianity on the road to Damascus.[27] Thus, the olive branch is held out to the population, offering them salvation from their fascist sins if they are willing to join the winning side after the war and the strict leadership of the party. The presentation of antifascist themes was basically constant throughout the existence of the GDR, as can be seen in chart 9, except in the earliest years, when few films were made. Antifascism in East German film has been discussed extensively by other authors.[28] I have selected only a few examples here to highlight some of the main themes.

One early example is Wolfgang Staudte's *Rotation*.[29] The film focuses upon the life of Hans, an apolitical worker who struggles to provide for his small family during the economic downturns of the Weimar Republic and becomes involved with the National Socialists without reflecting upon the ideology of the party. He then witnesses the destruction of the war and the deportation of his Jewish neighbors and is finally drawn into the resistance by Kurt, his brother-in-law, who is then captured by the Gestapo and murdered in Sachsenhausen. The film appears ready to begin another rotation at the end when Hans's son, Helmut, meets a woman at a crossing gate just as he had met his wife at the beginning of the film. The woman says, "Everything repeats itself," to which Helmut replies, "No, for those who want peace, they can now work for it." They then walk into the woods but take a different path; they take the path to the left rather than the one to the right, as Hans had at the opening.

The film includes a number of key themes. First, Communism will overcome the rotation of history and the ever-recurring economic crises, which have led to so much destruction and loss of life. There is also an East German version of the terror state represented by the Gestapo, who appear in the film as unnamed figures in leather coats. The character of Kurt celebrates the martyrdom of the Communist resistance fighter. Finally, although discussion of the Holocaust will soon disappear with the arrival of the anticosmopolitan purges, Staudte again inserts several scenes referring to the persecution of the Jews and a reference to 11 million killed in the concentration camps.

Other antifascist films also play with the theme of conversion, as the main character learns about the true nature of fascism. In *Die Abenteuer der Werner Holt* [Adventures of Werner Holt] (1964),[30] Werner Holt finally turns a machine gun on the SS, not ordinary German soldiers, to prevent them from committing further crimes. His father had tried to tell him earlier in the film that the Nazis were using poison gas to murder thousands in the concentration camps, but Werner had refused to believe him. His first act of resistance occurs when he refuses to obey an order to shoot two civilians, who may have killed a German soldier in self-defense. Although regular army units often participated in the execution of civilians in the occupied territories, both East and West German films are almost completely void of such killings. Rather than doing one's duty and following orders, the on-screen soldier never shoots the innocent or the unarmed. They always find a way to resist or subvert the order to kill. It is the brutal crimes of the SS that finally allow Werner to turn his gun against other Germans.

The film highlights the extreme level of tension that existed within the discursive field of resistance and collaboration as German-on-German violence becomes a morally legitimate position only once the German agents have placed themselves outside the boundaries of all civilized behavior in specific instances. Although these narratives rail against abstract fascism, only specific Germans can be marked for death at the hands of other Germans.

Im Sonderauftrag [Special Mission] (1959)[31] combines the themes of antifascism in the present with wartime resistance. The film opens in the postwar present when two wartime comrades confront each other on opposite sides of the German divide. Fischer is now the captain of a mine sweeper, which is still clearing the waters from World War II, when he receives a request from the border police to help them intercept a small fishing vessel, which has crossed illegally into East German waters. Onboard the small ship he confronts Wegner, his old wartime comrade, who is now living in the West. At first, Wegner is suspected of nothing more than running a small-time smuggling operation, but by the end of the film we discover that he had worked for the Gestapo during the war, had betrayed Fischer and others, and is now working as a spy for the fascist West German state.

Another important example is Konrad Wolf's autobiographical *Ich war neunzehn* [I Was Nineteen] (1968).[32] In an interview published several years after the film's release, Wolf claimed that 1.7 million had seen the film within three months of its release.[33] If his claim is true, the film had a success in East Germany that rivaled that of the West German resistance film *Canaris* (1954). The interviewer asked Wolf whether or not the film could have been made ten years earlier; Wolf responded that the film's attempt to portray the everyday criminality of the regime, rather than of just the Nazis and SS, could not have been shown, but that by 1968 the audience should not have any trouble identifying with the main character, a German who fights alongside the Russians, as a hero rather than a traitor.

In the film, Wolf tells of his experiences as a young soldier in the Soviet army at the end of the war. The film shows the main character, Gregor, as working with the Russians, but not shooting at Germans. Only at the very end does Gregor pick up a gun and shoot at some SS in the distance, after they shoot his friend. Despite Wolf's claim that the film opened new ground, the portrayal of resistance remained very restrained. But Gregor clearly wrestles with his role as a potential traitor. During a dreamlike opening sequence we see a floating gallows on a field of water with a sign hanging around the dead man's neck, "Deserteur—Ich bin ein Russen knecht" [Deserter—I Am a Russian Slave]. Gregor fantasizes about his own death at the hands of his countrymen, but the film's narrative is carefully crafted to limit reactions that might lead the audience to label him a traitor.

If the film is critical of the German soldiers' "insane" willingness to continue the fight at all costs, the Russian soldiers are rarely portrayed in a manner that could be reproached by a German unaware of the savage acts of revenge carried out by the Soviet army. When a former concentration camp prisoner suggests that now is the time for revenge, a Russian officer contradicts him, "Revenge is a poor preparation for the future." The Russian soldiers are also shown giving food to those in need. Many of the newspaper articles around May 8, which I will discuss later, include pictures of Russian soldiers' feeding the starving population of Berlin. This icon of the Russian as provider and liberator is used to try to displace the memories of the wartime atrocities carried out against German soldiers and the civilian population. We will return to the portrayal of the Russians in German war films later.

Gregor struggles throughout the film with his multiple identities and potential national loyalties. His foreignness to the Germans he encounters is emphasized throughout the film by his speaking in Russian to the other Russian characters. In the version I viewed, there were no subtitles for the Russian. The conversations were probably of a very basic nature, and an East German audience may well have been able to understand the Russian in the film as the Russian language was a compulsory subject in school. Nonetheless, Gregor is seen as a foreigner by the other German characters, someone whom they struggle to categorize. At one point, a young German woman confronts him and asks him whether he is German. Gregor refuses to answer her, and it is only by the end of the film and having experienced all that he has that he is willing to state to the audience as a disembodied voice, "I am German. I was nineteen."

July 20 in the West: A Failed Foundational Myth

The twentieth was from the beginning of the new Federal Republic a day of national remembrance for the resistance against Hitler. Other segments of the resistance were slowly blended with the coup plotters, including resistance by the church, ordinary Germans, soldiers, socialists, and eventually Communists, but the coup attempt remained almost the sole focus of official ceremonies as it offered at least a partial reprieve for the German military as a legitimate institution of a new democratic German state. At the same time, many of the authors, directors, and producers attempted to construct a narrative of an inner resistance within the discursive field of resistance to the Nazis to explain the "passivity" of the masses.

West German Newspapers

As seen in chart 8, there was only one brief article marking the fifth anniversary of the coup attempt. Writing in *Die* Zeit in 1949, Johann A. Graf Kielmansegg wrote a detailed account of the events and noted that W. E. Schäfer had already created a dramatic portrayal of the events in a play called *Die Verschwörung* [The Conspiracy].[34] By 1954, the political sphere had become fully engaged in commemorating the day. Since the West German leaders had direct access to some of the original sites associated with the coup in Berlin, they returned to these locations year after year. Chancellor Adenauer and Federal President Heuss both participated in a memorial service at Plötzensee, the Berlin site where the Nazis executed many of the conspirators. This early participation by prominent politicians stands in marked contrast to their late and tentative involvement with the memory work for November 9 or May 8. Some aspects of the past were more usable than others.

In his speech, President Heuss tried to disentangle the praise that was being given to the coup plotters from a general moral responsibility to resist Hitler. As he put it in his speech, a career officer, whom he did not know beforehand, went to him and asked him not to condemn the soldiers who had continued the fight against the allies before and even after the failed coup attempt. Heuss then continued:

> I could only ask him not to take me for so stupid and unjust. I would have to accuse indeed friends and relatives, who hated Hitler and National So-

> cialism, but as they died must have believed, could have believed, that their struggle perhaps would save Germany from the worst. And the good troop officer thought of his people. . . . The spiritual situation from hundreds of thousands, from millions of soldiers, was horrible, because they were not the fanatical National Socialists in the field, but rather also German men, among whom were many who throughout the war were marked by their steadfastness and courage while also constantly accompanied by an inner conflict.[35]

Heuss attempted to drive a rhetorical wedge between the fanatical Nazi and the ordinary German, one of the central themes of all postwar discourse. In a Bundestag speech in 1952, Chancellor Adenauer had argued for just such a separation between Germany and Hitler.[36] As with the so-called passive crowds, which sometimes watched and sometimes cheered the burning of the synagogues in November 1938, German memory and official commemorative practice wanted to believe and invoke an ever-present inner resistance. But what evidence do we have of this inner conflict? The scant empirical data that we have about the soldier in the field suggest a very different picture, because as a group, they were the most negatively oriented in their evaluation of the twentieth. In June 1951, while 30 percent of the general population still rejected the attempted assassination of Hitler, 59 percent of former career soldiers did not recognize the legitimacy of the coup plotters' goals.[37] Obviously the inner conflict to which Heuss makes reference did not reach as deep as one might have wished.

In fact, although this inner conflict certainly did eventually manifest itself in Claus von Stauffenberg and others, Stauffenberg had been willing to support the Nazi war effort during the early years when Germany had its military successes. He even endorsed parts of the Nazi's racial view toward the Slavic people in the east. In a letter to his wife in 1939 during the Polish campaign, Stauffenberg wrote the following: "The population [here in Poland] is an unbelievable rabble, there are a lot of Jews and a lot of cross-breeds. It is a people that only feels good when it is under the whip. The thousands of prisoners will do our agricultural economy good. They are certain to be put to good use in Germany [and will be] industrious, willing and easily satisfied."[38] As is always the case with the instrumentalization of history for political purposes and the creation of heroic figures, the ambiguity of Stauffenberg's earlier behavior is left out of the picture. The newspapers remained, for the most part, captivated by the elite political discourse and avoided these ambiguities.[39]

There is no question that the early essays were primarily interested in the national conservative side of the resistance. For example, Carl Goerdeler is the most often cited resistance figure, rather than Stauffenberg, in 1954. Goerdeler had been the mayor of Leipzig from 1930 to 1937. He resigned after the Nazis removed a statue of the Jewish composer Felix Mendelssohn from the front of the city hall. However, Goerdeler was also a problematic resistance figure for canonization. The Federal Republic required good democratic heroes, but Goerdeler was not particularly predisposed toward democratic institutions. Nonetheless, postwar politicians claimed that the national-conservative resistance wanted a democratic state and a united Europe and recognized the true dangers of Soviet Communism, unlike the allies, who permitted the division of the country.

Rather than recognize the unrealistic demands that the resistance made in their terms for surrender to the western allies, many postwar German commentators blamed the allies for having isolated the resistance with the demand of unconditional surrender, a claim popularized in the film *Canaris* among others. Anglo-Saxon historians have also criticized the demand for unconditional surrender, but most of them agree that in the end it really had no important impact on the outcome of the war.[40] Prior to the demand of unconditional surrender agreed to by Churchill and Roosevelt in 1943, the peace proposals being sent out from the German resistance were hardly satisfactory from the perspective of the allies. In 1941, a proposal formulated by Goerdeler demanded that Germany retain the borders of 1914 with France, Belgium, and Poland. Furthermore, the prewar annexation of Austria and the Sudetenland was also to be accepted. In the early summer of 1944, the Stauffenberg proposal failed to make any major improvements on the points that the allies clearly had objected to in 1941.[41] Contrary to German popular memory and public discourse, the resistance was not isolated because of the policy of unconditional surrender but rather because of its own unrealistic expectations of what the allies should accept. When the German commentators write that the resistance tried "to save that which remained to be saved," they fail to mention that this included a great deal of what Nazi Germany had already gained on the battlefield.

The year 1954 also saw the first proclamations of collective innocence and redemption to counter the German perception that foreigners, in particular Jews, were trying to saddle the German nation with collective guilt. Elfriede Kaiser-Nebgen wrote, "The political meaning of the 20th of July lies foremost in the revelation that the Hitler-system with all of its crimes to a large extent was the fate and not the fault of the German nation."[42] The absurdity of collective guilt is easily transformed into collective innocence, victimhood, and self-pity. Rather than a narrative that leads to asking difficult questions, July 20 offered redemption for the German nation. As another commentator claimed, millions of Germans would have supported the coup, "But the nation was certainly with its true leaders."[43]

Marion Gräfin Dönhoff was a member of the Prussian aristocracy who knew some of those who were involved in the coup attempt. After the war, she became an editor at *Die Zeit* and wrote many editorials for the paper on the subject over the years. Her personal experiences and her public standing provide an interesting example of how certain voices were able to find their way into the public space while others were much more muffled or distant. Her background in no way disqualifies her as a legitimate commentator on the twenieth, but her unique position as an editor of a prominent German newspaper was directly related to her social standing. The other chief editor of *Die Zeit*, Theo Summer, was also from a well-to-do German family, and his parents had enrolled him in one of the most elite schools offered by the Nazis so as to assure his future success. The point is not to praise or condemn certain perspectives or individuals but rather to underscore the observation that elite German newspapers included in this study carry a clear class or status bias more sympathetic to the conservative resistance. Writing in 1954, Dönhoff highlighted the position of the church vis-à-vis the state during the National Socialist times.[44] The title of her essay, "The Conscience Stands Up," was taken from a book of the same title. The rehabilitation of the church as an institution through the few well-known acts of resistance that occurred was very popular at the time, for the church appeared to be one institution to which the population could cling during the postwar period of economic and moral uncertainty.

The most important political speech given in 1959 was by General Inspector Heusinger, and the most important political symbol was the inclusion of Bundeswehr soldiers dressed in civilian clothing in the ceremonies in Berlin. Marion Gräfin Dönhoff praised Heusinger for his speech, in which he again criticized the collective guilt that foreigners tried to place upon the German nation saying, "They [the men of the twentieth] are the most distinguished witnesses against the collective guilt of the German nation, their spirit and behavior are examples for us."[45] She then went on to lash out at the Nuremberg trials and judges for having created this charge of collective guilt. "They [the judges at the Nuremberg trials] portrayed everyone who had not deserted [the German army] as a cad and stamped each who had stood up to the enemy [the allies] a moral coward. How incomprehensible must that have been for all those who had endured and believed they had only done their duty."

In one of the rare articles that sought to portray the complexity of the resistance's history, Helmut Krausnick, the then-recently-assigned director of the Institute for Contemporary History in Munich, wrote a detailed essay about the relationship between the state and the army.[46] He wrote openly about the *Einsatzkommandos* and the mass shootings of Jewish civilians in the east, but more importantly he noted that the military had not only accepted such criminal actions passively but participated directly in their execution. This was not a fact that was accepted by the broader public, and his passing reference to the complicity and active involvement of the military in war crimes was left at that. But this was an issue that would not die despite a political sphere and a popular culture that continually tried to reinforce the wall separating the Nazis from the Germans, a point we will return to in chapter 6.

By 1964 the official recognition of July 20 had been fully institutionalized. The sites of the memorial services were now firmly fixed at the Bendlerblock in Berlin and Plötzensee. In his speech at the Free University of Berlin, Federal President Lübke compared July 20, 1944, with June 17, 1953, by noting that both dates showed the uprising of the conscience against totalitarian oppression in the German capital.[47] He also offered a positive reading of the vast majority of Germans, who had always resisted Hitler spiritually and from within, often in a passive manner. Thus, he offered all Germans the chance to feel that they too had participated in the spirit of the twentieth even if they had been unable to carry out the assassination of Hitler because of their own personal remoteness from the affairs of state. He also sought to highlight the fundamental democratic spirit of the German nation, a theme that is often linked to June 17. Surprisingly for the time, Lübke was also willing to recognize the resistance of the Communists, who had acted as idealists and not simply as puppets at the command of a foreign power. Although his attempt to include the early Communist resistance in the narrative fabric of July 20 failed, the same issue would flare up again thirty years later in 1994.

Almost all of the essayists, political leaders, and commentators were careful to underscore the moral legitimacy of the coup plotters' actions, for their primary ambition had been to save Germany and the good name of the German nation. However, the Holocaust and the mass slaughter of innocent civilians had up to 1964 not been integrated into the narrative of the twentieth as a possible motive for the coup plotters. This is not hard to understand given the relative public silence on the Holocaust as demonstrated in the previous chapters. Thus, according to the resistance narrative up to 1964, the failure of the coup plot led to millions of more deaths for both the Germans and the allies, but not specifically the Jews.

Why were the commentators so reluctant to draw upon the Holocaust as a clear moral justification for the actions taken by the coup plotters in defense of "the other Germany"? In large part, the answer lies with the role of the military in perpetrating crimes against civilian populations and Jews. Once German society recognized the true implications of the Holocaust, it could no longer easily defend the role of the individual soldiers and offer a blanket excuse that they must have suffered a "severe inner conflict." When doing one's duty begins to include the shooting of innocent civilians and the facilitation of Jewish deportations to death camps, it becomes more difficult to keep the Nazis and the Germans separated. Once one recognizes these crimes, the clear divisions between good and evil begin to spill into each other, and the political mythology begins to weaken.

Thus, it is of note that a Jewish rabbi was invited to speak and that his words were reported in *Der Tagesspiegel.* Rabbi Friedländer had been born in Berlin and fled after 1938. Twenty years after the actual events, he was the first commentator I found in my research to draw an explicit link between the resistance and Auschwitz. "Friedländer reminds us that he cannot speak of the 20th of July without thinking about Auschwitz. . . . According to Friedländer, everybody in the Third Reich should have noticed this poison in the air. One must however full of sadness recognize how few noticed this poison."[48] Once again, it took a Jewish survivor with a specific and unique Jewish frame of memory to draw this connection in public. But as a Jew speaking in the 1960s, he had a perspective that was still easily marginalized and not a threat to the central postwar mythologies.

The year 1974 probably would have passed quietly with the same state ceremonies if the president of the Bundestag, Hans Filbinger, had not been invited to speak at one of the ceremonies in Berlin. According to Filbinger, he had been a member of the resistance from the first moment. But "new" evidence suggested otherwise. The Berlin *Jungdemokraten* [Young Democrats] charged that Filbinger had continued to administer Nazi-style justice even after the war. Apparently, he had sentenced a soldier to six months in prison for having removed a swastika from his medals and cap on May 20, 1945, that is, twelve days after the end of the war.[49] Yet, Filbinger could point to a August 4, 1972, ruling from a court in Stuttgart, which stated that he was, in fact, "a declared and active opponent of the NS-regime, and therefore suffered personal disadvantages, and had used his position as a navy judge at risk to his own limb and life to block expected death sentences or those executions already rendered."[50] The courts had declared him innocent, a resister, and a victim of the regime.

The controversy surrounding Filbinger probably made him a very poor choice as a speaker for the July 20 ceremonies, but in the past, the president of the Bundestag had often been included. His speech was interrupted throughout with calls of "hypocrite," "Nazi," and "liar."[51] Filbinger's party, the CDU, stood firmly behind their man. Most Germans probably also had no idea what the fuss was about except that the students were once again going after their elders. In a short and tersely worded report, "What the SFB and ZDF Silenced," a *Tagesspiegel* reporter wrote that the TV stations noted the disruptions during the speech but said nothing about the reason for the protests.[52] The *Frankfurter Allgemeine* provided no coverage of the charges against Filbinger and chose instead only to quote the Stuttgart ruling, which defended him. *Die Zeit* also ignored the students' charges and merely regretted that he had been selected as a speaker. Germany's elite media sources, both Left and Right, turned a blind eye to Filbinger's potentially troubled past. However, this past returned with a vengeance in 1978.

In 1974, the German media seemed to share the government's embarrassment at having a keynote speaker remembering the resistance having been called a Nazi. Filbinger tried to portray himself as the victim of a public smear campaign being led by radicals at the universities. However, by 1978 some of the old postwar mythologies that had protected individuals like Filbinger had begun to crack. The restructuring of Germany's history within the public sphere around the Holocaust created the possibility for new political dynamics in which Filbinger's past actions could be seen as at least morally reprehensible if not criminal. There is no question that Filbinger could have weathered the storm in previous decades, but by the late 1970s, the cultural matrix had greatly expanded the rhetorical space within which his antagonists could challenge his legitimacy.

A fair amount of the media reporting in 1978 revolved around what became known as the "Filbinger Affair," which ended with Hans Filbinger's resignation in August 1978. Interestingly, Filbinger's past came to light primarily through a play by Roth Hochhuth, who had long used a drama genre known as documentary drama to investigate Germany's Nazi past. In his 1978 play *The Lawyers* or *Jurists*, Hochhuth revealed that Filbinger, who had been a military lawyer in the navy, had ordered the execution of Walter Gröger, a sailor, because of desertion at the very end of the war. Because of the scandal, Filbinger was forced to resign as the minister president of Baden-Würtenberg.

The postwar myths continued to crumble. In his essay in the *Frankfurter Allgemeine*, Jürgen Busche was one of the first essayists to begin breaking free of the terror state myth. "The vast majority of the German nation was mixed up in the unjust system to such an extent, that, as horrible as this may be, the total defeat, the complete subjection to the will of the victors was necessary in order to destroy every halo around the Third Reich."[53] Busche began to question the traditional meaning of German "passivity" during the Nazi era, as well as the innocence of the "vast majority." The lines between Germans and Nazis, good and evil, began to blur significantly compared to the rhetoric of the 1950s and the 1960s. This was encouraged, in no small part, by the arrival of the Holocaust narrative within the public sphere by the late 1970s. This narrative of horrendous crimes began to collide with the mythology of German resistance. The past now had to be reevaluated in light of the Holocaust, and the national-conservative resistance needed some inspiring story of their attempt to save the Jews. But the evidence was simply not there. The myth's credibility was in danger of collapse.

Critics of memory studies or culture-based approaches to politics will sometimes note that history can be made to say anything the powerful wish, and therefore it is only instrumentalized by the powerful. Would it not simply be better to study power in the first place rather than the epiphenomenon of culture and memory? But the arrival of the Holocaust narrative in the 1970s became a force that different social actors arguing for a different interpretation of the past could then utilize. The point is that the potential for this narrative had always been there as well as actors willing to use it, as seen with *Long Is the Way.* However, it was only within a cultural matrix more open to such narratives that these stories themselves could have any significant effect. Up until this point, politicians like Filbinger had been safe. Now all this was changing, and rapidly. Until 1974, Jews had played basically no role in remembering the German resistance. The two narrative threads had appeared to have nothing to do with each other. After 1978, the two crashed into each other.

In 1979, Heinz Galinski was invited to speak again after his first appearance in 1974, but this time he was much more critical of the resistance's refusal to acknowledge more serious consequences of the persecution of the Jews, which had begun in 1933. In fact, Galinski argued that history provided little to no evidence that the resistance had shown any sense of outrage or concern about the persecution and mass murder of the Jews, and if it occurred, it occurred only too late.[54] Other commentators agreed. In a book review, Peter Gralla noted that the question of the coup plotters' relationship to the persecution of the Jews and the concentration camps remained unresolved.[55] He speculated that the ugly truth probably was that this was of little immediate concern to them.

The new conservative coalition led by Helmut Kohl's CDU arrived in 1982 and began to dig in their heels. Dönhoff compared Hitler to a

Rattenfänger, a literary allusion to the Pied Piper of Hamelin, who had hypnotized an innocent German public, thus making resistance impossible.[56] On the other side, the Left began to demand recognition of the socialist and Communist resistance.[57] The SPD established a discussion forum called "The Unknown Resistance," where members of the SPD and KPD during the Nazi regime could give personal testimony of their activities.[58] These issues had been boiling below the surface since 1983, when the then-mayor of Berlin, von Weizsäcker, had called in Professor Peter Steinbach to Berlin to rework the exhibit space in the Bendlerblock, which had first opened in 1968. Steinbach was given responsibility for updating it with the latest historiographical research. Chancellor Kohl was not at all pleased with the proposed inclusion of Communists in the new exhibit and even wrote to Steinbach in 1987 demanding their removal. Kohl's interference almost led to Steinbach's resignation, but the exhibit's director convinced him to stay on. The exhibit's director wrote to Kohl criticizing his position by noting that one could not project the current totalitarian outcome in the East back into 1944.[59] The expanding notion of resistance led to the Green Party's 1989 proposal that desertion should also be recognized as a form of resistance.[60] Their proposal did not gain much support at the time.

The intensity of the debates in 1994 must be seen against the backdrop of German reunification and the struggle between traditional Right and Left factions over the old totalitarian debate. In the most basic terms, the political Right wanted to damn the Communist resistance in its entirety as having been just as totalitarian as the fascism that it sought to overthrow. The political Left sought to keep the Communist resistance in historical perspective, stating that they were not directly responsible for all that followed under Stalin's leadership. In the end, even conservatives recognized that the traditional recognition of the coup plotters as unquestioned heroes of "the other Germany" was no longer sustainable. Kohl's attempt to maintain their centrality to the discourse on resistance began to appear anachronistic. It was now openly recognized by those on the Right that even Stauffenberg had celebrated Hitler's earliest victories and was intent on maintaining these in any peace settlement with the allies.[61] Even Joachim Fest, the well-known conservative historian, had taken a more critical position vis-à-vis the coup plotters. In his review of Fest's then-most-recent book, Wilhelm von Sternburg wrote:

> The leadership of the *Wehrmacht* did not move against Hitler because of his terror- and extermination-state, but rather revolted in quick order only when his war plans appeared too risky to them. It is to the strength of Fest's

> book about the story of the 20th of July that this disastrous political and moral failure is not minimized but shown clearly. It could also be formulated even more pointedly than the author does. Because the research has since shown that the Wehrmacht leadership not only tolerated the inhuman mass shootings in the captured territories but also took active participation.[62]

The debates of 1994 had exhausted the participants. In 1999, only one brief article appeared in the *Frankfurter Allgemeine*, and the ceremonies appeared to have lost their emotional edge. The Communist issue had disappeared except for a few demonstrators who again tried to disrupt the ceremonies at the Bendlerblock. For *Die Zeit* and *Der Tagesspiegel* the twentieth was no news at all, either in terms of reporting on the public sphere or having an essayist evaluate the history. Was this just an off-year similar to 1979? Had all of the issues of 1994 been resolved or simply forgotten? With the Nazi generation now all but gone, we can probably expect some of the intensity in these debates to fade. Perhaps the weight of the Holocaust and the crimes of the Wehrmacht had simply become too much for the day to bear. Traditional supporters of the heroic interpretation of the coup attempt simply began to abandon the cause.

West German Television: Broadcasting the Resistance

There is no question that state television took an early interest in dealing with the question of resistance during the National Socialist years. Classen found no fewer than thirty-one programs dealing specifically with the twentieth between 1955 and 1965. He notes that many of these programs were shown around the twentieth, thus validating my choice of using commemorative dates to locate valuable material.[63] Overall, eighty-nine programs dealt with resistance in some form, accounting for 11 percent of all programs dealing with National Socialism. This was also roughly the same number of programs that dealt with Nazi era persecutions. By far the most common themes were the results of the war and the war itself, which together accounted for 40 percent of all the programs. In contrast, very few programs tried to deal with National Socialism itself, its structures (2 percent), its antecedents (4 percent), or everyday life (1 percent). These patterns of avoidance indicated in Classen's research reinforce the conclusions drawn here.

Within the programming directed at the theme of resistance, there was a very strong bias toward the national-conservative resistance (33 percent) and the church (20 percent), which together accounted for half the programming. The resistance efforts of individuals or foreigners accounted for the other half of the programming. Only two programs of eighty-nine addressed the resistance efforts of the socialists, while the Communist resistance was completely absent.[64] The key theme that appeared to run through almost all of these programs was the moral position of the individual vis-à-vis National Socialism. Each of the programs can be seen as a German challenge to a perceived charge of collective guilt.

There is very little information about the earliest television programs, several of which shared the same title, *Aufstand des Gewissens*[65] [Uprising of the Conscience]. Classen identified three other programs with the same title in his research.[66] In 1959, the ARD presented a discussion group[67] and a drama entitled *Mann ohne Namen* [Man without Name].[68] From a write-up on the drama, we know that the narrative dealt with the question of a soldier's duty to obey orders when those orders conflicted with his own conscience.[69] The ZDF also began its first year of programming with dramatic portrayals of the twentieth and the resistance. In 1963 the ZDF broadcast the 1955 G. W. Pabst film *Es Geschah am 20. Juli* [It Happened on the 20th of July] followed by a discussion round.[70] The overall viewership for the film of 15 percent requires a brief clarification in that in 1963 not all households could receive the ZDF, which had yet to extend fully its network of relay stations.[71] Of those who could receive both the ARD and ZDF, 34 percent opted for the ZDF program.

The audience survey material for Pabst's film is revealing, for it shows that the public was more willing to engage the discursive field of resistance and collaboration when questions relating to the Jews were removed. This helps to explain why the narratives of resistance and the Holocaust remained divided until the 1970s. As the previous chapter has shown, programs that tried to engage the persecution of the Jews or the crimes of the Nazis often received negative comments from around 20 percent of the viewers along the lines "One should finally stop showing such stuff" to even more anti-Semitic comments such as "Enough with the Jews already." This caught the attention of the *Infratest* author as well, who noted with surprise that such comments were somewhat more subdued. Still, 11 percent of the comments showed a fair amount of reserve vis-à-vis the topic of the film. But the overwhelming response was very positive. The viewers liked the "objectivity" of the film, probably a response to Pabst's use of a pseudo-documentary style. Almost the majority of viewers made comments along the lines of "Finally we see how it really was" and "Such material is particularly important for the young generation or young people today." Such comments are rather curious, for the film certainly shows events that no living German had witnessed. So what was it about the film that "showed it as it really was"? Viewed in isolation, the comments may appear quite ambiguous, but if one views this film alongside other films of resistance, it is clear that the audience is quite receptive of the resistance narrative. "How it really was" includes upstanding Germans who risked their lives to fight the Nazi leadership. While it is logically inconsistent to praise the resistance while also believing that National Socialism was a good idea, such is the nature of mundane political culture.[72]

Some scholarship on July 20 has tended to underestimate its importance. Regina Holler concludes her extensive newspaper survey writing, "It [the 20th] was celebrations without a population, just as the 20th was a resistance without a nation. The 20th of July also like the 17th of June became a cliché, a burdensome duty, whose origin hardly anyone knew. The government celebrated itself."[73] Such a conclusion certainly holds for the state ritual, but the message of redemption offered in the popular culture was certainly welcomed by many, particularly the older generation.

In November 1964, the ZDF broadcast a two-part docudrama, *Der Fall Nebe* [The Nebe Case],[74] which was extremely well received by the public. Both parts of the program were given a +6 rating, rather rare, and had a good viewership of 39 percent and 37 percent. The *Infratest* report was also extensive, as were the comments of viewers, which often went beyond the usual "That was interesting."[75] For the ten years covered by Classen's research, this was the only television program that took a former elite Nazi official, Arthur Nebe, and showed him as a member of the resistance.[76] The fact that such heroic Nazis were more common in commercial films suggests again that this medium was closer to popular attitudes and the market than television. For the most part, the television audience embraced Nebe as a good German.

Although such "ambivalent" elite Nazis were commonly found in the illustrated press of the 1950s such as *Stern* and *Quick* or little booklets that glorified the war such as *SOS Schicksale Deutscher Schiffe* [SOS Fate of German Ships] or *Der Landser* [The Private], which were often the basis for many of the war films of the 1950s and 1960s, Classen writes that such material was rare on television. Michael Schornstheimer, who wrote a study of the portrayal of National Socialism and the war in *Stern* and *Quick*, estimated that one third of the reading public saw each magazine edition with a combined weekly circulation of over 2 million in 1960.[77] His work reveals the same themes and mythologies discussed in the present study, such as the mythical wall between Nazis and Germans. For example, at the end of Roland Hardt's *Der letzte Kampf* [The Final Struggle] the evil SS appear to execute the honorable German captain and shoot an innocent woman.[78]

Arthur Nebe was a SS general and the head of the Kriminalpolitzei, or criminal police (KRIPO), from 1933 to 1945. He entered the Nazi

Party, the SS, and the SA in 1931 after a distinguished career as a civilian police officer after World War I. As the head of the KRIPO and a top Gestapo official, Nebe was largely responsible for instituting the terror state, which crushed the socialist and Communist resistance, and worked tirelessly for the deportation of the Jews. Yet, at the same time, Nebe began to pass classified information to the military resistance as early as 1938. Later during the war, Nebe was also given command of Einsatzgruppe B, an extermination group, between June and November 1941. During these five months in 1941, forty-five thousand people were murdered in the area under his command. Despite all of this, or perhaps because of it, Nebe may have been involved in the July 20 coup plot. Like much of Nebe's life outside his murderous public record, even his time of death and possible execution are in doubt, as some have claimed to have seen him in the 1950s.[79] With so much uncertainty surrounding Nebe except for his participation in some of the worst crimes of the regime, the choice to make him into a possible figure of the resistance is indeed curious. The ZDF's own write-up on the program is problematic. Because of his German nationalist worldview Nebe "succumbed very soon to the seduction of the National Socialist movement."[80] Such a statement emphasizes his passivity and lack of will. The report continues, "Arthur Nebe . . . saw himself in war year 1944 entangled in the guilt of the regime, in whose service he had, like numerous other Germans, placed himself as a professional."[81] These professional duties, unmentioned in the write-up, included eliminating socialists, Communists, and Jews.

The attraction of the docudrama was so strong for one viewer that he made a special trip to the pub to watch the program. One commented, "Such things must be shown," and another said, "We discussed the program at the firm." Still others felt that they had gained some "objective" insight into what had happened behind the scenes during the Nazi times.[82] Clearly the program had entered into the mundane political culture for a time. Such comments remind one of the social roles that film, television, and newspaper articles play in the daily discussions among individuals. Individual interaction with macrolevel social productions thus feeds back into the microworld on a daily basis and thus guides and structures the daily discourse and the formation of opinions.

The reception of any given cultural product is never universal, and too much work in cultural studies has tried to theorize reception on the basis of a universal viewer. Although generational data are usually not given in the early West German television data, this time there was a significant difference between viewers over the age of fifty and others. Those over the age of fifty, all of whom belonged to the Nazi generation, gave the program a lower rating than younger viewers, and they also rejected the theme of National Socialism out of hand.[83]

While some expressed either pity for Nebe or doubt that such men had actually existed in the SS leadership, the majority of comments made suggestions of having had one's eyes opened to the way it really was at the time. Others talked of finally being able to see behind the facade. Some praised the "objectivity" and "reality" of the docudrama, which showed that not all Nazis and SS members had been evil. As one viewer put it, "One learns that the leading people at that time indeed also had a conscience."[84] "It is good that in those times there were still such individuals, who had a heart, even when they were not able to push through their opinion."[85]

What was this facade that had been stripped away? What was this new-found objectivity? It may well have been what many Germans perceived as the illegitimacy of the Nuremberg trials as well, perhaps, as the Frankfurt Auschwitz trials, which were ongoing during the broadcast. This was not only a resistance from below. The moral legitimacy of the Nuremberg trials, if not their legal legitimacy, had been drawn into question by Marion Gräfin Dönhoff.[86] Soon after the end of the war in October 1946, 78 percent of Germans claimed that the Nuremberg trials were legitimate, but by late 1950 this support had evaporated to only 38 percent.[87] In 1952, the majority of Germans felt that Albert Kesselring, Karl Dönitz, and Albert Speer had been unjustly convicted of war crimes. A majority of Germans thought Rudolf Hess and Baldur von Schirach had been unjustly convicted or were uncertain of the justice of the conviction.[88] Kesselring had been convicted of murdering 335 Italian civilians in retaliation for partisan attacks against German troops in the Ardeantine cave massacre. Albert Speer had been responsible for the organization and use of slave labor. Rudolf Hess had been third in command of the Nazi regime, although he later became mentally unstable. Baldur von Schirach had been the Nazi youth leader, the Hitler Youth leader, and had deported sixty-five thousand Jews from Vienna while governor. Only Dönitz could be said to have had a normal military career absent the excesses of the others, although he had always remained loyal to Hitler.

In short, the facade that *Der Fall Nebe* tore down was "the sham" of Nuremberg. The public of the 1950s and 1960s rarely embraced the prosecution of even the worst Nazi criminals. In 1960, a majority of Germans were either opposed to or undecided about the justice of Adolf Eichmann's abduction by the Israelis.[89] Eichmann had been responsible for organizing the deportation of the Jews to the death camps in the east. In 1965, 60 percent of Germans were against extending the statute of limitations.[90] In 1969, 67 percent were opposed to the same extension. In November 1978, the number was still 62 percent, but there was a precipitous 12 percent drop between then and February 1979, after the showing of the television series *Holocaust* in January 1979.[91] This final shift in public opinion might have been enough to save the SPD vote with minimal CDU and FDP support.

There were also other sites of individual resistance in the Protestant and Catholic Churches. We have already seen the fictionalized resistance work of Pastor Tornqvist in *Waldhausstr. 20.* There can be no doubt that the Confessional Church, led by the Protestant pastor Martin Niemöller, was a significant achievement of institutional independence during the Nazi years. There was also Dietrich Bonhoeffer, who worked directly with the resistance by aiding the escape of Jews and delivering messages from the resistance to the allies. Father Bernhard Lichtenberg, a Catholic priest in Berlin, had protested against the euthanasia program in 1941 and prayed openly for the Jews in October of the same year. This act of defiance led to his arrest and imprisonment, during which he died.

As with every other aspect of life during National Socialism, the history of church institutions is indeed complicated and conflictual. While, on the one hand, one can point to the traditional theological anti-Jewish message of both the Catholic and Protestant Churches, which created part of the cultural basis for the Holocaust, one had individuals working within the structures of the church to save Jews. Yet, one also had church-run orphanages collecting the Jewish children before they were sent to the death camps, as seen in *Leni.* While one had some leaders such as Niemöller standing forth and decrying the euthanasia program of the Nazis, the very institutions where the killings took place were often church-run charities staffed with Christian nurses. Indeed, by the time Niemöller and others had put pressure on the regime to end the euthanasia program in 1941, the goals set for the program by Hitler had already been achieved.[92] In the postwar period, some church leaders did not hesitate to aid in the rehabilitation of former Nazis and Gestapo officials.[93]

The ZDF television drama *Bernhard Lichtenberg*[94] was shown as part of the station's programming dedicated to July 20. As was usually the case, 18 percent of the viewers rejected the theme of National Socialism outright. Overall though, the program was well received with a +5 rating and an audience share of 28 percent. The write-up in the *Infratest* report again showed the producers' awareness of the difficulties they faced in presenting themes related to the Nazi period. The authors then noted that the selection of Bernhard Lichtenberg was a wise choice because it helped to break down the defensive reactions of the audience due to its own "guilt complex."[95] In general, the press reviews were positive, but only one of them threw open the larger question of what would have happened had more Catholic priests behaved as Lichtenberg had.[96]

In 1969, the ARD/NDR broadcast a program focused upon the lives of the children of those fathers who had been executed in connection with the coup attempt. *Im Schatten der Väter*[97] [In the Shadow of the Fathers] avoided a retelling of the July 20 narrative and instead was based solely on the interviews with the sons and daughters of the executed resistance fighters. The program received a low +2 with an audience share of 24 percent. The same evening the ZDF broadcast their documentary entitled *Deutsche gegen Hitler* [Germans against Hitler],[98] which received a paltry 5 percent of the viewers but a better +4 rating.[99] The interviews with the sons and daughters revealed little. The documentarians did not ask the hard questions such as "How does it feel to live in a society that by and large once supported a regime that killed your father?" When one of the daughters makes an insightful statement about her difficulty in teaching the National Socialist period to her students because she might be challenging the moral position of their parents and grandparents, the interviewers fail to pick up the thread.

Although German television stations certainly continued to generate new programs during the 1970s, my research did not uncover any significant trends during that decade. Following the trends marked off by the Bendlerblock debate, members of the Communist resistance gained new attention. For example, in 1984, the ZDF returned with a new two-part documentary, *Warum habt ihr Hitler widerstanden?*[100] [Why Did You Resist Hitler?] and a rebroadcast of the 1955 film *Der 20. Juli*.[101] The documentary received an audience of 3–5 percent.[102] The ZDF received its regular barrage of hate calls, stating that one should finally stop praising these "traitors of the fatherland" (the Communists) who were responsible for the loss of the war and the death of German soldiers.[103]

Perhaps again because it was an off year, 1989 did not attract any new programming,[104] while 1994 ran parallel to the newspaper debates about the proper location of the Communist resistance. The ARD presented a new documentary, *Netzwerk—Adam von Trott zu Solz und der 20. Juli 1944* [Network—Adam von Trott zu Solz and the 20 of July 1944],[105] which took a closer look at the role Trott had played in trying to communicate with the allies about the German resistance. Beginning in June, the NDR had broadcast a multipart series, entitled *Widerstand—Kampf gegen Hitler* [Resistance—Struggle against Hitler].[106] Part 6, entitled *Aufstand der Offiziere* [Uprising of the Officers], is a shocking departure from the narratives about the twentieth from the 1960s. The interviewees continued to try to maintain a distinction between the Wehrmacht, on the one hand, and the Nazis, the SS, and the Holocaust, on the other. But whereas the documentaries and docudramas of the 1960s about resistance had marginalized or ignored the Holocaust, in 1994 the Holocaust had collided not only with the narrative of resistance, as a point of motivation, but also with the role of the Wehrmacht in the perpetration of mass murder. The film shows images of German soldiers participating in the deportations and shooting helpless individuals on the eastern front. Although the narration clearly states the role of the Einsatzgruppen and SS, there is no doubt left in the viewer's mind that the Wehrmacht, as an institution, also played a key role in the war crimes.

There was also growing interest in individual acts of resistance. Although Georg Elser's story had been known for many years, historians either had ignored his assassination attempt or had believed the various pieces of misinformation, that he was either a Nazi or British agent. In fact, Elser was a skilled tradesman who had experience with carpentry and clocks. He was motivated primarily by his dislike for the extreme nationalism of the Nazis and the threat of war. His timed bomb missed Hitler by ten minutes but killed seven and wounded sixty-three on November 8, 1939.

The inclusion of Elser's story within the narrative of the resistance helps us to see how membership in the resistance had expanded rapidly more recently in large part as a reslut of a change in historiographical methods. The study of everyday life had expanded during the 1970s, as had the research on National Socialism. The truth behind Elser's story was discovered in 1970, when a historian working on Nazi justice came across the protocol for his interrogation by the SS. Eva Witte sought to learn more about him in her documentary *Einer aus Königsbronn: Der Widerstandskämpfer Georg Elser* [One from Königsbronn: The resistance fighter Georg Elser].[107] Her interviews with those who knew Elser in his village revealed little else about him, as most were still reluctant to talk. His story was also dramatized in the 1989 film *Georg Elser—einer aus Deutschland* [Georg Elser—One from Germany].[108]

West German Cinema and the Resistance

Narrative themes of resistance are common throughout West German cinema, but the nature of that resistance changed dramatically between the 1950s and the 1980s. The portrayal of resistance was often the central theme and reason for the action of many of the films. In the 1950s, the military resistance against Hitler is almost exclusively shown, although this resistance is divided between high-ranking officers and common soldiers. By the 1980s, the conservative military resistance had almost disappeared from the cinema while numerous portrayals of resistance in everyday life outside the military had become much more common. As with the other mediums, the cinema maintained a clear division between Nazis and Germans. By maintaining the division between the light and dark, between noble officers and sadistic black-clad SS officers, between good and evil, the German cinema worked to help reconstruct a clear vision of the good moral German community. Part of that strategy involved separating the soldier from the Nazi regime. The films struggled to portray the nobleness of resistance while not questioning the righteousness of the common soldier's struggle to defend the fatherland. Many of these films were extremely popular, suggesting again that rather than silence there was highly selective engagement with the past.

I have divided the films into the subcategories of elite resistance and individual resistance. Before moving on to these two categories, it is worth noting again the highly unique portrayal of violent Jewish resistance in *Lang ist der Weg*. It is ironic that the clearest portrayal of Jewish armed resistance to the Nazis should appear in the most conservative early postwar years. To this day, David's off-screen killing of a German soldier remains a unique act of resistance in mainstream German cinema. His other acts of sabotage and killing are only hinted at in the film, but it is clear that these acts are *not* the "other Germany" with which audiences wished to identify. Jewish resistance is not part of the German narrative.

Elite Resistance to the Nazis

A core narrative dilemma for these films is how to portray resistance while not harming Germans or Germany. Yet, how then was one to offer resistance? One of the rhetorical advantages of trying to hold to the traditional narrative of July 20 was that the coup plotters only acted directly against the Nazi leadership without immediately endangering the lives of soldiers at the front. Carl Zuckmayer tried to deal with this latter question in his play *Des Teufels General* [The Devil's General] (1954),[109] which premiered in Zurich in 1946. In the play, the character of Oderbruch is responsible for the death of German pilots at the front because he has intentionally sabotaged their planes. To achieve his goal of resistance, Oderbruch is willing to work with a resistance group and to sacrifice the lives of his own friends. The deep and difficult moral dilemma that Oderbruch represents in the play was removed from the film version.[110] In the film, the test pilots jump to safety before the planes crash, and General Harras, aware of Oderbruch's actions, works to prevent the planes from being sent to the front. The contrast between the play and the film highlights the memory-market dictum.

Although the *Des Teufels General* was only a moderate success in 1955 and was ranked as the twenty-third most successful film for the year,[111] the film was very well received by the ZDF television audience when it was broadcast in 1967.[112] It received an audience share above 50 percent and a high +6 rating. A very small minority of the film's audience, about 5 percent, rejected the war theme or the portrayal of the Nazi era. Of greater significance is the fact that very few rejected the film solely for its Nazi era content, which tended to be much higher when films dealt more directly with Jews.

Canaris (1954) follows a similar pattern to the other July 20 films.[113] Based upon the real-life person Wilhelm Canaris, who was an admiral and the chief of the military intelligence service, the film portrays his resistance efforts. Although *Des Teufels General* had been a moderate success in 1955, *Canaris* was ranked fifth for the same year and both films received the recognition of the FBW as, respectively, "valuable" and "especially valuable," which guaranteed the films' producers further financial benefits.[114] *Canaris* was even awarded a Bambi for the most financially successful film of 1955.[115] It was estimated that 4 million Germans had seen the film between its opening on January 13, 1954, and the beginning of February 1955.[116]

Press reaction to the film was generally positive. Many were willing to accept the narrative of the film as more or less the historical truth even though the same reviewers acknowledged that little was actually known about Canaris. As one reviewer put it, "If he really was so, little depends upon it." For as the reviewer went on to note, what was really important was to show that even during Hitler's reign of terror there were powerful and influential men who followed their conscience.[117] Still, at the same time, another reviewer called it a propaganda piece designed to smooth over the entrance of Hitler's old officer corps into the new Bundeswehr.[118] From what we know of Canaris today, the skepticism of the second reviewer, the minority view, appears more than justified. Canaris had served in the navy during World War I. After the war, he participated in the 1920 Kapp putsch, which was the most serious attempt at a coup d'état during the Weimar Republic carried out by rightist forces in Germany. Although he disliked the mob tactics of the Nazis, he served as the head of the Abwehr, or military intelligence, from 1935 until his removal in February 1944. One of his most lasting contributions to the iconography of the Holocaust was the proposition that Jews be identified with a yellow star. Forcing Jews to wear distinctive markings was a century-old practice in Europe.[119] His deep fear of the eastern Communist threat kept him on the side of the Nazis, but he did become involved in the July 20 coup attempt, for which he was captured and executed.[120]

In the film, Canaris is a much less ambiguous figure, who is generous, fair, and willing to take risks to help friends. The good, noble, and all-seeing Canaris is set in opposition in the film to the dark and evil Reinhard Heydrich. The film attempts to build up a nearly flawless character whose sympathetic nature is enhanced through his love of dogs and his loyalty to his friends. The spy business, which he directs, does not appear to harm anyone at all. We see his spies at work in Paris and London, but we witness nothing more than documents being exchanged. In London, one of the spies, whose true identity is not known to those around him, is warned by a servant, "Sir, did you hear the air raid warnings?" The spy then turns to his female companion and notes in a cavalier manner, "Ach, this happens about five times a day!" The audience is spared images of the German aerial bombardment.

In another scene, Canaris is shown in Franco's Spain while trying to meet with a representative from the allies. Before he meets with the Swedish official, Canaris takes some time to be entertained in a club by a sexy Spanish dancer. Fascist Spain appears to have been a nice location for a vacation. Then he meets with the Swedish official, who informs him that the allies do not believe in the existence of the resistance and are determined to maintain their demand for unconditional surrender. The scene is shot with Canaris speaking directly to the audience with a close-up shot, while the Swedish official is cold and distant as he stands with his back to the camera. Canaris responds, "They must know that we cannot accept such conditions! This will result in millions of additional deaths on both sides!" Soon afterward Canaris is arrested. In a final scene of sentimentality and pathos, the car carrying Canaris and the SS is shown driving into the woods, a common ending for the *Heimatfilme*, with the car being chased by his two loyal little dogs. The film has had an extensive afterlife on television: the ZDF has shown the film five times since its original release, three times in the 1990s.[121]

Two films were released in 1955 that attempted to portray the specific events of the twentieth, G. W. Pabst's *Es geschah am 20. Juli* [It Happened on July 20][122] and Falk Harnack's *Der 20. Juli*,[123] but I want to discuss instead a film from Harald Reinl as his films often attempted to combine the theme of resistance with Nazi war heroes, not unlike the ZDF's *Der Fall Nebe*. Reinl followed in the tradition of showing high-level resistance with *U47—Kapitänleutnant Prien*.[124]

Reinl was one of the most important directors of West German postwar cinema, and he made a series of extremely popular westerns based upon the writings of Karl May. At the time of his death in 1986, one obituary noted that some of his work revealed his political naiveté, including *U47*.[125] What the obituary was stating much too politely was that some of his films were ugly apologies for the Nazis and their heroes. *Solange du lebst* [As long as you live] (1955),[126] which is set during the Spanish civil war, is clearly profascist in its message. At the time, the conservative press simply praised the film's anti-Communism.[127] The same noble fascists battle the Americans in Italy in a defensive battle to save great artistic treasures in *Die grünen Teufel von Monte Cassino* [The Green Demons from Monte Cassino] (1958).[128] The film opens with soldiers being rousted from their vacation time in France.

In defense of his work, Reinl claimed to be the innocent artist, much like Leni Riefenstahl, with whom he worked during the Nazi years. Riefenstahl's defense of her work for the Nazis, including most importantly the propaganda film *Triumph of the Will* (1934),[129] has always been that of the innocent artist.[130] She has always maintained that she knew nothing of the regime's dark side. Yet, when she had volunteered to go to the front in Poland in 1939 as a reporter, she most likely witnessed the killing of Jews in the village of Konskie on September 12, 1939.[131]

U47 is a film about the submarine lieutenant commander Günter Prien, the Nazi hero of Scapa Flow. In October 1939, Prien carried out an extremely dangerous mission against the British navy and was successful. He was awarded the Iron Cross First Class and a private audience with Hitler. Prien's exploits on the high seas have all of the makings for a classic war film with heroism, danger, and masculine camaraderie, but there is nothing in Prien's biography that would lead one to believe he was somehow secretly opposed to the Nazis. Yet this resistance narrative is tagged to his life in the film. Besides the huge success of his memoirs in Germany, Prien was the subject of postwar stories of military heroism and glory.[132]

The film's promotion did run into problems with the FSK. One of the proposed film posters for the film showed Prien in the foreground with his National Socialist honors highlighted on his chest with a diving U-boat and sinking enemy ships in the background. The FSK had rejected the poster because of its suggestive glorification of the Nazi regime.[133] The FSK also originally refused to release the film for young audiences, below the age of twelve, because the film failed to demonstrate the importance of making choices based upon one's conscience. After some changes, the film was released for youth after the offending glorification of the war was removed.[134] One wonders whether the resistance theme, which feels carelessly added on in the film, was included solely to smooth the film's release.

The theme of elite military resistance to the Nazis disappears after the end of the 1950s. Although the ZDF's *Nebe* program proved that such material was still very popular in the 1960s, the German war film genre had already largely disappeared from the cinemas. Although there were war films made after the mid-1960s, they were less common than in the early postwar years. In general, these films have not become so-called classics of German cinema in the same way that John Wayne war films have found an afterlife on video and television in the United States.

Acts of Individual Resistance

One of the most important films to deal with individual resistance is Falk Harnack's *Unruhige Nacht* [The Restless Night] (1958), for it deals with the question of desertion.[135] Whether the act of desertion in the film actually constitutes an act of resistance is questionable, but the position of deserters in the German legal system was straightforward until 1997. Up until 1997, desertion from the Wehrmacht was a crime, and all those who had deserted were still marked by a criminal record. Deserters were almost universally condemned throughout the history of the Federal Republic as having abandoned their comrades and having behaved in a selfish manner. German elites and the general public continuously condemned the deserters and the allies' claim that desertion was an act of resistance and a moral responsibility in Hitler's Germany.

In such commentaries, one often encounters a note stating that desertion is a crime in all the armies of the world and that military discipline demands that deserters be punished. What such commentators regularly ignored was that German military justice during World War II was particularly brutal. While the Anglo-Saxon allies carried out only one execution as a result of desertion during the war, German military justice led by judges such as Filbinger executed no fewer than ten thousand German soldiers.[136] German attitudes toward desertion only began to change once citizens and their leaders began to view the Nazi system as fundamentally unjust (see chart 1). The German historian Manfred Messerschmidt has argued that the executions were part of the Nazi biological worldview. More than simply maintaining military discipline, desertion marked one as biologically and psychologically unfit for the new German race.[137]

Such attitudes had real political consequences for the deserters who were not executed and their families after the war. In the 1950s and 1960s, the German justice system was granting full pensions to former leading members of the Gestapo who had built their careers on the deportation of the Jews at the same time it was denying the deserter's wife and children the normal pension granted to a family after the death of the husband.[138] Rather than recognize the injustice of the original sentence, the courts ruled that the sentence had legal merit. This is hardly surprising when one considers the fact that the justice system had never been purged of judges who had worked during the Nazi years. In large part because of dramatic changes in the portrayal and reception of National Socialist history in the 1980s and 1990s, and growing debates surrounding the crimes of the Wehrmacht, all of the major parties (CDU/CSU, SPD, and FDP) recognized in May 1997 that the military justice of the Wehrmacht during the war vis-à-vis the deserters was unjust, and in December of the same year the surviving deserters or their family members received a onetime restitution payment. Changes in the cultural matrix had opened up new possibilities and realities within the sphere of politics and policy formation.

With these past debates in mind, one can better appreciate the potentially radical and subversive nature of a film that dealt with the question of desertion in the late 1950s. In a decade filled with war films that tried to glorify the war and the noble sacrifice of one's life for Germany, while also separating the war from the fascist cause, Harnack's film had the potential to expose the narrative division between the military and the fascists as a myth. Several Berlin newspaper reports noted that the audience at the premiere of the film in Berlin was very quiet and perhaps shocked after the presentation before finally thanking the actors and the director, who were present for the premiere.[139] The film certainly made some people uncomfortable. One former soldier wrote a letter to his local paper reaffirming the justice of the deserter's execution, although he places *just* in quotation marks. He then wrote, "Please understand me correctly—I do not want to sanction the military justice," but continued, "I feared for my own life in the partisan fighting; in the summer of 1942 Baranowski [the deserter in the film] would have found no mercy, not for one moment understanding."[140] One wonders, would the author then have willingly participated in the execution squad shown in the film?

In the film, Baranowski is to be executed for desertion. We learn about his case through a priest, played by Bernhard Wicki, who has arrived to comfort him before the execution. The priest spends a restless night reading Baranowski's file. Through a series of flashbacks, we learn that Baranowski is a decorated soldier, who was severely wounded in the knee. Because of this, he was given the job of going into the villages to collect food from civilians for the soldiers.

While the film does confront the issue of military justice and executions, it does not deal critically with the occupation policies of the German military. In fact, German occupation policies are almost never addressed in German cinema. It is therefore particularly poignant that the film is actually set in Ukraine during the summer of 1942. Although there were military regulations that prohibited the looting of food and clothing from the local populations, the shortages that developed during Operation Barbarosa in 1941, the attack on the Soviet Union, soon led to widespread looting by the soldiers. Furthermore, the capture of the Ukraine was intended not only to supply the occupying military, but also to help prevent shortages at home. Bread was shipped back to Germany from the front. As the invasion of Russia went drastically wrong, lasting not twenty weeks but rather the rest of the war, the discipline of the army continued to deteriorate into the winter of 1941. The measures against the civilian population also grew increasingly brutal. Many starved as a result of the food's being shipped back to Germany. Others were shot when they left the cities illegally to search for food in the countryside. They were considered partisans or vagabonds, although they were only wandering the countryside in search of food.[141]

In the film, Baranowski's requisition activities are orderly as he writes a receipt for each item taken from the civilian population. He assures them that they will be fairly compensated. In one of the houses he enters, he meets a woman whose husband has been killed in the fighting, and he begins a relationship with her and her son. One day the SS arrive and decide to tear the place apart, for no apparent reason, and they find letters that Baranowski had sent to the woman. The criminal actions of the SS contrast with the proper behavior of Baranowski vis-à-vis the civilian population, thus reinforcing the evil Nazi and good German myth. As a punishment, he is to be placed in one of the infamous punishment battalions, which were made up of criminals, Communists, socialists, and other social outcasts. The punishment battalions were used basically as canon fodder by the military. The fate of one such battalion is dramatized in the kitsch film *Strafbataillon 999*.[142]

Rather than be sent away from a woman with whom he is now in love, he flees the battalion and returns to her but is eventually found again by the SS. By showing him dedicated to the theme of love in the midst of war, the film's narrative tries to make his insubordination sympathetic to the audience and his execution unjust. How can one be against love? If his actions had been motivated by politics rather than love, the filmmakers knew they would lose a large portion of their potential audience. The film closes with Baranowski's execution, and we see the priest being given a ride by another military official, who refused Baranowski's request for a pardon. The two confront each other over their conflicting views of the justice of the execution, and the priest demands that he be let out of the car, saying, "And when this war is over, people will ask us what we did during those days." He leaves the car and walks out into a cemetery with row upon row of small white crosses.

Given the times within which it was made, Harnack's film is surprisingly daring for a commercial enterprise. Although the film failed to deal with the true nature of the occupation policies of the Wehrmacht in the Ukraine, and the SS play the bad guy once again, it did raise serious questions regarding the morality of Nazi wartime justice. But it failed to wed this execution to the Nazi ideal of racial purity. It was also a rather solitary voice in an era when deserters were almost universally seen as having betrayed the nation. Even in later years, one could read from Dönhoff and others that one could not treat the deserters as a whole as either good or bad. One needed to search for their individual motivations. At the same time, commentators would assure their audience that at least the majority of the soldiers in the Wehrmacht had always had an inner struggle against Hitler. The burden of proof was never the same. In the end, it is not a surprise that the film was not a commercial success, but it remains an important attempt to expand the cultural matrix surrounding the Nazi years.[143] It is therefore surprising that it has thus far been ignored in the film literature.

Non-German Resistance: The Partisans

Up to this point, all of the films have focused upon German resistance to the Nazis, which helped to reaffirm the moral goodness of the Germans and Germany vis-à-vis the evil and corruption of the SS and Nazis. Soldiers shown fighting at the front are not depicted as supporting Nazi policies, either tacitly or explicitly. In fact, many of the films have been de-Nazified except for the SS and the occasional sadistic and idiotic Nazi officer. But the narratives again become more difficult to construct once one opens the question of resistance to the German army in the occupied countries. To the extent that a legitimate and moral partisan resistance is recognized as having existed in these countries, the German-Nazi division becomes more difficult to defend.

What is interesting and disheartening to observe is that the same process of dehumanization that occurs in war, perhaps as a psychological necessity to justify the killing of other human beings, is almost always continued in every national cinema's portrayal of the enemy years after the end of the conflict. This is hardly a fact that is unique to German cinema, but its realization helps us to understand the additional cultural barriers that exist to a process of reconciliation. One might have hoped that once humans were removed from the actual process of killing each other in massive numbers, the humanity of the other might be more readily recognized. Unfortunately, the process of dehumanization usually continues well after the war so that the moral nature of one's own soldiers is not drawn into question. The justifications, rationalizations, subterfuge, and stereotypes continue.[144] One example of the typical portrayal of the partisans can be seen in *Strafbataillon 999* (1959), which shows them as cowardly, dirty fighters who ambush German soldiers. At one point in the film, one of the Asiatic partisans rapes a woman.

Despite the usual portrayal of the partisans as fighting dirty, being dirty, and constituting a constant threat to German soldiers, there are two notable films that provide a human face for the foreign resistance to the Germans rather than just the Nazis. They also show the narrative complexities that exist in trying to maintain a human face for such resistance while not denigrating the German soldier.

In *Die letzte Nacht* [The Last Night] (1949),[145] from Eugen York, a French noblewoman risks her own life in not only distributing anti-German propaganda pamphlets but also blowing up a dam so that the retreating German forces are trapped. They will most likely be captured, rather than killed, thus blunting the violence of her act. The French noblewoman is simply identified as Madame, and she exudes a sense of grace and an appreciation for high culture, which may make her more sympathetic for the audience. In contrast, her other helpers are more similar to the portrayal of the partisans as rough-looking street toughs.

The retreating German officers are to be housed at Madame's large estate for at least the evening. It is the same evening on which Madame makes her dangerous sortie to blow up the dam. She is successful, but she is discovered by the Germans and sentenced to death. Although military justice is harsh, the German officers are all very cultured and polite. Bruckner, one of the German officers, goes to comfort Madame after her sentence. At this point, the film fails to create a credible motivation for Madame, and when she speaks of her act it sounds like what Germans might want to hear rather than what a French resistance fighter might say. She says, for example, "I don't hate you, your uniform, your country, the officers downstairs. I don't hate the general who has sentenced me to death. What I hate is the war." Bruckner takes pity on her and confronts the general. He pleads on her behalf, but the general will not rescind his order.

Bruckner returns to Madame, and they continue their discussions. She speaks perfect German, having once studied in Freiburg, and she gives Bruckner a copy of Goethe, which a university friend had once given her. Would he please return it for her? Although her comments continue to be abstract, her character then speaks of the importance of not only loving peace and freedom but also fighting for it. Her actions in the movie do not directly threaten the lives of the German soldiers, who we are told will only be captured. What else might a willingness to fight entail? Bruckner decides that he too will fight for freedom, and the two hatch a plan to help her escape. Her escape is successful, but now Bruckner is sentenced to death in her place. The last image of the film is a haunting misty morning with Madame walking down along the train tracks away from us into the distance.

A rare example of the brutality of German occupation is shown in *Am Galgen hängt die Liebe* [Love Hangs on the Gibbet] (1960).[146] In this film, the German military is clearly shown executing innocent civilians in retaliation for partisan activities. This is only the second suggestion of such war crimes' being committed by regular German soldiers in West German cinema that I found in the secondary literature or my own viewing of films. The other film is *Das Haus in der Karpfengasse*, in which we are only told that Czech students were taken away and shot as a collective punishment for rioting. The only film that actually shows the killing of innocent civilians by regular army troops is the DEFA film *Die Mörder sind unter uns*.

The story focuses upon an old bickering couple, Nikolaos and Marulja, and the aid that they give to both a partisan commander and two German soldiers in Greece during the war. We are quickly introduced to the fighting between the partisans and the Germans. The partisan leader, Petros, seeks shelter at the simple home of the old couple. Although the Germans arrive, search the place, and threaten Nikolaos with death, they fail to find Petros's hiding place. The couple also later hides two Germans from Petros, one of whom escapes to warn the other German forces.

Now Nikolaos realizes that the Germans will enter the village and kill some hostages in retaliation. He rushes to the village to try to warn the inhabitants, but he is too late. The Germans have arrived in the village to carry out their vengeance upon the innocent population. Thirty men not under the age of eighteen are to be executed. In an extremely gripping scene, the men are lined up against the wall in the darkness with women screaming and chaos all around. The selections are made, and the men are loaded on the truck and taken away to be shot. Although the actual executions are not shown, the scenes in the village are very intense, and we have no doubt about the men's fate after they are taken away. Petros knows that Nikolaos has lied to him about hiding the Germans and returns to execute the old couple.

Conclusion

The leaders of both East and West Germany faced similar problems in the immediate postwar years. There had been a high level of collaboration with the previous fascist regime by much if not most of their respective populations. This collaboration did not necessarily manifest itself in the direct carrying out of criminal acts, but as do the villagers in the film *Leni*, almost all bore some level of responsibility. Although the postwar leaders in both societies attempted to cover over this widespread collaboration and admiration for the dictator and his policies, the German society of 1945 was not seized by revolutionary fervor at having defeated the enemy. Hitler, the Nazis, the SS, Germany, and the Germans had been defeated.

A society that had shown enthusiastic support for the regime up until 1941 later viewed itself as the primary victim of barbaric criminals and outside occupiers. But the exact identity of those criminals was rarely clear and often shifting. As the success of the TV program *Der Fall Nebe* or the film *Canaris* demonstrated, there was a great desire to believe that even within the very center of the corrupt and evil regime there had been good men who had tried to prevent worse from happening. Such acts had redeemed the true Germany.

In the East, an official state-led antifascism became the central theme and founding myth for the new society. The state offered a second chance to the members of its society to defeat fascism once and for all. Perhaps one had collaborated or been indifferent in the past as was Hans in *Rotation*, but by joining the modern socialist movement and the true antifascist state one could help atone for past misdeeds through good work.

In the West, the socialist and Communist resistance was largely forgotten for most of the cold war. Rather than the official antifascism of the GDR, West German elites tried to develop popular interest in the national-conservative and military resistance to Hitler. Political leaders, filmmakers, and newspaper editors invited all to identify with this narrow segment of the resistance as having redeemed the nation through their blood sacrifice. Their sacrifice, it was argued, had shown to the world that Germany was never truly Hitler's and that the "other Germany" had always existed.

A more curious question, which is not easy to answer, is the absence of democratic or liberal resistance figures. One might have assumed that such figures were destined to become the heroes of the new democratic West German state. Many of these more liberal figures were, however, tainted because they had fled Germany before the war. Willy Brandt was not able to draw upon his participation in the liberal democratic resistance for political advantage largely because of his time spent in exile. As they did the deserter, the general public viewed those who had fled into exile as having abandoned Germany in the moment of greatest need. Indeed, Brandt's political opponents, including Konrad Adenauer, used this time in exile as a political weapon against him. There was a great deal of public resentment of those who had not suffered the deprivations of the war. The fact that they had often worked in the West rather than the East only made them slightly better than the Communists. The fact that liberal democratic resistance fighters were not openly embraced shows the low level of legitimacy that West Germany's democracy suffered from in the earliest years.

The data that we have for West Germany suggest a significant level of ambivalence toward the theme of resistance, especially in the 1950s and 1960s. A substantial segment of the population refused to identify the National Socialist regime as a criminal regime for many years (see chart 1), and the negative view of the military resistance among the majority of former soldiers has already been shown. In general, any discussion of resistance was always hampered by its implied critique of those who had not resisted. This was a particularly sensitive issue for former soldiers.

Although similar data are lacking for East Germany, it is reasonable to assume that for the 1950s and 1960s similar trends could have been found among the Nazi generation in that society as well. As for the following generations in the East, they were often encouraged through East Germany's popular culture to question their parents and to throw their support behind the socialist regime as a way of overcoming the past. Wolf's *Ich war neunzehn* was a popular success with its antifascist themes for just this generation. Although the official antifascism often appeared ridiculous and overdrawn, it also offered a guilt-free past.

While the official antifascism of the East German state remained largely unaltered over the years, the national-conservative resistance that the West celebrated began to run into trouble with the emergence of the Holocaust narrative in the 1970s. As the Holocaust narrative began to dominate the public discourse of the late 1970s and 1980s, the moral imperative for having resisted the Nazis in some form became ever more compelling. It also became more and more difficult to defend the leaders of the national-conservative resistance, whose primary motivation did not appear to have been derived from the persecution of the Jews.

Whereas other countries were able to embrace their wartime resistance to the German occupation and thus paper over the collaboration of local populations with the Nazis in the extermination of the Jews, Germany's relationship to its own history of resistance would always be problematic. In trying to establish a resistance narrative, German society tried yet again to drive a wedge between the moral community of the Germans and the moral abyss of the Nazis. Germans needed to mourn the loss of their husbands and sons as soldiers in the war and the loss of other family members and property in the bombing raids. From the perspective of many Germans, the allies had unjustly punished the German nation, the "other Germany" celebrated in the resistance narratives, by dividing it between East and West. But as chapter 6 will demonstrate, the end of the war was greeted not as liberation, but rather as defeat. The first forty-five years of postwar history were dedicated to defending the soldier-father and the soldier-son as having done their duty for Germany, but in the end the most difficult questions remained. What had they been fighting for?

5

Division and Unity: A Revolutionary People Unites Itself

THIS CHAPTER IS DESIGNED TO HIGHLIGHT HOW THE TWO GERman states and societies reflected upon the division and unity of the German state and nation. I have used June 17 as a national holiday in West Germany and its celebration as a means to locate debates within the discursive field of division and unity. How was the division of the country discussed in both parts of Germany? What was said about the unity of the German nation or people despite this political division? In the West, the theme of resistance to tyranny, Communist and fascist, appeared regularly within the discursive field of unity and division. From the Western perspective, the German nation was destined to be united within a democratic rule-of-law state. This was the natural order of things, which had been upset by the Communist puppet state in the East.

Much of the discussion that surrounded the division of the country was focused upon how this was an unnatural state of affairs. Neither side could risk stating that the division of the German nation was a natural and inevitable outcome of the war. Rather than focusing on the root causes of the war and German fascism as the reason for the division, both states blamed the other and their cold war allies for the division. Both sides argued vociferously that the unity of the nation could only be regained under the banner of either democratic liberalism or socialism, depending on where one stood.

The democratic state argued that democracy was the natural endpoint of a revolutionary people and a revolutionary movement dating back to the nineteenth century. In contrast, the socialist state tried to show that socialism was the true heir of that same nineteenth-century revolutionary movement and that only socialism could restore love to human relationships. Love and the nurturing of human bonds became themes and leitmotifs of political speeches as well as films. The nation was a family that had been torn apart by political forces beyond its control or understanding.

In the rest of this chapter, I will first outline the most general discussions about the division of the country as either unnatural or natural. Most of the discussion in this first section will be focused upon West Germany, as June 17 was officially ignored in the East. In the final section of the chapter, we will look at a collection of East and West German films that deal with the division of the country. These "films of division" can help us to understand the Eastern perspective. While the SED regime avoided almost all reference to June 17, the party was fairly willing to engage the theme of division and try to justify the division to its citizens.

The History

On the morning of June 17, 1953, in East Berlin and throughout East Germany there was widespread unrest in the streets with striking workers, strike leaders, curiosity seekers, solidarity marchers from West Berlin, and people simply passing by who decided to join the various marches, demonstrations, and riots. Current estimates suggest that 500,000 demonstrators were involved throughout East Germany, with major disturbances in 373 different cities and more than 600 separate factory strikes. At some point during the day, Walter Ulbricht and Otto Grotewohl, the two most powerful members of the SED, were flown out of Berlin to Karlshorst under the protection of the Soviet military. By one in the afternoon on the seventeenth, the Soviet military authority had declared a state of emergency, and the tanks began to roll through the streets of Berlin. Soviet soldiers also began to disperse the demonstrators at the other locations throughout East Germany. Although disturbances continued for over a week, the revolt in the streets of Berlin was basically over within a forty-eight-hour period. Considering the number of demonstrators involved, the revolt was put down with relatively little violence. One report listed fifty-one demonstrator casualties. The legal proceedings that followed were much more extensive with over fifty-six hundred cases brought against those involved in the disturbances.[1]

For a period of hours, the SED had lost control, and the regime would have collapsed if it had not been for the intervention of Soviet military forces on its behalf. In 1953, the SED still lacked a proper military, and the demonstrators had quickly disarmed the Volkspolitzei, or People's Police. At first, even the Soviet soldiers had refused to fire upon the masses, as they broke into prisons and demanded the release of political prisoners. But with the imposition of the state of emergency, the Soviet military was able again to bring the situation under control.

The immediate and primary cause for the mass uprising was an increase in the work norms by 10 percent, which, when combined with other reductions in subsides, had caused some workers to lose 25 percent of their purchasing power during 1953. Even with the death of Stalin in March 1953, Ulbricht and the SED had continued to move forward with a radical Stalinization of the economy. There was widespread unrest in rural areas as a result of forced collectivization, and the party was asking urban workers to increase their productivity to try to save an economy that was struggling under state command. Conditions had become so bad that in May the SED leaders had been summoned to Moscow and told to reverse course immediately. At the beginning of June, the party admitted its mistakes to the public and originally expected to be embraced by a thankful populace. Instead a revolt broke out. At some point during the demonstrations in East Berlin, the demands began to shift from removal of the work norm increases toward more political demands for free elections and the removal of party leaders.

There were two important long-term consequences for those living in the East. First, the Soviet suppression of the 1953 East German revolt showed that the Soviet Union was prepared to use military force to defend its interests in Eastern Europe. During the same summer of 1953, the United States and its allies were in the final stages of extricating themselves from the Korean peninsula, where the first attempt to roll back Communism had failed after a three-year war. On June 17, the United States and its allies did everything they could to minimize the involvement of West Berliners in the disturbances.

The second consequence was the development of the police state. Up to 1953, the East German state's capacity for monitoring internal dissent had not been particularly well developed. There was a clear policy of repressing political dissent, but a widespread net of informers had yet to be developed; June 17 showed the SED leaders that their attempts at trying to bring the population on-board the train of the socialist revolution through propaganda had largely failed. From that day forward, there was a permanent wall of mistrust between the rulers and the ruled, and the development of the Ministry for State Security, or Stasi, began in earnest. The development of internal state security under the direction of Erich Mielke certainly did become an exercise in paranoia. At one point a committee for radio and television in Poland had sent a 1965 calendar to some of their colleagues in East Germany. Someone noticed that June 17 was marked in red as a special holiday and thought this of such great importance that the calendar eventually ended up on Mielke's desk. He even filed the calendar away. However, rather than a Polish attempt to overthrow the regime by reminding

East Germans of the revolt, the day simply marked a well-known Polish holiday.[2]

An Unnatural Division

While elites of both parts of the truncated German nation-state often spoke about the possibility and need for reunification, neither side was willing to sacrifice its vision of the good society in the deal. In the beginning, except for some socialists, West German elites and the United States would only accept a capitalist democracy, and East German elites and the Soviet Union would only accept a Communist or perhaps an ill-defined neutral Germany. Once the idea of a neutral Germany was dropped by the Adenauer administration in 1952, under clear pressure from the United States, reunification was out for the foreseeable future.

For West German elites, many civil society organizations, and certainly the vast majority of Germans, the division of the country was an unnatural situation. Within the ceremonies marking June 17, West German elites never failed to proclaim that the nation remained as one, despite the political division. In 1963, Vice Chancellor Erhard spoke along with Willy Brandt, the mayor of Berlin at the time, before a crowd of around 100,000 in Berlin. Erhard spoke of "the 'open wound' on the body of the German nation."[3] At another ceremony that same year, Chancellor Adenauer commented, "The residents of the tattered part are no communists and never will become communists."[4] The Eastern part had been torn away violently from the natural whole, taking on the imagery of a family, body, or lost homeland.[5]

The loss of the Sudetenland to Czechoslovakia and Austria to neutrality, two of Hitler's greatest achievements in the eyes of many Germans, was also accepted more easily than the division between East and West. Nonetheless, the loss of East Prussia and the Sudetenland remained politically important because the refugees from these lands had organized themselves into a powerful lobby force. They became particularly influential in Bavaria, through their participation in the CSU, which is Bavaria's unique wing of the CDU. Elite public pronouncements about German nationalism after 1945 in West Germany often addressed the unity of the nation despite political division, but the goal of reunification was generally limited to East Germany. Although some would continue to dream of the return of lost territory, elites rarely tried to articulate such claims.

Overcoming the division of the country was a top political priority for many Germans between 1955 and 1963.[6] But by 1976, this wish had a clear generational divide.[7] Younger Germans who grew up with the division were more likely to accept it as the natural state of affairs. West Germany's political elite were aware of this danger and often admonished younger Germans to take an interest in the unity of the country and to work for unity. But what exactly the German youth should do, except think good thoughts, was never clearly articulated.

An Unnatural but Necessary Division

The SED's official party line explained the uprising as having resulted from provocative fascist agents who had entered the East through West Berlin. This position never wavered, and as one East German commented, it was not a topic that was openly discussed in the schools. The teacher simply delivered the party line and then refused to answer questions or discuss the issue.[8] My search of *Neues Deutschland* did not uncover any discussion of June 17, even the party line, after the actual event. But the seventeenth was discussed in the popular press from time to time, and articles may well have appeared in *Neues Deutschland* at other times of the year. The newspaper clippings archive at the DRA did have a slim folder with some articles about the uprising published in later years. In June 1978, *Die Wahrheit* [The Truth], one supposes a not ironically titled publication, ran a series of articles on the so-called Day X, which continued to repeat the old party line of Western agent's having been responsible for the uprising.[9]

East German elites saw their part of Germany as the culmination of natural historical forces, which had finally led to a true Communist revolution. Their claims to speak for the entire German nation were, however, much more muted in the beginning and then nonexistent. After June 17, they certainly realized that their popular legitimacy was weak. But even before the popular revolt, the East German elite viewed itself as on the edge of progressive world history, and they recognized that not everyone was spiritually prepared for the difficult struggle of building socialism.

This can be seen in many of the East German films of division, which show characters making a conscious choice to continue living in the East based on political principle and the importance of human love, which could only flourish within socialism. By contrast, in the West, greed and lust for power had caused people to renounce love. As Alberich's renunciation of love allows him to seize the Rhinemaidens' gold in Wagner's *Das Rheingold*, capitalism had corrupted the human capacity for love. As we will see later, the theme of love and the natural bond between humans is corrupted and crushed by those driven for money and power.

It is therefore ironic to find passages referring to the need to work for national unity in the pages of *Neues Deutschland* just before the popular revolt in 1953. For example, one article makes several references to the "struggle for Germany's unity." In an article entitled "The Workers Will Fully Support the Measures," published on the sixteenth, one can read, "The financial and economic relief for all farmers gives us a powerful impetus to support even more the struggle for the establishment of Germany's unity."[10] The relief referred to in the quote was the party's capitulation before the farmers' resistance to collectivization, but what this might have had to do with Germany's unity is anyone's guess. Yet, the rhetorical flourishes are important for they show that even the SED felt the need to present itself as concerned about Germany's unity.

June 17 as a West German National Holiday

June 17 as a national holiday in Germany is a perfect example of how the state's attempt to invent tradition can almost completely fail. After the original uprising, the West German parliament declared the seventeenth an official federal holiday, making it a day off from work with pay. As politicians never tired of repeating in the following years, they expected citizens to participate in mass demonstrations and "to work for the unity of Germany." How the masses were exactly to work for this unity was never explained; nor did the political leaders appear to have any solution themselves. Needless to say, the masses often spent the holiday in the park. The day remained an official federal holiday until the collapse of the GDR, when it became a *Gedenktag*, or memorial day.

Chancellor Adenauer sought first to integrate West Germany within the Western alliance. Unification was, from the beginning, a distant goal. The CDU/CSU then launched vicious attacks against the SPD and Kurt Schumacher for their willingness to flirt with the idea of accommodation with the East. The SPD, in turn, attacked the Christian Democrats for having abandoned those living in the East. In 1955, the Hallstein doctrine, articulated by the Christian Democrats, stated that official recognition of East Germany would be seen as an unfriendly act by the West German state. Beginning in 1969, the SPD, led by Chancellor Willy Brandt and Egon Bahr, took a different approach, which became known as *Ostpolitik*. Brandt had begun to articulate the idea of *Ostpolitik* while he was the mayor of Berlin in the 1950s. The basic principle of *Ostpolitik* was to accept the international political reality and to work toward improving the personal contacts across the border, while also improving the life of those living in East Germany.

It would be a mistake to view June 17 as simply an example of everyday politics, money, and free time, for the unity of the nation and the reunification of the country were very passionate political topics for many Germans. As with July 20, it is necessary to separate stale state ceremony from the historical narrative of unity and division, which did resonate with the general public. The *Kuritorium Unteilbares Deutschland* (KUD) [Committee for an Indivisible Germany] was formed on June 14, 1954, near the first anniversary of the uprising, and it became the most prominent civil society organization dedicated to German unity. The original 128 members were drawn from West Germany's political, economic, and social elite. The committee participated regularly in political events marking June 17, while also taking out special newspaper advertisements and organizing other community-level events. A working group within the KUD called *Widerstandskämpfer des 17. Juni* [Resistance Fighters of the 17th of June] took a special interest in introducing the story of the seventeenth into the schools so that the next generation would not forget the sacrifices of the previous generation.

The *Arbeitsgemeinschaft 13. August* [Working Society 13th of August] opened a museum called Haus am Checkpoint Charlie on June 15, 1963, to show visitors the human costs of the division. Some of the most popular exhibits at the museum, which had up to 1973 averaged eight hundred visitors a day, were actual artifacts from different successful escape attempts out of the East.[11] The theme of escape became a leitmotif in many West German films. The museum continued to attract visitors well after the reunification of the country in 1990. Still other civil society organizations worked to help refugees from the East and to demand the reestablishment of human rights such as the *Gesamtverband der Sowjetzonenflüchtlinge* [General Association of Soviet Zone Refugees][12] and the *Vereinigung der Opfer des Stalinismus* [Union of Victims of Stalinism].

The day also became a rallying point for extreme nationalists, which occasionally led to violent clashes with police and far Left demonstrators. Little of their activity was regularly reported in the mainstream press, but the far Right did make the papers a couple times during the late 1970s and early 1980s. As has been shown in chapter 3, it was also during these years that the Holocaust had become a much more prominent topic of public discussions. The 1978 riot that destroyed a good part of central Frankfurt was related to the police's attempt to protect a gathering organized by the NPD, a far Right organization, from a group of antifascist demonstrators. The entire scene simply descended into chaos with eighty-six injuries and extensive damage to property.[13]

On June 17, 1983, in Berlin, about eight hundred took part in a march organized by the *Konservativen Aktion* [Conservative Action], which attacked detente with the East and sought to intimidate Turks living in Kreuzberg, a part of Berlin with a large Turkish population.[14] Once again fights broke out among police, counterdemonstrators, and the far Right demonstrators. Rather than trying to link themselves explicitly in any manner to June 17, the far Right groups simply tried to turn the day into a nationalist event.

There were also certainly many individuals who marked the day in a more personal manner, which simply escaped the attention of the television and newspapers. *Der Tagesspiegel* reported a couple times on small informal gatherings in which individuals joined to mourn the division of the country or the separation from family on the other side of the border or to demonstrate their solidarity with those on the other side.[15]

Each of these groups used the day in ways partially in line with the wishes of the state but also at cross-purposes with the nationalism that mainstream politicians hoped to stir. Vacationers flaunted their indifference to politics; civil society organizations used the day as a rallying point to motivate members to keep memories alive; far Left and far Right demonstrators used the day to fight each other and the police; individuals took time to participate in larger demonstrations or more private ceremonies. It is important to keep the multiple uses and meanings of the day in mind, for if one simply looks to the state, and official ceremonies and pronouncements, one can be misled into thinking that all this was nothing more than political hot air or at the same time take the political pronouncements as somehow being equivalent to mass opinions. For their part, the official state ceremonies for June 17 quickly settled into a very regular, passionless pattern of wreath ceremonies and small marches. Except for ceremonies in 1963, which drew close to 100,000 demonstrators in Berlin, the gatherings were often much more modest, with often no more than a couple of thousand participating. The large turnout in Berlin in 1963 marking the tenth anniversary can probably be explained by the then-recent construction of the Berlin wall.

In addition to frequently criticizing the masses as being apolitical pleasure seekers, politicians and newspaper columnists began to draw some interesting historical parallels between June 17 and other important dates in German history. There was a concerted effort on the part of elites and intellectuals to show June 17 as part of a long history of Germans offering valiant resistance against tyranny despite impossible odds. Consider this passage from one such essay: "This 17th of June was the only complete glorious chapter in the most recent German history; it has washed clean the German name before the whole world from the appearance that we are a people of will-less servants, that we deserve nothing other than a dictatorship."[16] Notice the parallels with some of the rhetoric surrounding July 20 in that the German name has been washed clean. Rather than simply a group of riotous workers primarily upset about wages, the uprising was sewn into the narrative fabric of resistance. By assigning democratic demands to the June 17 uprising, West German elites could claim to speak for the East German population and use the ritual to portray the Germans as a revolutionary people dedicated to democracy.

According to other political figures, this long tradition of resistance has always been working for the goal of a democratic Germany, with West Germany the final culmination of a century-long struggle. For example, Federal President Lübke used the entrance hall at Munich University to speak about the uprising and the tradition of resistance in German history. The selection of that stage for the political drama was loaded with symbolism, for it was within this entrance hall that the student members of the White Rose resistance group had thrown their anti-Nazi propaganda leaflets just before their capture.[17] Lübke also made direct reference to July 20 in his speech, saying that what the White Rose and the workers had begun was not yet completed because of the division of the country.[18]

This theme of resistance against tyranny throughout German history was taken up in every single year in some form or other. When the SED regime was finally toppled in 1989, this was seen as the culmination of what had begun in 1953, if not 1848. The historical pathway to democracy within a unified Germany, the goal for which the workers had gone on strike according to the commentators, had finally been realized.[19] Thus, June 17, according to the German elite, showed to history that the German people were actually a people of resistance and democratic spirit. The democratic spirit that had been shown during the European revolutions of 1848 had finally been realized within the new German state unified once again in 1990. The natural end point of history had finally been realized. In this manner, the national narrative surrounding June 17 proved to have much more in common with the discursive field of resistance and collaboration than I originally had anticipated finding.

I was somewhat surprised by the almost complete absence of any linkage drawn between the crimes of the Third Reich and the division of the country. In all of the material incorporated in this research, I found very few references that tried to tie the division of the country to the history of National Socialism and World War II. The two events appeared, by and large, to be disconnected from each other. This is true for the films of division as well as the newspaper reports. The only such clear reference I found in all of the newspaper material was an essay published in *Die Zeit* in 1978, in which Karl-Heinz Janßen mused: "Do we still want a common German state? Or have we forfeited the moral right for that through the crimes of the Third Reich?"[20] Again, it is interesting to note that the author articulated such thoughts in the late 1970s, when the extent of those crimes was becoming common public knowledge.

But this was never more than a minority position and nothing short of apostasy for the vast majority of Germans. Those intellectuals on the Left who flirted with such thoughts were pummeled repeatedly in the national press after reunification as if they alone had been responsible for delaying the reunification of the country. The Green Party was also hurt severely at the ballot box because of its open questioning of the reunification agenda set by Chancellor Helmut Kohl in 1989.[21] Günter Grass, Germany's best known living writer and then later Nobel laureate, was the most vocal opponent to reunification because he thought that Auschwitz had shown for all time that a single German state was too dangerous for the world to risk.[22] But only his immense stature in German society even allowed him to articulate such a position, and he was, for the most part, alone.

Leaving aside Grass's and Janßen's argument that the division was a punishment, and perhaps a divine one, why did the most obvious root cause of Germany's division, the war and Nazi leadership, play such a minor role in the narratives surrounding the country's division? One reason is that the division of the country immediately became entangled with the political struggles surrounding the cold war. Rather than looking for the root causes of the division as having grown out of Nazi foreign policy and a lost war, West German society tended to focus on the failures of the allies to stand up to the Soviets and for having agreed to the division of the country in the first place at Yalta.

The Films of Division

In approaching these films, I applied the same open coding technique of content analysis I used with the rest of the material.[23] With these films, I was even more interested in both manifest and latent elements in the narratives.[24] The most common manifest elements involved political attacks on the opposing side by linking capitalism with fascism, from the Eastern perspective, or using the iconography of the Nazis to mark the Communists, from the Western perspective. One of the most striking latent elements involved a high level of uniformity in how gender was discussed and portrayed in both the East and the

West. I return to each of these manifest and latent elements in the discussion that follows.

Before turning to a brief theoretical reflection on the nature of borders from an anthropological perspective, I want to highlight some of the key themes addressed in these films of division. Both national cinemas directly engaged the political reality of the division in a manifest manner. The GDR cinema struggled to justify the division and the closing of the border to its population and to win them over to the building of a new and better socialist reality. In DEFA films, the division and then the dramatic closure of the border were necessary for the defense of socialism against capitalist fascism. At first, the more market-oriented West German cinema took the division as a temporary necessity forced upon the German nation by the cold war. Later, it simply became a German reality. Neither national cinema attempted to trace the division back to World War II. Both national cinemas played a role in constructing separate national identities for East and West Germans, which obviously varied in their intensity, coherence, and staying power.[25]

Although the interpretations of cold war politics in the two national cinemas obviously clash, there are also a number of interesting similarities. The division of families begins to dramatize the division of the national family. Love and lovers try to transcend the political border and often fail, or the love is transformed in crossing the border. In order to realize love, characters often attempt to cross the border, but the border becomes a location of extreme violence, which can destroy that very possibility.

Women are most often the victims. In fact, women survive the border crossing less frequently than men. The female characters are weaker and perish. Both national cinemas also tend to gender the East as female and the West as male. Men desire to be in the West so they can prove their masculinity in competition, while women are drawn to the protective and more nurturing state in the East.

Both national cinemas began to establish a set of stereotypes of what life was like on the other side over time. One clearly sees the traits that become associated with *Ossis*, or Easterners, and *Wessis*, or Westerners, being portrayed in the films. Easterners become more depressed, withdrawn, alcoholic, and indifferent. Westerners are shown to be aggressive, pushy, dominating, and uncaring. Although cinema is only one agent among many in the process of socialization, it became an important space within which the two halves could encounter each other, especially after the building of the Berlin wall in August 1961.[26] But as the prewall films demonstrate, the division began long before the most dramatic symbol of the nation's division.

The last uniting feature of the films of division is the motif of movement across the border. Whether this is portrayed as an escape from a repressive regime, the Western perspective, or a flight from responsibility and a sign of egoism, the Eastern perspective, the transcending of the border is common to all these films. One could say that the border's existence is recreated and restructured again and again as characters attempt to transcend its power to slow, stop, or kill their movement.

Border Crossings: A Theoretical Note

There was, of course, the very real and literal existence of a violent political border between East and West Germany, but it was also a border imbued with symbolic significance and cultural meaning.[27] Anthropologists have long recognized that the boundaries between different communities can be marked by both territorial markers as well as cultural ones.[28] Both Arnold Van Gennep, in his classic work on rites of passage, and Victor Turner, who expanded on Van Gennep's work, spoke of territorial passage, or the movement between "states," in their discussion of the cultural similarities that exist in the rites of passage from one social category to another, for example, from single to married or from life to death.[29] Van Gennep recognized a general pattern surrounding the rites of passage, which he classified in three stages: (1) rites of separation, (2) rites of transition, and (3) rites of incorporation.

The film narratives are often marked by these three stages of crossing the German-German boundary. The form of the three rites changes over time. In the prewall films, characters move rather seamlessly back and forth. But as the border becomes more closely guarded, the characters must prepare for the separation by organizing for the journey and perhaps attempting to disguise their disappearance from the East, representing a loss of or shedding of a previous identity. Then the character enters the liminal state of moving between the two communities, which is represented as a time of danger. There is, of course, the literal narrative of a state border marked by violence. But the border also takes on symbolic meaning in that men more often then women are able to attempt and survive the transition from one state to another. The crossing of the border and the character's transition into the liminal state is gendered in both the East and West German films.

Finally, there are a series of incorporation rituals. There is the literal narrative of the refugee camps in the West to deal with the flow from the East or the difficulty of integrating into a new society. But these camps also take on male characteristics in the East films, as in *Berlin—Ecke Schönhauser* (1957), and West films, and they emphasize the foreignness of the East Germans who arrive in the West, who need to be categorized and given a proper status before they are incorporated.[30] The fact that integration is necessary highlights again the nature of the cultural and political border that has developed. If the border was only political and without cultural significance, then there would be no need for a set of integration rituals. These are rites of incorporation of both a practical political nature and a symbolic nature. Before the East Germans can be incorporated into the body of the Western nation, they must be cleaned of any contaminating pollution that they might have carried with them. The East German films repeat over and over that those who do leave will face rejection or endangerment of their lives in the West. Rather than simply rites of so-called primitive tribes, these three stages of border crossing play key roles in modern societies as well, as do cultural practices surrounding purity and danger.[31]

What follows is an analysis of boundary maintenance between East and West as constructed in the narratives of a genre I have termed the *films of division*. Although there have been limited and more extensive treatments of some of the films mentioned here, there is no exclusive study of the division as a theme in German cinema covering the entire time of the separation.[32] I have chosen these films solely on the basis of their narratives about the internal division of the German nation. I am not primarily interested in traditional questions of film study such as artistic quality, production history, actors, directors, or film theory. Rather, this is a middle-level research program of posttheory in which I use the films as cultural artifacts to help us gain insight into how Germans discussed and conceptualized the division of the national body.[33]

West German Films of Division

One of the first West German films to deal directly with the issue of division was *Himmel ohne Sterne* [Sky without Stars] (1955).[34] The film opens with scenes of a group of refugees trying to cross illegally the German-German border during the night. The viewer's sympathy for the refugees is increased by their innocence, as the group consists only of an old man, an old woman, a young woman, and other nonthreatening characters. They encounter a group of border guards from the East, who ask them for their papers. The old man suffers a heart attack out of shock and fear, and this distraction provides the young woman with the opportunity to dive into the river. One of the guards shoots at her before the other stops him. The young woman is Anna, one of the two main characters in the film. Lightly wounded in the leg, she is found the next day by Karl, who is a West German border guard. Since she has left illegally, he must take her to the refugee camp. She must be properly categorized and incorporated into the West. Yet, Anna manages to escape him as well. She has another goal rather than escape. But Karl and Anna's story does not end here.

Anna is going to her in-laws, who have custody of her son, Joachim, because her husband was killed in the war, and they do not want him to live in the East. This is one of the very rare references to the war in any of these films. She wants to take her son back to the East, where her elderly parents, who do not want to leave, still live. The story is unique in that it begins with the attempt of Anna to return to the East with her son on the basis of motherly love, absent of politics. But eventually she sees the hopelessness of life in the East. Her working conditions in the factory are shown in a harsh realist mode with uncaring coworkers and a lazy boss. The poverty of the East is also shown in the home and lifestyle of the people. The film works to portray the growing differences between East and West, and in particular the better quality of life in the West.

Anna becomes torn between her love for her parents and love for Karl. Almost all of the films about division in both the East and West focus upon personal relationships to draw the audience into the story and to elicit an emotional attachment to the characters. In addition to being a common narrative tool to pull the audience into the film, this is how ordinary Germans directly experienced the division of the nation-family; although it was also a political division, it was the invasion of politics and political consequences in a very personal and intimate sphere.[35] Thus, such narrative structures would have resonated deeply at the level of the individual, as the audience could quickly identify with the plight of the characters in the story. The reality displayed in this film, although heightened for dramatic impact, often matched the real experiences of the audience.

Anna and Karl find a meeting place in the no-man's-land between the two Germanys where they can carry on their love relationship. He has grown deeply attached to Anna and has even helped take Joachim to live with her in the East. But the situation calls for some sort of resolution. Anna finally agrees to move to the West when her in-laws agree to give her legal custody of her son, on the condition that she leave the East. With the help of a friendly Russian soldier, Misha, Anna hopes to take her parents and Joachim out of the East legally with the papers Misha has promised. She will have to try to escape again with Karl. However, both of them are killed during the attempted escape in the no-man's-land in a very dramatic scene with guard dogs barking and gunshots fired from both sides. The camera shows their hands inches apart from each other in death as a closing text is shown: "It can still happen even today, because there is a border, a dark line that divides Germany from Germany." The final shot is of a new orphan, Joachim, as he jumps out of the truck, which has taken him safely into the West. He walks away from us into an uncertain future, partially redeemed or saved through the death of his mother.

The film is relatively unique in its sympathetic portrayal of a Russian soldier, while the East German guards, in contrast, are shown to be quite brutal and indifferent to human life. The East German guards have taken on the cinematic traits of the Gestapo agents from other German films. One German character in the film says, "Our guards are the worst," suggesting that the Russians are not nearly as bad. Another early division film in the West, *Weg ohne Umkehr* [Way of No Return] (1953), also has a main character who is a sympathetic Russian who escapes to the West.[36]

With the deepening of the cold war and the building of the Berlin wall, the West German films began to portray ever more sinister forces in the East. *Flucht nach Berlin* [Escape to Berlin] (1961) is a rather bizarre film.[37] It swerves so much in the direction of anti-Communist propaganda that in viewing the film today one is unsure at first whether it is not some sort of parody or comedy. The film is filled with party fanatics who will stop at nothing to socialize a small farming community. The characters are so overdrawn that they appear comical from today's perspective. The film again focuses upon the recurring escape motif, as one East German farmer tries to escape with his family to the West through Berlin. East Germans are shown to live in extreme poverty and technological backwardness. More importantly, the socialist system has made them mean and uncaring. The socialist system has turned them into subhuman creatures, void of human intimacy or love. For example, as the German farmer tries to finish his escape to the West with the aid of a boatman and a Swiss journalist, an East German drunk falls into the water. It appears that he may even drown. The Swiss woman comments on how sad it is that he is drunk, to which the farmer replies, "It's Saturday night, what else is he to do?" The boatman then takes a drink from his flask and passes it to the farmer. He also takes a long drink. No one attempts to save the drowning man.

One central motif that runs through all of the films is that of escape. The East is a totalitarian system from which thousands want to escape. *Tunnel 28* (1962) is basically just an escape film, that plays with the dramatic tension of such an escape.[38] *Der Mann auf der Mauer* [The Man on the Wall] (1982) plays with the theme of escape by having the main character moving back and forth across the border more or less at will, through comical situations.[39] This same theme of movement across the border will also be played out in East German films, but with a very different moral lesson.

The cold war also led to its own entertainment spy genre in West German film alongside the international success of the James Bond and other spy films. One example from the German genre is *Lieb Vaterland, magst ruhig sein* [Dear Fatherland, Rest Peacefully] (1976).[40] The main character, Bruno, turns from being an East German agent to work with the Americans because as he says sarcastically, he "wants to be on the right side this time." The Communists are now shown to be rather ruthless, cold fanatics. In one scene, a captured Communist begins to sing an anthem while being hauled away by Western authorities. Once again, the attempted escape from the East turns deadly, as Bruno's chance for personal happiness with his wife is destroyed when she is shot trying to escape to the West. In a similar postunification film, . . . *und der Himmel steht still* [The Innocent] (1993), the espionage drama is used again along with a love story.[41]

But by far the most common element in all of the West German films dealing with division is the separation of friends, family, and lovers from each other. *Westler* (1985) explores this theme with a couple of young gay males.[42] Thanks to Chancellor Brandt's *Ostpolitik*, West Germans could, with limits, transcend the border for visits, particularly between the two halves of Berlin. The two young men meet when the West German goes with another friend to visit East Berlin. He then returns regularly to the East to meet with his new lover.

The film also follows another pattern common to most East and West German films in that the characters from the East are most often women. The East becomes associated again and again with female characters, who are or become more passive, nurturing, or victimized. The West is often associated with maleness, aggressive behavior, and harsh competition. In *Westler*, the gay male in the East is more feminine in demeanor, but also in his situation. He must constantly wait for the initiative of the other young man because he is unable to call or act. His feminine passivity is forced upon him by his situation. It is interesting to note that this pattern of gendering both the East and the West is fairly consistent through both East and West German films. One significant exception to this rule is Margarethe von Trotta's *Das Versprechen* [The Promise] (1995), in which Sophie proves more decisive and stronger than her boyfriend, Konrad, as she manages the escape from East to West while he remains behind.[43] In the film, she becomes the conquering and competitive Westerner, while Konrad grows more feminine and passive in his role in the East.

Another characteristic common to almost all of the West German films of division is their tendency to portray the West as the better place to live, if not the ideal place. There are a couple of notable exceptions.

The role of the media in stirring tensions between the two sides is critiqued in *Lieb Vaterland, magst ruhig sein*, *Der Mann auf der Mauer*, and *Eisenhans* [Iron Man Hans] (1982).[44] The other exception is *Anna* (1975), in which the main character leaves the East but then decides to return, offering a partial critique of capitalism.[45]

In conclusion, the West German films mentioned here do not show direct state interference, but they do follow the political developments closely and generally support the state in defining the West as the better place for security in personal relationships and material comfort. As the cold war progressed and the Berlin wall was built, the anti-Communist message of the films in the 1960s and 1970s began to equal the anticapitalist message from the East. The films also began to portray an ever-more stereotyped Easterner as passive, poor, subhuman, and forced to work in harsh conditions. Furthermore, except for *Himmel ohne Sterne*, East Germans are shown to be careless and indifferent workers when in fact they were often highly skilled in solving the problems created by the command economy. It was often the resourcefulness of the workers and managers that prevented complete collapse despite the difficult conditions created by the command economy. Nonetheless, these stereotypes generated in the films played a role in shaping how East German workers would be treated during the unification process.

East German Films of Division

In the East, there were a surprising number of films that dealt not only with the division of the country but also with the building of the wall, including a comedy, and stories of attempted escape. However, the moral of the tales is quite different from that in the West. The films can be put into two analytic categories, pre- and postwall (August 1961). The earlier prewall films show the characters making conscious choices about where they want to live, across an increasingly closed and dangerous border. In the postwall films, now that this choice has been severely limited, there is an attempt to justify that division and to show the costs associated with ignoring the political realities of a divided Europe.

I also find it useful to refer to the prewall films as *new society films*, because they all attempt to portray the new socialist reality, which at least some of the characters eventually decide to help build. They follow the social-realist movement of trying to show how the socialist reality will look, even if this is at some future date. Such films often have a "working toward the future" feeling, which is always upbeat in their closing. We are never presented with a final shot as in *Himmel ohne Sterne* with a small boy walking away from us into an uncertain future. The Eastern message is clear, simple, and didactic. "The socialist future is bright and just around the corner."

The first such film is *Irgendwo in Berlin* [Anywhere in Berlin] (1946), in which a returning POW, Karl, must rediscover his will to carry on and rebuild after the devastation of the war.[46] Before he can rebuild his external world, he must reconstruct himself as a man. Karl even states in the film, "I'll learn what it means to be a human being again." This inward and outward collapse is dramatized through the film's being shot among the actual ruins of destroyed Berlin. After a number of adventures, which show the heartlessness of those obsessed with money, Karl begins working with the children in the film to rebuild the garage where he used to work before the war.

Unser täglich Brot [Our Daily Bread] (1949) also focuses upon the theme of rebuilding, even without immediate financial rewards.[47] Again, the film is filled with numerous side adventures and the development of a personal love relationship between Inge and Peter, the director of a factory. But the struggle to keep the factory going is central to the action of the film. The workers cannot be paid at first, and Peter must struggle to keep them together. Skilled workers such as the factory's engineers decide to leave for the West because they want to earn more. They are shown as selfish egoists. Ernst, Inge's brother, is constantly badgered by the father about leaving the factory and earning money rather than working on some silly socialist project. But Ernst, along with the other workers, decides to stay and build the factory, "their factory." By the end of the film, Peter has the factory in full swing, and instead of the pots and pans that it was producing at the beginning of the film, the factory is now producing tractors.

Roman einer jüngen Ehe [Novel of a Young Marriage] (1952) also shows artists and actors who have to make decisions about living and working in the East or the West.[48] The film focuses on Annes and Joachim, two actors struggling to survive in postwar Berlin. The two meet in Berlin and marry, not in a church, and begin their lives in a simple apartment. The quality of the consumer goods in their lives improves slowly throughout the film, although the East German films always have an ambivalent relationship toward consumption. The individual's desire for a better consumer society is constantly recognized, but the excesses of the West are always shown as decadent and extravagant. The message is "Consumption, but not at the cost of others."

Annes and Joachim take work at the Northwest German Radio studio, located in the West, on what they believe to be an antifascist radio play. But they are tricked by the Western producers, and the radio play turns out to be anti-Communist propaganda. They have used the money they earned from the job to purchase new furniture and a radio for their apartment, but Annes seems displeased with the new consumer goods, knowing how they have earned the money. Joachim is less concerned. Again, the gendering of East and West becomes apparent in the female and male characters of the film.

The further division of the city is dramatized by the currency reform in the West, without mentioning the blockade of Berlin. The city is being torn apart, but the two characters recognize that "we must stay together." Ignoring the growing divisions within their city, the two look for a new apartment in the East but find only old war-damaged buildings. That the GDR government will not tolerate such circumstances is shown by the end of the film.

Outside political forces are driving the two characters to make a conscious choice of where they wish to live and work. Joachim is unable to find work and begins to take jobs in the West, which Annes finds morally questionable. In contrast to her husband, she decides to make a film in the East, and the two begin to drift apart. We see Annes participating in the celebration of the opening of Stalin Avenue, which was a much trumpeted attempt by the GDR government to solve the housing shortage in the East. On the other hand, Joachim's moral descent continues as he has even agreed to work for an old Nazi filmmaker now working in West Berlin. His separation from Annes appears to be complete. But while walking to their meeting for a divorce, he helps break up a fight started by Western agents who have descended upon an East German peace demonstration in an attempt to start a riot. Finally, he has his socialist epiphany, and he recognizes that only greed and manipulation rule in the West. He returns to Annes in the East, to the nurturing arms of the socialist state. They decide to stay together and begin a new life in the new society.

The same basic theme of having to decide between two different societies and visions of the future is portrayed in three other prewall films. In *Sein großer Sieg* [His great victory] (1952) a cyclist must decide where he wants to make his career, with the factory team in the East, where the camaraderie is good but the pay is poor, or in the West, where the money is good but the respect for the health of the cyclist is low.[49] Again, the profit motive is put before the health and safety of the workers, in this case an athlete. The cyclist eventually returns to his girlfriend in the East. The same choice is played out in *Der Fall Dr. Wagner* [The case of Dr. Wagner] (1954), when a talented scientist is tricked into going to the West to work.[50] However, he finally discovers how manipulative and greedy those in the West are. In the end, Dr. Wagner also returns to the East and completes his experiments successfully for the benefit of all mankind.

The last such new society film is *Eine Berliner Romanze* [A Berlin Romance] (1956), which focuses less on the choice of the characters for the new socialist society than the love relationship of the two main characters.[51] In this way, the film delivers its message in a less obvious and didactic manner than the other films, as the explicit political messages retreat to the background. But in the end, the young couple discover they can only find mutual happiness in the East.

Another film that deals with the issue of skilled professionals' leaving the East is *Das Leben Beginnt* [Life Begins] (1960).[52] The film is similar to *Eine Berliner Romanze* in that the main characters are teenagers caught in the political tension of a world divided by forces that they do not fully understand or even perceive. Dr. Schenk takes his daughter, Erika, with him to the West for reasons that are clearly individualist and selfish. Meanwhile, Erika discovers the wonders of the West as a paradise of consumption in which she eventually loses herself, literally. The film ends with her attempted suicide and Rolf, her boyfriend, by her bedside telling her that they can begin again. The film's ending is different from that of many of the new society films because of its ambiguous conclusion. If she survives her suicide attempt, that new life will be in the East. Although the gender roles are partially reversed in this case, as Rolf has to prove his manhood in the East and resolve a conflict with his father, Erika is pulled to the West not by an individual choice, but rather by the egoism of her father. And like many women in East German films, she is tempted and almost destroyed by the consumer society. Rather than being integrated into Western society, she is nearly destroyed by it.

In all of the prewall films, the division of the city is shown graphically again and again as characters move back and forth across the border crossings, or the narrator will remind us that this is a divided city with two passports and two police forces. Maps of the city are occasionally shown with the different sectors outlined. The fact that there are two different currencies is also often portrayed as those from the East are only able to use their money at specific shops in the West.

The East is also identified with female characters in the films, just as in the films by the West. In four of the films, a central female character remains in the East and eventually draws her male partner back to it. The East is shown to be more nurturing and caring than the cold male world of the West, which is driven by profit, greed, and indifference to human life. The women who flee to the West are nearly destroyed by consumerism, while the men are ground under through brutal competition.

In these prewall films, the influence of the state in directing the message of the film through willing participants in the film industry is very clear, and sometimes much too obvious. The *Parteilichkeit*, or partisanship, of the films is often drawn in such an obvious way that it makes the propaganda effort much too obvious. Some of the films contained much less explicit partisanship. *Eine Berliner Romance* is a much slicker production where the message is hidden more in the background, so that during the first viewing, the film offers a love story of a young man and woman. It is a clear attempt to address a young audience and their hopes and fears for the future. The film also demonstrates the sensitivity of Eastern filmmakers to changes occurring in the West. The first films focusing upon the life of teenagers were also appearing in the American market a year or two earlier: Marlon Brando in *On the Waterfront* (1954) and *The Wild One* (1954) and James Dean in *East of Eden* (1954) and *Rebel without a Cause* (1955).[53]

Without exception, the prewall films offer support for the Communist Party's nation building agenda. The films are not wholly uncritical of life in the East, but in the end the problems that exist are corrected through the hard work of individuals and less frequently by the direct assistance of the party. For example, in *Sein großer Sieg*, Hans decides to take his cycling career to the West in part because his Eastern derailleur has failed in a key race. The technology in the East is not on a par with that in the West. But by the end of the film, other factory riders are winning races on the new equipment designed at the East German factory. These new society films are often about where the East German society is heading but has not yet arrived. The films also clearly show the attraction of the consumer culture in the West but also make an effort to emphasize that the same consumption opportunities are arriving in the East without the downside of capitalism.

What impact did these films have on their audience? Obviously the reality outside the cinema played a far larger role than the hopes and dreams represented by the filmmakers at DEFA. Throughout the 1950s many skilled workers continued to leave for the West, a theme that the film *Der Fall Dr. Wagner* tries to explain as an example of Western agents' tricking talented scientists to leave for the West. By 1953, more than 1 million East Germans had left for the West, and by 1961, when the wall was built, 2.7 million had left.[54] Still, the films also show why most chose to remain. They reminded the audience of the personal ties and human intimacy that surrounded them in the East. A move to the West was not without its own uncertainties and risks. These relationships could be lost or damaged if one left; only by returning could the relationship be restored. Certainly the number of individuals leaving for the West was significant and extremely damaging to the economy in the East, but the majority remained and made the necessary accommodations with the Communist system.

In creating a filmography for the genre of division in German cinema, I was surprised to find a number of East German films made after 1961 that dealt directly with the wall's being built. I had gone into the research expecting that the wall would have been a taboo subject similar to the June 17, 1953, uprising. One film from 1962, *. . . und deine Liebe auch* [. . . and Your Love Also], offers a better picture of individual lives trapped by political forces remote from their individual lives.[55] The story centers on a love triangle between two brothers, Ulrich and Klaus, and their common love for Eva. The film opens with a map of the world on the wall of Ulrich's apartment, and we hear his disembodied voice saying that he needs Berlin to live. Klaus, on the other hand, is always on the hunt for more money. He meets Eva, a postal worker, when she delivers him 500 DM in cash. The three go out to the Cafe Budapest to celebrate and later return to Ulrich's apartment. It is August 12, 1961, and later in the evening Ulrich is called to service at the border as a guard. The first barbwire fences are being thrown up. Klaus later confronts his brother at the border, demanding that he be allowed to go to the West for money. Ulrich turns him away.

Later, we again see Ulrich at the border with Alfrado, a Cuban friend, and they begin singing songs together. The border with the West may have closed, but the world is still partially open. Alfrado takes the magazine from a machine gun and begins to bang on it as if it were a drum. The weapons of war are turned into instruments for the peace-loving Communists of the world. Alfrado wants Ulrich to visit him in Cuba. So while some borders have been closed others remain open. Later in the film, we see Ulrich's enjoying a trip in Cuba with his Cuban friend. Travel outside Eastern Germany remains possible; not much has changed, the film seems to promise.

There is also a sequence of several scenes that emphasize the perspective of the main characters as common individuals caught in the storm of world events beyond their control. In one such scene, we are shown a military parade in the East over which Ulrich comments, "Next to our little story, the big history continues." We even see Walter Ulbricht, the leader of East Germany at the time, on a platform while another political figure is speaking. Then later we see Ulrich and Eva lost in a large crowd in the Lustgarten in East Berlin while Ulbricht is speaking. These scenes allow the government and the personality of Ulbricht to appear popular and still in control of a dangerous situation, which could explode into another war. While the common individual cannot control these events, the film tries to reassure the viewers that their leaders are in control and watching out for their interests. The actual appearance of Ulbricht and other top party officials in this film is rather unique, as the party is rarely directly seen in any of these films.

The film leaves no doubt about the source of the threat of war. An off screen narrator comments, "In August we said, Stop! The class enemy will not come through. In our Germany we will decide for ourselves." We then see Eva lost again in the streets of the city. She watches as American tanks drive aggressively up to the border painted on the road and then slam on their brakes. American troops are shown moving along the border. Eva's distress in the scene is further emphasized by her verbalized decision not to have children in the future. An off screen narrator repeats again and again in the film, "Somewhere there must be a border." The border appears to refer not only to the political borders between the two Germanys, but also to the personal relationships between the characters and Eva's love for the two brothers. Ulrich uses the line when talking about Klaus's philandering and affair with Eva.

The dramatic tension in the film reaches its climax as Ulrich realizes that his brother is planning to try to escape to the West to get 5,000 DM which he has there. Ulrich rushes to the cemetery where Klaus has placed a ladder against the cemetery wall and is starting to climb over. At this point it is not clear why Ulrich wants so desperately to prevent Klaus from leaving, but they fight in the cemetery and Klaus begins to make his way over the wall. In a grotesque twist of the border's reality, the East German border guards fire a warning shot while the police in the West fire at the two brothers on the wall, wounding both of them. We then hear Eva commenting, "We have to know where we belong."

Klaus is put on trial for trying to escape, and Ulrich even testifies against his brother. But Klaus is now thankful that he can begin a new life and turns to his work at the rock quarry where he has been sent to do his penitence. "Somewhere there must be a border," Klaus comments. As does Winston Smith in *1984*, he is learning to love Big Brother. The film closes with Ulrich now wearing a jacket with a party pin. Then there is a shot of the Warschauer Bridge in East Berlin with people moving back and forth. The camera then pans from the bridge to the buildings of East Berlin in the background, providing us with an open space for a closed land. What else could one want? And we are reminded of Ulrich's comment at the beginning of the film that he needs Berlin to live.

Ulrich's party membership is never discussed at any other point in the film, and his presence at the very end of the film with a party pin in his coat comes as a surprise. The film does a much better job of trying to present the party's view of why the wall had to be built, "Somewhere there must be a border." Indeed. The film emphasizes that borders in both politics and personal relationships help to minimize conflict, while the scene with the tanks and the American soldiers leaves no question as to where the potential for war exists. Klaus, the more Western of the two brothers, clearly abuses the borders of personal relationships with his crass treatment of Eva and his willful ignoring of his brother's love for her. With the border now secured, Eva is prepared to have her child and be with Ulrich. The hope for a new world will be reborn with her child. As with the other films, escaping the East remains an issue, but now the consequences have turned even deadlier, and those who ignore this will be shot, by the West.

Two other films in the early 1960s also address the building of the wall. In *Kinnhaken* [The Punch to the Jaw] (1962), Caroline, a prostitute living in East Berlin, awakens one morning to find the border sealed.[56] Cut off from her work in the West, she is befriended by Manfred, a border guard, with whom she falls in love and decides to remain in the East. In *Der geteilte Himmel* [Divided Heaven] (1964), Konrad Wolf, East Germany's best known film director, turns Christa Wolf's famous novel into a film.[57] In the story Manfred decides he must leave for the West as his proposals at work are refused without explanation, while his girlfriend, Rita, remains in the East, a pattern in gender roles common to many of the films.

One of the most daring films dealing with the division of the country is a comedy called *Sonntagsfahrer* [Sunday drivers] (1963).[58] Humor was also used to address the painful division of the country in one West German film, *Genosse Münchhausen* [Comrade Münchhausen] (1962), but was generally avoided.[59] In *Sonntagsfahrer* a group of families plan a "trip" together while actually planning to escape to the West through West Berlin. One of them has seen a letter suggesting that the war between the East and West will arrive later that summer and that the West is prepared to use nuclear weapons. The son of one family, Gernold, falls in love with the daughter of another family, Sabine, and they decide that they want nothing to do with their crazy parents. They leave the group to continue their affair in the East, and through their abandonment of their parents the tension between the two generations is clearly portrayed. This conflict between the generations is a theme that is common to both East and West German films and reflects the societal realities.[60]

The parents encounter one detour after another on their way and eventually spend the evening lost in the woods. When they see the East German tanks moving for the border, they believe the war between the two sides has already begun. Someone has a bottle of schnapps, so they spend the evening getting drunk. In the process, some ugly truths rise to the surface. One wife no longer loves her husband, and one of the husbands betrays his sympathies for Hitler. The film ends with all of the parents returning home with their lives greatly disrupted after the evening in the woods. In contrast, Gernold and Sabine return to the university, where the professor welcomes them back, from what he hopes has been a peaceful weekend. He then begins a philosophical lecture on "the reason of humanity."

The last film to deal directly with the building of the wall is *Geschichte Jener Nacht* [Every Night Stories] (1967).[61] The film is actually composed of four shorter films, each of which takes place on August 12 and 13, although some mainly incorporate flashbacks. In the third segment of the film, entitled "Materna," the main character, who is a border guard, comments as he patrols, "13 August 1961, perhaps it will be written in the history books that at that time in August the back door was slammed shut, lightning fast, over night, in exactly the right moment . . . so that the war could not come in. So that all which we had built in all the years could no longer be plundered. . . . This border has thousands of faces . . . bitter and joyful, true and untrue, they know courage and cowardliness, the true and the traitor."

The same film segment also has one of only two film scenes that directly address the events of June 17, 1953, when there were mass riots and worker strikes throughout the GDR in protest of the increased work norms set by the party. But rather than trying to clarify anything, even from the party's perspective, the scene from 1953 appears to suggest that the strikes and riots began as a sort of drunken brawl, and the character comments, "There are things that just happen which you can't explain." There are no Soviet tanks rolling into his memories of 1953. The guard's closing comment for the scene is just as enigmatic as his other statements: "After I came back from the war, I decided never to wear a uniform or to carry a gun again. But then I had to decide just one more time. And that is all." Except for vague references to the possibility that war was averted through the building of the wall, one sees in these films the difficulty the party had in justifying its existence to its own population. The East German regime struggled to construct a credible narrative of the division and its legitimacy.

After *Geschichte Jener Nacht* (1967), there are very few films that deal with the division so explicitly. In *Die Flucht* (1977), Dr. Schmidt has decided to try to flee to the West.[62] He has developed a technique that helps premature babies to survive, but his research plans are being blocked by the state bureaucracy. The attraction of the West for some of the other doctors is clearly shown as a couple of them discuss the fact that Western doctors earn five to ten times more, but the female director for the clinic reminds them of their collective duty to the community: "But think of what the state has done for you!"

Schmidt becomes romantically involved with one of the nurses, Catharine, and this love interest, as in the other films, causes him to begin reconsidering his decision. The escape to the West is being organized by a mysterious Mr. X, who appears from time to time to talk with Schmidt about his planned escape. Schmidt ignores the first signal for the designated meeting point and is put under pressure from Mr. X to go to the West. "We've invested a great deal in you," he reminds him. But the power that Mr. X has over Schmidt is never made clear. There are only vague threats, and the narrative makes little sense. Finally, Schmidt decides to go and tries to take Catharine with him. They are at a remote highway stop and are supposed to wait for a cargo truck to stop and pick them up. Catharine was not told of the plan beforehand and panics, running off. The truck driver has become suspicious and pushes Schmidt from the truck. He dies from the fall. He also dies a symbolic death for his moral failings.

Conclusion: The Political Consequences of Cultural Narratives: Identity

With these examples in mind, we can now ask the question, how has culture worked in this case?[63] In films both from the East and the West, the filmmakers aided their respective states in helping to clarify the "us and them" of the German-German conflict. The films from the West direct their antagonism against the foreign regime, which has led to the division of the nation. The early films tend to be sympathetic toward the East Germans themselves, except the fanatic party members and vicious border guards. The message is clear: "They are like us and are trapped within an evil regime. We should help them in every way possible." The division is a political one from the Western point of view. Personal relationships should remain intact. This is most clearly portrayed in the relationship between Karl and Anna, and Anna and her son in *Himmel ohne Sterne.*

The East German films, in contrast, constantly cast doubt on the moral character of those who live in the West and those who want to live in the West. Not only is the regime evil and polluted with former Nazi Party members, but it also attracts greedy individualists who will stop at nothing to get what they want. The heroes in the film may wander from the socialist path but are eventually led back to the East, often through their female partners. The films recognize the attraction of the consumer society but also show the commodification of women, the abuse of alcohol, and the lack of care given to the way workers are treated.

Both East and West films portray the other political regime in openly hostile terms, helping to establish a nationalist division. *Anna,* a self-critical assessment of the West, remains the exception that proves the rule. The postwall films in the East actually spend a great deal less time in the West trying to show how terrible the conditions can be. The exit option has been removed. Rather, they focus on the costs of trying to leave or try to justify the building of the wall as the only way to prevent a war with the West. Only in *Die Flucht* does the main character die as a result of his attempt to flee. Furthermore, he dies at the hands of a truck driver and not an East German border guard. In . . . *und deine Liebe auch*, Klaus and Ulrich are shot while Klaus is trying to escape, but by West German border guards.

What then was the effect of these films on the construction of East and West German identities? I do not want to claim too much authority for the cinema alone in shaping the impressions that East and West Germans developed of each other and themselves. Rather, I want to emphasize that the images and impressions that were being generated in both national cinemas were reinforced by other mediums of experience such as the print media, television, and personal experience.

With the building of the Berlin wall in August 1961, personal experience as a medium for knowing about "the other" was greatly reduced on both sides. Eventually with the arrival of Chancellor Willy Brandt in the late 1960s and his policy of *Ostpolitik*, the movement of people back and forth across the border slowly increased, but never was it what it once had been in the open city of Berlin. Even before the building of the wall, the crossing of the border had become increasingly difficult except within the city of Berlin; that is why the wall was eventually built there. The rest of the border had closed long before 1961, as dramatized in *Himmel ohne Sterne*.

With the loss of personal experience except for letter writing, the imagined community of the respective national media became almost the sole means by which the two sides were able to interact with each other.[64] After the collapse of the Berlin wall and the reunification of the German nation within a single sovereign state, a new vocabulary developed for talking about the other, *Ossi* (Easterner) and *Wessi* (Westerner).[65] Rather than a set of stereotypes developed out of disappointments with reunification,[66] the Ossi and Wessi social categories had been prepared in the respective national media during the time of division. While the political borders dramatically disappeared, the cultural boundaries remained.

The Ossi and Wessi discussions followed much the same lines and stereotypes that were developed in both of the national cinemas during the period of division. The first personal interactions between the two sides that took place on a mass scale, particularly in Berlin, were filled with the expectations that had been generated by the national cinemas, television stations, and newspapers. Eastern access to the Western media and Western ignorance of the Eastern media did not prevent the stereotypes from being cemented in the now-unified national consciousness. While the stereotypes of greedy Western capitalists in the East German cinema often appear laughable and overdrawn, it was exactly these stereotypes and expectations through which the East Germans tended to view the West. The two sides encountered each other through the cultural lenses that their respective national cultures had developed over the course of the division and the cold war. Once the microlevel interactions had been largely blocked, there was no other experience with which to counter the macrolevel presentations. Both national cultures had developed stereotyped views of what to expect from the other once the border fell.

6

Defeat and Liberation: Ending the War

THE CENTRAL DISCURSIVE FIELD FOR THIS CHAPTER IS THAT OF liberation-defeat, but as with the other chapters, the relationship between the two can only be understood when seen in relation to the other discursive fields. As we will see, there is a clear narrative shift from that of defeat and bitterness to one of liberation in West Germany. Perhaps a similar pattern would have developed in East Germany had the regime not dominated the macrosocial space with its antifascist liberation rhetoric.

One should view the dominance of the defeat theme in the earliest sources as linked directly to that of a German sense of victimization. To understand this apparent contradiction of how the Germans were able to see themselves as victims of the regime but unable to celebrate its demise, one must see how, from the German perspective, Germany had been defeated along with Hitler. It was for Germany that the Germans had made their sacrifices, not for Hitler. The noble and just sacrifices in the extreme violence of war had been for Germany, while the unjust suffering borne by the German nation had been imposed by Hitler's madness. The narratives surrounding the end of the war reinforced the mythical division between Germans and Nazis, as constructed in the terror state mythology. Although West German society would recognize the unique status of the Jew as a victim of National Socialism by the late 1970s, the society never relented in portraying Germans as victims, if not the primary victims, of the regime. This was particularly true for elite and popular reflections upon the role of the Wehrmacht.

Recognizing the crimes of the Holocaust was a relatively easy task compared to identifying the perpetrators and discussing issues of guilt and justice. Although the crimes and the victims were, in a public sense, still being uncovered throughout the 1980s, the perpetrators remained mostly obscured. The standard narratives had either reduced them to Hitler and a few dedicated followers or abstracted them beyond recognition. If the speaker, journalist, writer, film, or television program wished to identify the perpetrators outside Hitler himself, the black-clad Gestapo and SS were always present to represent the demonic forces of evil at work. For most of the postwar history, the soldiers of the Wehrmacht were seen as one of the primary victims of Hitler's madness. The potential links between the Wehrmacht and the Holocaust remained untouched for almost two decades after the Holocaust had entered the public consciousness on a mass scale. The mythical barrier between Nazis and Germans had been challenged but remained in place.

Since reunification in 1990, there has been a great deal of discussion about to what extent Germany was now a normal country. As we have seen in chapter 5 on the division of the country, there was an overwhelming sense that Germany and the Germans had finally reached the democratic end point of a long historical trajectory toward which they had been moving since the nineteenth century. Outside forces such as Napoleon and Stalin and internal madmen such as Hitler had frustrated this trajectory time and again, but by 1990 that point had finally been reached. Yet, this normalcy has remained elusive. There were two cultural shocks to the emergence of normalcy in unified Germany, which both hit in the mid-1990s. The first was a German photography exhibit, and the second was a book by Daniel Goldhagen, an American political scientist.

I will just add a few words here to the reception of Goldhagen's book *Hitler's Willing Executioners*,[1] as there is already an extensive secondary literature about the book and its reception in Germany.[2] I have included a discussion of his work in this chapter because of what it says about the nature and identity of the perpetrators. Obviously this material overlaps with the chapters on the Holocaust, but I want to deal with the discussions of the Wehrmacht in a separate chapter. There are a couple key points that have emerged from these discussions. The basic thesis of the book is that German culture, and thus by extension all or most Germans, have for centuries harbored an extreme form of eliminationist anti-Semitism. Goldhagen claims to have opened up a new field of Holocaust research, which had up to the time of the publication of the book been ignored by other scholars. With his research, Goldhagen reveals that ordinary Germans willingly participated in the perpetration of the Holocaust. The rest of the book is a catalog of the horrors of the Holocaust and many disturbing tales of both organized German persecutions and random acts of vicious violence against Jews. Thus, his book was an open assault on two of the treasured postwar mythologies. First, his research attacked the terror state mythology by showing that more than a few Germans willingly killed Jews without state-imposed sanctions. Furthermore, by identifying these perpetrators as ordinary Germans rather than Nazis, Goldhagen challenged the rhetorical distinction between Germans and Nazis, which German narratives were almost always careful to maintain.

The first point of interest is that of the German reaction that, since the end of the war, has faced this same charge in different forms from different authors. In his book, Goldhagen takes a clear primordialist view of culture: that is to say, he reifies German culture and hints at an unchanging "German character" through the ages. This has been the foundation of much of the academic criticism of the book. Such a claim, of course, again drew forth a resounding chorus of German commentators who criticized the book as yet another incarnation of the collective guilt thesis. In its uglier forms, this criticism carried with it stereotypes of the avenging American Jew.

The second point of interest is Goldhagen's response to his German critics when he sought to set aside the collective guilt thesis by suggesting that democracy had already healed the German nation and culture of this century-old malaise. Despite the fact that such a claim clearly ran contrary to the central thesis of the book and the supposed primordial nature of German cultural anti-Semitism, Goldhagen was quickly embraced by the German public and some academics. He still received a fair amount of criticism from some historians, who were sometimes booed or shouted down during public appearances with Goldhagen during his tour of the country. Goldhagen had told German society what it was longing to hear from an American Jew, that they were now a unified nation, a good nation, a democratic nation, and that the wounds of the past were now healed.

In contrast to Goldhagen's book, the cultural legacy of the photography exhibit that opened in March 1995 has been less discussed and remains much more open ended as it has only recently reopened after having been closed for two years. The exhibit, which became simply known as the Wehrmacht exhibit, showed with visual evidence the actions of the German army during the Second World War. With each photograph, the division between the Nazis and the Germans grew thinner and thinner. The authentic visual evidence was powerful, and many of the younger visitors to the exhibit went looking for their parents or other relatives. Some visitors found close relatives in the photographs of the perpetrators.

After discussing the exhibit and its impact in some detail, I return to the history before 1995 to show how German society defended the soldiers in the Wehrmacht and showed them to be another of Hitler's victims. The mythical division between the community of good Germans and evil Nazis was also constructed and maintained within the narratives surrounding the end of the war. In the second section of the chapter, I will also draw a comparison between East and West Germany along the narrative thread of defeat and liberation. As will be seen, the legacy of the war's end was a difficult burden for the West German society, and a pompous empty celebration for the East German state.

The Wehrmacht Exhibit

Interestingly enough, the German perpetrators had been archiving the evidence of their crimes for almost fifty years in countless shoe boxes and photo albums. By the beginning of the 1990s, the documents and photographs of former Wehrmacht soldiers were circulating more freely within their families and the society. Scholars used these photographs, taken for the most part by the soldiers themselves, their diaries and letters, to begin a new phase of scholarly research into the history of the Wehrmacht during World War II.

As with other areas of historical writing in the 1970s, which began to take a bottom-up view of historiography and employed new methodologies, scholars had also begun to write more of an everyday history of the Wehrmacht, which differed significantly from the traditional approach to military history and its focus upon tactics and strategy. The image that began to emerge from this research was not of a "clean Wehrmacht," which had remained free of Nazi ideology and had fought a noble and fair fight against worthy enemies. Rather, scholars were uncovering a Wehrmacht that had not only worked closely with the regime in fighting a race war, but also aided directly in the extermination of European Jewry. The change in perspective was dramatic and placed a severe strain on the mythology of good Germans and evil Nazis. As Omer Bartov has observed, "The political impact of these works is of course immense, since they not only call for a profound reevaluation of the meaning and implications of the Nazi regime for German society during and after the war, they also discredit some of the most dearly held assumptions on the ability of postwar Germany to 'come to terms' with its past."[3]

Although scholars had been publishing academic books on the topic of war crimes and the Wehrmacht since the late 1960s, this information rarely found itself circulating among the general public. Instead, as will be seen, television programs, films, political ceremonies, and newspaper articles associated with May 8 focused upon German victimhood and the suffering of German soldiers on the eastern front. Within families, fathers or grandfathers rarely, if ever, discussed in any detail the fighting. And to the extent such discussions did take place, the bonds of loyalty within the family often caused the younger generations to reinterpret what they heard to protect their loved relative and the unity of the family.[4] The memories and the history of that period had effectively been sealed off within both public and private space. In 1957, when those under the age of twenty-five were asked what subjects they had discussed with their parents from a specific list, only 18 percent responded that they had discussed "the persecution of the Jews under Hitler," but nearly half had discussed the end of the war or the results of the war in some form.[5] As in the broader society, the Nazi past was not so much wholly repressed as discussed within certain bounds.

Although photographic evidence of these crimes had been in archives in Eastern Europe as well as Germany and Austria, the individual photo albums or shoe boxes spread around Germany and Austria were certainly the largest archive of all. These more private archives began to open in the 1990s as the older generation began to die. A significant amount of this evidence was then collected by the researchers at the Hamburg Institute for Social Research, who in March 1995 opened their photography and document exhibit in Hamburg entitled, *Vernichtungskrieg: Verbrechen der Wehrmacht 1941 bis 1944* [War of Extermination: Crimes of the Wehrmacht 1941 to 1944].

In this manner, established institutions dedicated to the investigation of historical truth were indispensable in placing the bottom-up history before the public. Without their work, the history that the photographs tell would have remained hidden or hopelessly fragmented. In this manner, the Hamburg Institute put the message of the photographs' microhistory in focus so that the entire society could literally see, in many ways for the first time, what had actually happened during the war. However, the photographs do not speak for themselves, and the narratives attached to them by the Hamburg Institute were not without great controversy or methodological shortcomings.

At first the exhibit did not attract national attention. It was a traveling exhibit of photographs and documentary evidence, which focused on a couple of cases in which significant numbers of Wehrmacht soldiers participated in committing war crimes, either by aiding the SS or Einsatzgruppen or carrying out reprisals against civilian populations under the direct orders and initiative of Wehrmacht commanders. For example, while regular Wehrmacht soldiers did not man the death camps in the east, they would encircle Jewish villages and force the Jews to the train station to be deported. At other times, Wehrmacht soldiers participated in the mass shooting of civilians in retaliation for partisan resistance. The exhibit, however, challenged some dearly held myths about the behavior of German soldiers, and thus not just Nazis, during the war. If the Wehrmacht could be shown to have participated in the perpetration of the Holocaust along with other crimes, the wall between Nazis and Germans might collapse. The stakes, personal and political, were extremely high.

Almost exactly two years after the exhibit had opened in Hamburg, it arrived in Munich in 1997. By this time, the exhibit had become the focus of a national debate on the role of the Wehrmacht during the Third Reich. Peter Gauweiler, a member of the Christian Social Union, began to mobilize other politicians and far Right civil society groups against the exhibit. The political controversy drove public interest and even more people, many of them between the ages of sixteen and thirty along with members of the older generation, began to line up for hours to see the exhibit. Debates about the exhibit even spilled onto the floor of the German Bundestag on March 13, 1997.[6] From this point forward perhaps the most important struggle over the representation of the National Socialist past had begun. If Germans began to recognize publicly that the roots of *Volkish* and racial thought were present within parts of the society and segments of German culture, then perhaps a fuller accounting of the past might become possible.[7] The exhibit aided this growing realization.

The exhibit continued to tour and draw significant crowds. By fall 1999 the exhibit had visited thirty-three locations in Germany and Austria, and by July of that year approximately 860,000 individuals had visited the exhibit. To put that number into some perspective, the exhibit had drawn a larger audience than any single German film of light entertainment can usually attract to the movie theater in any given year. In addition to the number of visitors who actually saw the exhibit, there was extensive reporting in the media about the exhibit, its perspective, and the opinions of those who supported the exhibit or sought to challenge it. The demonstrations by far Right groups even went so far as to attack the exhibition space itself in Saarbrücken with a bomb.

Critics of the exhibit were mostly from the more conservative sides of German society, including politicians in the CDU, FDP, and Republican Party. The defensiveness that marked the conservative reaction mirrored what we have already seen with the construction of the so-called collective guilt. They charged that the exhibit failed to differentiate or led to the impression that the Wehrmacht as a whole was a criminal organization and defamed the honor of those who had served their country, although this is never suggested in the exhibit.[8] Even more centrist politicians such as the former SPD chancellor Helmut Schmidt, himself a former soldier of the eastern front, attacked the exhibit, arguing that those in the younger generation had been taking an unfair moral high ground vis-à-vis their elders.[9] But Schmidt's criticism begs the question of why the older generation had never been able to take a more critical perspective.

The reactions of those who actually visited the exhibit are hard to quantify, and many were certainly drawn to the exhibit as a dramatic event. The Hamburg Institute is in the process of evaluating the reaction to the exhibit and may later offer further insights into the views of the visitors. One clear effect of the exhibit for many visitors was that they turned over yet more photographic and textual evidence from their personal shoe box archives. Visitors, young and old, wanted the story to be told even more fully then in its current form and often requested how they might contribute other personal artifacts.[10] But other visitors, many of them from the Nazi generation, reacted in a very defensive manner and often showed no ability to identify with the victims in the photographs.[11] Generational divisions remained clear as 80 percent those in their twenties reported that the National Socialist period was still not a closed chapter in Germany's history, and 41 percent of them thought the exhibit had changed their worldview in some manner.[12] At the same time, however, they were not interested in a complex view of history, which might allow the older generation to share their views and experiences. Bernd Greiner, one of the institute's researchers, concluded that hope of an intergenerational discussion were soon crushed as the divisions between young and old remained much too wide.[13]

Part of the animosity aroused by the exhibit can also be traced back to the history of the Hamburg Institute for Social Research and its founder and director, Han Philipp Reemtsma. He is a member of the 1968 generation, which inspires a great deal of resentment among members of the older generation. He also inherited a vast family fortune at a relatively young age. In the 1980s, he was seen as a "cranky guy with a lot of money," and some argue the institute has become his personal vehicle for causing trouble rather than a serious scholarly organization.

In addition to the ad hominem arguments against Reemtsma, some historians had begun to question the validity of some of the exhibit's photographs, many of which were merely marked "location unknown." The exhibit's organizers had yet to overcome many of the methodological problems of working with photographs, and they had left themselves exposed to serious scholarly critiques. In fall 1999, Bogdan Musial, a Polish historian, had identified nine photographs in the exhibit that showed the crimes of the Soviet NKWD rather than the Wehrmacht. The results of his research were published in a prestigious historical academic journal[14] and quickly picked up by the popular press. The exhibit was rapidly heading for trouble.[15]

After the appearance of Musial's article, there was a rapid exchange of editorials and articles between the Left and Right press giants of the *Frankfurter Allgemeine* and the *Süddeutscher Zeitung*. Based upon Musial's evidence, a *Frankfurter* article four days later openly questioned the overall validity of the exhibit's thesis that the Wehrmacht had participated in committing war crimes. Was this not clear evidence of manipulation? Was this not most likely only the tip of the iceberg of falsified photographic evidence?[16] Johannes Willms of the *Süddeutscher Zeitung* responded the next day that Musial's critique raised only the methodological problems of working with photographs and did not challenge the thesis of the exhibit or the historical evidence of the crimes.[17]

The *Frankfurter* shot back immediately the following day, charging that further research indicated that only 10 percent of the pictures in the exhibit actually showed any specific crimes of the Wehrmacht at all.[18] On the same day the paper's editorial charged that the entire exhibit had been instrumentalized by those of the political Left for their own selfish ideological goals. "One knows something of a similar nature only from state directed disinformation campaigns," the editorial charged.[19] But the charge that only 10 percent of the photos clearly showed criminal acts of the Wehrmacht said absolutely nothing at all, unless one wanted to read the evidence through an ideological filter, which had already damned the exhibit. For example, one of the more powerful displays in the exhibit confronts the viewer with a wall of simple portraits of individual civilians murdered by the Wehrmacht in reprisal for partisan attacks while fighting in Serbia. The portraits are sixty of the more than twenty-three hundred civilians shot in Kragujevac as a "punishment" for partisan resistance to the occupation. It is a haunting moment, for it restores the individual identity of some of those who were murdered by Wehrmacht soldiers under orders from General Böhme.

Musial's charges were serious, but the exhibit organizers and most likely Reemtsma himself delayed any organized response. Finally, in November 1999 the exhibition's organizers reacted by closing the exhibit. A planned trip to New York City, the first outside Germany and Austria, was also canceled. A catalog for the exhibit had already been released in English with the misidentified photographs. One of them even appears on the cover of the catalog.[20] Something had to be done immediately.

The organizers had finally recognized the need to change course radically before more damage was done. Over the following months a commission of historians was organized to look at the entire exhibit from its basic thesis to the history of individual photographs. Their evaluation was that the general thesis of the original exhibit was correct, that the Wehrmacht had committed numerous war crimes and had participated willingly in the Holocaust, but that there were a number of failings in how the photographs and documents had been displayed in the exhibit.[21] An entirely new exhibit twice the size of the original reopened in 2001 in Berlin and again went on tour.[22]

This social investigation into the identity of the perpetrators has only just begun, but the narrative dynamics are beginning to develop in a similar manner to those of the Holocaust in the mid-1970s. Rather than remaining tied specifically to the exhibit, the discussions of the Wehrmacht exhibit began to spill over into other contexts, changing the boundaries of the cultural matrix. Whereas the Holocaust film narratives could aid in the construction of the mythical barrier between Nazis and Germans by allowing good Germans to hide Jews from evil SS and Gestapo agents, a true cinematic encounter with the crimes of the Wehrmacht has no positive payoff for supporting the postwar mythology. We have yet to see the filming of a narrative along the lines of Christopher Browning's *Ordinary Men.*[23] Some director may eventually wander out and develop a German version of *Apocalypse Now,* but such extreme nihilism cannot sustain itself within mass popular culture and the ideology of the marketplace.[24]

Nonetheless, whereas critical comments about the role of the Wehrmacht are virtually absent for the first fifty years of postwar German history, the more critical evaluation supported by the Wehrmacht exhibit has begun to shape public discussions. A not so faint echo from 1995 could be found in some of the commentaries surrounding May 8, 2000. Although he did not dwell upon the crimes of the Wehrmacht, Heribert Prantl mentioned the exhibit in his essay in the *Süddeutscher Zeitung.*[25] *Der Tagesspiegel* published a short book review that looked at the everyday life of the soldiers through their photographs and correspondence with home, some of which clearly showed the racism of some soldiers along with the killing of Jews.[26] In *Die Zeit,* Wolfram Wette wrote an essay that was very critical of the Wehrmacht leadership and noted that they were an important and willing pillar in the National Socialist system, although he tended to excuse the behavior of the soldiers, who knew that the war was lost in the end and were merely trying to survive.[27] In contrast to its vigorous attacks against the exhibit and its central thesis in 1999, the more conservative *Frankfurter Allgemeine* almost retreated entirely from marking May 8, 2000. The paper's only comment about the end of the war in that year (Chancellor Schröder's speech in Berlin was not even reported) was to publish an essay by Erika Steinbach, who was at the time the president of the Federation of the Refugees, which represents those Germans driven from the eastern lands at the end of the war. Her essay attempted to move the focus back to the suffering of the Germans, which she claimed had become a taboo subject. Returning to the narratives of the 1950s, she directly compared German and Jewish suffering with a compete lack of historical perspective.

Going Back

The rest of this chapter is divided into three sections. I dedicate one section each to East and West Germany before 1990 and then one final brief section to the memory of May 8 after reunification. Whereas May 8 became a pompous state ceremony of liberation in the East, the memory of the day in the West revealed the truer sentiments of the society as it was at first either ignored or treated as a day of capitulation, defeat, and shame, but also as a day that offered the chance for a new beginning.

The East German State: Long Live the Weapon Brotherhood with the Glorious Soviet Army!

For the East German state, the eighth was *the* high state holiday. While it is literally impossible to quantify the amount of material published or broadcast on the topic, it is relatively easy to state the central message, as it was repeated over and over again without any significant changes for the entire history of the GDR. In chart 11, I did not include any data for *Neues Deutschland* prior to 1990, as it is impossible to quantify the amount of material that appeared in this single publication during the GDR times. For the three days that I searched each year, basically the entire newspaper was dedicated to this national holiday and the end of the war, but the reporting about the end of the war stretched well beyond my concentrated three-day search window. The evidence from the newspaper archive on May 8 collected at the DRA suggests that such publications in a key memorial year sometimes began at least as early as March.

This state monopoly on public representations of the past was not without some consequences for individual memories, especially for the postwar generation. As seen in table I, East Germans, in contrast to West Germans, overwhelmingly viewed the Soviet Union as having played the most important role in the victory over Nazi Germany.[28] While table II shows that it was more difficult to make East Germans accept the presence of Soviet troops in their country, the state had managed to weaken any open resistance.[29] Perhaps the masses did not warmly accept the party's line of the Soviets as only brothers and friendly liberators, but many did view them as necessary for maintaining peace in Europe.

Table I
Who Played the Key Role in the Defeat of Nazi Germany? (values in percentage with more than one answer possible)

April 1995	Totals	West Germans	East Germans	Russians
Russia	39	24	87	96
USA	61	69	23	9
England	13	18	9	6
France	7	8	9	4

Source: Noelle-Neumann and Köcher, 1997, 522.

Table II
East German Views of the Soviet Occupiers (values in percentage)

	Political Party				
September 1994	Average	CDU	SPD	Greens	PDS
More as friends and allies	32	17	36	30	62
More as an occupation force	42	58	36	35	15
Undecided	26	25	28	35	23
Total	100	100	100	100	100

Source: Noelle-Neumann and Köcher, 1997, 546.

Regina Mönch, who grew up in the GDR, testified to the influence of these state ceremonies upon their own worldview.[30] Thinking back upon their own childhoods, she and her friends never connected the brutality of the German soldiers portrayed in East European films with their own fathers. The state-organized ritual surrounding the eighth was just part of growing up and helped to smooth over these images of the war. The first time she seriously questioned the state version of history was when she had direct personal contact with other East Europeans. A trip in Poland and her interaction with the people there forced her to begin reevaluating the history she had been taught. But since the topic of National Socialism was a taboo subject within her family, the state perspective dominated her worldview of the past. Regina's testimony fits well with one of the main theses of this project. When the microlevel of the family is closed off to the past, the state or other social institutions can readily fill in the blanks with whatever version of the past they wish. I will offer further evidence of how state propaganda was not without some effect on the general population when we look at the Soviet film *Blokada* later in this section.

For the antifascist state and its leadership returned from exile, the meaning of the day was never in question. From the very beginning to the very end, the day marked the national liberation from the chains of fascism and its roots within the capitalist economic system.[31] There were two key elements to the celebrations, which were repeated over and over again with basically no perceptible change in emphasis. First and foremost, the day was a celebration in praise of the Soviet Army, which had defeated Hitler fascism but not the German people, which had been liberated and not defeated. The praise was not only from the leaders through official speeches, but also through Soviet films and television programs, which sought to give Germans the Soviet perspective. Of secondary importance was the celebration of the antifascist resistance and the triumph of the German working class, but this narrative was always less important than the brotherhood between Germans and the Russians. One example of this can be seen in the television program *Strasse zur Freiheit*, which follows three Russians, a widow and two former soldiers, back to Germany, where they are greeted enthusiastically by mostly younger Germans.[32] The international Communist brotherhood with the Soviet Union at the head was always the central focal point of the day. In this sense, the day was never a national holiday so much as a celebration of the Soviet empire.

As we can see, the East German state also constructed a mythological division between Germans and Nazis in its postwar narratives.[33] The result was also the same. Both the Communist East and the democratic West sought to reintegrate as many members of the previous regime as possible with the minimal amount of social friction. To push this process forward, both states sought to isolate the crimes of the regime to the Nazi elite. The cost of such an approach was that Germans in both halves of Germany were given an easy out from examining the social and cultural roots of National Socialism.

On the topic of the international Communist brotherhood, one of the most important photographic icons of the liberation was that of Soviet soldiers helping to feed Germans, particularly children, in the streets of the destroyed cities.[34] These same photographs reappear again and again over the years along with personal testimonies from Germans who tell of how the soldiers gave them bread rather than sentiments of revenge.[35] The German acceptance of this image of the Soviet soldier as both liberator and savior was always at risk because it required that one also accept the Soviet victory over the German Wehrmacht. The liberator had to appear to have defeated Hitler, but not without undue cost of life to German soldiers, who belonged to the community of the good Germans. Thus, characterization of the fighting of the Soviet troops against the Wehrmacht always entailed extreme tension. On the one hand, the authorities had the obligation to praise the victory of the Soviet Army over Hitler, but at the same time it also had to maintain the image of the liberator while not casting too much doubt upon the position of the Wehrmacht soldier. The answer to this dilemma was to blame the western allies for the bombing of the cities and the terrorization of the civilian population, which played into the ready sentiments of victimhood that were widespread in the German population, while minimizing actual portrayals of the fighting done by the Soviet troops. This sentiment was captured in a supposed letter from a reader whose subtitle read, "After days and nights under American bombs the Soviet army brought the first bread."[36] In this manner, the state tried to have the images of the Soviet soldiers with food displace the brutality of the fighting. But this was always an ambiguous image. Since many of the television programs and Soviet films sought to capture the actual fighting from the Soviet perspective, confrontations with German soldiers were inevitably shown.

The brutality of the early occupation months and mass rapes were, of course, not discussed.[37] One early article even tried to suggest that local populations in Poland and Czechoslovakia did not take personal revenge against local German populations, although the same article fails to explain what, then, the refugees were actually fleeing.[38] In later years, the state did not even try to address the question of the refugees or the brutality of the early months of the occupation. Official state silence and silence within families about rape allowed the state to shape the national historical consciousness of the younger generations. Those with living memories of these events could easily dismiss the state's message. When living memories conflicted with public narratives, provided by either a democratic civil society or a dictatorial state, the living memories held sway over the individual. But once the living memories had passed away, the state or society gained new authority over the interpretation of history. Yet this new authority was never absolute, and pockets of resistance remained even in a situation where the state dominated almost all public space, as seen with the oral history surrounding June 17.[39]

The central site for the East German celebrations was Treptow Park in East Berlin, which includes a gigantic memorial to the heroic struggle of the Soviet army against German fascism. The park still exists today. At one end of the park is a massive thirty-eight-foot-tall statue of a Soviet soldier carrying a giant broadsword in his right hand and a small child, whom he is protecting, in his left. Under his foot is a smashed swastika. Standing opposite the statue across a long open field are two abstract triangular monuments on another platform. Between the two ends of the memorial, there are a number of individual rectangular monuments with quotations from Stalin and images from the heroic struggle.[40] The Trepow Soviet soldier became an icon of the eighth. The park was often the site of official state ceremonies and had been the location in previous years for live television broadcasts.[41] In 1985 the FDJ, or Free German Youth, held a torch-lit gathering at the memorial.[42] Although the ceremony was broadcast in prime time on East German television, it had a viewership of only 6 percent.[43] One can assume from this a general social fatigue among almost all vis-à-vis the ossified state ceremonies. The organization of the ceremony encapsulated the entire message of May 8 for the East German state. With the sun setting, the torch light grew stronger, and the red flags flying all around the memorial took on a powerful glow.

Had it always been the case that the official state ceremony had been met with general public apathy? Was the cynicism about official pronouncements as great in the 1950s as it was in the 1980s? The most boring and tedious of all the state broadcasts were the political speeches given during the Central Committee's official ceremonies. In the 1960s, these ceremonies praised the Soviet Union and the success of the SED and included a smattering of current political concerns.[44] To try to gauge public interest or support for the SED along with official state ceremonies connected with May 8, I tried to create a simple comparison between viewership at the earliest possible point in 1970 and then in 1985 for the same type of program. I assumed that only the most hard-core supporters of the SED would have willingly exposed themselves to such programming. The difference in viewership is dramatic, although the overall viewership is small in both cases. In 1970, the official Central Committee ceremony attracted a viewership of 12.8 percent,[45] while the same program attracted a viewership of between 1.7 percent and 4.2 percent in 1985 at two different broadcast times during the day.[46] If we take the FDJ broadcast viewership of 6 percent in the evening as the best comparison, as it was shown in prime time, the hard-core viewership for SED state ceremony was half what it had been in 1970. Even the state's core supporters appeared tired and had drifted away.

This ossification of state ceremony and with it party support during the final years of the GDR is symbolized on the cover of *Neues Deutschland* from 1986 to 1989 when the same group photograph of Honecker, other SED leaders, and some Soviet military officials appeared year after year. Even the editors at the party's leading newspaper could no longer find more stirring images of socialism's final victory. Instead, the old men grew older each year.[47] In the end, even the party could hardly rise to the occasion of its own high holiday.

But as I have shown in the chapters on July 20 and June 17, indifference toward official state ceremony should not lead us to assume that the essential message of those days, their narrative core, was without meaning for the general population. The state ceremonies around July 20 in West Germany soon took on as much spontaneous joyful participation as any state ceremonies organized by the SED in the GDR. While the public did not rally around official state ceremonies, the message of redemption through the July 20 resistance was very warmly embraced by the vast majority of the West German public, as seen in their positive reactions to such films as *Canaris*, *Des Teufels General*, and the ZDF's *Der Fall Nebe*. Therefore, one should not be too dismissive of the GDR's state propaganda, for the message of liberation and the promise that one was now fighting on the right side of history certainly could hold a deep attraction for some old Wehrmacht soldiers but also, more importantly, for the next generation.

To answer this question, we again need to turn to the field of popular culture, where the basic state message was replicated in a more popular format. Tables I and II show that the various states had had some success in shaping general historical attitudes. However, these data provide no evidence of a generational memory divide. The television survey data can help clarify this. From May 2 to 6 in 1980 the Soviet film *Blokada*[48] by the Russian director Michail Jerschow and based upon the novel of the same name by Alexander Tschakowski was shown on East German television in four parts. The film retells the three-year battle for Leningrad during the Second World War from the siege of the city to the Russian operation Iskra, which sought to break the siege. The film emphasizes the heroic efforts of the citizens and the soldiers of Leningrad. As Alexander Tschakowski commented, "Our land and our people survived this war against a cruel enemy, because they were convinced that they were fighting for a just cause."[49] If the Russian cause was just, then the Nazi-German cause was unjust.

Viewer opinion data are only available for the final two segments of the film. In terms of total viewers, the film scored fairly high for a Soviet film with the third part capturing 20.4 percent and the fourth part 17.7 percent. What was more surprising was the polarization of views over the quality of the film. Viewers were asked to rate the program on a 5-point scale with 1 being the best. The average viewer response to the movie was an average to below-average 2.98 and 2.82 for parts 3 and 4, respectively. However, while the intelligentsia gave the film a 1.06 and 1.00 rating, and students a 1.54 for the fourth part, those over the age of sixty-five gave the film a 5.00 rating for both parts.[50] Clearly there was a sharp polarization in the society of views of the war and the Soviet army!

These data help to show again the ability of the state to penetrate the microworld of the individual and to socialize the individual to certain cultural-ideological principles. At the same time it shows the importance of age and personal experience in resisting the state's ideological message. For those who had joined the intelligentsia of the new Communist state or were seeking to join the intelligentsia through advanced education, the film obviously inspired their respect for the Soviet soldiers and citizens. This same ideological support of the intelligentsia for state perspectives was seen in the data for the television film *Die Bilder des Zeugen Schattmann*. This co-opting of the intelligentsia can also be seen in other East European states.[51]

None of this, however, could prevent the eventual collapse of the GDR, whose vanguard party had failed time and again to restructure the economy or to liberalize the society enough to permit at least some critical voicing of concerns. What is interesting to see in the postunification publications of *Neues Deutschland* is how transfixed the PDS, the successor party of the SED, and its membership still were with the antifascist history of the earlier state. As chart 11 shows, *Neues Deutschland* published nearly as much material as the other three papers combined. This is even more amazing when one considers that it is by far the smallest newspaper of the three. Old antifascist fighters are still interviewed.[52] Other articles warn of the rise of "everyday fascism" in Germany,[53] while another author questioned the real reasons behind the fact that May 8 was still not a national holiday in unified Germany.[54] There were even still articles that presented the Russian point of view and tried to maintain the mythical brotherhood between the two peoples forged in the GDR times.[55] The PDS is holding dearly to some of the most cherished traditions from the old GDR.

West Germany: The Myth of the Clean Wehrmacht

For those of us who grew up outside West Germany, several afternoons with German war films will create the impression of having entered an altered reality. Defeats are turned into victories or at least modified defeats. The ultimate victory of the enemy in the east is often portrayed as the defeat of the Wehrmacht by the Russian winter. If the narrative turns to the western front, the allies are shown to be at blame for the extended fighting because of their ridiculous demands for unconditional surrender. If the Wehrmacht is ultimately defeated, it is due to Hitler's madness. In the end, Hitler is defeated, not Germany.

While tracing the developments within the liberation-defeat narrative, we will also have a chance to view the changing portrayal of the Wehrmacht. The postwar representations of the Wehrmacht became one of the central narrative fields in which the division of Nazis and Germans was secured in German popular culture. In the early years, not only was the Wehrmacht innocent of any serious war crimes, its members were often portrayed as the victim of Hitler's madness. To illustrate this point, I will first turn to the narratives surrounding the battle for Stalingrad, which would symbolize Hitler's insanity and the victimization of ordinary soldiers. Then I will return to a chronological analysis of May 8 to examine the narrative changes, which move from defeat to liberation.

Stalingrad: Hitler's Madness Consumes an Army

West German films set during the war almost always focus on the last two years of fighting. If the early victories and quick occupation of most of Europe are referred to at all, they are usually only shown briefly through the use of old Nazi newsreels. In German cinema, World War II became primarily a defensive war. By portraying Germans as fighting in defense of the homeland, the films helped to deflect difficult questions about the beginning of the war. These same patterns are reflected in German oral histories.[56]

The narrative focal point of the Wehrmacht's victimization at the hands of an insane Führer turns around the battle for Stalingrad in 1942. In August 1942, nearly 250,000 German troops began an all-out assault on the city of Stalingrad, which was a strategic military target. The capture of the city would have allowed the Germans to control all of the transport routes on the Lower Volga. No sooner had the Germans finally captured the city in extremely brutal fighting at close quarters then the Red Army launched a massive counterattack and trapped most of the German forces in the city. By the time the German forces surrendered in February 1943, there were only 100,000 starved and frozen German troops left alive. The Soviet casualties were even more horrendous. The battle of Stalingrad cost the Red Army more lives than the United States lost during the entire war.[57] Stalingrad marked the turning point for the war in the east, and from that point forward the Germans were mostly on the defensive for the final two years of the war. In the postwar years, the battle for Stalingrad and the narratives surrounding it reached mythical proportions.[58] In almost all films set at least in part in 1943, there is some reference to Stalingrad, which symbolized the beginning of the end.

There is a substantial amount of cultural material that deals directly with the battle for Stalingrad, and we will touch upon only a few examples here. One of the first of these to appear was Frank Wisbar's film *Hunde, wollt ihr ewig leben?* [Dogs, Do You Want to Live Forever?]

(1958).[59] Lieutenant Wisse enters the story a young idealist dedicated to fighting for his country, but he is transformed by the battle for Stalingrad into a harsh cynic who shoots his dedicated Nazi commanding officer in the back, once he proves to be a coward. As with almost the entire West German war film genre, the film is almost completely drained of all ideological concerns. The soldiers are shown fighting for their lives and displaying a dedication to each other until death. In general, the men show only contempt for those leaders who have sent them into this hellhole.

From the outside and our current perspective such sentiments appear entirely plausible. However, it was not the reality of Hitler's army, which was highly ideologically motivated. Many bore the worst fighting of Stalingrad while still praising Hitler for his brilliant leadership. In his work on the ideological motivation of the Wehrmacht officers and soldiers, Omer Bartov notes, "The Field Post Inspection Office (FPP) of 4 Panzer Army examined over 11,237 letters sent to and from Stalingrad between December 20, 1942, and January 16, 1943, and noted that almost until the very end the soldiers kept expressing their loyalty to and belief in Hitler."[60]

The same sort of division between the common soldiers and the criminally insane leadership back in Berlin is the subject of *Stalingrad* (1963), which was a theater piece produced for television.[61] The innocence of the common soldier vis-à-vis the ideologically driven leadership is part of the Stalingrad mythology. During the first ten years of German television there was a fixation upon the fighting in the east and in particular the mythical struggle for Stalingrad.[62] A 1963 documentary entitled *Eine Armee wird mißbraucht* [An Army Is Abused] focused solely upon the destruction of the sixth army at Stalingrad.[63] The documentary leaves no doubt as to the true identity of the criminals as Hitler's smiling face is shown in an ironic fashion at a couple of points during the documentary. Interestingly, the documentary does not portray Stalingrad as military madness, but rather as a calculated risk to defeat the Russians quickly now that the Americans had entered the war. Although the entire documentary has been building toward the point of condemning the senselessness of their deaths at Stalingrad, the camera then offers praise to the noble sacrifice of the soldiers as we are shown their graves with the words "They died so that Germany may live." As we will see in other examples, the theme that the Nazi leadership misused the Wehrmacht will return again and again.[64]

In a 1965 documentary entitled *Hitlerjugend—Mißbrauch einer Generation* [Hitler Youth—Misuse of a Generation], the director focuses upon the coercive power of the state rather than upon the cooperation that had existed between state and society.[65] Classen notes that this failure to identify the historical antecedents and cultural support for National Socialism in German society is an endemic problem with German television between 1955 and 1965.[66] I certainly draw the same general conclusion after having watched many such programs, but I differ with Classen's assessment of this documentary, which he thinks worked against this general trend.[67] The documentary never discusses the role of the family, the decisions of the parents, nor their willing co-optation by the state. Nor is the history of *Volkish* bourgeois youth movements prior to 1933 discussed.[68] In the end, the documentary only works again to heighten the German sense of abuse at the hands of Hitler.

Although German-produced war films almost completely disappeared from the screens after the early 1960s, there are a few important exceptions. *Stalingrad* (1992) is one of those exceptions, and the film proved to be a major success with the German public.[69] Set for release in January 1993 on the fiftieth anniversary of the battle for Stalingrad and with a budget of 20 million DM, a vast sum of money by German industry standards, the film was set to become a media event. The high production quality of the film and the gripping battle scenes coupled with the promise of "showing how it really was" pulled more than 1.3 million Germans into the theater. It is also a film that fits squarely within the narrative traditions surrounding the Stalingrad mythology.

German soldiers of various backgrounds and ideological persuasions fight it out against the Russians in the bitter cold and frozen wasteland of the city. There are love stories, the crazed Nazi fanatics, the camaraderie of the common soldiers, and their suffering at the hands of a criminal regime in Berlin. As with the earlier films, the ideological fervor of some of the soldiers reflected in Bartov's work is again missing. Rather, the soldiers are shown to be the victims of distant powers in Berlin represented by a sadistic group of officers.

At each moment when the German soldiers are placed in a morally tense situation, they successfully resolve the situation so as not to disappoint the audience. For example, rather than showing any of the soldiers carrying out any atrocities whatsoever, they are shown as being forced by their officers to execute Russian POWs under the threat of shooting or being shot. In the tradition of the Stalingrad myth, the heroic soldiers and Germany are not defeated by the Russians but rather by the winter and the criminal stupidity of the Nazi leadership. Thus, Germany remains, in a sense, undefeated in a fair fight against the Russians. Rather than forcing the audience to face difficult truths about how the sixth army even arrived in Stalingrad as part of a brutal war of racial extermination, Germans were again allowed to see themselves as victims of the Russians, the Nazis, and the winter.

A Chronology of May 8 in West Germany: From Defeat and Capitulation to Liberation

Because the Jewish experience of liberation clashed with the German sense of defeat and shame, Jews, for the most part, never played an important role in marking May 8. Thus, one potential source of a liberation narrative was silenced from the beginning along with that of the German resistance. Because of the state's silence on the ending of the war, the first five-year anniversary passed with barely a note in the papers. There were only a couple of very brief reports noting that the end of the war was marked as a day of liberation in the East.[70] Media interest in the East German national celebration of the day of liberation remained a central feature of each year's reporting. In a rare display of constitutional patriotism, the *Frankfurter Allgemeine* ran a short story praising the development of West German democracy five years after the end of the war by marking the one-year anniversary of the constitution.[71]

The ten-year anniversary generated more press, but reporting remained relatively sparse as the state did not seek to mark the day with any official ceremonies. Besides a continuing interest in the East German national celebration of liberation, three narrative strands appeared in 1955 and continued for many years. First, there was the retelling of the capitulation in often extensive detail.[72] While this retelling of the history was sometimes quite neutral, many essayists used May 8 as a chance to attack the unfair treatment of Germany at the hands of the allies. A second narrative thread developed around the theme of German victimhood that resulted from the suffering during the war and the end of the war. The final narrative thread was one of triumph over adversity in which Germans were encouraged to celebrate what they had made of their new beginning in a democratic state.

The bitterness in two of the 1955 essays is palpable. Joachim Bölke blamed the allies and in particular President Roosevelt for the disastrous outcome of the war. Germany, Bölke argued, was sacrificed so that the new United Nations (UN) could be formed. Furthermore, the demand for unconditional surrender had only increased the suffering of the Germans.[73] Writing in the *Frankfurter Allgemeine*, Erich Dombrowski was even less restrained in his attacks against the allies, who, "as the victors of the German people, in contrast to the truth, wanted to burden them with collective guilt, in order to ostracize them for all time."[74] Dombrowski made clear that not only the civilian population had been the victim of Hitler's policies, but also the Wehrmacht as well. Despite all this and the repressive guilt placed upon the Germans by the allies, the success of postwar German society was a tribute to the German's love for his *Heimat* and *Vaterland*. This triumph of having rebuilt after the end of the war became a safe expression of German nationalism and was expressed in a collection of photographs published in *Der Tagesspiegel*, which told a story of Germany's defeat and the success of German industry.[75] Each of the three narrative threads mentioned can be clearly seen in these articles and many others.

What do these articles say about the narrative division between defeat and liberation? The authors of most of the articles tended to avoid using either term. The writers only mentioned liberation in relationship to the ceremonies in the East. Rather than discussing defeat, most authors referred to the unfair capitulation forced upon Germany by the allies. While the journalists and essayists were quick to criticize the celebrations in the East as false state pathos, they were just as swift to defend the reason why West Germans did not seek to celebrate the end of the war. "What was there to celebrate?" was the typical rhetorical question. There were potential countermemories embodied in German resistance fighters and Jews, but these groups remained marginalized until the late 1970s.

The absence of official state ceremony stood in contrast to various movements within civil society to mark the end of the war. In 1955, the membership of the Union of Home-Comers [*Verband der Heimkerer*] placed large burning pylons in several major German cities in the form of memory candles to remind Germans of those who had not yet returned from the priosner of war (POW) camps.[76] The Frankfurt paper also mentioned a church service in the Paulskirche dedicated to "the victims of terror."[77] Although there were very few newspaper reports of such events, it is clear that various groups within the civil society marked the end of the war independently of the state.

One of the most popular films dealing with the end of the war and its consequences was the film *Der Arzt von Stalingrad* [The Doctor from Stalingrad] (1958), which focused upon German soldiers in a Soviet POW camp.[78] Along with *Haie und kleine Fische* [Sharks and Small Fish] (1957),[79] *Der Arzt von Stalingrad* proved to be one of the top ten films in Germany in 1958.[80] Both films take the war and its consequences as their subject matter. *Der Arzt von Stalingrad* tells the story of a group of German POWs who fall into Soviet hands after the collapse of Stalingrad in 1943. In the beginning of the film we see the words *Stalingrad 1943* in flames, along with wounded soldiers who have been burned or shot or are still bleeding while one of Hitler's triumphant speeches can be heard in the background. The main character in the story is Dr. Böhler, whom we see working to save the life of a wounded German soldier when the Russians break into the room and pull the wounded German soldier aside so that the doctor can care for a wounded Russian soldier. Throughout the film, the Russians are shown in morally compromising positions while the German heroes strive to maintain their humanity in the face of eastern barbarism. The otherness of the eastern peoples is also stressed in the film through racial differences and their crude, mechanical, almost robotlike behavior, which suggests ideological indoctrination.

The film's clear anti-Soviet message drew both praise and condemnation in the German press.[81] A typical conservative reviewer of the film in the *Stuttgarter Zeitung* had the following to say: "Flight, persecution and Russian captivity, postwar experiences that have left inextinguishable marks upon millions of Germans, were until now a taboo in German film."[82] The film was designed to show Germans again as the victims of not only Hitler but also eastern barbarism, which, incidentally, Nazism had set out to destroy. Indeed, some essayists in the 1950s came close to suggesting that the allies should have worked with the Nazis to defeat the Soviets, as the July 20 conspirators had proposed. It is interesting to note that today, the issue as to whether or not German suffering had ever been a taboo subject has been raised again.[83]

This film and others also portrayed a long-lasting obsession within German society about the preservation of the *Volk* in the face of challenges from racial others. The fact that those from the east were often portrayed as racial others is an interesting point that cannot be simply dismissed as part of the film's realism or historical accuracy. These racial views and traditions also cannot simply be blamed upon the propaganda of National Socialism. Rather, they are part of German nineteenth-century nationalism upon which National Socialism was later able to establish itself.[84] The use of racial others in the films is not in and of itself a negative factor, but the Asiatic-looking Soviets often behave in a much cruder, primordial and animallike manner. This is true even in the DEFA classic from Konrad Wolf, *Ich war neunzehn*, in which the cultured Russians are portrayed by European racial types, while the comrades of Gregor who are Asiatic-looking remain more foreign and distant. They are good comrades and war buddies, to be sure, but they lack the European sophistication of the white Russians. This racial otherness was extended to Jews as well. In 1961, 73 percent of Germans believed that Jews were of a different race.[85]

A different approach to a war film from the same period is taken by *Haie und kleine Fische*, based upon a book by Wolfgang Ott. Ott's book had not been well received by navy veterans, for the author's intention had been to destroy the romantic image of war on the high seas.[86] In contrast to the praise for a Nazi war hero in *U47—Kapitänleutnant Prien*, this film tries hard to remove the veneer of romantic excitement of war at sea, but at the same time the film praises the camaraderie of those small fish who man the submarines of the German navy. In this manner, the film is not unlike the later film *Das Boot* (1981), which was a significant international success.[87] Unlike in *U47*, there are not any parades or a hero's welcome to greet the sailors when they return from a hard tour of duty at sea. Rather, there are only girlfriends, alcohol, and prostitutes. While the film attempts to portray the sailors in a less heroic fashion, their struggle for survival is not contrasted with a clear understanding of what they are fighting for. The film is generally void of any political or ideological concerns except in one brief scene in which Teichmann, the main character, discovers that the father of one of his comrades has just died in a concentration camp because he was Jewish. Rather than portraying individuals who are capable of making moral decisions, the film turns more on the issue of fate and being lost in a vast sea. The images of the sailors once they have abandoned their damaged submarine are striking as they float in an immense empty space, not unlike the snowstorm at the end of *Stalingrad* (1992).

By 1965 more divergent views of what May 8 meant or should mean for German society began to appear. While the Berlin CDU continued to call the eighth a day for inward reflection, the Landesjugendring, a local youth group, called for Germans to recognize the day as marking the end of a period of bondage and the chance for a new beginning.[88] By referring to a period of bondage, the youth group began to suggest a theme of liberation.

The year 1965 also marked the first time the federal government officially recognized the end of the war. In Bonn, Federal President Lübke and Chancellor Erhard along with thirty members of the Bundeswehr in uniform placed a wreath in Bonn at a memorial for the Victims of War. Although Chancellor Erhard's speech was broadcast on radio and television, it was not well reported in the print media.[89] This year also provided the potential for a breakthrough in terms of a Jewish perspective on the end of the war with the well-reported Auschwitz trials, which had been taking place in Frankfurt for over a year and a half by this time.[90] Despite this first major public discussion about the Holocaust, the trial had little to no social resonance outside the regular reports from the trials themselves. This conclusion is supported by the evidence in chart 4 of the radio broadcasts related to reports on Kristallnacht and Auschwitz. I found only a couple of lines in one article in which a Jewish survivor of the deportations was asked about them by a journalist for *Die Zeit*.[91]

The question of German guilt for the war continued to be a point of obsession with which the state television industry had to deal. The *Infratest* report on a televised discussion between two historians, Walther Hofer and A. J. P. Taylor, about the causes of the war stated that the viewers followed the discussion with great interest. The report concluded that Taylor's comments were readily accepted by the viewers because his arguments took part of the guilt for the war off the shoulders of the Germans.[92] *Das letzte Kapitel* was another ZDF documentary that was well received by the audience and broadcast on the twentieth anniversary of the capitulation.[93] Once again the *Infratest* report noted that the typical defensive reactions of the audience were avoided because questions of guilt were never addressed. In fact, as did most narratives, which focused solely on the end of the war and the final days of the conflict, the program allowed Germans to view themselves solely as victims.

In 1970, Chancellor Willy Brandt, who had worked in the German resistance while in exile in Sweden, addressed the German parliament. In his speech, he focused more upon the need for reconciliation with the East, reflecting the then-current struggles over his foreign policy of *Ostpolitik*.[94] But Federal President Heinemann did hint at the theme of liberation in his speech in which he noted that the criminal despotism of National Socialism had been taken from the German people.[95] But his speech did not make much of an impact as it was extremely short and placed well away from the media spotlight. Despite the fact that Brandt's speech dealt primarily with current foreign policy, the CDU and CSU had protested his plans to speak before the German parliament on the day of the capitulation: "One does not celebrate defeats."[96] Richard von Weizsäcker was also invited to speak on behalf of the conservative opposition in the parliament.[97] Von Weizsäcker, who delivered a much celebrated speech fifteen years later marking the end of the war, blamed the crimes on National Socialism. He then used the rest of his speech to question Brandt's *Ostpolitik*.

Meanwhile, other small steps within the civil society to recognize the liberation perspective of the German resistance and Jews continued to move forward. At the Jewish Community Center in Berlin, the Federation of Victims of Political, Racial and Religious Persecution [Bund politisch, rassisch und religiös Verfolgter] had organized a postage stamp exhibit showing how twenty-two different countries had recognized the role of resistance fighters.[98] In a separate ceremony, a former resistance fighter was recognized for his work by the mayor of Berlin.[99]

The year 1975 marked yet another struggle between more conservative politicians and the new federal president, Scheel, who delivered a powerful speech in commemoration of the capitulation at the church of the Bonn University. Leaders of the opposition even refused to attend Scheel's speech.[100] In his speech, Scheel emphasized the theme of liberation, but liberation produced outside Germany. Even more striking was Scheel's willingness to identify the society's open participation in the plans of the National Socialists: "He [Hitler] had changed our land into a gigantic war machine and each of us was a wheel in that machine. This was recognizable. But we closed our ears and eyes, hopeful, that it might be otherwise." Scheel also assaulted the German obsession with throwing off the question of guilt after the war. "After the war there was an excited discussion about whether or not there was a collective guilt. Today we have enough distance to recognize: Hitler became our fate, because we—in a time of great emergency—did not give freedom and the rule of law enough vlaue, as the constitution required." Of equal importance was Scheel's attack on the traditional May 8 narratives: "But the German tragedy began in 1933, not in 1945."

Scheel's speech pushed to widen traditional interpretations of the day, but his words were delivered at a time when the society was still largely deaf to them. As chart 2 reminds us, at the time of his speech, the esteem for Hitler in the general public was still rising and the criminal nature of the National Socialist regime was still rejected by one third of the population. The full impact of the Holocaust narrative had not yet hit the public, which included some very well-entrenched and powerful pockets of conservative nationalists. One must remember that in 1975, the opposition leadership thought they could benefit politically by ignoring Scheel's speech altogether. Chancellor Schmidt's speech, in contrast, lacked all of Scheel's demands for a more intense and painful reflection upon the past.[101] When he did turn his attention to the past, Schmidt attempted to sound a triumphal tone: "We have since then not repressed the years of darkness, rather we have cleared up in our consciousness of this epoch of our history in an often painful process." Whereas Scheel recognized that a great deal of memory work remained, in fact was only beginning, Schmidt was already willing to declare victory. Instead, he declared that the vast majority of Germans were born after 1933 and therefore could not possibly bear any guilt for the Nazi regime. This comment did not draw any critical fire from commentators, although Chancellor Kohl was later roundly attacked for making a similar statement several years later. In the context of 1975, this comment was well within the bounds of the cultural matrix.

While the Jewish perspectives remained completely absent in *Die Zeit* and the *Frankfurter Allgemeine*, the unique position of the Jewish community in Berlin allowed a bit of the Jewish voice to come through, but only on the margins. Mayor Schütz not only placed wreaths at a military memorial and at Plötzensee but also in the memorial courtyard of the Jewish Community Center in the Fasanenstraße.[102] During the ceremony in the Fasanenstraße, both Mayor Schütz and the Jewish community leader Galinski spoke. In contrast to Schmidt's triumphant tone, both sounded words of warning. Galinski's words were perhaps the more pointed of the two as he appeared to question Schmidt's observation that most Germans then were born after 1933 when he noted that only a few of the older generation had fully severed their ties to the most damaging period in German history.[103] Galinski reiterated these concerns in 1980, noting that some Germans still failed to recognize the criminal nature of the Nazi regime, although this situation was rapidly changing during these very same years (see chart 1).

Perhaps because 1980 was an off year in the memory calendar, there was almost nothing to report, and unlike in earlier years other commentators or essayists were not called in to voice their opinions. In this manner, 1980 represented the calm before the storm of Bitburg in 1985. In 1975, the CDU under Helmut Kohl's leadership had bitterly resisted then-Federal President Scheel's attempt to refocus the nation's attention upon the past. While Scheel's speech fell into the media void, others echoed his criticisms in later years once the Holocaust became more widely discussed during the 1980s.

In 1985, Chancellor Kohl made a bid to put the historical narrative of National Socialism back under control by trying to return Germany to the narrative patterns of the 1950s and 1960s. Whether it was the ceremony at Bitburg or the attempt to create a new central national memorial with the *Neue Wache* in 1993, Kohl was attempting to level the historical playing field once again by allowing Germans to see themselves as one of the primary victims of National Socialism.[104] For most conservatives, this was a necessary strategy to counter what they viewed as the Left's attempt to suppress all forms of German nationalism, which kept the country weak and without a strong national identity.[105]

Much has already been written about Bitburg, so I will pass over it fairly quickly here.[106] In 1985, Chancellor Kohl suggested that he and the U.S. president Reagan visit a German military cemetery as a national act of reconciliation forty years after the end of the war. Controversy over the visit erupted when it was revealed that members of the SS were also buried in the same cemetery. This then expanded into a dispute about the different levels of victimization and different burdens of guilt for various perpetrators. Political pressure for and against the ceremony mounted. Kohl was warned not to turn his back on German soldiers by many German commentators and at the same time heavily criticized by Jewish groups and Holocaust survivors for his willingness to continue with the ceremony. The response of the government was to organize a separate trip for both Kohl and Reagan to the Bergen-Belsen concentration camp.

In the end, most in the German press concluded that both Kohl and Reagan had found the right words and tone for the ceremony in Bitburg and Bergen-Belsen. An editorial in *Der Tagesspiegel* suggested that those who continued to criticize the two leaders had other political agendas.[107] Günther Gillessen drew much the same conclusion in his editorial for the *Frankfurter Allgemeine*.[108] He noted that if it had not been the graves of the Waffen-*SS* in the cemetery, the critics would have found something else to complain about. In the end, he decided, as many had since the end of the war, that the central question of Bitburg was not that of the Holocaust but rather the unfair charge of collective guilt. If Kohl and Reagan had ignored Bitburg, then they would have placed a collective guilt upon all of the innocent regular soldiers who were also buried there.

Marion Gräfin Dönhoff also maintained a similar defensive line in her editorial in *Die Zeit*.[109] She listed the various reasons why May 8 could never be celebrated in Germany: the massive flight and expulsion of Germans from the east, the destruction of the cities, the division of the country, the loss of one's *Heimat*, the many fallen soldiers, and the execution of still others. But why was it then that Jews and resistance fighters were able to accept the destruction of their homes in Berlin because they knew that each bomb moved their liberation closer? As seen in the previous chapters, Dönhoff was never able to abandon her image of Hitler as the central evil of National Socialism, who was somehow disconnected from the rest of German history. She continued to maintain that it was only the clever propaganda of the state and his dual strategy of terror and military success that had kept the population in line. But if the Germans celebrated his successes, did they then not also celebrate his goals of enslaving and destroying the Slavic people? If the military victories were interpreted as "success," did they not then reflect the hopes and wishes of the German nation?

Such positive and defensive evaluations of the visit ignored the bitter and angry reaction of many Jews. The then-Israeli defense minister Rabin said that "the equality of victims and murders" represented in Reagan's visit to Bitburg would not be forgiven nor forgotten by Jews and humanity.[110] Speaking in Berlin at the Jewish Community Center, thus making the story only of "local interest," as it was not covered in the other national papers, Galinski praised the growing recognition of those unsung heroes who had hidden persecuted Jews during the Nazi years.[111] But he was much less sanguine about the success of Germany's encounter with its past. He noted that former members of the SS continued to meet to celebrate their war deeds and that the German youth still lacked any clear perspective on the Hitler years. Willy Brandt joined the chorus of the critics, saying that perhaps one third of the CDU was almost incapable of learning anything from history, as he stated angrily that the Nazi crimes were not just committed "in the name of the Germans" but rather "by Germans."[112] Such language was nothing new for the former German chancellor, who had knelt at the Warsaw ghetto memorial in atonement for the collective horrors of his nation.

The most praised and well-reported speech of 1985 was without a doubt the one delivered by the then-federal president, Richard von Weizsäcker.[113] The most important and most often quoted sections of the speech, however, made exactly the same points that Scheel had made ten years earlier in 1975. As had Scheel, von Weizsäcker called upon Germans not to separate 1933 from 1945, and he also stated clearly that there was no collective guilt or innocence but rather a collective responsibility of a community to recognize its history. Guilt and innocence remained an individual issue. Von Weizsäcker was more forceful in calling the eighth a day of liberation, a perspective he then encouraged the younger generation to embrace. But unlike Scheel, von Weizsäcker still sought to keep the majority of Germans separate from Nazis by noting that they had fought and suffered for their country in what they considered a just cause. It was only later, he argued, that the German nation discovered it had been misused by the Nazi leadership.

This continued shifting of responsibility can be seen in other speeches given by various religious leaders. During the official state ceremony in the Cologne Cathedral, Cardinal Höffner and Bishop Lohse tended to retreat into the same vague language of "crimes done in Germany's name" during their speeches. Collective guilt was again rejected as a regular part of the ceremony, and individual guilt appeared to be a matter to be settled only between the individual and his or her God. As Cardinal Höffner put it, all guilt is already forgiven through Christ's mercy.[114] Writing about the religious ceremonies, Karl-Alfred Odin repeated this Christian perspective, noting that only God can stand in judgment of individuals and their actions, for only he knows their true motivations. The need for reconciliation and forgiveness was being recognized by the Germans, and he wondered why Jews and Americans lacked the same willingness to forgive.[115] In contrast to these commentators, Pastor Heinrich Albertz, speaking in Berlin, admonished Germans to remember that the majority of them had turned their backs on National Socialism not out of conviction but rather because of the total war and the absolute defeat of the nation.[116]

After Reunification

As with 1980, the off year anniversary of 1990 passed without any significant activity in the newspapers except a couple of brief reports from Jews as the Jewish World Congress had gathered at the Wannsee Villa in Berlin to mark the end of the war. Elie Wiesel spoke for the group with his characteristic directness in which he sought to overturn the common German formulation of stating that the crimes had been "committed in Germany's name." Wiesel said, "What the Germans sought to extinguish here [at the Wannsee Villa], was the history of the Jews. What Germany wanted to destroy for eternity, was the memory of the Jews."[117] While Wiesel's powerful words were reprinted verbatim in *Der Tagesspiegel*, the more conservative *Frankfurter Allgemeine* only reprinted one abstract statement from Wiesel and ignored the rest of his speech.[118] Jews had gained a greater voice since the late 1970s, but by no means a decisive voice.

Marking the fiftieth anniversary of the ending of the war, May 8, 1995, was an important date for all of Europe. It also marked the first major anniversary of the war's ending on which all of Europe appeared to be moving toward greater unity with the end of the cold war. Thus, high state ceremony had the perhaps the highest profile in this year compared to all previous years. Federal President Roman Herzog delivered his speech before numerous world leaders including the then very ill French president François Mitterrand in the Berlin Schauspielhaus. His speech followed in the traditions of former Federal Presidents Scheel and von Weizsäcker except that whereas von Weizsäcker had maintained a more strict division between Nazis as perpetrators and Germans as victims, Herzog clearly began to label the perpetrators not as Nazis but as Germans.[119] Herzog had finally dropped the phraseology of "done in Germany's name" for actually naming the perpetrators. But his main purpose was not to dwell upon the past, but rather to focus upon his metaphor of May 8 as having been the opening of a door into a new future for Germany.

These subtle shifts in the narratives around the eighth were noticeable in other ways as well. First, as in previous years, German victimhood was placed alongside the growing presence of both Nazi and German perpetrators. Second, along with the growing Jewish presence on the day was the combining of the Holocaust and liberation themes on a date that had previously been reserved almost solely for remembering German suffering. Last, the impact of the Wehrmacht exhibit was already making its presence known even though it had just opened in March of the same year. Wolfram Wetre reviewed a book about the exhibit in *Die Zeit* and other essayists referred to the exhibit's message.[120] One poll cited at the time showed that a full 80 percent of the Germans now saw the day as a day of liberation.[121] This change in historical consciousness was created in part by the most recent German generations' having passed through the national narrative changes of the Holocaust of the mid-1970s to the present day. The more or less ambivalent sentiments about the criminal nature of the National Socialist regime were in full retreat by 1995 as the Nazi generation continued to withdraw from public life (see chart 2).

The conservative reaction to this change was anything but hospitable. The leading editorial by Johann Georg Reißmüller in the *Frankfurter Allgemeine* again noted all of the reasons Germans had for not celebrating the day.[122] He then spent the second half of his essay decrying the long existing taboo of Germans' not being able to discuss their own status as victims after the war at the hands of the Russians or the killing and expulsion of civilians from the East. Despite the fact that such a taboo never existed, the theme that Germans had been denied their own sense of victimhood is a very current topic today.

Despite such dissenting voices, one important political and cultural consequence of this shift toward a liberation narrative was that it gave a new discursive space into which Jews and resistance fighters could step to present their version of history. Perhaps for the first time since the end of the war, Jewish narratives of liberation became more common as they became more accepted by the general population. The counternarratives became integrated into the mainstream.

For example, instead of waiting until November 9 or another day to open the new Centrum Judaicum in the Oranienburger Strasse, which was connected to the old Jewish synagogue, major political figures including Chancellor Kohl and Ignatz Bubis, the leader of the German Jewish community, celebrated the opening along with the end of the war.[123] The new center was to become a new meeting place in the city for Jews and non-Jews while providing some exhibition space. Writing in *Der Tagesspiegel*, Malte Lehming tried to put all of this celebration of Jewish life back into perspective by noting that Berlin's Jewish community now only numbered around ten thousand, six thousand of them recent immigrants from Russia. In terms of absolute numbers, that placed the size of the Jewish community between that of the Greek Orthodox and Jehovah's Witnesses.[124] Lehming's article also suggested the beginning of a period of mourning for Germany's destruction of its Jewish neighbors. Indeed, as Jerzy Kanal, the new leader of the Berlin Jewish community, stated, "We can again build up the houses, but we can never replace the people."

More than in any previous year, the German papers and television stations shared narratives of liberation provided from a Jewish or resistance perspective. Hans-Peter Messerschmidt, a Jewish survivor from Theresienstadt, told of his liberation and the loss of his family members, but also his search for former German Berlin classmates of his 1935 graduating class.[125] Thomas Lackmann not only told the story of his father's survival and liberation from the Dachau concentration camp but took a bold stand on the issue of resistance: "But each soldier that shot Hitler's soldiers, each German, that as a deserter or normal coward or clever opportunist worked so that the war did not last a day longer is on MY side."[126] Wolfgang Ebert remembered similar sentiments in his Jewish family when the Americans arrived in Bavaria. He recalled his father's screaming, "We are free, free!"[127]

One final example helps to illustrate how the Holocaust narrative had begun to find its way into personal narratives and memories; how some individuals had begun to integrate macrolevel narratives of the Holocaust into their own personal memories and stories. Manfred Sack had written a brief essay in *Die Zeit* in 1975 as well as 1995.[128] While the core of the personal narrative remained unaltered over this twenty-year period, the 1995 version was significantly different as Sack admitted that his pride and dedication to National Socialism, learned in his youth, had blinded him to the fate of the Jews around him. He also admitted in the later story that he even had joined the SED in East Berlin after the war because of his sense of guilt and despair at the end of the war, although he later left the party. While it is difficult to determine how frequently this occurred, the aggregate data presented in chart 2 suggest that the post-1975 Holocaust narrative probably had a similar effect upon others as well.

Public television also picked up on the liberation theme. Similarly to the story of Hans-Peter Messerschmidt, Erwin Leiser, who was a Berlin Jew and a student at a German high school from 1932 to 1938, went in search of his former classmates to probe their memories of those years. In talking about his documentary film *Pimpf war jeder* [Each was a Pimpf],[129] Leiser said he wanted to know what conclusions his classmates had drawn from their experiences first in the Hitler Youth and then in the war.[130] One television program was simply called *Die Befreiung* [The liberation].[131] As in previous documentaries about the end of the war, the film's makers sought out those who had experienced the end of the war in different locations, but this time Jewish perspectives were clearly given, and they conflicted with those of people who had served in the military or had experienced the end of the war through the occupation of the Red Army.[132]

Both ARD and ZDF presented major film productions focusing upon the final days of the war and what followed. ARD presented a film, *Drei Tage im April*, which covered the end of the war from the perspective of a young German woman and her discovery of the regime's worst crimes. The film was significant, for it combined the narratives of May 8 with that of the Holocaust. The ZDF presented a more lengthy three-part film, *Deutschlandlied* [literally, the title of the German national anthem], which told the story of the final days of the war and the early period of the American occupation.[133] Themes of de-Nazification, the black market, and race relations were dealt with in the film. The latter theme was explored through a love relationship between a black American soldier and a German woman.[134] Unlike earlier ZDF films or documentaries on the Nazi past, the film did not elicit a large number of phone calls or strong opinions.[135]

Conclusion

In terms of the liberation-defeat narrative, the comparison of the East and West German cases is instructive. In the East, the state-driven interpretation of liberation was accepted by the intelligentsia, party members, and many in the younger generation, while it was largely rejected by the older generation. Since the state dominated the macrolevel, the counternarrative of defeat was never allowed into public discussions. In contrast, the openness of the Western state-society relationship permitted competition among different interpretations. There is no question that the older generation overwhelmingly viewed May 8 with bitterness and defeat, while the younger generation, resistance fighters, and Jews struggled to place the theme of liberation in the public space.

As with the July 20 and resistance narratives, the narratives surrounding May 8 were transformed through the ever-increasing public knowledge of the Holocaust, which began to emerge around 1975. The position of German victimhood was thrown into question at the same time a renewed search for the identity of the perpetrators began. This search for the perpetrators has culminated most recently and explosively in the narratives surrounding the Wehrmacht exhibit and public debates surrounding Goldhagen's book. It is difficult to predict the long-term impact of the Wehrmacht exhibit and the emerging perpetrator-oriented narratives. From the practical perspective of justice, there is almost nothing that can be done, as many of the perpetrators are already too old or are dead. The same is true for almost all of the witnesses to the crimes, except for the witness offered by the perpetrators' own photographs. But there is no question that the issue remains one of not only historical and scholarly concern as the political and social spheres have been fully engaged by the topic.

One can see how politicians become engaged in the construction of their own societal and political culture not solely motivated by an intent to manipulate history for instrumental gains at the ballot box. Rather, they are emotionally and passionately moved by these topics, because of direct personal experience or emotional connections to others within their own families or circles of friends. The universal human dilemma remains as to how one is to mourn death in war and at the same time encounter the collective horrors of the nation.

7

Conclusion—Mourning, Loss, and the Difficulty of Remembering

Introduction

Individual Germans, societal groups, and both German states have been processing and reworking the history and representation of the war and the Holocaust since 1945. Rather than maintaining silence and refusing to engage the past, we have seen that Germans were actively engaged in interpreting the past and struggling over those interpretations. If "the past" is not reduced to the Holocaust, there is anything but silence or repression. Instead, there is a vibrant and lively discussion. The German engagement with each of the discursive fields explored in this research varied over time, and the interaction of the different narrative threads with each other has had an important impact on the outcome thus far. For example, the deep entrenchment of the Holocaust narrative in West German culture during the 1980s put severe strains on the primary resistance narrative in the West, which had focused on the July 20 plot. Once it was revealed that the elite resistance had hardly been motivated by the crimes of the regime, it became more difficult for their blood sacrifice to redeem the nation.

What is important to realize is that the various actors in this story played out their engagement with these symbolic narratives and mythologies in a bounded cultural matrix, in which the different groups were either advantaged or disadvantaged vis-à-vis others. The symbolic power and influence that shifted in the direction of Jews, socialists, and Communists in the later years was a result of the boundaries of the cultural matrix shifting to incorporate and lend more support to their version of how to get history right. It was in this changed narrative context that West German youth could more easily challenge a political figure like Filbinger, in the late 1970s. It became more difficult to argue for a statute of limitations on crimes against humanity in 1979, causing enough conservative Christian Democratic members of parliament to break ranks with their party to support the Social Democrats and their legislation for abolishing any such limits on prosecution. When Chancellor Kohl sought to establish his new war memorial at the *Neue Wache* in 1993 with its ambiguous inscription *To the Victims of Tyranny*, Jewish groups were able to challenge him and the national conservatives in their attempt to return to the language and rituals of the 1950s. Jews were able to draw upon new sources of symbolic power and legitimacy to speak and be heard in public. This was rooted in the changed cultural matrix after the wave of Holocaust memory from the late 1970s and throughout the 1980s, which gave Jews a different status in German society. In the earlier postwar years, their voices would have been much more muted.

This concluding chapter draws together the core points of this book, especially those observations that are relevant to other similar cases of societies dealing with their difficult pasts. The West German example is, today, often held up as a positive model for others to follow. But as has been shown here, the path to the present fuller engagement with the history of National Socialism is relatively recent. While certainly a positive example given today's perspective, the West German case shows us that it may indeed take an extended period to deal with the deep wounds of war and genocide. These lessons are for all of us, for all human societies have been founded upon, on the one hand, human creativity, art, beauty, and culture, but on the other, the destruction, humiliation, and elimination of others and their cultural heritage. Dealing with, if not overcoming, this contradiction is a burden we all share.

Postwar Mythologies and the Ethnocentrism of Death and Suffering

Stretching across all of the discursive fields presented here are two central postwar myths, which originally eased the crushing defeat of Germany in 1945. In both the East and the West, Germans developed different versions of the terror state mythology to explain the "passive" German population and the lack of widespread resistance to what was increasingly seen as a criminal regime. Both halves of the nation also carefully maintained distinctions between Germans and Nazis, between fighting for Germany and fighting for Hitler, between the fulfillment of one's duty and the perpetration of criminal acts.

The mourning for destroyed cities; for lost sovereignty and national unity; for dead soldiers, fathers, sons, mothers, daughters; for the expulsion from homes in the East; and for the silent and depressive legacy of mass rapes, had all added mortar to the wall between Nazis and Germans and thus led to only a partial accounting for the National Socialist past. Both German societies spent fifty-five years constructing this mythology, and it is primarily during the past decade that serious social and cultural challenges to this myth have been raised, especially with regard to the "clean Wehrmacht." These general observations hold true for both East and West German postwar societies.

This book has been about the German case of dealing with a difficult past and the potential for reconciliation, but its conclusions are far more general. One should not dismiss the very human need to mourn such massive loss of life and home. The struggle and difficulty we all face is to recognize our own suffering and loss, while also recognizing the harm that we, in a collective if not personal sense, have caused others. The problem is that this need to mourn our loses and to try to find a positive meaning in the deaths of our side puts severe limits on what we can accept in terms of evaluating the meaning of what the victims of our own violence have experienced. We say to ourselves: "All of this death and suffering must have been for something. It *must* mean something. It *must* have been for a good cause." The thought that all the suffering may have made no difference whatsoever is unbearable. The fact that all this destruction was for an unjust cause is nearly unthinkable.

The German encounter with the past was in part limited by their "inability to mourn" the loss of Hitler as their ego ideal, as proposed by the Mitscherlichs. Yet, rather than only a denial of the past as suggested by the Mitscherlichs,[1] Germans also sought to make the past usable and meaningful to their process of mourning. The work presented here emphasizes that the process of mourning individual losses in families was critical to the formation of the postwar mythologies and narratives about the past. This microlevel dynamic of mourning had consequences for the entire society. To rescue positive meanings from the massive death and destruction, one had to separate the death or loss, in whatever form, from whatever crimes could be attached to the regime and the abstraction of National Socialism. From the earliest years to roughly the mid-1970s (see chart 1, appendix), this also included decriminalizing the regime or blaming certain excesses on a limited group. The popularity of films such as *Canaris* or the television series *Der Fall Nebe* shows the extent to which West Germans wished to find active resistance among elite Nazis. These resistance narratives had the potential symbolic power of redeeming the nation with these blood sacrifices. We need only contrast these film narratives with those of the Wehrmacht exhibit to see how stark the changes in the cultural matrix had become over a thirty-year period. The redefinition of perpetrators and victims has been a slow and very painful process.

Democratic versus Authoritarian Memory Regimes and Generational Turnover

Generational turnover is an important mechanism that creates new opportunities in the struggle over symbols and the representation of the past. The transference of values and meaning from one generation to another is central to the ability of a society to reproduce and regenerate itself. But each new generation comes of age in a different historical and political context, thus offering a chance for change. The burden of the past, the mourning of death, and the ethnocentrism of death will find some resonance with new generations as well, but they may also take some greater emotional distance from past events. This provides a chance for a new framework of interpretation to be put in place, for the boundaries of the cultural matrix to be redrawn.

One criticism of a generational explanation for postwar reinterpretations of the Holocaust and war in East and West Germany is that generational change is gradual, while the narrative shifts have sometimes been rather abrupt. Insofar as the changes can be abrupt, as with the arrival of the Holocaust narrative in the mid-1970s, this does require further explanation. But that does not mean that generational turnover is not a core mechanism for change. For example, was it reasonable to believe that such a massive narrative shift could have occurred in the 1950s? The possibility was there with a film like *Lang ist der Weg*, immediately after the war, but the Jewish perspective of the film was largely rejected by Germans at the time. The film was very much on the periphery of the cultural matrix, although it also sought to reshape the same. There is nothing automatic about generational turnover's causing a reevaluation of the past, but it does create new opportunities. The comparison of East and West Germany is instructive on this point, as generational turnover in the East failed to generate the same responses as in the West. To understand why, we need also to consider the role of regime type alongside generational turnover, the ethnocentrism of death, and the memory-market dictum.

For example, the East German state was relatively successful in constructing a framework of the past that many East German youth embraced, at least in part. While the East German state certainly failed to instill a sense of celebratory ecstasy in its achievements, it nonetheless had established traditions that helped alienate and isolate the individual within the society and thus minimized the risk of social unrest. While the state failed to create spontaneous celebrations for the Soviet army in the country, it was at least able to create ambivalent sentiments in the population and to prevent outright hostility. The state had also successfully closed off the public space to countermemories of the war.

Nonetheless, the state suffered a severe crisis of legitimacy in terms of trying to justify the division of the country, the highly restricted free movement outside the country, and the ever-weakening economic performance of the command economy. The past can be one source of legitimacy; it cannot be the only source. The antifascist legacy helped to launch the East German state and indeed gave it legitimacy in the eyes of many in the immediate postwar years, but this narrative alone could not sustain it indefinitely. The state's growing weakness throughout the 1970s and 1980s was perhaps most in evidence in its attempts to maintain the rituals of the antifascist state.

The West German case, in contrast, provides a much more dynamic relationship among the society, generational turnover, the state, and the economic system. The West German society of the 1950s and 1960s was filled with German victims and German resistance fighters, who were often drawn from the noble, courageous, and dutiful Wehrmacht, which had never become Hitler's army. These narratives filled not only the popular culture of film, but also public television and independent newspapers. Until well into the 1970s, May 8 was either avoided or used to play up German sentiments of victimhood, which were almost always detached from the history and antecedents of National Socialism except to blame Hitler's insanity.

The German cases should offer a cautionary tale to those who try to engineer confrontations with difficult pasts and criminal regimes. Although the Nuremberg trials are generally seen in a positive light in American society and even mythologized in American popular culture, which has an obsession with courtroom dramas, as the triumph of justice, the rule of law, and a history lesson for the Germans, West German elites and the general public largely rejected the trials as "victor's justice." The popular culture and elite press derided and ridiculed the trials. Clearly victims of criminal regimes will cry for justice, and there may very well be good reasons for proceeding with trials and truth and reconciliation commissions, but we should not delude ourselves into thinking that other didactic goals are also being served. Instead, such trials may produce lingering resentment and bitterness and entrench a resistance to internal critiques of the past.[2]

The German cases also demonstrate some of the limits on the openness and plurality of democratic societies. The memory-market dictum offers a way to generalize this point across democratic and authoritarian societies: the more capital intensive a given medium, producing a film compared to writing a book, and the more dependent it is on market success, the less challenging the material produced. Market forces can have their own censoring effect upon the process of collective memory formation. Market-based societies are not free of ideological constraints. In the East, the ideology of the authoritarian state set clear limits on how the past could be discussed, and this propaganda was not without some effects on the population, although the state never extinguished the memory of June 17 nor compelled a love for the Soviets among the older generation. But in the West as well, the ideology of the market, with its dedication to profit and sometimes efficiency, set clear limits on what could be said by whom and where. The more exposed a given medium or product was to market forces, the more sensitive its producers had to be to the prevailing cultural attitudes and values. It is certainly incorrect to suggest that the ideology of the market was as limiting as the ideology of the East German state, but one should note that there are clear limits to the plurality that the market will support. One need only contrast the rejection of *Lang ist der Weg* in 1948, the cinematic failure and then the public television triumph of *Das Haus in der Karpfengasse* in 1965, and finally the wide acceptance of *Holocaust* in 1979. Over time, the market-based democracy in the West proved by far the more dynamic of the two cases, in terms of permitting struggles over getting history right. An important part of that process was the medium of public television, which was somewhat insulated from the ideology of the market. West German public television proved to be an important player in opening debate about the past and indeed increasing the plurality of the discussion.

Symbolic and Political Power, and the Need to Engage Popular Culture

Another central pont is that the cultural matrix can be an extremely dynamic field for social scientific investigation. As argued by Abner Cohen, social scientists need to recognize both symbolic and political power as relevant to their work.[3] The actors in the story told here vary from extremely large institutions, such as the two German states, down to individuals who have a shoe box filled with wartime photographs or a memoir to write. For all of these actors, the past is not simply instrumentalized to achieve other material goals, be it an electoral victory or the profits from the sale of a book or movie. Rather, getting history right matters to the individual on an emotional level, and, by extension, this has consequences for the entire society. It is a struggle over identity and defining oneself or the nation. And struggles over identity and the contours of the cultural matrix are political acts; they are attempts to define groups and the symbolic borders of the group. Are Jews part of the Germany community, on the fringes of the German community, or central to the self-understanding and life of that German community? Who were the Nazis; who were the Germans? To what degree does such a distinction even make sense? What is one to make of former officials within the Nazi bureaucracy? Were those who deported Jews and worked for the SS really Nazis? Or were they perhaps actually members of the "other Germany" and thus Germans rather than Nazis? Again, the identity of these actors as either "Nazis" or "Germans" has significant political implications. From 1945 to 1974, Hans Filbinger was a German with a record of resistance certified by a German court; after 1974, his legitimacy and political career began to collapse under the weight of the label *Nazi*. The symbolic struggles over the past had redefined the boundaries of the cultural matrix and made the downfall of a major political figure possible. This is a clear example of how culture and politics intersect. The struggle over getting history right is a struggle for a scarce resource. It is a struggle for legitimacy to be heard and to have influence over current events.

Both German states have played their role in getting history right and in ascribing identities to different social actors, but we miss a great deal of what is happening within the process of collective memory if we only turn to the official and public memory. The rituals around July 20 are a very good example of how official state ceremony can ossify and fail to have much dynamic resonance with the general public. But if one turns toward the popular culture and the discursive field of resistance and collaboration embodied within the July 20 narrative, one finds a very dynamic and passionate discussion about the German resistance to the Nazis or even Nazi resistance to the Nazis, as seen with *Canaris*. The study of the process of collective memory formation should not be limited to elite pronouncements, parliamentary debates, and official state ritual. Scholars should still engage these data sources, but we also need to broaden our potential sources of data to oral history and popular culture. By studying film and television, scholars can gain new insights into the diversity of audience reactions and draw upon research in mass communication.

For example, the television viewer surveys from East Germany provide a window on public attitudes toward the Nazi past not seen before. East German citizens were willing to say things about television programs that they probably would not have said to a pollster. The diametrically opposite reactions to the Soviet war film *Blokada* by the older generation, on the one hand, and the younger generation, intellectuals, and party members, on the other, provide some important insight into East German society.

In the West, there was a more open process of change in which individuals, groups, political parties, and institutional actors struggled to get history right. The state quickly dominated discussions about resistance and collaboration. In contrast, smaller social groups first memorialized the persecution of the Jews. But whatever the agents and their tools of rhetorical engagement, the slow and ever-changing makeup of the society through generational turnover played a key role in the changing boundaries of the cultural matrix (see chart 2). The passing of the Nazi generation, a generation that had directly experienced the Nazi regime as at least young adults, from the labor force in the 1980s and the society as a whole in the 1990s significantly opened the possibilities for reinterpreting the past. As this research has shown, this generation was anything but homogeneous, but nonetheless had some general common traits that, among other things, promoted the development of the two central postwar mythologies. As they left their leadership positions in the political parties, the directorships of the public television stations, the editorial boards of the leading newspapers, and the controlling factors of the movie industry, individuals without living memories of the war and the Nazi regime were being handed the reins of the institutions that guide a great deal of social discussion about the past. This generational turnover is a gradual process, and there is no neat or clean separation from one group to the next as many of the values and perspectives of the older generation are transmitted to the younger generation. It is then this new generation, without lived experience in the Nazi past, that will only be able to formulate a sense of self vis-à-vis the national past as a mediated experience. This can be mediated to them through societal level discussions at the macrolevel or through discussions within more intimate spheres at the microlevel. A very similar process can be seen with Israel's new historians, who have set about challenging many of the foundational myths of the state or the situation in France during the 1970s, when the French began to reevaluate the period of the Vichy regime.

In the end, the fascination that drew me into this project at the beginning remains. Why should the past for the individual or the collective matter as much as it does? Why do we appear incapable of mastering or overcoming our pasts? How do we set about reinterpreting our individual histories as well as those of our communities? Many, if not all, of us have difficulty avoiding the role of the fool in the old Jewish proverb "Only a fool trips over what is already behind him." It seems that most of us and our societies continue to stumble forward, bound by a need to understand ourselves as rooted in the past but also, at times, wanting to set ourselves free of it. Nations are nothing unless they are rooted in the past and seen as a continuous historical community. Individuals cannot have any sense of self without memory. The process by which individuals and collectivities come to see themselves and to identify themselves are bound up with each other. This is the process of formulating collective memories and getting history right.

Appendix: Charts and Chart Notes

CHART 1

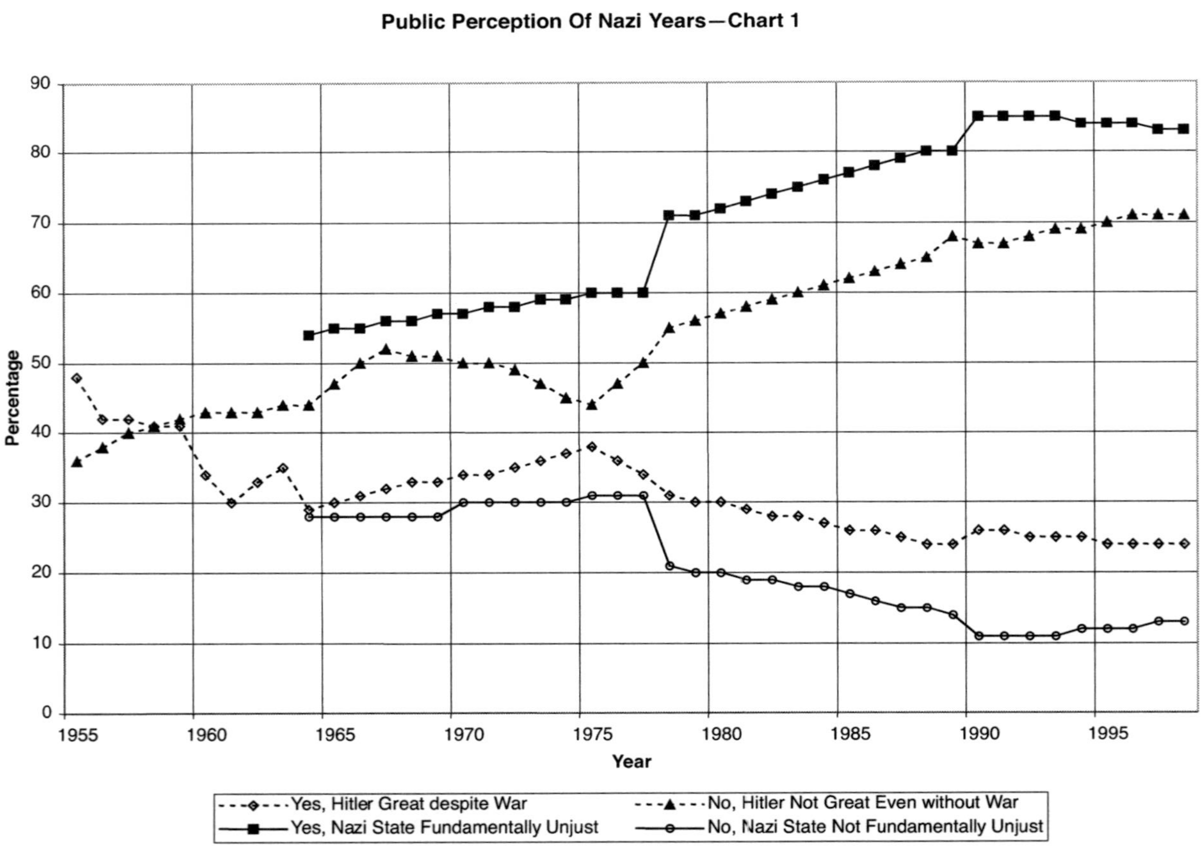

Public Perception Of Nazi Years—Chart 1
Percentage
90
80
70
60
50
40
30
20
10
0
1955
1960
1965
1970
1975
1980
1985
1990
1995
Year
Yes, Hitler Great despite War
No, Hitler Not Great Even without War
Yes, Nazi State Fundamentally Unjust
No, Nazi State Not Fundamentally Unjust

Question 1: “Everything which was built up between 1933 and 1939 and much more was destroyed through the war. Would you say that Hitler, without the war, would have been one of the greatest German statesmen?”

Full Series Titles:
Yes, Hitler one of Germany’s greatest statesmen.
No, Hitler not one of Germany’s greatest statesmen.

Question 2: “When someone says, the National Socialist state was an unjust state, a criminal regime: after what you know today about the Hitler times or have experienced personally, would you say that it is true to say it was an unjust state, a criminal state, or can one not say that?”

Full Series Titles:
National Socialist State was unjust.
National Socialist State was not unjust.

Source: Elisabeth Noelle-Neumann and Renate Köcher eds., *Allensbach Jahrbuch der Demoskopie 1993–1997* (Munich: K.G. Saur, 1997), 514–15.

Chart 2

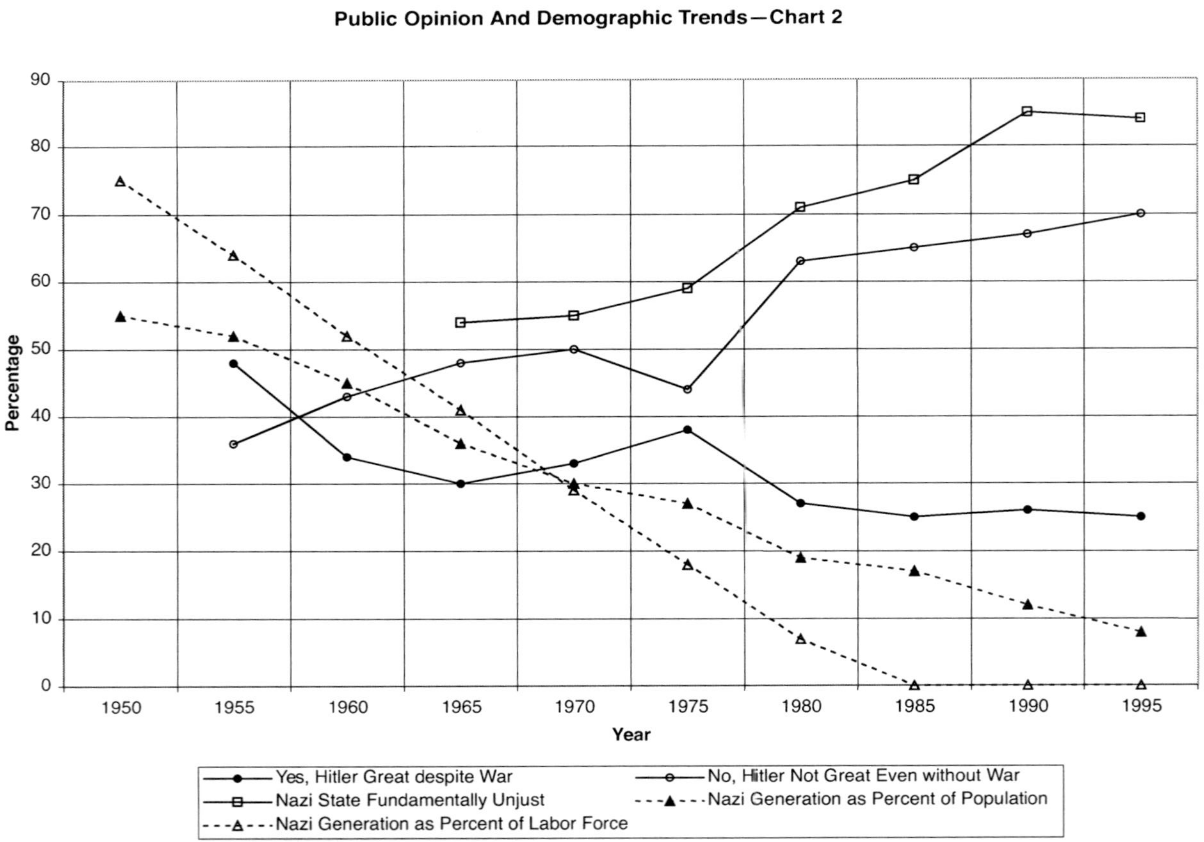
Public Opinion And Demographic Trends—Chart 2
Percentage
90
80
70
60
50
40
30
20
10
0
1950
1955
1960
1965
1970
1975
1980
1985
1990
1995
Year
Yes, Hitler Great despite War
No, Hitler Not Great Even without War
Nazi State Fundamentally Unjust
Nazi Generation as Percent of Population
Nazi Generation as Percent of Labor Force

Full Series Titles:

Yes, Hitler one of Germany's greatest statesmen.
No, Hitler not one of Germany's greatest statesmen.
National Socialist State was unjust.
National Socialist State was not unjust.
Nazi Generation as Percent of the Total Population
Nazi Generation as Percent of the Total Labor Force

Source: Demographic data based upon U.S. Bureau of the Census, International Data Base; online source: http://www.census.gov/cgi-bin/ipcsprd.

Chart 3

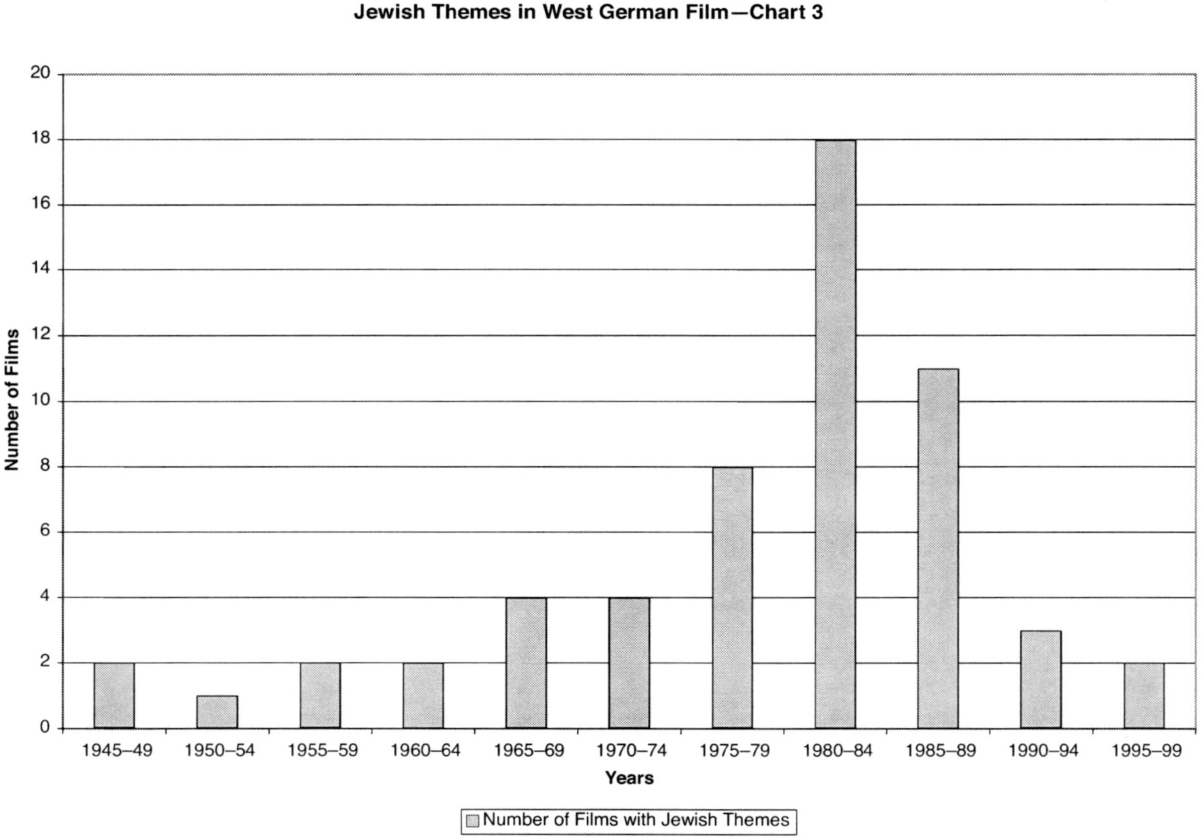

Sources: See filmography section of bibliography

CHART 4

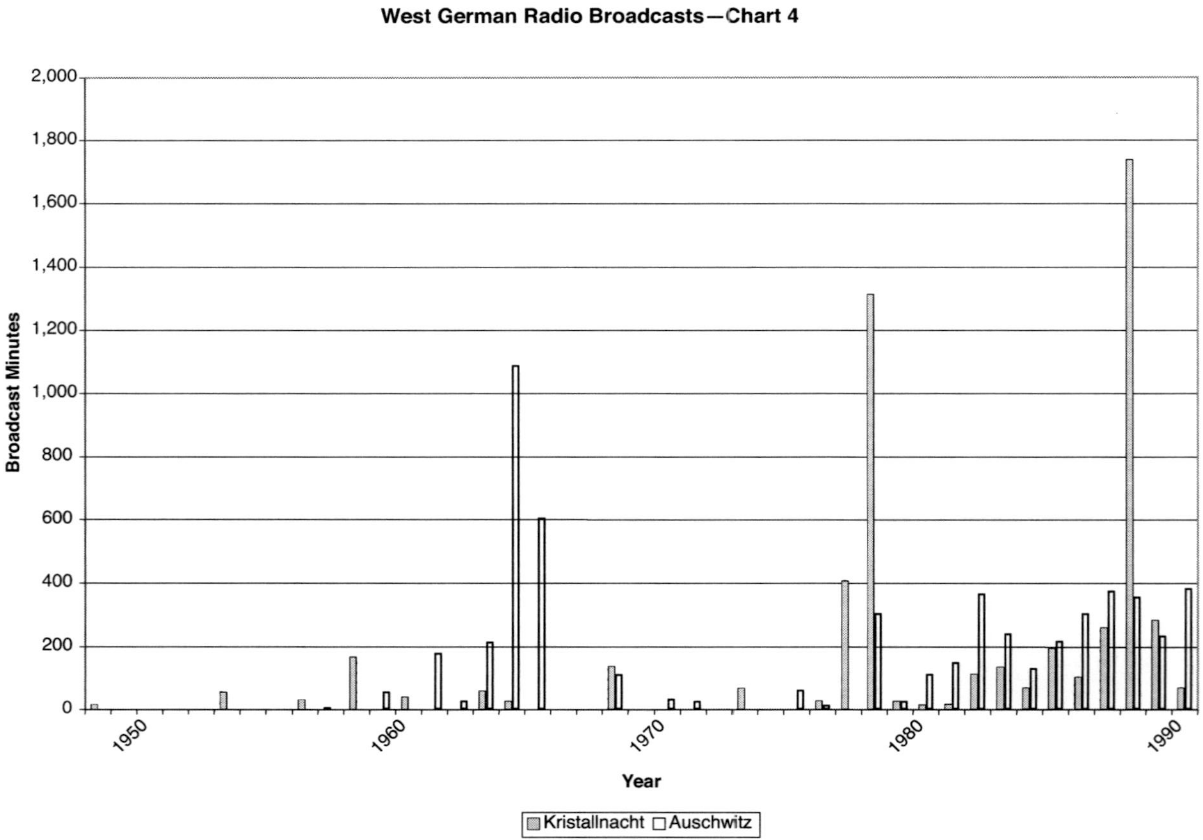

West German Radio Broadcasts—Chart 4
Broadcast Minutes
2,000
1,800
1,600
1,400
1,200
1,000
800
600
400
200
0
1950
1960
1970
1980
1990
Year
Kristallnacht
Auschwitz

Source: Data compiled from

Judeverfolgung und jüdisches Leben unter den Bedingungen der nationalsozialistischen Gewaltherrschaft: Tondokumente und Rundfunksendungen 1947–1990. Zusammengestellt und bearbeitet von Felix Kresing-Wulf unter Mitwirkung von Eva-Maria Mühlmann. Veröffentlichungen des Deutschen Rundfunkarchivs Band 8 (Verlag für Berlin-Brandenburg, 1997).

Important: This chart includes only those radio broadcasts that are still in the archives. Not all of the material was archived. This is particularly true for the 1950s and 1960s, but much less so for the later years. The chart shows the number of archived program minutes related to either Kristallnacht or Auschwitz.

CHART 5

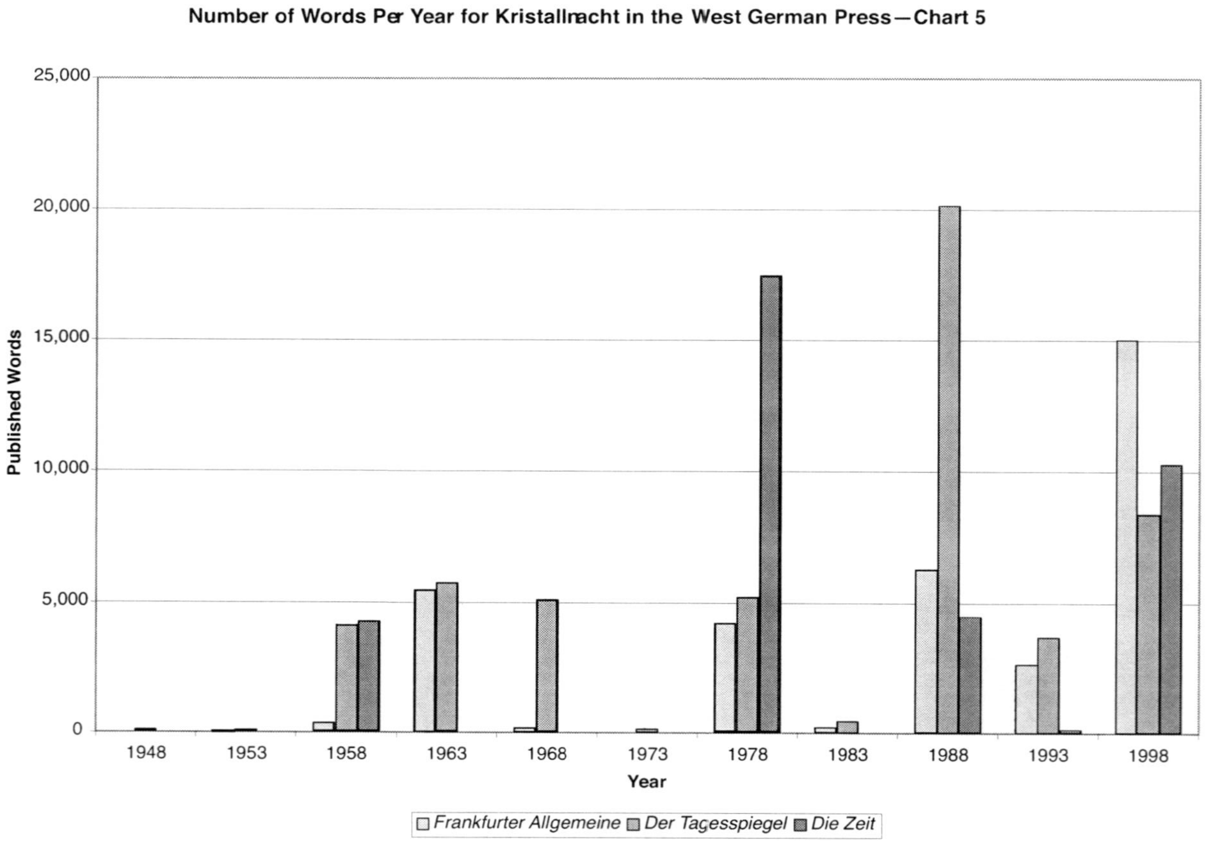
Number of Words Per Year for Kristallnacht in the West German Press—Chart 5
25,000
20,000
15,000
10,000
5,000
0
Published Words
1948
1953
1958
1963
1968
1973
1978
1983
1988
1993
1998
Year
Frankfurter Allgemeine
Der Tagesspiegel
Die Zeit

CHART 6

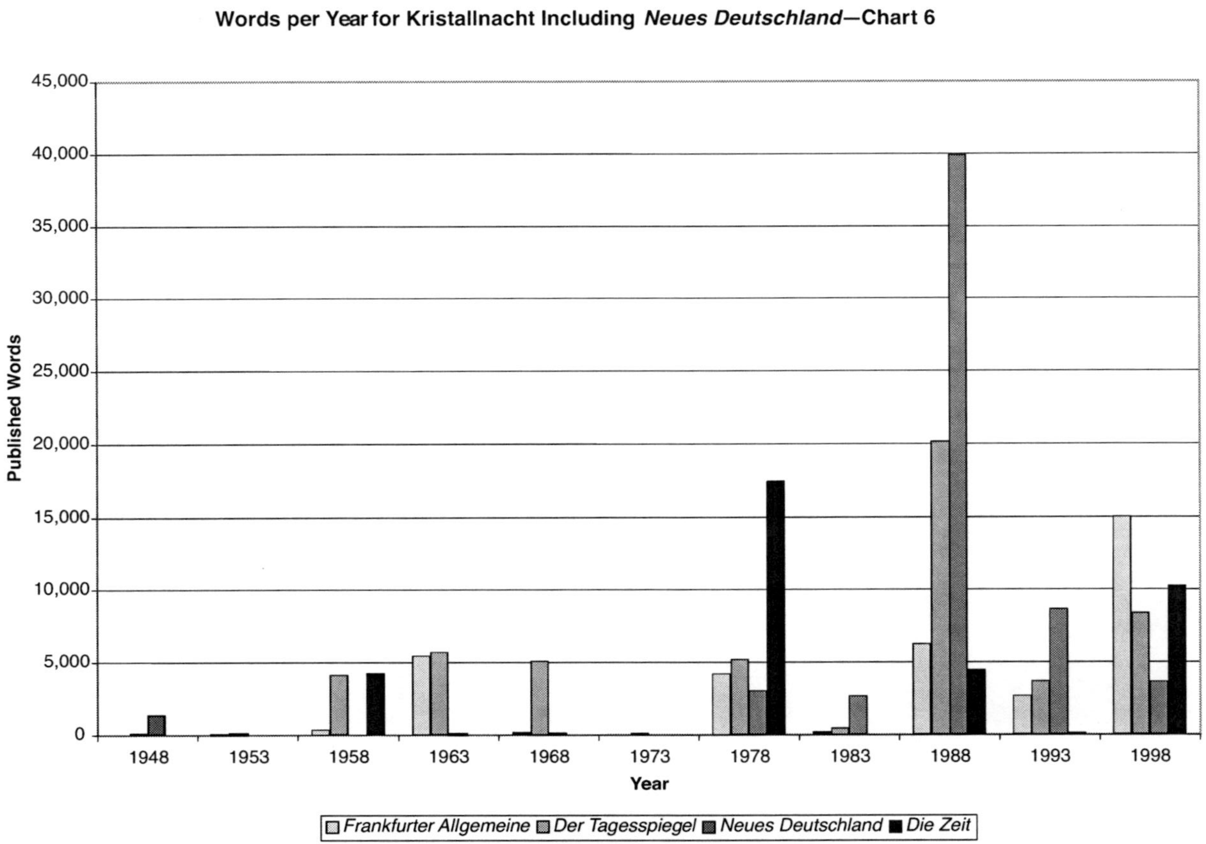
Words per Year for Kristallnacht Including *Neues Deutschland*—Chart 6
Published Words
45,000
40,000
35,000
30,000
25,000
20,000
15,000
10,000
5,000
0
1948
1953
1958
1963
1968
1973
1978
1983
1988
1993
1998
Year
Frankfurter Allgemeine
Der Tagesspiegel
Neues Deutschland
Die Zeit

CHART 7

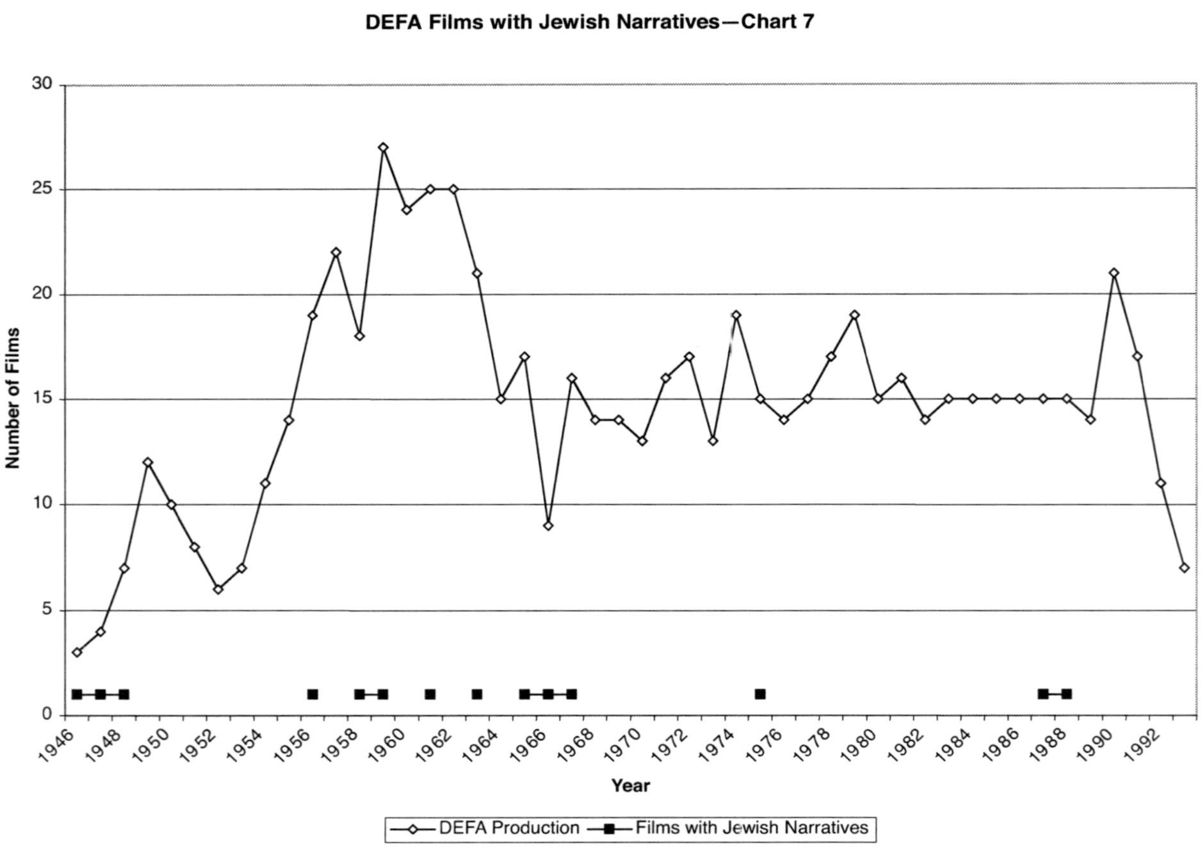

Source: See filmography section of bibliography

CHART 8

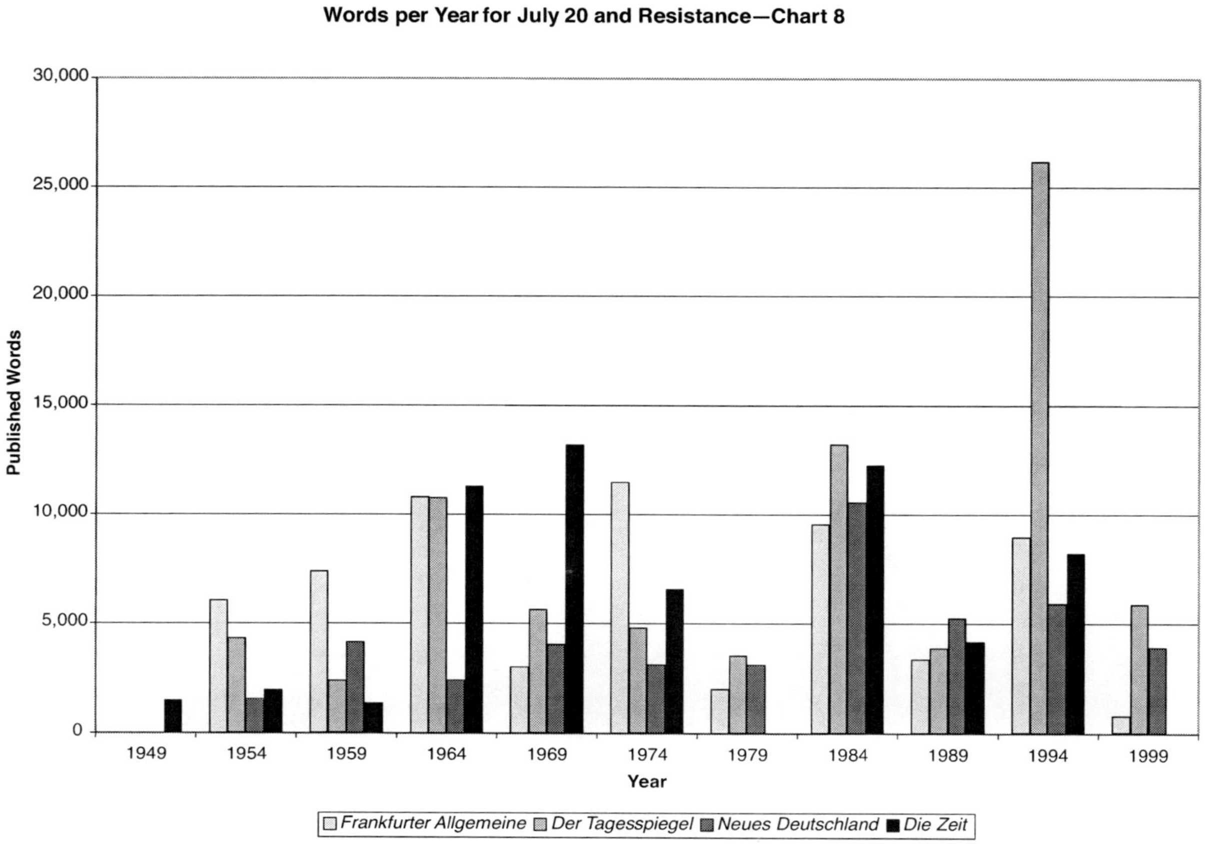

Words per Year for July 20 and Resistance—Chart 8
Published Words
30,000
25,000
20,000
15,000
10,000
5,000
0
1949
1954
1959
1964
1969
1974
1979
1984
1989
1994
1999
Year
Frankfurter Allgemeine
Der Tagesspiegel
Neues Deutschland
Die Zeit

CHART 9

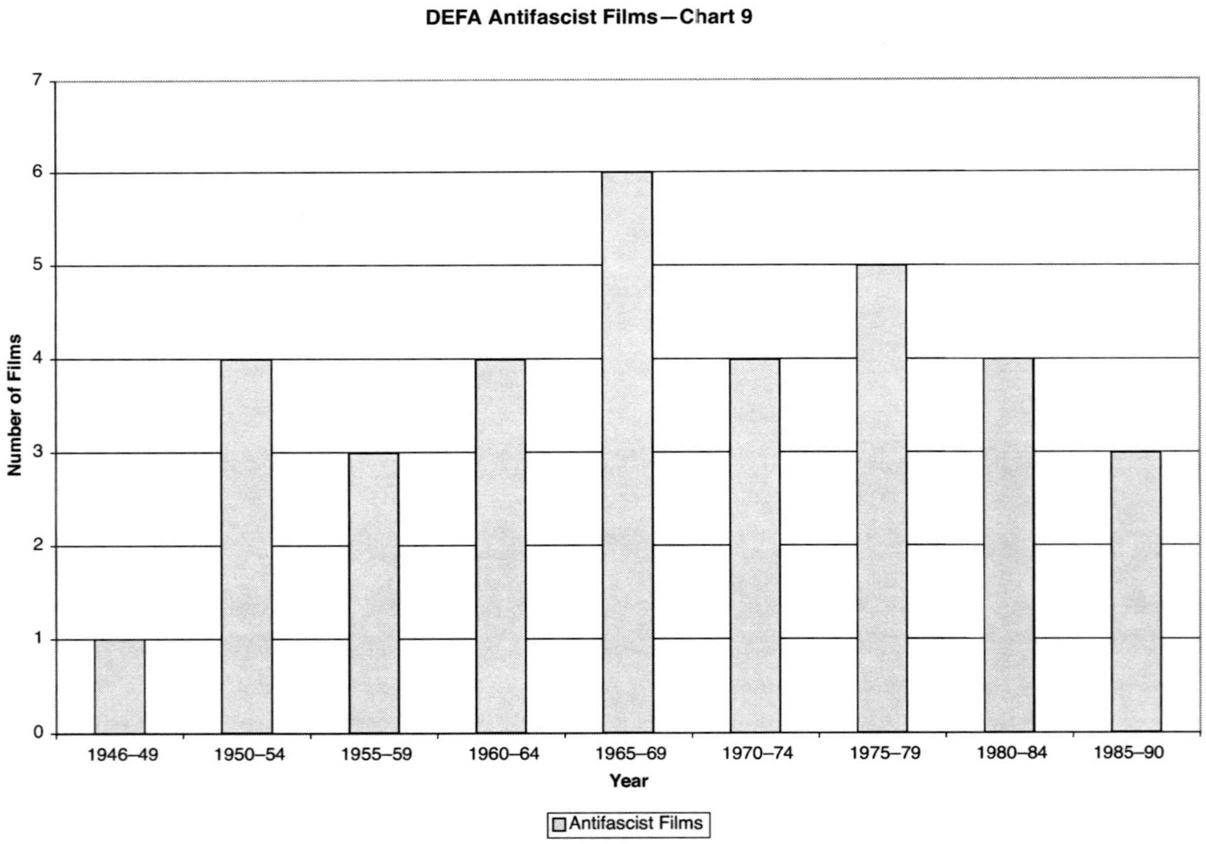

Source: See filmography section of bibliography

Chart 10

Words per Year for June 17 and Division/Unity—Chart 10

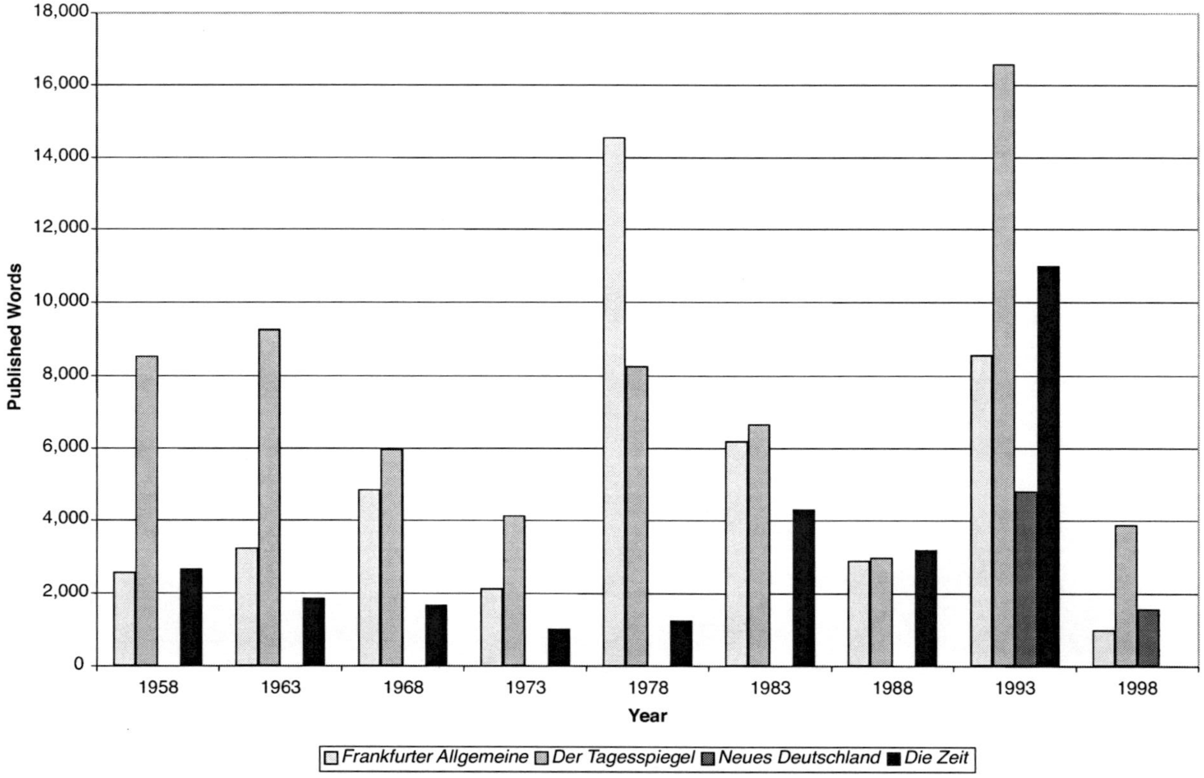

CHART 11

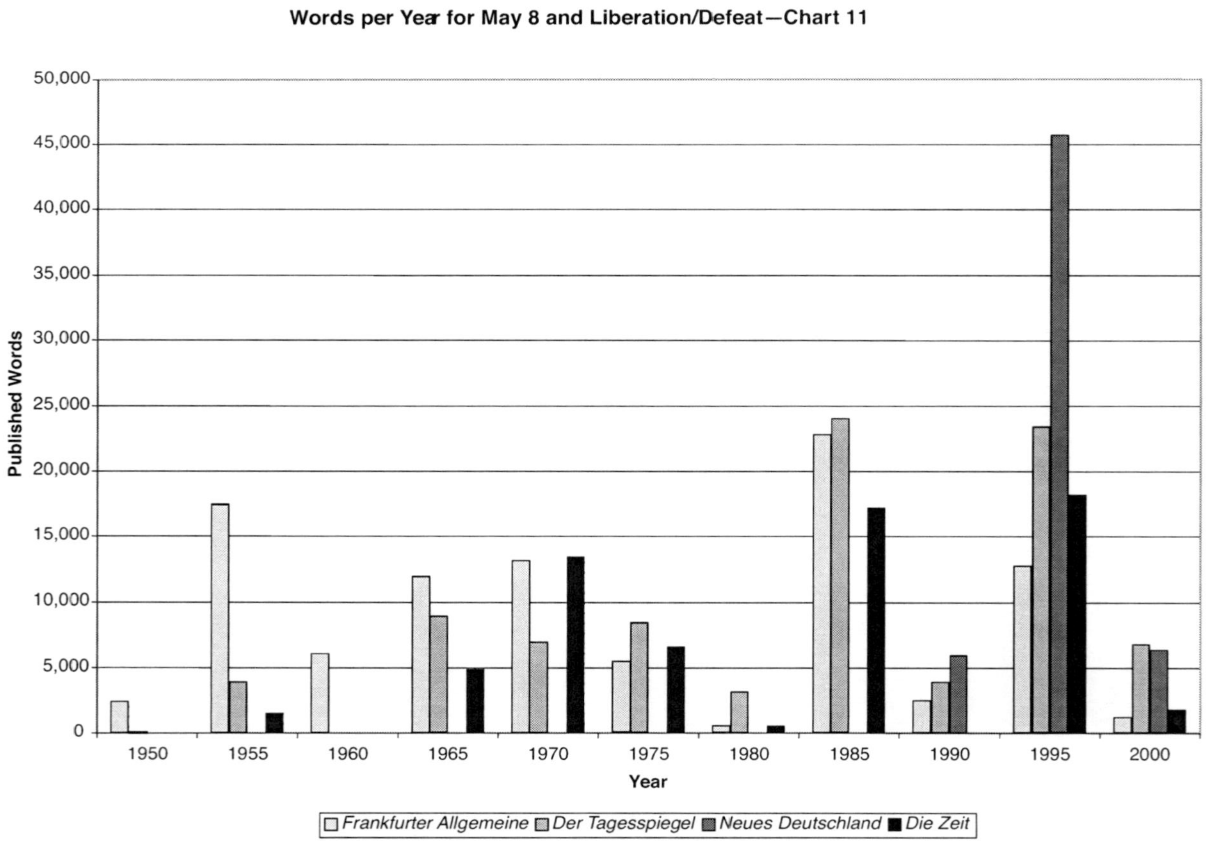

Neus Deutschland data only included for 1990, 1995, and 2000. See page 185.

Notes

Chapter 1. Collective Memory

1. Ann Norton, *95 Theses on Politics, Culture, and Method* (New Haven, CT: Yale University Press, 2004), 1–12. Jeffrey C. Alexander, "Analytic Debates: Understanding the Relative Autonomy of Culture," in *Culture and Society: Contemporary Debates*, ed. Jeffrey C. Alexander and Steven Seidman (Cambridge: Cambridge University Press, 1990), 1–27.

2. Ronald Inglehart, *Culture Shift in Advanced Industrial Society* (Princeton, NJ: Princeton University Press, 1990). Gabriel A. Almond and Sidney Verba, *The Civic Culture: Political Attitudes and Democracy in Five Nations* (Princeton, NJ: Princeton University Press, 1963).

3. Mary Douglas, *Natural Symbols: Explorations in Cosmology* (London: Barrie & Rockliff, 1970; London: Routledge, 1996), 7; see also Claude Lévi-Strauss, *Structural Anthropology*, trans. Claire Jacobson and Brooke Grundfest Schoepf (New York: Basic Books, 1963), 230.

4. There is a vast collective memory literature today. Particularly notable works include Henry Rousso, *The Vichy Syndrome: History and Memory in France since 1944*, trans. Arthur Goldhammer (Cambridge, MA: Harvard University Press, 1991); Yael Zerubavel, *Recovered Roots: Collective Memory and the Making of Israeli National Tradition* (Chicago: University of Chicago Press, 1995); Jeffrey K. Olick, ed., *States of Memory: Continuities, Conflicts and Transformations in National Retrospection* (Durham, NC: Duke University Press, 2003); Paul Ricoeur, *Memory, History, Forgetting*, trans. Kathleen Blamey and David Pellauer (Chicago: University of Chicago Press, 2004); Anne Dolan, *Commemorating the Irish Civil War: History and Memory, 1923–2000* (Cambridge: Cambridge University Press, 2003); Richard Ned Lebow, Wulf Kansteiner, and Claudio Fogu, eds., *The Politics of Memory in Postwar Europe* (Durham, NC: Duke University Press, 2006).

5. Andrei S. Markovits and Simon Reich, *The German Predicament: Memory and Power in the New Europe* (Ithaca, NY: Cornell University Press, 1997); Anne Sa'adah, *Germany's Second Chance: Trust, Justice, and Democratization* (Cambridge, MA: Harvard University Press, 1998); Paloma Aguilar, *Memory and Amnesia: The Role of the Spanish Civil War in the Transition to Democracy*, trans. Mark Oakley (New York: Berghahn Books, 2002); David Art, *The Politics of the Nazi Past in Germany and Austria* (New York: Cambridge University Press, 2006); Marc Howard Ross, *Cultural Contestation in Ethnic Conflict* (Cambridge: Cambridge University Press, 2007); Martin O. Heisler, ed., "The Politics of History in Comparative Perspective," special issue, *Annals of the American Academy of Political and Social Science* 617 (May 2008).

6. Mark A. Wolfgram, "Das kollektive Gedächtnis als theoretisches Konzept aktueller Forschung," trans. Cornelia Dörries, *Berliner Journal für Soziologie* 9, no. 4 (1999): 567–75.

7. Marc Howard Ross, "Culture and Identity in Comparative Political Analysis," in *Comparative Politics: Rationality, Culture, and Structure*, ed. Mark Irving Lichbach and Alan S. Zuckerman (Cambridge: Cambridge University Press, 1997), 42–80.

8. Other examples include Jeffrey Herf, *Divided Memory: The Nazi Past in the Two Germanys* (Cambridge, MA: Harvard University Press, 1997); Sa'adah, *Germany's Second Chance;* Mary Fulbrook, *German National Identity after the Holocaust* (Cambridge, UK: Polity Press, 1999).

9. Wulf Kansteiner, *In Pursuit of German Memory: History, Television, and Politics after Auschwitz* (Athens: Ohio University Press, 2006); Art, *Politics of the Nazi Past.*

10. Mark A. Wolfgram, "The Holocaust through the Prism of East German Television: Collective Memory and Audience Perceptions," *Holocaust and Genocide Studies* 20, no. 1 (Spring 2006): 57–79.

11. Daniel Jonah Goldhagen, *Hitler's Willing Executioners: Ordinary Germans and the Holocaust* (New York: Vintage Books, 1997).

12. Peter Novick, *The Holocaust in American Life* (Boston: Mariner Books, 1999), 213.

13. Robert G. Moeller, *War Stories: The Search for a Usable Past in the Federal Republic of Germany* (Berkeley: University of California Press, 2001); Rudy Koshar, *From Monuments to Traces: Artifacts of German Memory, 1870–1990* (Berkeley:University of California Press, 2000).

14. Eric Hobsbawm and Terence Ranger, eds., *The Invention of Tradition* (New York: Cambridge University Press, 1983). For a very helpful theoretical overview of the field, see Barbara A. Misztal, *Theories of Social Remembering* (Maidenhead, UK: Open University Press, 2003), especially chapter 3.

15. Ross, *Cultural Contestation in Ethnic Conflict*, xiv.

16. Abner Cohen, *Two-Dimensional Man: An Essay on the Anthropology of Power and Symbolism in Complex Society* (Berkeley: University of California Press, 1974), 7–8.

17. Ibid., 13.

18. Ibid., 23.

19. Jeffrey C. Alexander and Jason L. Mast, "Introduction: Symbolic Action in Theory and Practice: The Cultural Pragmatics of Symbolic Action," in *Social Performance: Symbolic Action, Cultural Pragmatics, and Ritual*, ed. Jeffrey C. Alexander, Bernhard Giesen, and Jason L. Mast (Cambridge: Cambridge University Press, 2006), 16.

20. Jeffrey C. Alexander, *The Meanings of Social Life: A Cultural Sociology* (Oxford: Oxford University Press, 2003), 12.

21. David I. Kertzer, *Ritual, Politics, and Power* (New Haven, CT: Yale University Press, 1988), 12.

22. W. J. T. Mitchell, *Picture Theory: Essays on Verbal and Visual Representation* (Chicago: University of Chicago Press, 1994).

23. Norton, *95 Theses*, 2004.

24. Ian Lustick, "History, Historiography, and Political Science: Multiple Historical Records and the Problem of Selection Bias," *American Political Science Review* 90, no. 3 (September 1996): 605–18.

25. F. R. Ankersmit, *Narrative Logic: A Semantic Analysis of the Historian's Language* (Boston: Kluwer, 1983); Hayden White, *Metahistory: The Historical Imagination in Nineteenth Century Europe* (Baltimore: Johns Hopkins University Press, 1973); Hayden White, *The Content of the Form: Narrative Discourse and Historical Representation* (Baltimore: Johns Hopkins University Press, 1987).

26. Gary King, Robert O. Keohane, and Sidney Verba, *Designing Social Inquiry: Scientific Inference in Qualitative Research* (Princeton, NJ: Princeton University Press, 1994).

27. Pierre Bourdieu, *Language and Symbolic Power/Pierre Bourdieu*, ed. John B.

Thompson, trans. Gino Raymond and Matthew Adamson (Cambridge, MA: Harvard University Press, 1991); Anthony Giddens, *Central Problems in Social Theory: Action, Structure and Contradiction in Social Analysis* (Cambridge: Cambridge University Press, 1979).

28. Eric A. Johnson, *Nazi Terror: The Gestapo, Jews, and Ordinary Germans* (New York: Basic Books, 1999); Mark A. Wolfgram, "Rediscovering Narratives of German Resistance: Opposing the Nazi 'Terror-State,'" *Rethinking History* 10, no. 2 (June 2006): 201–19.

29. Herf, *Divided Memory*, 1997. For another study of elite discourse, see Art, *The Politics of the Nazi Past*, 2006.

30. Gesine Schwan, *Politik und Schuld: Die zerstörische Macht des Schweigens* (Frankfurt am Main: Fischer Taschenbuch Verlag, 1997); Harald Welzer, Sabine Moller, and Karoline Tschuggnall, *"Opa war kein Nazi": Nationalsozialismus und Holocaust im Familiengedächtnis* (Frankfurt am Main: Fischer, 2002).

31. Douglas James Davies, *A Brief History of Death* (Malden, MA: Blackwell, 2005).

32. Leon Festinger, *A Theory of Cognitive Dissonance* (Stanford, CA: Stanford University Press, 1957); Carol Travis and Elliot Aronson, *Mistakes Were Made (But Not by Me): Why We Justify Foolish Beliefs, Bad Decisions, and Hurtful Acts* (Orlando, FL: Harcourt, 2007).

33. Jay Winter, *Remembering War: The Great War between Memory and History in the Twentieth Century* (New Haven, CT: Yale University Press, 2006).

34. Jeffrey C. Alexander and Bernhard Giesen, "From Reduction to Linkage: The Long View of the Micro-Macro Debate," in *The Micro-Macro Link*, ed. Jeffrey C. Alexander, Bernhard Giesen, Richard Münch, and Neil J. Smelser (Berkeley: University of California Press, 1987), 1–42; Margaret S. Archer, *Culture and Agency: The Place of Culture in Social Theory*, revised edition (Cambridge: Cambridge University Press, 1996).

35. Other scholars have focused on the role of school textbooks and educational trips to the concentration camps. Therefore, I have not engaged school textbooks directly in my own work. For a study of the minimal effect trips to a concentration camp had on youth, see Renata Barlog-Scholz, *Historisches Wissen über die national-sozialistischen Konzentrationslager bei deutschen Jugendlichen* (Frankfurt am Main: Peter Lang, 1994). For studies of textbooks, see Dr. Rudolf Raasch, *Zeitgeschichte und Nationalbewußtsein* (Berlin-West: Hermann Luchterhand Verlag, 1964); Peter Dudek, *"Der Rückblick auf die Vergangenheit wird sich nicht vermeiden lassen": Zur pädagogischen Verarbeitung des Nationalsozialismus in Deutschland (1945–1990)* (Opladen: Westdeutscher Verlag, 1995).

36. Wulf Kansteiner, "Finding Meaning in Memory: A Methodological Critique of Collective Memory Studies," *History and Theory* 41 (May 2002): 179–97; Mark A. Wolfgram, "Das kollektive Gedächtnis als theoretisches Konzept aktueller Forschung," trans. Cornelia Dörries, *Berliner Journal für Soziologie* 9, no. 4 (1999): 567–75.

37. Daniel L. Schacter, *Searching for Memory: The Brain, the Mind, and the Past* (New York: Basic Books, 1996); Daniel L. Schacter, ed., *Memory Distortion: How Minds, Brains and Societies Reconstruct the Past* (Cambridge, MA: Harvard University Press, 1997).

38. Maurice Halbwachs, *On Collective Memory*, ed. and trans. Lewis A. Coser (Chicago: University of Chicago Press, 1992).

39. Andrea Liss, *Trespassing through Shadows: Memory, Photography, and the Holocaust* (Minneapolis: University of Minnesota Press, 1998).

40. Arnold van Gennep, *The Rites of Passage*, trans. Monika B. Vizedom and Gabrielle L. Caffee (London: Routledge & Kegan Paul, 1960); Victor Turner, *The Forest of Symbols: Aspects of Ndembu Ritual* (Ithaca, NY: Cornell University Press, 1967), 93–94; Anthony P. Cohen, *The Symbolic Construction of Community* (London: Routledge, 1985); Clifford Geertz, *The Interpretation of Cultures* (London: Hutchinson, 1975).

41. Rogers M. Smith, *Stories of Peoplehood: The Politics and Morals of Political Membership* (Cambridge: Cambridge University Press, 2003), 160.
42. *Lost King of the Maya*, Dir. David Stewart. Nova-PBS, April 16, 2002.
43. David Lan, *Guns and Rain: Guerrillas and Spirit Mediums in Zimbabwe* (Berkeley: University of California Press, 1985), in particular chapter 4, "The Great Spectacle of the Past."
44. Barry Schwartz, *Abraham Lincoln and the Forge of National Memory* (Chicago: University of Chicago Press, 2000).
45. Bruce L. Berg, *Qualitative Research Methods for the Social Sciences*, 5th ed. (Boston: Pearson, 2004), 265–97.
46. *Kristallnacht* is the term the Nazis originally gave to these events, which focuses attention on the crimes against property rather than persons. See the discussion in chapter 3.

Chapter 2. View from the East

1. Gerhard Paul and Klaus-Michael Mallmann, eds., *Die Gestapo: Mythos und Realität* (Darmstadt: Wissenschaftliche Buchgesellschaft, 1995).
2. Eric Johnson, *Nazi Terror: The Gestapo, Jews and Ordinary Germans* (New York: Basic Books, 1999), 18–20.
3. Ibid., 261, 321, and 325. See also Eric A. Johnson and Karl-Heinz Reuband, *What We Knew: Terror, Mass Murder, and Everyday Life in Germany* (Cambridge: Basic Books, 2005), chapters 9, 12.
4. Robert Gellately, *Backing Hitler: Consent and Coercion in Nazi Germany* (Oxford: Oxford University Press, 2001), chapter 10.
5. Norbert Frei, ed., *Hitlers Eliten nach 1945* (Munich: Deutscher Taschenbuch Verlag, 2003), 270.
6. Peter J. Humphreys, *Media and Media Policy in Germany: The Press and Broadcasting since 1945*, 2d ed. (Oxford: Berg, 1994), 286.
7. Anja Kreutz and Susanne Vollberg, *Beiträge zur DDR-Fernseh- und Magazingeschichte: Eine kommentierte Auswahlbibliographie* (Frankfurt am Main: Peter Lang, 1998), 13.
8. Heinz Niemann, *Meinungsforschung in der DDR: Die geheimen Berichte des Instituts für Meinungsforschung an das Politbüro der SED* (Cologne: Bund-Verlag, 1993).
9. Gunter Holzweissig, *Massenmedien in der DDR* (Berlin: Verlag Gebr. Holzapfel, 1989), 62.
10. Christa Braumann, "Fernsehforschung zwischen Parteilichkeit und Objektivität: Zur Zuschauerforschung in der ehemaligen DDR," *Rundfunk und Fernsehen* 42 (1994): 533.
11. DRA ArNr: H008–02–04/0050 loose material. Braumann, "Fernsehforschung," 531.
12. Christa Oehme, "Die Zuschauerforschung als ein Instrument der Leitung, Planung, Programm- und Sendungsgestaltung des Fernsehens der DDR—ihre Möglichkeiten und Grenzen—dargestellt an empirischen Forschungsergebnissen" (dissertation, Akademie für Gesellschaftswissenschaften beim ZK der SED, Institute für Marxistisch-Leninistische Kultur- und Kunstwissenschaften [Berlin, 1978]), 114.
13. Wolfgram, "Holocaust through the Prism," 57–79.
14. Elisabeth Noelle-Neumann, *The Spiral of Silence: Public Opinion, Our Social Skin* (Chicago: University of Chicago Press, 1993).

15. Lutz Niethammer, "Erfahrungen und Strukturen: Prolegomena zu einer Geschichte der Gesellschaft der DDR," in *Sozialgeschichte der DDR*, ed. Hartmut Kaelble, Jürgen Kocka, and Hartmut Zwahr (Stuttgart: Klett-Cotta, 1994), 111.

16. Braumann, "Fernsehforschung," 528.

17. I have offered a more detailed critique of the data elsewhere. Wolfgram, "Holocaust through the Prism," 57–79.

18. Michael Meyen, *Einschalten, Umschalten, Ausschalten? Das Fernsehen im DDR-Alltag* (Leipzig: Leipziger Universitätsverlag, 2003), 10.

19. Ibid., 95.

20. Ibid., 93.

21. Mark A. Wolfgram, "The Legacies of Memory: The Third Reich in Unified Germany," *German Politics & Society* 21, no. 3 (Fall 2003): 89–100.

22. "Gedenkgottesdienst in den Synagogen," *Neues Deutschland*, November 9, 1948: 6.

23. Herf, *Divided Memory*, 40.

24. Ibid., 99.

25. Paul Merker, "Die Hintergründe der Kristallnacht," *Neues Deutschland*, November 10, 1948: 3.

26. Anna Foa, *The Jews of Europe after the Black Death*, trans. Andrea Grover (Berkeley: University of California Press, 2000); Ruth Gay, *The Jews of Germany: A Historical Portrait* (New Haven, CT: Yale University Press, 1992).

27. Thomas C. Fox, *Stated Memory: East Germany and the Holocaust* (Rochester, NY: Camden House, 1999), 27–30.

28. Herf, *Divided Memory*, 160.

29. Günter Morsch, ed., *Von der Erinnerung zum Monument: Die Entstehungsgeschichte der Nationalen Mahn- und Gedenkstätte Sachsenhausen* (Oranienburg: Stiftung Brandenburgische Gedenkstätten, 1996).

30. "Gedenkstunde im jüdischen Friedenstempel," *Neues Deutschland*, November 10, 1968: 2.

31. *Die Bilder des Zeugen Schattmann*, Dir. Kurt Jung-Alsen. DEFA, 1971. DRA Lagernr.: AC 5040 (part 1), AC 5041 (part 2), AC 5042 (part 3), and AC 5043 (part 4).

32. Peter Edel, *Die Bilder des Zeugen Schattmann: Ein Roman über deutsche Vergangenheit und Gegenwart* (Berlin: Verlag der Nation, 1969).

33. Peter Edel, "An meine Leser, Hörer und Zuschauer: Zur Wiederaufführung des vierteiligen Fernsehfilms 'Die Bilder des Zeugen Schattmann,'" *FF Dabei* no. 46, November 8–14, 1982: 6–7.

34. Norbert Frei, ed., *Hitlers Eliten nach 1945* (Munich: Deutscher Taschenbuch Verlag, 2003).

35. Heide Fehrenbach, *Cinema in Democratizing Germany: Reconstructing National Identity after Hitler* (Chapel Hill: University of North Carolina Press, 1995), 5.

36. Historians now dismiss this as a myth. Novick, *Holocaust*, 23.

37. DRA ArNr: H 008–02–04/0052. Report from June 6, 1972, dated June 13, 1972.

38. Programmdirecktion Zuschauerforschung dated June 5, 1972. DRA ArNr: H 008–02–04/0052, 10–11.

39. "Jüdischer Friedhof wird würdig ausgestaltet," *Neues Deutschland*, November 10, 1978: 8.

40. "Berliner Synagoge wurde umfassend rekonstruiert," *Neues Deutschland*, November 9, 1978: 8.

41. Professor Kurt Pätzold, "Der Pogrom, der Profit und der Weg in den Tod," *Neues Deutschland*, November 9, 1978: 4.

42. *Die Nacht der Pogrome*, DDR-F, 1982. DRA Lagernr.: FAZ 02198.

43. *Als die Synagogen brannten*, Dir. Guenter Wittenbecher. DDR-F, 1988. DRA Lagernr.: AC 0364.

44. DRA, "Bericht der 47. Programmwoche (14. 11.–20.11. 1988)." ArNr.: H 023–00–02/0122, 5.

45. Lutz Niethammer, "Juden und Russen im Gedächtnis der Deutschen," in *Der historische Ort des Nationalsozialismus: Annäherungen*, ed. Walter H. Pehle (Frankfurt am Main: Fischer Taschenbuch Verlag, 1990), 132.

46. "Der jungen Generation Erfahrungen weitergeben," *Neues Deutschland*, November 10, 1988: 3.

47. Dieter Brückner, Günter Stechow, and Wolfgang Spickermann, "Bewegende Begegnung Erich Honeckers mit jüdischen Persönlichkeiten im Staatsrat," *Neues Deutschland*, November 9, 1988: 1.

48. Erich Honecker, "Verpflichtung zu einer Politik des Humanismus, des Friedens und der Völkerverständigung," *Neues Deutschland*, November 9, 1988: 2.

49. Marie Lavigne, "The Economics of the Transition Process: What Have We Learned?" *Problems of Post-Communism* 47, no. 4 (July/August 2000): 16–23.

50. Jörg Roesler, "Privatization by Treuhand and the Restructuring of East German Industry—a Model for Middle Europe?" (paper, Prague, December 7–9, 1993).

51. Humphreys, *Media*, 314.

52. Ibid., 296, 300.

53. Hermann Kant, "Hauptsachen," *Neues Deutschland*, November 9, 1993: 3.

54. René Helig interview with Uli Faber, "Die, die nicht sehen die Schrift an der Wand . . ." *Neues Deutschland*, November 8, 1993: 3. For a more detailed discussion of this debate and many others since unification, see Bill Niven, *Facing the Nazi Past: United Germany and the Legacy of the Third Reich* (London: Routledge, 2002).

55. Jürgen Amendt, "'Verziehen, nicht vergessen,'" *Neues Deutschland*, November 8, 1993: 3.

56. Helfried Liesch, "Auf dem Weg ins 4. Reich?" *Neues Deutschland*, November 9, 1993: 1.

57. Professor Dr. Wolfgang Benz, "Der Novemberpogrom," *Neues Deutschland*, November 9, 1993: 9.

58. "Bubis: Neue Kultur des Wegschauens," *Neues Deutschland*, November 9, 1998: 4; "Gedenken zum 60. Jahrestag der Pogrome," *Neues Deutschland*, November 10, 1998: 1.

59. Wolfgang Hübner, "Sonntagsreden," *Neues Deutschland*, November 10, 1998: 2.

60. *DEFA* is the acronym for *Deutsche Film AG*, or German Film Inc.

61. Conflicting dates are given for this. Some sources list May 13, 1945 while others list May 17.

62. Thomas Heinmann, *DEFA, Künstler und SED-Kulturpolitik: Zum Verhältnis von Kulturpolitik und Filmproduktion in der SBZ/DDR 1945 bis 1959*. Beiträge zur Film- und Fernsehwissenschaft BFF, ed. Peter Hoff and Dieter Wiedemann (Potsdam: Hochschule für Film und Fernsehen 'Konrad Wolf,' 1994), 25–26.

63. Martin Brady, "Discussion with Kurt Maetzig," in *DEFA: East German Cinema, 1946–1992*, ed. Seán Allan and John Sandford (New York: Berghahn Books, 1999), 83.

64. Heinmann, *DEFA*, 130.

65. Brady, "Discussion," 85.

66. Seán Allan, "DEFA: An Historical Overview," in *DEFA: East German Cinema, 1946–1992*, ed. Seán Allan and Joahn Sandford (New York: Berghahn Books, 1999), 12–13.

67. Wolfgang Kohlhaase, "DEFA: A Personal View," in *DEFA: East German Cinema, 1946–1992*, ed. Seán Allan and John Sandford (New York: Berghahn Books, 1999), 121.

68. Kohlhaase, "DEFA," 125.

69. Rousso, *Vichy*, 226–40.

70. *Die Mörder sind unter uns*, Dir. Wolfgang Staudte. DEFA, 1946.

71. Hamburg Institute for Social Research, ed., *The German Army and Genocide: Crimes against War Prisoners, Jews, and Other Civilians, 1939–1944* (New York: New Press, 1999).

72. Joe Hembus and Christa Bandmann, *Klassiker des deutschen Tonfilms, 1930–1960* (Munich: Goldmann, 1980), 153.

73. Klaus Sigl, Werner Schneider, and Ingo Tornow, *Jede Menge Kohle? Kunst und Kommerz auf dem deutschen Filmmarkt der Nachkriegszeit* (Munich: Filmland Presse, 1986), 162. *Grün ist die Heide*, Dir. Hans Deppe. Berolina, 1951. There is an extensive literature on the *Heimat* genre. One key work is Anton Kaes, *From Hitler to Heimat: The Return of History as Film* (Cambridge, MA: Harvard University Press, 1989). For an in-depth discussion of the concept of *Heimat* see part 1 in Alon Confino, *Germany as a Culture of Remembrance: Promises and Limits of Writing History* (Chapel Hill: University of North Carolina Press, 2006).

74. *Ehe im Schatten*, Dir. Kurt Maetzig. DEFA, 1947. Robert C. Reimer and Carl J. Reimer, *Nazi-Retro Film: How German Narrative Cinema Remembers the Past* (New York: Twayne, 1992), 133. Wolfgang Becker and Norbert Schöll, *In jenen Tagen . . .: Wie der deutsche Nachkriegsfilm die Vergangenheit bewältigte* (Opladen: Leske+Budrich, 1995), 55–56.

75. Fox, *Stated Memory*, 111.

76. Sigl et al., *Jede Menge*, 123.

77. *Die Affäre Blum*, Dir. Erich Engel. DEFA, 1948.

78. The Sigl volume gives some sense of how successful individual films were by ranking them according to their success as perceived by numerous cinema owners who were polled on a yearly basis. These rankings are far from perfect as films that were released late in the year will have their "perceived successfulness" divided between two separate years. But these are the best data available as attendance figures and other information are often nonexistent.

79. *Chronik eines Mordes*, Dir. Jo Hasler. DEFA, 1965. *Der Prozeß wird vertagt*, Dir. Herbert Ballmann. DEFA, 1958. *Zwischenfall in Benderath*, Dir. János Veiczi. DEFA, 1956.

80. F. B. Habel, *Das große Lexikon der DEFA-Spielfilme* (Berlin: Schwarzkopf & Schwarzkopf, 2001), 99–100.

81. *Lebende Ware*, Dir. Wolfgang Luderer. DEFA, 1966.

82. *Das Tal der sieben Monde*, Dir. Gottfried Kolditz. DEFA, 1967.

83. *Stielke, Heinz, Fünfzehn*, Dir. Michael Kann. DEFA, 1987.

84. *Die Schauspielerin*, Dir. Siegfried Kühn. DEFA, 1988.

85. *Sterne*, Dir. Konrad Wolf. DEFA, 1959. *Professor Mamlock*, Dir. Konrad Wolf. DEFA, 1961.

86. *Nackt unter Wölfen*, Dir. Frank Beyer. DEFA, 1963. *Jakob der Lügner*, Dir. Frank Beyer. DEFA, 1975.

87. Marc Silberman, "Remembering History: The Filmmaker Konrad Wolf," *New German Critique* 49 (Winter 1990): 163–91.

88. Dieter Wolf, "Gesellschaft mit beschränkter Haftung," in *Babelsberg: Ein Filmstudio 1912–1992*, ed. Wolfgang Jacobsen (Berlin: Argon, 1992), 257.

89. Hans Müncheberg, *Blaues Wunder aus Adlershof: Der Deutsche Fernsehfunk: Erlebtes und Gesammeltes* (Berlin: Das Neue Berlin, 2000), 151–53.

90. David A. Hackett, "Buchwenwald: Symbol and Metaphor for the Changing Political Culture of East Germany," in *Changing Identities in East Germany: Selected Papers*

from the Nineteenth and Twentieth New Hampshire Symposia, Studies in GDR Culture and Society 14/15, ed. Margy Gerber and Roger Woods (Lanham, MD: University Press of America, 1996), 127–142; Bill Niven, *The Buchenwald Child: Truth, Fiction and Propaganda* (Rochester, NY: Camden House, 2007).

91. Elisabeth Noelle-Neumann and Renate Köcher, eds., *Allensbach Jahrbuch der Demoskopie 1993–1997* (Munich: K.G. Saur, 1997), 522.

92. This is entirely realistic. As Gerda Beer reported in her interview, there was a great deal of uncertainty and unease among the passengers, but she recalls finding the black humor of a fellow passenger and a friend as helping to ease some tension. She also reports having been seated during the journey. LBS TA-Nr.: 8713, 9 (Interview 106).

93. *Life Is Beautiful* [La Vita è bella], Dir. Roberto Benigni. 1997.

94. Wolfgram, "Holocaust through the Prism," 57–79.

CHAPTER 3. VIEW FROM THE WEST

1. Gary Herrigel, *Industrial Constructions: The Sources of German Industrial Power* (Cambridge: Cambridge University Press, 1996).

2. This summary is based upon Peter J. Humphreys's excellent history, *Media and Media Policy in Germany: The Press and Broadcasting since 1943* (Oxford: Beg, 1994), chap. 4 "Controversies over the Public-Service Broadcasting System."

3. Ibid., 167.

4. Ibid., 51.

5. Michael Schornstheimer, *Bombenstimmung und Katzenjammer: Vergangenheitsbewältigung—Quick und Stern in den 50er Jahren* (Cologne: Pahl-Rugenstein, 1989).

6. This section is based upon Heide Fehrenbach's history of film regulation, *Cinema in Democratizing Germany: Reconstructing National Identity after Hitler* (Chapel Hill: University of North Carolina Press, 1995), 77–91.

7. Ibid., 83.

8. Ibid., 143.

9. Anton Kaes, *From Hitler to Heimat*, 14–15; Fehrenbach, *Cinema*, 8–9.

10. Scholars of collective memory have by and large failed to give enough attention to the role of the market and the ideologies of the market. For an exception, see Jay Winter and Emmanuel Sivan, "Setting the Framework," in *War and Remembrance in the Twentieth Century*, ed., Jay Winter and Emmanuel Sivan (Cambridge: Cambridge University Press, 1999), 29; Jay Winter, *Remembering War: The Great War between Memory and History in the Twentieth Century* (New Haven, CT: Yale University Press, 2006), 276, 279ff.

11. Festinger, *Theory of Cognitive Dissonance.*

12. Humphreys, *Media*, 272.

13. "Das deutsche kernproblem," *Der Tagesspiegel*, November 9, 1948: 1; "Zum Gedenken an die 'Kristallnacht,'" *Der Tagesspiegel*, November 9, 1948: 6.

14. For discussion about the use of the terms *collective memory* and *collective remembrance*, see Jay Winter and Emmanuel Sivan, "Setting the Framework," 6ff.

15. Joachim Bölke, "Dreimal 9. November," *Der Tagesspiegel*, November 9, 1958: 3.

16. "Zeugnis der neuen deutschen Demokratie," *Der Tagesspiegel*, November 11, 1958: 9.

17. "Adenauer zur 'Kristallnacht,'" *Frankfurter Allgemeine*, November 8, 1958: 1.

18. "Neue Synagoge für Hamburg," *Frankfurter Allgemeine*, November 10, 1958: 4.

19. Hans J. Robinsohn, "Ein Versuch, sich zu behaupten," *Die Zeit*, November 7, 1958: 4.

20. Y. Michal Bodemann, "Reconstructions of History: From Jewish Memory to Nationalized Commemoration of Kristallnacht in Germany," in *Jews, Germans, Memory: Reconstructions of Jewish Life in Germany*, ed. Y. Michal Bodemann (Ann Arbor: University of Michigan Press, 1996), 179–223.

21. *Deveti Krug*, Dir. France Štiglic. Jadran Film (Yugoslavia) 1960. Daniel J. Goulding, *Liberated Cinema: The Yugoslav Experience, 1945–2001*, 2nd ed. (Bloomington: Indiana University Press, 2002), 49–50.

22. "'Moralische Enttrümmerung streckengeblieben,'" *Der Tagesspiegel*, November 9, 1963: 7.

23. Isabelle Engelhardt, *A Topography of Memory: Representations of the Holocaust at Dachau and Buchenwald in Comparison with Auschwitz, Yad Vashem and Washington, DC* (Bruxelles: P.I.E.-Peter Lang, 2002).

24. "In Dachau entsteht eine Sühne-Christi-Kirche," *Frankfurter Allgemeine*, November 11, 1963: 3.

25. I define the Nazi generation more specifically in the final section of this chapter. It comprises all individuals who were at least thirteen years of age in 1933. The term signifies only membership in this age cohort, not an ideological allegiance.

26. "Sühne-Kirche für Dachau," *Fankfurter Allgemeine*, November 9, 1963: 17.

27. Hermann Graml, "Goebbels' Pogrom," *Frankfurter Allgemeine*, November 9, 1963: 'Bild und Zeiten' 3.

28. Ibid.

29. Ibid.

30. Ernestine Schlant, *The Language of Silence: West German Literature and the Holocaust* (London: Routledge, 1999), 54–55.

31. "Gedenkfeiern für Opfer der Juden-Verfolgung," *Frankfurter Allgemeine*, November 11, 1968: 1.

32. "Schmidt bittet Juden um Versöhnung," *Der Tagesspiegel*, November 10, 1978: 1.

33. "Großer Bußgottesdienst in der Festhalle," *Frankfurter Allgemeine*, November 8, 1978: 41.

34. "Scheel: Den November 1938 nicht vergessen," *Frankfurter Allgemeine*, November 9, 1978: 1.

35. "Rede Scheels zum 40. Jahrestag des Pogroms der 'Kristallnacht,'" *Der Tagesspiegel*, November 9, 1978: 1.

36. "Gottesdienste zum 9. November," *Der Tagesspiegel*, November 9, 1978: 11.

37. Herf, *Divided Memory*, 342.

38. In 1980, 25 percent of the total West German population belonged to the Nazi generation.

39. Joachim Fest, "Gedanken zu Erinnerungen," *Frankfurter Allgemeine*, November 9, 1978: 1.

40. Rolf Zundel, "Schlußstrich unter die Vergangenheit?" *Die Zeit*, November 10, 1978: 9.

41. Ulrich Völkein, "Nochmal nach Theresienstadt," *Die Zeit*, November 10, 1978: 10.

42. Charles S. Maier, *The Unmasterable Past: History, Holocaust, and German National Identity* (Cambridge, MA: Harvard University Press, 1988).

43. "Vor Aller Augen," special insert to *Der Tagesspiegel*, November 8, 1988: 1–12.

44. Ibid., 7.

45. Ibid., 10.

46. Günter Beukert, "Als Bildjournalist in der 'Reichskristallnacht,'" ibid., special section, "Vor Aller Augen," 4.

47. Shimon Sachs, "Berliner erinnerungen eines Israeli," *Der Tagesspiegel*, November 10, 1988: 12.

48. Wolfgang Lehmann, "9. November 1938: Vor Aller Augen," *Der Tagesspiegel*, November 8, 1988: 12.

49. Ian Buruma, *The Wages of Guilt: Memories of War in Germany and Japan* (Middlesex, England: Meridian, 1995), 244; see the chapter "A Normal Country" for further discussion.

50. "Ringsum Peinlichkeit," *Frankfurter Allgemeine*, November 11, 1988: 1.

51. Chancellor Helmut Kohl, "Die Menschen von heute sind nicht besser oder mutiger als damals," *Frankfurter Allgemeine*, November 10, 1988: 5.

52. "Mahnung, nicht Schuld," *Frankfurter Allgemeine*, November 10, 1988: 1.

53. Robert Leicht, "Im Schatten der Schande," *Die Zeit*, November 11, 1988: 1.

54. Gerd Langguth, *In Search of Security: A Socio-Psychological Portrait of Today's Germany*, trans. Dirk Johnson (Westport, CT: Praeger, 1995). Langguth refers to the Holocaust as a tragic "aberration" of German history and culture, thus placing it "outside" German history.

55. "Ein Datum," *Die Zeit*, November 12, 1993: 1; "Historische Unpäßlichkeit," *Frankfurter Allgemeine*, November 9, 1993: 1; Hermann Rudolph, "Was der 9. November uns zu sagen hat," *Der Tagesspiegel*, November 9, 1993: 1; "Gedenken an den 9. November 1938," *Der Tagesspiegel*, November 9, 1993: 10; "Süssmuth: Kein Schlußstrich unter die Vergangenheit," *Der Tagesspiegel*, November 10, 1993: 1.

56. "Neue Wache 'kein Mahnmal,'" *Der Tagesspiegel*, November 10, 1993: 9; "Demonstranten ketten sich am Eingang der Neuen Wache an," *Der Tagesspiegel*, November 10, 1993: 1.

57. Ann Norton, *95 Theses on Politics, Culture, and Method*, (New Haven, CT: Yale University Press, 2004), 1–2.

58. Victor Klemperer, *I Will Bear Witness*, trans. Martin Chalmers (New York: Random House, 1998).

59. "Eine Synagoge am alten Ort," *Frankfurter Allgemeine*, November 9, 1998: 4; "Zerstört, entweiht, wiederentdeckt und renoviert," *Frankfurter Allgemeine*, November 9, 1998: 13. Both rebuildings are also mentioned in Ralf Hübner, "Ausdruck des Neubeginns," *Der Tagesspiegel*, November 10, 1998: 5.

60. "Löschen nur mit Erlaubnis: Freiwillige Feuerwehren in der Pogromnacht," *Frankfurter Allgemeine*, November 9, 1998: 13.

61. Werner Schmidt, "Den Nazis entgegengestellt," *Der Tagesspiegel*, November 10, 1998: 16.

62. Hanne Bahra, "'Synagogen sofort niederbrennen . . .'" ibid., 18.

63. Aleander Pajevic, "'Sag beim Abschied leise . . . Shalom!'" ibid., 16.

64. Title story, "Ist die Schuld verjährt?" *Der Spiegel*, November 30, 1998. The debate has been covered in great detail in the literature; see Bill Niven, *Facing the Nazi Past*, chap. 7, "The Walser-Bubis Debate." Frank Schirrmacher, ed., *Die Walser-Bubis Debatte: Eine Dokumentation* (Frankfurt: Suhrkamp, 1999).

65. Roger Cohen, "Germany Searches for 'Normality,'" *New York Times*, November 29, 1998: 10.

66. Niven, *Facing the Nazi Past*, 191.

67. *Schicksalstag 9. November.* ARD, November 9, 1953.

68. "9 November ein 'verflucht deutscher Tag,'" *Frankfurter Allgemeine*, November 9, 1998: 1; "Ein deutsches Datum," *Der Tagesspiegel*, November 9, 1998: 8.

69. *Schicksalstag des deutshcen Volkes.* ARD, November 9, 1958.

70. Christoph Classen, *Bilder der Vergangenheit: Die Zeit des Nationalsozialismus im*

Fernsehen der Bundesrepublik Deutschland 1955–1965 (Cologne: Böhlau Verlag, 1999), 49, 87.

71. Ibid., 50. *Night and Fog*, Dir. Alain Resnais. 1955. BR, April 18, 1957.

72. Classen, *Bilder*, 91.

73. See the later discussion of Kurt Hoffmann's film *Das Haus in der Karpfengasse.*

74. W. M. Hamdorf, "Der Holocaust im Film," *Filmdienst* 20 (1995): 38.

75. I was unable to locate any audience survey from 1957.

76. *Waldhausstr. 20*, Dir. John Olden. NDR, October 23, 1960. NDR Archive Nr.: 45927/03.

77. Classen, *Bilder*, 83.

78. Yael Zerubavel, *Recovered Roots: Collective Memory and the Making of Israeli National Tradition* (Chicago: University of Chicago Press, 1995), 147.

79. *Das schreckliche Mädchen.* Dir. Michael Verhoeven. 1990; *Leni.* Dir. Leo Hiemer. DAZU Film/SDR/arte/WDR, 1994.

80. David I. Kertzer, *The Popes against the Jews: The Vatican's Role in the Rise of Modern Anti-Semitism* (New York: Knopf, 2001).

81. *Bilanz eines Verlustes: Jüdische Mitbürger in Deutschland—gestern und heute.* ZDF, November 8, 1963. *ZDF Presse Programm* 45/63, November 8, 1963.

82. *Stuttgarter Zeitung*, November 12, 1963. *Kölner Nacht*, November 11, 1963. Both in ZDF press reaction archive.

83. *Infratest*, November 4–10, 1963: 56–57.

84. *Die verschlossene Tür*, Dir. Dieter Lemmels. ZDF, March 10, 1965. *ZDF Presse Programm* 11/65, March 10, 1965.

85. *Infratest*, March 8–13, 1965: 35–37.

86. *Das Haus in der Karpfengasse*, Dir. Kurt Hoffmann, WDR, March 7, 9, and 11, 1965.

87. Sigl et al., *Jede Menge*, 106.

88. *Wir Wunderkinder*, Dir. Kurt Hoffmann. Filmaufbau, 1958. Reimer and Reimer, *Nazi-Retro*, 117–22.

89. M. Y. Ben-Gaviel, *Das Haus in der Karpfengasse* (Berlin: Colloqium-Verlag, 1957).

90. "Tschechische Hilfe für Kurt Hoffmann," *Neue Zürcher Zeitung*, February 24, 1962. LBS newspaper clipping archive.

91. Several of these historical details are drawn from Peter Daniel, "Kurt Hoffmanns 'Das Haus in der Karpfengasse,' " *Die Andere Zeitung* (Hamburg). LBS newspaper clippings archive.

92. Sigl et al., *Jede Menge*, 47.

93. Inge Deutschkron, *Mein Leben Nach Dem Überleben* (Munich: Deutscher Taschenbuch Verlag, 1995), 130–31.

94. The term literally means "nest dirtier." Its use in such cases means that Germans should not be fouling their own "nest."

95. Sigl et al., *Jede Menge*, 102.

96. Ibid., 139.

97. *Filmgutachtungskommission für Jugend und Schule* Berlin 21, Levetzowstr. 1–2. The document is marked "confidential" and is undated. LBS newspaper clippings archive.

98. I viewed the film version, which was shortened from the original television broadcast.

99. Inge Deutschkron, . . . *denn ihrer war die Hölle. Kinder in Gettos und Lagern* (Cologne: Verlag Wissenschaft und Politik, 1965).

100. *Denn ihrer war die Hölle*, Dir. Horst Siebecke. BR Archive Number 8210/42058.

101. *Ein Tag*, Dir. Egon Monk. NDR, May 6, 1965.

102. *Juden in München*. BR, April 3, 1972. BR Archive Nr.: 314300/14414. I probably was not shown the broadcast copy of the film as it ran well over the fifty-seven minutes shown in the archive records.

103. Henry Rousso, *The Vichy Syndrome: History and Memory in France since 1944*, (Cambridge, MA: Harvard University Press, 1991), chapter 4.

104. Ibid., 226–27. Michel Foucault, "Film and Popular Memory," in *Foucault Live: Collected Interviews, 1961–1984*, ed. Sylvère Lotringer, trans. Lysa Hochroth and John Johnston (New York: Semiotext(e), 1989), 122–132.

105. *Lacombe Lucien*, Dir. Louis Malle. 1974. *The Sorrow and the Pity*, Dir. Marcel Ophuls. 1971.

106. *Shoah*, Dir. Claude Lanzmann. 1985.

107. Peter Novick, *The Holocaust in American Life* (Boston: Mariner Books, 1999), 207.

108. *Das letzte Ghetto*, Dir. Arno Rattay. ZDF, November 8, 1978.

109. *ZDF Presse Programm* 45/78, 27.

110. "Der Kritiker meint," *Frankfurter Rundschau*, November 13, 1978. Eckhart Schmidt, "Stichwort-Sauce statt Trauerarbeit," *Süddeutsche Zeitung*, November 10, 1978. "Blinder Eifer," *Kölner Stadt Anzeiger*, November 10, 1978. All ZDF press reaction archive.

111. Eckhart Schmidt, "Aspekte deutscher Sünde," *Süddeustche Zeitung*, November 13, 1978. Michael Schwarze, "Von Bad König nach Auschwitz," *Frankfurter Allgemeine, Zeitung*, November 11, 1978. Dorothee Hammerstein, "Entrüstung genügt nicht," *Badische Zeitung*, November 11, 1978. All ZDF press reaction archive.

112. *Als sie in Deutschland mit Steinen nach uns warfen*, Dir. Rolf Seelmann-Eggebert. NDR, November 10, 1978. NDR Archive Nr.: 1034282.

113. *Holocaust*, Dir. Marvin Chomsky. Robert Berger, 1978. For additional comments, see Anton Kaes, *From Hitler to Heimat: The Return of History as Film* (Cambridge, MA: Harvard University Press, 1989).

114. "Fernsehen: Gaskammern a la Hollywood?" *Der Spiegel*, May 15, 1978: 228–31.

115. Y. Michal Bodemann, "The Uncanny Clatter: The Holocaust in Germany before Its Mass Commemoration," in *Remembering the Holocaust in Germany, 1945–2000: German Strategies and Jewish Responses*, ed. Dan Michman (New York: Peter Lang), 43–53.

116. "'Holocaust': Die Vergangenheit kommt zurück," *Der Spiegel*, January 29, 1979: 17–34. Wieslaw Kielar, "'Niemand kommt hier raus,'" *Der Spiegel*, February 5, 1979: 36–49.

117. Friedrich Knilli and Siegfried Zielinski, eds., *Betrift, "Holocaust": Zuschauer schreiben an den WDR: Ein Projektbericht* (Berlin: V. Spiess, 1983). Yizhak Ahren et al., *Das Lehrstück "Holocaust": Zur Wirkungspsychologie eines Medienereignisses* (Opladen: Westdeutscher Verlag, 1982).

118. "Fernsehen: Nachwirkungen von 'Holocaust,'" *Der Spiegel*, May 7, 1979: 202, 205.

119. Andrei S. Markovits and Simon Reich advance a strong instrumentalist argument in *The German Predicament: Memory and Power in the New Europe*, (Ithaca, NY: Cornell University Press, 1997), 15, 18.

120. Norton, *95 Theses*, 2–7.

121. *Die Verschwindenen Stetl*, Dir. Karl Nikolaus Renner. BR (broadcast date known only to be in the 1980s). BR Archive Number 70403.

122. *Reichskristallnacht: Die November-Pogrome 1938*. BR, November 9, 1988. BR, Archive Number 80285.

123. *Als die Synagogen brannten . . .* ZDF, November 8, 1988.

124. *Die Bertinis.* ZDF, October 31, 1988 (part 1); November 1 (part 2); November 6 (part 3); November 7 (part 4); November 8 (part 5).

125. "Fernsehen: Nachwirkungen von 'Holocaust,'" *Der Spiegel,* May 7, 1979: 205.

126. Fehrenbach, *Cinema,* 91.

127. The West German film database that I created for this project is based upon the information gathered from the following sources: Richard C. Helt and Marie E. Helt, *West German Cinema since 1945: A Reference Handbook* (Metuchen, NJ: Scarecrow Press, 1987); Richard C. Helt and Marie E. Helt, *West German Cinema 1986–1990: A Reference Handbook* (Metuchen, NJ: Scarecrow Press, 1992); Daniel Lopex, *Films by Genre* (Jefferson, NC: McFarland, 1993); Sheba F. Skirball, *Films of the Holocaust: An Annotated Filmography of Collections in Israel* (New York: Garland, 1990); Steven Spielberg Jewish Film Archive, The Hebrew University of Jerusalem—Institute of Contemporary Jewry, http://www.spielbergfilmarchive.org.il/; Erika Gregor, Ulrich Gregor, and Helma Schleif, eds., *Jüdische Lebenswelten im Film* (Berlin: Freunde der Deutschen Kinemathek, 1993); Heiko R. Blum, ed., *30 Jahre danach: Auseinandersetzung mit dem Nationalsozialismus im Film 1945 bis 1975* (Cologne: Horst May Schnelldruck & Verlag, 1975). For films after 1990, I used primarily two sources: (1) the *Fischer Film Almanach* of various years and (2) the *Filmstatistische Taschenbuch,* ed., Spitzenorganisation der Filmwirtschaft, Wiesbaden 1952–.

128. Sigl et al., *Jede Menge,* 160–61.

129. *Filmstatistische Taschenbuch* (Frankfurt am Main: Fischer Taschenbuch Verlag, 1995), 36. *Schindler's List,* Dir. Steven Spielberg. 1993.

130. *Lang ist der Weg,* Dir. Herbert B. Fredersdorf and Marek Goldstein. IFO-Film, 1947.

131. For a good history of film clubs in Germany, see Fehrenbach, *Cinema,* 170–92.

132. LBS TA-Nr.: 8616, 11 (Interview 58).

133. "*Lang ist der Weg*/zu einer Film-Diskussion," *Der Kurier,* October 11, 1948. LBS newspaper clippings archive.

134. "Ein Film—politisch gesehen," *Berliner Zeitung,* September 8, 1948. The article is presented as a letter, although the authorship is hidden behind the initials F. T. So-called letters in East German papers must be treated with extreme skepticism. See also Hugo Hermann, "Ein Film klagt an," *Tägliche Ründschau,* September 5, 1948. LBS newspaper clippings archive.

135. *Nacht fiel über Gotenhafen,* Dir. Frank Wisbar. DFH, 1959. Robert C. Reimer and Carl J. Reimer, *Nazi-Retro Film: How German Narrative Cinema Remembers the Past* (New York: Twayne, 1992), 68.

136. Ruth Klüger Angress, "A 'Jewish Problem' in German Postwar Fiction," *Modern Judaism* 5 (1985): 215.

137. Ernestine Schlant, *The Language of Silence: West German Literature and the Holocaust* (London: Routledge, 1999), 168.

138. "Lang ist der Weg," *Westfälische Rundschau* (Dortmund), January 24, 1955. LBS newspaper clipping archive.

139. "Lang ist der Weg," *Westfalenpost* (Hagen), September 23, 1952. LBS newspaper clipping archive.

140. *Ich weiß, wofür ich lebe,* Dir. Paul Verhoeven. Neubach-Film, 1955.

141. *Filmdienst* 4070.

142. *Friedericke von Barring,* Dir. Rolf Thiele. 1956.

143. *Ein Lied geht um die Welt (Die Joseph-Schmidt-Story),* Dir. Geza von Bolvary. Neubach, 1958.

144. *Liebling der Götter*, Dir. Gottfried Reinhardt. CCC, 1960.

145. "Kriegsverbrechen," *Der Spiegel*, June 15, 1960: 20–33.

146. *Rosen für den Staatsanwalt*, Dir. Wolfgang Staudte. Kurt Ulrich, 1959. Sigl et al., *Jede Menge*, 134. Sigl ranks the film 113 of 522 in 1960. The film was also given second prize for the best film of the year by the Interior Ministry.

147. *Zeugin aus der Hölle*, Dir. Zica Mitrovic. CCC and Avala, 1965.

148. Irmtrud Wojak and Susanne Meinl, "Forschungskolloquium: Der erste Frankfurter Auschwitz-Prozeß, Geschichte und Wirkungsgeschichte," *Newsletter: Informationen des Fritz Bauer Instituts* (Fall 1999): 16–17.

149. Thomas Elsaesser, *New German Cinema: A History* (New Brunswick, NJ: Rutgers University Press, 1989). Julia Knight, *Women and the New German Cinema* (London: Verso, 1992).

150. *Wie ein Hirschberger dänisch lernte*, Dir. Rolf Busch. 1968.

151. *Stern ohne Himmel*, Dir. Ottokar Runze. Ottokar Runze, 1980. *Filmdienst* 23,000.

152. *Blutiger Schnee (Zu Freiwild verdammt)*, Dir. Jerzy Hoffman. CCC-Filmkunst/SFB/PRF Zespoloy Filmowe Zespol "Zodiak," 1983.

153. *Bittere Ernte*, Dir. Agnieszka Holland. CCC-Filmkunst, Admiral-Film, 1984.

154. *Versteckt*, Dir. Anthony Page. Jodack-Decade/Forstater/Clasart/Anthea/Stella, 1984. *Filmdienst* 25,313.

155. *Die Wannseekonferenz*, Dir. Heinz Schcik. Manfred Korytowski/Infafilm GmbH Munich/ORF/Bavarian Broadcasting Corporation, 1984.

156. Reimer and Reimer, *Nazi-Retro*, 138.

157. *David*, Dir. Peter Lilienthal. Von Vietinghoff/ Pro-ject / ZDF, 1978. Reimer and Reimer, *Nazi-retro*, 142–45; Annette Insdorf, "A Passion for Social Justice," *Cineaste* 11, no. 4 (Winter 1982), 36–38. Annette Insdorf, "*David:* A German-Jewish Film about the Holocaust," *Martyrdom and Resistance* 8, no. 2 (March–April 1982), 4.

158. The film was ranked 123 of approximately 400 films in 1979. Sigl et al., *Jede Menge*, 153.

159. Annette Insdorf, *Indelible Shadows: Films and the Holocaust*, 2d ed. (Cambridge: Cambridge University Press, 1989), 223–25.

160. *Dark Lullabies*, Dir. Irene Lilienheim Angelico. National Film Board of Canada, 1993.

161. Zerubavel, *Recovered Roots*, 192.

162. *Auf Wiedersehen Amerika*, Dir. Jan Schütte. Novoscop/Pandora/arte/Casting S.F./WDR, 1993. *Filmdienst* 30,723.

163. Peter Gay, *My German Question: Growing Up in Nazi Berlin* (New Haven, CT: Yale University Press, 1998). See in particular chapter 10, "On Good Behavior."

164. *Shtetl*, Dir. Marian Marzynski. Marz Associates/WGBH/Frontline, 1996.

165. Dan Bar-On, *Legacy of Silence: Encounters with Children of the Third Reich* (Cambridge, MA: Harvard University Press, 1989).

166. *Leni*, Dir. Leo Hiemer. DAZU Film/SDR/arte/WDR, 1994.

167. *Heimat*, Dir. Edgar Reitz. 1984.

168. http://www.german-cinema.de/archive/l/leni_E.html.

169. *Aimée and Jaguar*, Dir. Max Fäberböck. Senator, 1998.

170. Elisabeth Noelle and Erich Peter Neumann, *The Germans: Public Opinion Polls 1947–1966* (Allensbach: Verlag für Demoskopie, 1967), 315–16.

171. Potential labor force is defined here as ages twenty to sixty-four.

172. Noelle-Neumann and Köcher, *Allensbach Jahrbuch* (1997), 514–15.

173. Ibid., 504.

Chapter 4. Blood and Redemption

Parts of this chapter have already appeared in Mark A. Wolfgram, "Blood and Redemption: German Collective Memory of the Elite Resistance against the Nazis," *Journal of Political and Military Sociology* 35, no. 1 (Summer 2007): 63–84.

1. Leviticus 17:11–12. All Bible passages taken from *Good News Study Bible* (Nashville: Thomas Nelson, 1986).
2. Hebrews 9:22.
3. Stalingrad, Dir. Joseph Vilsmaier. Royal/Bavaria/B.A./Pevathon, 1991–92.
4. See Henry Rousso, *The Vichy Syndrome: History and Memory in France since 1944*, (Cambridge, MA: Harvard University Press, 1991), 100ff.
5. Ruby Rohrlich, ed., *Resisting the Holocaust* (Oxford: Berg, 1998).
6. Robert Gellately, *Backing Hitler: Consent and Coercion in Nazi Germany* (Oxford: Oxford University Press, 2001), 224.
7. Josie McLellan, *Antifascism and Memory in East Germany: Remembering the International Brigades 1945–1989* (Oxford: Oxford Unviersity Press, 2004).
8. Günter Paulus, "Der 20. Juli 1944—ein Versuch zur Rettung des deutschen Imperialismus vor der Niederlage," *Neues Deutschland*, July 20, 1954: 3.
9. Dr. Lothar Berthold, "Heusingers hündische Heuchelei," *Neues Deutschland*, July 19, 1959: 4.
10. Martyn Housden, *Resistance and Conformity in the Third Reich* (London: Routledge, 1997), 112.
11. Willi Arnold and Gertrud Glondajewski, "Magnus Poser—treuer Sohn der Arbeiterklasse," *Neues Deuschland*, July 21, 1959: 4.
12. Dr. Bruno Löwel, "Am 20. Juli vor 20 Jahren," *Neues Deutschland*, July 19, 1964: 3.
13. *Revolution am Telefon.* Directors Günter Stahnke and Karl Gass. DEFA-Studio Dok.-Filme, 1964. (1) "Das Attentat und der Prozeß" DRA Lagernr.: AC 12716, (2) "Legende und Wirklichkeit" DRA Lagernr.: AC 12717.
14. LBS TA-NR 8572, 10–11 (Interview 1).
15. Prof. Dr. Kurt Finker, "Am 20. Juli vor 40 Jahren," *Neues Deutschland*, July 20, 1984: 3.
16. Peter Jochen Winters, "Koalition der Vernunft," *Frankfurter Allgemeine*, July 21, 1984: 25.
17. *Das Attentat auf Hitler*; Dir. Rolf Schnabel. DEFA-Studio Dok.-Filme, 1984. DRA AC 2246.
18. *Wir haben nichts zu bereuen*, Dir. Ulrich Teschner. DDR-F, 1984. DRA AC 1169.
19. *Stauffenberg: 13 Bilder über einen Täter*; Dir. Erich Thiede. DDR-F, 1989. DRA AC 1685. "Fernsehen der DDR 1. und 2. Programm Gesamtsehbeteilung, 19.7.89–22.7.89," 1b. DRA ArNr: H 023–00–02 0123.
20. *Leutnant Yorck von Wartenberg*, Dir. Peter Vogel. DEFA-Studio Spielfilme, 1981. DRA AC 7315.
21. "Fernsehen der DDR, 1. und 2. Program, 18.7.84–21.7.84," 1b. DRA ArNr: H023–00–02/0118.
22. "Fernsehen der DDR, 1. und 2. Program, 18.7.84–21.7.84," 1b. DRA ArNr: H023–00–02/0118.
23. "Fernsehen der DDR, 1. und 2. Program, 18.7.84–21.7.84," 1b. DRA ArNr: H023–00–02/0118.
24. "Berlin (West): Ausstellung über Kampf gegen Faschismus," *Neues Deutschland*, July 20, 1989: 7.

25. Dr. Kurt Finker, "Der Versuch einer Wende?" *Neues Deutschland*, July 20, 1994: 3.

26. Günther Rüther, *"Greif zur Feder, Kumpel": Schriftsteller, Literatur und Politik in der DDR 1949–1990* (Düsseldorf: Droste, 1991); Wolfgang Emmerich, *Kleine Literaturgeschichte der DDR* (Leipzig: Gustav Kiepenhauer, 1996); Alf Lüdtke, "Helden der Arbeit"—Mühen beim Arbeiten. Zur mißmutigen Loyalität von Industriearbeitern in der DDR," in *Sozialgeschichte der DDR*, ed. Hartmut Kaelble (Stuttgart: Klett-Cotta, 1994), 188–213.

27. Acts 9:1–19; Acts 22:6–16; Acts 26:12–18.

28. Joachim Schmitt-Sasse, ed., *Widergänger: Faschismus und Antifaschismus im Film* (Münster: MAkS Publikationen, 1993); Antonia Grunenberg, *Antifaschismus—ein deutscher Mythos* (Reinbeck bei Hamburg: Rowohlt, 1993).

29. *Rotation*, Dir. Wolfgang Staudte. DEFA, 1949.

30. *Die Abenteuer der Werner Holt*, Dir. Joachim Kunert. DEFA, 1964.

31. *Im Sonderauftrag*, Dir. Heinz Thiel. DEFA, 1959.

32. *Ich war neunzehn*, Dir. Konrad Wolf. DEFA, 1968.

33. Sigrid Schmitt, "Konrad Wolf: Assoziationen zur Gegenwart," in *30 Jahre danach: Auseinandersetzung mit dem Nationalsozialismus im Film 1945 bis 1975*, ed. Heiko R. Blum (Cologne: Horst May Schnelldruck & Verlag, 1975), 29.

34. Johann A. Graf Kielmansegg, " 'An jedem anderen Tag, nur heute nicht . . .' " *Die Zeit*, July 21, 1949: 10.

35. Federal President Heuss, "20. Juli 1944—Grenzsitutation der sittlichen Entscheidungen: Aus der Rede des Bundespräsidenten . . ." *Der Tagesspiegel*, July 20, 1954: 3.

36. Manfred Messerschmidt, "Zur neueren Diskussion um Opposition und Verweigerung von Soldaten, Deserteure, Zersetzer und Verweigerer," in *Der 20. Juli. 'Das andere Deutschland' in der Vergangenheitspolitik nach 1945*, ed. Gerd R. Ueberschär (Berlin: Elefanten Press, 1998), 392.

37. Erich Peter Neumann and Elisabeth Noelle, *Antworten: Politik im Kraftfeld der öffentlichen Meinung* (Allensbach: Verlag für Demoskopie, 1954), 33.

38. Housden, *Resistance and Conformity*, 100.

39. Regina Holler, *20 Juli 1944 Vermächtnis oder Alibi? Wie Historiker, Politiker und Journalisten mit dem deutschen Widerstand gegen den Nationalsozialismus umgehen: Eine Untersuchung der wissenschaftlichen Literatur, der offiziellen Reden und der Zeitungsberichterstattung in Nordrhein-Westfalen von 1945–1986* (Munich: K. G. Saur, 1994).

40. R. R. Palmer and Joel Colton, *A History of the Modern World*, 8th ed. (New York: McGraw-Hill, 1995), 862.

41. Housden, *Resistance and Conformity*, 108–10.

42. Elfriede Kaiser-Nebgen, "Mut und Tragik um den 20. Juli," *Frankfurter Allgemeine*, July 20, 1954: 2.

43. Paul Sethe, "Für immer gescheitert?" *Frankfurter Allgemeine*, July 20, 1954: 1.

44. Marion Gräfin Dönhoff, "Das Gewissen steht auf," *Die Zeit*, July 15, 1954: 17.

45. Marion Gräfin Dönhoff, "Heusingers Tagesbefehl," *Die Zeit*, July 17, 1959: 1.

46. Helmut Krausnick, "Im Zwiespalt von Soldateneid und Gewissen," *Frankfurter Allgemeine*, July 20, 1959; 9.

47. "Lübke nennt den 20. Juli ein Symbol der Selbstachtung," *Frankfurter Allgemeine*, July 20, 1964: 1.

48. "Trauer gilt den menschen, nicht den Symbolen: Rabbiner Friedländer zum 20. Juli 1944," *Der Tagesspiegel*, July 20, 1964: 10.

49. "Verteidigungsminister Leber zum 20. Juli," *Der Tagesspiegel*, July 19, 1974: 2.

50. "Gedenkfeiern zum 20. Juli," *Frankfurter Allgemeine*, July 22, 1974: 5.

51. "Gedenkfeier zum 20. Juli mit Protesten gegen Filbinger," *Der Tagesspiegel*, July 20, 1974: 1.
52. "Was SFB und ZDF verschwiegen," ibid., 2.
53. Jürgen Busche, "Schwieriger Gedenktag," *Frankfurter Allgemeine*, July 20, 1979: 21.
54. "Kohl: Attentat vom 20. Juli 1944 Symbol für ein anderes Deutschland," *Der Tagesspiegel*, July 20, 1984: 2.
55. Peter Gralla, "Widerstand gegen den NS-Staat," *Der Tagesspiegel*, July 20, 1984: 10.
56. Marion Gräfin Dönhoff, "Verschwörer gegen das Unrecht," *Die Zeit*, July 20, 1984: 3.
57. "Diepgen und Rasch würdigen Rolle des Widerstands gegen die Hitler-Diktatur," *Der Tagesspiegel*, July 19, 1984: 8.
58. "Der alltägliche Widerstand," *Der Tagesspiegel*, July 21, 1984: 12.
59. Bernhard Schulz, "Grenzen des Darstellbaren," *Der Tagesspiegel*, July 19, 1989: 3.
60. "Kohl dankt den Widerstandskämpfern des 20. Juli," *Frankfurter Allgemeine*, July 20, 1989: 1.
61. Jacques Schuster, "Nur eine Generalsrevolute?" *Frankfurter Allgemeine*, July 20, 1994: 10.
62. Wilhelm von Sternburg, "Ein Flammenzeichen," *Die Zeit*, July 15, 1994: 16.
63. Classen, *Bilder*, 47.
64. Ibid., 80.
65. *Aufstand des Gewissens*, Dir. Hannes Huepper. ARD, July 20, 1954.
66. Classen, *Bilder*, 238.
67. *Gespräch des Monats*, Discussion Leader Fritz Bruehl. ARD, July 20, 1959.
68. *Mann ohne Namen*, Dir. Curt Goetz-Pflug. ARD, July 20, 1959.
69. J. Hyzdal von Miserony, *Mann ohne Namen*, in *Hören und Sehen*. ARD, July 20, 1959.
70. *Widerstand—eine Diskussion*. ZDF, July 20, 1963.
71. *Infratest*, July 15–21, 1963: 59–60.
72. Richard M. Merelman, "The Mundane Experience of Political Culture," *Political Communication* 15, no. 4 (October/December 1998): 517.
73. Holler, *20 Juli 1944*, 292.
74. *Der Fall Nebe I*, Dir. Georg Tressler. ZDF, November 18, 1964, *Der Fall Nebe II*, Dir. Georg Tressler. ZDF, November 19, 1964.
75. *Infratest*, November 16–22, 1964: 29–37.
76. Classen, *Bilder*, 101.
77. Michael Schornstheimer, *Bombenstimmung*.
78. Roland Hardt, *Der Landser #1122: Der letzte Kampf* (Rastatt: Erich Pabel Verlag, 1979), 65–66.
79. Robert Wistrich, *Who's Who in Nazi Germany* (London: Routledge, 1995), 177–78.
80. *ZDF Presse Programm* 47/64, November 18, 1964.
81. *Ibid.*, November 19, 1964.
82. Infratest, November 16–22, 1964: 30.
83. Ibid., 31.
84. *Infratest*, November 16–22, 1964: 34.
85. Ibid., 36.
86. Marion Gräfin Dönhoff, "Heusingers Tagesbefehl," *Die Zeit*, July 17, 1959: 1.
87. Anna J. Merritt and Richard L. Merritt, eds., *Public Opinion in Semisovereign Germany: The HICOG Surveys, 1949–1955* (Urbana: University of Illinois Press, 1980), 101.

88. Erich Peter Neumann and Elisabeth Noelle, eds., *The Germans: Public Opinion Polls 1947–1966* (Allensbach: Verlag für Demoskopie, 1967), 202.

89. Ibid., 193.

90. Ibid., 316.

91. Elisabeth Noelle-Neumann, ed., *The Germans: Public Opinion Polls, 1967–1980* (Westport, CT: Greenwood Press, 1981), 114.

92. Housden, *Resistance and Conformity*, 62–63.

93. Johnson, *Nazi Terror*, 482.

94. *Bernhard Lichtenberg*, Dir. Peter Beauvais. ZDF, July 20, 1965.

95. *Infratest*, July 19–25, 1965: 17–20.

96. ZDF press reaction archive. W. M. G., *Bernhard Lichtenberg*, *Süddeutscher Zeitung*, July 24, 1965.

97. *Im Schatten der Väter*, by Walter Leo and Lothar Janßen. ARD, July 20, 1969. NDR Archive 1025003.

98. *Deutsche gegen Hitler: Ein Rückblick auf den Widerstand im Dritten Reich*, from F. A. Krummacher. ZDF, July 20, 1969.

99. *Infratest*, July 14–20, 1969: 28.

100. *Warum habt ihr Hitler widerstanden? 1. Das andere Deutschland.* From Guido Knopp and Ralf Piechowiak. ZDF, July 18, 1984. *Warum habt ihr Hitler widerstanden? 2. Das andere Deutschland im Exil.* From Achim Gerloff. ZDF, July 19, 1984.

101. *Der 20. Juli*, Dir. Falk Harnack. CCC, 1955.

102. *Teleskopie*, July 18, 1984. The general audience data were missing for this year; thus the 3–5 percent is based upon data for Bavaria and the NDR viewer area. This is only for the first part of the documentary.

103. ZDF Telfon-Protokoll File, *Warum habt ihr Hitler widerstanden*, July 18 and 19, 1984.

104. The ARD rebroadcast the *Er wollte Hitler töten* documentary very late in the evening. *Er wollte Hitler töten*, by Juergen Engert. ARD/SFB, July 20, 1989.

105. *Netzwerk—Adam von Trott zu Solz und der 20. Juli 1944*, by Henric Wuermeling. ARD, July 20, 1994. BR Archive Production Number 95553.

106. *Widerstand—Kampf gegen Hitler.* NDR Archive 1062093 for parts 6 and 7.

107. *Einer aus Königsbronn: Der Widerstandskämpfer Georg Elser*, from Eva Witte. ARD/SDR, November 7, 1998.

108. *Georg Elser—einer aus Deutschland*, Dir. Klaus Maria Brandauer. Söhnlein / Borman Prod. / Mutoskop Film / Saturn, 1989.

109. *Des Teufels General*, Dir. Helmut Käutner. Real-Film, 1954.

110. Becker and Schöll, *In jenen Tagen*, 88–90.

111. Sigl et al., *Jede Menge*, 129.

112. *Infratest*, April 24–30, 1967: 5–6.

113. *Canaris*, Dir. Alfred Weidenmann. Fama, 1954.

114. Sigl et al., *Jede Menge*, 129.

115. Ibid., 20.

116. *Telegraf*, February 8, 1955. LBS newspaper clippings archive.

117. Rudolf Lange, "Canaris—Verräter oder Held?" *Die Welt*, January 3, 1955. LBS newspaper clippings archive.

118. Hans Stempel, "Canaris," *Deutsche Volkszeitung* (Düsseldorf), January 22, 1955. LBS newspaper clippings archive.

119. Anna Foa, *The Jews of Europe after the Black Death.*

120. Wistrich, *Who's Who in Nazi Germany*, 29–30.

121. ZDF, September 12, 1978. ZDF, May 13, 1981. ZDF, July 31, 1994. ZDF, October 15, 1995. ZDF, September 10, 1998.

122. *Es geschah am 20. Juli*, Dir. G.W. Pabst. Ariston/Area, 1955.

123. *Der 20. Juli*, Dir. Falk Harnack. CCC, 1955.

124. *U47—Kapitänleutnant Prien*, Dir. Harald Reinl. Arca, 1958.

125. "Harold Reinl wurde getötet," *Nürenberger Nachrichten*, October 10, 1986. LBS newspaper clippings archive.

126. *Solange du lebst*, Dir. Harald Reinl. 1955.

127. Heiko Blum, "Die Blonden sind blond," *Rheinische Post* (Düsseldorf) undated. LBS newspaper clippings archive.

128. *Die grünen Teufel von Monte Cassino*, Dir. Harald Reinl. Franz Seitz, 1958.

129. *Triumph des Willens* [Triumph of the will], Dir. Leni Riefenstahl. Leni Riefenstahl, 1934.

130. *The Wonderful Horrible Life of Leni Riefenstahl*, Dir. Ray Müller. Hans-Jürgen Panitz, Omega Films and Nomad Films, 1993.

131. Hamburg Institute, *The German Army and Genocide*, 26–27.

132. "'U 47'—Günter Prien," *SOS Schicksale Deutscher Schiffe* 15. (Munich: Arthur Moewig Verlag, n.d.).

133. Prüfverfahren, "betr. 1 Plakatfoto zu dem Film 'U47', Prüf.- Nummer: 17 935." LBS newspaper clippings archive.

134. Jugendprotokoll—Hauptauschuß der FSK, Prüfsitzung, September 20, 1958, Prüf.—Nummer: 17 935. Jugendprotokoll—Arbeitsauschuß der FSK, Prüfsituzung, October 6, 1958, Prüf.—Nummer: 17 935. Both in LBS newspaper clippings archive.

135. *Unruhige Nacht*, Dir. Falk Harnack. Real/Carlton/Filmaufbau, 1958.

136. Messerschmidt, "Zur neueren Diskussion," 392.

137. Ibid., 393–94.

138. Ibid., 395.

139. *Telegraf* (Berlin-West), November 1, 1958. LBS newspaper clippings archive.

140. Former Private First Class 246 Infantry Division, "Ein ehemaliger Soldat bittet um das Wort," *Der Mittag* (Düsseldorf), November 25, 1958. LBS newspaper clippings archive.

141. Hamburg Institute, *German Army and Genocide*, 102–14.

142. *Strafbataillon 999*, Dir. Harald Philipp. Willy Zeyn, 1959.

143. Sigl et al., *Jede Menge*, 132–33. Although the film opened in 1958, it was unranked in that year and ranked 193 of approximately 500 films in 1959.

144. For an example of how difficult it is to escape ethnocentric worldviews even during the process of building peace, see Gadi Wolfsfeld, *Media and the Path to Peace* (Cambridge: Cambridge University Press, 2004).

145. *Die letzte Nacht*, Dir. Eugen York. Real, 1949.

146. *Am Galgen hängt die Liebe*, Dir. Edwin Zbonek. Rex/Bloemer, 1960.

Chapter 5. Division and Unity

1. Karl-Heinz Janßen, "Die Revolution aus dem Stegreif," *Die Zeit*, June 18, 1993: 13–16.

2. Stefan Wolle, "Lebendiges Bewußtsein gegen paranoide Angst," *Der Tagesspiegel*, June 17, 1993: 6.

3. "Berlin gedachte des Volksaufstandes," *Der Tagesspiegel*, June 19, 1963: 5.

4. "Reste des Stalinismus Beseitigen," *Der Tagesspiegel*, June 19, 1963: 5.

5. Matthias Walden, "Spielende Kinder hinter dem Stacheldraht," *Der Tagesspiegel*,

June 16, 1963: 3, Heinz Kulke, "Auf den Bergen die Burgen," *Der Tagesspiegel*, June 16, 1963: 3.

6. Noelle-Neumann, *The Germans*, 127.

7. Ibid., 126.

8. RM, "Weitab vom Rias," *Der Tagesspiegel*, June 17, 1993: 9.

9. "Die Dulles waren auch dabei," *Die Wahrheit*, June 3/4, 1978 (DRA newspaper clippings archive); "Mörder, Schläger und Brandstifter," *Die Wahrheit*, June 10/11, 1978 (DRA newspaper clippings archive).

10. "Die Arbeiter werden die Maßnahmen voll unterstützen," *Neues Deutschland*, June 16, 1953: 1.

11. Rainer Hildebrandt, "Vom menschenrechtlichen Anliegen ist das politische nicht zu trennen," *Der Tagesspiegel*, June 17, 1973: 3.

12. East Germany was referred to in official documents and the popular press simply as "the zone" in the early years.

13. "Chaoten verwüsten die City und terrorisieren Unbeteiligte," *Frankfurter Allgemeine*, June 19, 1978: 29.

14. "Krawalle nach Gegendemonstration," *Der Tagesspiegel*, June 19, 1983: 15.

15. "Kranzniederlegungen," *Der Tagesspiegel*, June 19, 1968: 11; "Kranzniederlegungen am 17. Juni," *Der Tagesspiegel*, June 16, 1978: 10.

16. Thilo Koch, "Ist Deutschland doch teilbar?" *Die Zeit*, June 12, 1958: 3.

17. For additional reflections on political spectacles and symbolism, see Murray Edelman, *Constructing the Political Spectacle* (Chicago: University of Chicago Press, 1988).

18. "Bundespräsident Lübke ruft zur Einigkeit auf," *Der Tagesspiegel*, June 19, 1963: 5; "Hunderttausende bei den Feiern zum Nationalen Gedenktag," *Frankfurter Allgemeine*, June 19, 1963: 1.

19. Brigitte Grunert and Lothar Heinke, "Die späte Ehrung der Helden des 17. Juni," *Der Tagesspiegel*, June 18, 1993: 3.

20. Karl-Heinz Janßen, "Wollen wir noch eine Nation sein?" *Die Zeit*, June 16, 1978: 1.

21. Andrei S. Markovits and Philip S. Gorski, *The German Left: Red, Green and Beyond* (New York: Oxford University Press, 1993), conclusion.

22. Günter Grass, *Two States—One Nation?*, trans. Krishna Winston and A. S. Wensinger (San Diego: Harcourt Brace Jovanovich, 1990), 6.

23. Parts of this section appeared in Mark A. Wolfgram, "Gendered Border Crossings: Germany's Films of Division," *Symploke* 15, nos. 1–2 (2007): 152–69.

24. Bruce L. Berg, *Qualitative Research Methods*.

25. Alan Williams, "Introduction," in *Film and Nationalism*, ed. Alan Williams (New Brunswick, NJ: Rutgers University Press, 2002), 1–22.

26. Murray Edelman, *From Art to Politics: How Artistic Creations Shape Political Conceptions* (Chicago: University of Chicago Press, 1995). Peter L. Berger and Thomas Luckmann, *The Social Construction of Reality: A Treatise in the Sociology of Knowledge* (New York: Anchor Books, 1966).

27. Daphne Berdahl, *Where the World Ended: Re-Unification and Identity in the German Borderland* (Berkeley: University of California Press, 1999).

28. Anthony P. Cohen, *The Symbolic Construction of Community* (London: Routledge, 1985).

29. Arnold Van Gennep, *The Rites of Passage*, trans. Monika B. Vizedom and Gabrielle L. Caffee (London: Routledge & Kegal Paul, 1960); Victor Turner, *The Forest of Symbols: Aspects of Ndembu Ritual* (Ithaca, NY: Cornell University Press, 1967), 93–94.

30. Julie Gregson, "East or West—a Straight Choice? Representations of Masculinity and Constructions of National Identity in Wolfgang Kohlhaase and Gerhad

Kein's *Berlin Ecke Schönhauser,*" in *Millennial Essays on Film and Other German Studies*, ed. Daniela Berghahn and Alan Bruce (Oxford: Peter Lang, 2002), 68–9. *Berlin—Ecke Schönhauser*, Dir. Gerhard Klein DEFA, 1957.

31. Mary Douglas, *Purity and Danger: An Analysis of the Concepts of Pollution and Taboo* (London: Routledge & Kegan Paul, 1966), 40.

32. There are, of course, numerous texts dealing with German cinema, but few focus explicitly on the division theme. Deutsches Rundfunkarchiv, *In geteilter Sicht: Fernsehgeschichte als Zeitgeschichte—Zeitgeschichte als Fernsehgeschichte* (Potsdam: Verlag für Berlin-Brandenberg, 2003); also see Joshua Feinstein's chapter, "Straddling the Wall," in *The Triumph of the Ordinary: Depictions of Daily Life in the East German Cinema 1949–1989* (Chapel Hill: University of North Carolina Press, 2002); Hans Joachim Meuer, *Cinema and National Identity in a Divided Germany, 1979–1989: The Split Screen* (Lewiston, NY: Edwin Mellen Press, 2000).

33. David Bordwell, "Contemporary Film Studies and the Vicissitudes of Grand Theory," in *Post-Theory: Reconstructing Film Studies*, ed. David Bordwell and Noël Carroll (Madison: University of Wisconsin Press, 1996), 3–36.

34. *Himmel ohne Sterne*, Dir. Helmut Käutner. Neue Deutsche Filmgesellschaft, 1955.

35. Alex Neill, "Empathy and (Film) Fiction," in *Post-Theory: Reconstructing Film Studies*, ed. David Bordwell and Noël Carroll (Madison: University of Wisconsin Press, 1996), 175–94.

36. *Weg ohne Umkehr*, Dir. Victor Vicas. Occident, 1953.

37. *Flucht nach Berlin*, Dir. Will Tremper. Stun and Tremper, 1960.

38. *Tunnel 28*, Dir. Robert Siodmak. Hans Albin/Waller Wood, 1962.

39. *Der Mann auf der Mauer*, Dir. Reinhard Hauff. Bioskop / Paramount / ZDF, 1982.

40. *Lieb Vaterland, magst ruhig sein*, Dir. Roland Klick. Solaris/Cotta/Filmstudio Havelschaussee, 1975.

41. *. . . und der Himmel steht still*, Dir. John Schlesinger. Sievernich Film/Lakehart, 1993.

42. *Westler*, Dir. Wieland Speck. Searcher Filmproduction Sunger & Grüttgen/ZDF, 1985.

43. *Das Versprechen*, Dir. Margarethe von Trotta. Bioskop/J.M.H./Odessa, WDR, 1995.

44. *Eisenhans*, Dir. Tankred Dorst. Bavaria/WDR, 1982.

45. *Anna*, Dir. Uschi Reich. WDR, 1975.

46. *Irgendwo in Berlin*, Dir. Gerhard Lamprecht. DEFA, 1946.

47. *Unser täglich Brot*, Dir. Slatan Dudow. DEFA, 1949.

48. *Roman einer jüngen Ehe*, Dir. Kurt Maetzig. DEFA, 1952.

49. *Sein grosser Sieg*, Dir. Franz Barrenstein. DEFA, 1952.

50. *Der Fall Dr. Wagner*, Dir. Harald Mannl. DEFA, 1954.

51. *Eine Berliner Romanze*, Dir. Gerhard Klein. DEFA, 1956.

52. *Das Leben Beginnt*, Dir. Heiner Carow. DEFA, 1960.

53. *East of Eden*, Dir. Elia Kazan, 1954. *On The Waterfront*, Dir. Elia Kazan, 1954. *Rebel without a Cause*, Dir. Nicholas Ray, 1955. *The Wild One*, Dir. Laslo Benedek, 1954.

54. Albert Hirschmann, "Exit, Voice and the Fate of the German Democratic Republic," *World Politics* 45, no. 2 (January 1993): 173–202.

55. *. . . und deine Liebe auch*, Dir. Frank Vogel. DEFA, 1962.

56. *Kinnhaken*, Dir. Heinz Thiel. DEFA, 1962.

57. *Der geteilte Himmel*, Dir. Konrad Wolf. DEFA, 1964.

58. *Sonntagsfahrer*, Dir. Gerhard Klein. DEFA, 1963.

59. *Genosse Münchhausen*, Dir. Wolfgang Neuss. Satir, 1962.

60. Gesine Schwan, *Politik und Schuld: Die Zerstörische Macht des Schweigens* (Frankfurt am Main: Fischer Taschenhuch Verlag, 1997); Michael Schneider, "Fathers and Son's Retrospectively: The Damaged Relationship between Two Generations," *New German Critique* 31 (Winter 1984): 3–51.

61. *Geschichte Jener Nacht*, Dir. Karlheinz Carpentier. DEFA, 1967.

62. *Die Flucht*, Dir. Roland Gräf. DEFA, 1977.

63. Michael Schudson, "How Culture Works: Perspectives from Media Studies on the Efficacy of Symbols," *Theory and Society* 18 (1989): 153–80.

64. Benedict Anderson, *Imagined Communities: Reflections on the Origins and Spread of Nationalisms* (New York: Verso, 1991).

65. Leo Ensel, *Warum wir uns nicht leiden mögen: Was Ossis und Wessis voneinander halten* (Münster: agenda, 1993). Mathias Wedel, *Einheitsfrust* (Berlin: Rowohlt, 1994).

66. Andrea Rinke, "From Motzki to Trotzki: Representations of East and West German Cultural Identities on German Television after Unification," in *The New Germany: Literature and Society after Unification*, ed. Osman Durrani et al. (Sheffield, England: Sheffield Academic Press, 1995), 235.

Chapter 6. Defeat and Liberation

1. Daniel Jonah Goldhagen, *Hitler's Willing Executioners: Ordinary Germans and the Holocaust* (New York: Vintage Books, 1997).

2. Geoff Eley, ed., *The "Goldhagen Effect": History, Memory, Nazism—Facing the German Past* (Ann Arbor: University of Michigan Press, 2000); Martin Kött, *Goldhagen in der Qualitätspresse: Eine Debatte über "Kollektivschuld" und "Nationalcharakter" der Deutschen* (Konstanz: UVK Medien, 1999); Robert R. Shandley, ed., *Unwilling Germans? The Goldhagen Debate* (Minneapolis: University of Minnesota Press, 1998); Norman G. Finkelstein and Ruth Bettina Birn, *A Nation on Trial: The Goldhagen Thesis and Historical Truth* (New York: Henry Holt, 1998).

3. Omer Bartov, "Professional Soldiers," in *The German Army and Genocide: Crimes against War Prisoners, Jews, and Other Civilians, 1939–1944*, ed. Hamburg Institute for Social Research (New York: New Press, 1999), 13.

4. Harald Welzer, Sabine Moller and Karoline Tschuggnall, *"Opa war kein Nazi": Nationalsozialismus und Holocaust im Familiengedächtnis* (Frankfurt am Main: Fischer, 2002), 150–56.

5. Erich Peter Neumann and Elisabeth Noelle, eds., *The Germans: Public Opinion Polls 1947–1966* (Allensbach: Verlag für Demoskopie, 1954), 77.

6. Peter Schneider, "Der Bundestag wolle beschließen: Zur Debatte über die Ausstellung 'Vernichtungskrieg: Verbrechen der Wehrmacht 1941 bis 1944,'" in *Eine Ausstellung und ihre Folgen: Zur Rezeption der Ausstellung "Vernichtungskrieg: Verbrechen der Wehrmacht 1941 bis 1944,"* ed. Hamburger Institut für Sozialforschung (Hamburg: Hamburger Edition, 1999), 112–22.

7. For the importance of the *Volkish* tradition in creating the cultural basis for the rise of the National Socialists see George L. Mosse, *The Crisis of German Ideology: Intellectual Origins of the Third Reich* (New York: Universal Library of Grosset & Dunlap, 1964).

8. Birgitta Nedelmann, "Die Ausstellung 'Vernichtungskrieg: Verbrechen der Wehrmacht 1941 bis 1944,' und die Konstruktion öffentlicher Diskurse," in *Eine Ausstellung und ihre Folgen: Zur Rezeption der Ausstellung "Vernichtungskrieg: Verbrechen*

der Wehrmacht 1941 bis 1944," ed. Hamburger Institut für Sozialforschung (Hamburg: Hamburger Edition, 1999), 241.

9. Ibid., 243.

10. Bernd Greiner, "Bruch-Stücke," in *Eine Ausstellung und ihre Folgen: Zur Rezeption der Ausstellung "Vernichtungskrieg. Verbrechen der Wehrmacht 1941 bis 1944*," ed. Hamburger Institut für Sozialforschung (Hamburg: Hamburger Edition, 1999), 20.

11. Ibid., 35.

12. Ibid., 36.

13. Ibid., 39.

14. Bogdan Musial, "Bilder einer Ausstellung: Kritische Anmerkungen zur Wanderausstellung 'Vernichtungskrieg: Verbrechen der Wehrmacht 1941 bis 1944,'" *Vierteljahrshefte für Zeitgeschichte* 47, no. 4 (October 1999): 563–91.

15. Dominik Wichmann, "These richtig, Bilder falsch?" *Süddeutscher Zeitung*, October 16, 1999: 17.

16. "Fotos der Wehrmachtausstellung falsch zugeordnet," *Frankfurter Allgemeine*, October 20, 1999: 1.

17. Johannes Willms, "Erdrückende Beweislast," *Süddeutscher Zeitung*, October 21, 1999: 15.

18. "Zehn Prozent der Bilder zeigen eindeutig Taten der Wehrmacht," *Frankfurter Allgemeine*, October 22, 1999: 2.

19. "Bilder einer Ausstellung," *Frankfurter Allgemeine*, October 22, 1999: 1.

20. Hamburg Institute, *German Army and Genocide.*

21. Joachim Kaeppner, "Mehr Verbrechen," *Süddeutscher Zeitung*, November 24, 2000: 15. For a collection of these critiques see Christian Hartmann, Johannes Hürter, and Ulrike Jureit, eds., *Verbrechen der Wehrmacht: Bilanz einer Debatte* (Munich: Verlag C. H. Beck, 2005).

22. www.verbrechen-der-wehrmacht.de.

23. Christopher Browning, *Ordinary Men: Reserve Police Battalion 101 and the Final Solution in Poland* (New York: HarperCollins, 1992).

24. *Apocalypse Now*, Dir. Francis Ford Coppola. 1979.

25. Heribert Prantl, "Wie geht Erinnerung?" *Süddeutsche Zeitung*, May 8, 2000: 4.

26. "Der Krieg als Männerlandverschickung," *Der Tagesspiegel*, May 8, 2000: 7.

27. Wolfram Wette, "Als Deutschland sterben sollte," *Die Zeit*, May 4, 2000: 84.

28. Noelle-Neumann and Köcher, *Allensbach Jahrbuch*, 522.

29. Ibid., 546.

30. Regina Mönch, "Rechzeitig auf der richtigen Seite," *Der Tagesspiegel*, May 7, 1995: Welt Spiegel 11.

31. Arnold Zweig, "Enthüllter Rat der Götter," *Neues Deutschland*, May 7, 1950: 3.

32. *Strasse zur Freiheit*, Dir. Horst Schubert. DFF, May 8 or 13, 1970. DRA Lagernr.: AC 11659.

33. For example, "Ruhm und Ehre den Befreiern!" *Neues Deutschland*, May 7, 1950: 1.

34. "Nach der Befreiung," *Neues Deutschland*, May 7, 1950: 6.

35. "Ruhm dem Sowjetvolk, das uns vom Faschismus befreit hat," *Neues Deutschland*, May 8, 1968: 3; *Freie Welt* Number 8, 1975; "Schildern Sie uns Ihre Erlebnisse," *Berliner Zeitung*, January 14, 1975: 7; *Tribüne*, March 21, 1975: 5; Margarete Steinführ, "Ein ganzes Brot," *Neues Deutschland*, March 16/17, 1985: 9.

36. Lucie Scharfenort, "Berliner erinnern sich an den 8. Mai 1945," *Neues Deutschland*, May 7, 1950: 8.

37. Norman M. Naimark, *The Russians in Germany* (Cambridge, MA: Harvard University Press, 1995). Atina Grossmann, "A Question of Silence: The Rape of German Women by Occupation Soldiers," *October* 72 (April 1995): 43–63.

38. Franz Dahlem, "Tag der Befreiung," *Neues Deutschland*, May 7, 1950: 2.

39. Lutz Niethammer, Alexander von Plato, and Dorothee Wierling, *Die volkseigene Erfahrung: Eine Archäologie des Lebens in der Industrieprovinz der DDR* (Berlin: Rowohlt, 1991), 55–56.

40. For an excellent recent analysis of old and new monuments in Berlin, see Brian Ladd, *The Ghosts of Berlin: Confronting German History in the Urban Landscape* (Chicago: University of Chicago Press, 1997).

41. *Ruhm und Ehre den sowejtischen Helden*. DDR-F, May 8, 1960.

42. *Manifestation der FDJ und der Pionierorganisation "Ernst Thälmann" anläßlich des 40. Jahrestages des Sieges über den Hitlerfaschismus und der Befreiung des Deutschen Volkes*. DDR-F, May 7, 1985; DRA Lagernr.: FAZ 02634 or OVC 0704.

43. Fernsehen der DDR Programmdirektion dated May 20, 1985, 2. DRA ArNr.: H 023–00–02/0119.

44. *Festveranstaltung des ZK der SED der Regierung der DDR und des Nationalrates zum 15. Jahrestag der Befreiung*. DFF, May 7, 1960. DRA Lagernr.: 04429/93561. *Kundgebung anläßlich des Kapitulationsfeiertages*. DFF, May 7, 1965. DRA Lagernr.: 05368/94365.

45. Zuschauerforschung dated June 3, 1970. DRA ArNr.: H 008–02–04 / 0061.

46. Fernsehen der DDR Programmdirektion dated May 20, 1985, 2. DRA ArNr.: H 023–00–02/0119.

47. *Neues Deutschland*, May 9, 1986: 1; May 9/10, 1987: 1; May 10, 1988: 1; and May 9, 1989: 1.

48. *Blokada*, Dir. Michail Jerschow. 1974.

49. Alexander Tschakowski, "900 heroische Tage," *Sowjet Film* 1978 (9): 7.

50. Zuschauerforschung for May 5, 1980. ArNr: H 081–03–02 / 0074.

51. Katherine Verdery, *National Ideology under Socialism: Identity and Cultural Politics in Ceausescu's Romania* (Berkeley: University of California Press, 1991).

52. Karlen Vesper, "'Endlich waren wir wieder frei!'" *Neues Deutschland*, May 8, 2000: 3.

53. "8. Mai: NS-Opfer warnen vor Alltagsfaschismus," *Neues Deutschland*, May 8, 2000: 1.

54. Heinrich Fink, "Nachdenken zum 8. Mai," *Neues Deutschland*, May 6/7, 2000: 1.

55. Full page of articles, *Neues Deutschland*, May 9, 1995: 3.

56. Alexander von Plato and Almut Leh, *"Ein unglaublicher Frühling": Erfahrene Geschichte im Nachkriegsdeutschland 1945–1948* (Bonn: Bundeszentrale für politische Bildung, 1997).

57. R. R. Palmer and Joel Colton, *A History of the Modern World*, 8th ed. (New York: McGraw-Hill, 1995), 854.

58. Michael Kumpfmüller, *Die Schlacht von Stalingrad: Metamorphosen eines deutschen Mythos* (Munich: Wilhelm Fink Verlag, 1996).

59. *Hunde, wollt ihr ewig leben?* Dir. Frank Wisbar. DFH, 1958. See also Reimer and Reimer, *Nazi-Retro*, 62–64.

60. Omer Bartov, *Hitler's Army: Soldiers, Nazis and War in the Third Reich* (New York: Oxford University Press, 1992), 166.

61. *Stalingrad*, Dir. Gustav Burmester. NDR, January 31, 1963.

62. Classen, *Bilder*, 73.

63. *Eine Armee wird mißbraucht*, Dir. Jürgen Neven-Dumont. NDR, February 1, 1963.

64. Classen, *Bilder*, 75–76.

65. *Hitlerjugend—Mißbrauch einer Generation*, Dir. Horst Siebecke. BR, April 13, 1965. BR Production Number 37913.

66. Classen, *Bilder*, 99–100.

67. Classen's conclusions on the documentary were probably drawn from some very minimal program notes. He offers an excellent survey of German television over a decade, and it is not my intention to nit-pick his work.

68. See Mosse, *The Crisis of German Ideology*, chapter 9, "The Youth Movement."

69. *Stalingrad*, Dir. Joseph Vilsmaier. Royal/Bavaria/B.A./Pevathon, 1991/92.

70. "Die sowjetische Fahne an Privathäusern," *Frankfurter Allgemeine*, May 8, 1950: 4. "Von der 'Befreiungsfeier' befreit," *Der Tagesspiegel*, May 9, 1950: 3.

71. "Ein Jahr Grundgesetz," *Frankfurter Allgemeine*, May 8, 1950: 2.

72. Michael Freund, "Die Wochen, die ein Jahrtausend zerstörten," *Die Zeit*, May 5, 1955: 2.

73. Joachim Bölke, "8. Mai 1945–8. Mai 1955," *Der Tagesspiegel*, May 8, 1955: 3.

74. Erich Dombrowski, "8. Mai 1945," *Frankfurter Allgemeine*, May 7, 1955: 1.

75. "Der Weg zur Soveränität," *Der Tagesspiegel*, May 8, 1955: 25.

76. "Zum gedenken der Kriegsgefangenen," *Der Tagesspiegel*, May 8, 1955: 2.

77. "Schweigeminute zum 8. Mai," *Frankfurter Allgemeine*, May 9, 1955: 1.

78. *Der Arzt von Stalingrad*, Dir. Geza von Radvanyi. Divinia, 1958.

79. *Haie und kleine Fische*, Dir. Frank Wisbar. Zeyn/Seveerin, 1957.

80. Sigl et al., *Jede Menge*, 132.

81. "Völkerversöhnung muss anders aussehen," *Deutsche Woche* (Munich), August 6, 1958. "Lob für Stalingrad-Film," *Welt am Sonntag* (Berlin/West), July 27, 1958. Both LBS newspaper clippings archive.

82. "Der Arzt von Stalingrad," *Stuttgarter Zeitung*, February 22, 1958. LBS newspaper clippings archive.

83. Eric Langenbacher, "The Return of Memory: New Discussions about German Suffering in World War II," *German Politics and Society* 21, no. 3 (Fall 2003): 74–88.

84. Mosse, *Crisis of German Ideology*, chapter 5.

85. Neumann and Noelle, *Germans*, 127.

86. "Des Meeres und des Krieges Wellen," *Stuttgarter Zeitung*, August 30, 1957. LBS newspaper clippings archive.

87. *Das Boot*, Dir. Wolfgang Petersen. Bavaria/Radiant/WDR/SDR, 1981.

88. "Erklärungen zum 8. Mai," *Der Tagesspiegel*, May 7, 1965: 6.

89. "Erhard: Positive Mitarbeit im Interesse des Friedens," *Der Tagesspiegel*, May 8, 1965: 1.

90. "'Die Mörder von gestern,'" *Der Tagesspiegel*, May 8, 1965: 5; "'Die Wahrheit ist die härteste Anklage,'" *Frankfurter Allgemeine*, May 8, 1965: 17–18.

91. Dietrich Strothmann, "Haltungen—Fehlhaltungen," *Die Zeit*, May 7, 1965: 21.

92. *Infratest*, August 24–30, 1964: 42–43. *Hitler und der Zweite Weltkrieg*. ZDF, August 27, 1964.

93. *Infratest* 19, 1965: 59–61. *Das letzte Kapitel*, Dir. F. A. Krummacher. ZDF, May 8, 1965.

94. "Bundestag gedachte des 25. Jahrestages der deutschen Kapitulation," *Der Tagesspiegel*, May 9, 1970: 9; "Unsere Wirklichkeit durch Hitlers Niederlage entstanden," *Frankfurter Allgemeine*, May 9, 1970: 7.

95. "Der Wortlaut der Rede Heinemanns zum 25. Jahrestag des Kriegsendes," *Der Tagesspiegel*, May 7, 1970: 9.

96. Marion Gräfin Dönhoff, "25 Jahre nach Hitler," *Die Zeit*, May 8, 1970: 1.

97. "Weizsäcker: Der 8. Mai nicht das letzte Datum gemeinsamer Geschichte," *Frankfurter Allgemeine*, May 9, 1970: 7.

98. "Denkmale des Widerstandes," *Der Tagesspiegel*, May 9, 1970: 6.

99. "Propst Heinrich Grüber wurde Ehrenbürger von Berlin," *Der Tagesspiegel*, May 9, 1970: 5.

100. "Scheel warnt die Jugend vor Demagogen," *Der Tagesspiegel*, May 7, 1975: 5.

101. "Schmidt fordert zu entschlossener Wahrung der Verfassung auf," *Der Tagesspiegel*, May 8, 1975: 1.

102. "Gedenken und Kränze zum 8. Mai," *Der Tagesspiegel*, May 8, 1975: 12.

103. "Jüdische Gemeinde gedachte des Jahrestages des Kriegsendes," *Der Tagesspiegel*, May 10, 1965: 2.

104. Ladd, *Ghosts of Berlin*, 217–24.

105. Langguth, *In Search of Security*.

106. Charles S. Maier, *The Unmasterable Past*, 9–16.

107. J. B., "Bitburg und Mitterrand," *Der Tagesspiegel*, May 7, 1985: 1.

108. Günter Gillessen, "Verwandlungen eines Besuches," *Frankfurter Allgemeine*, May 8, 1985: 1.

109. Marion Gräfin Dönhoff, "Die Last der Kindeskinder," *Die Zeit*, May 10, 1985: 1.

110. "Kritik aus Israel an Besuch Reagans," *Der Tagesspiegel*, May 7, 1985: 7.

111. "Galinski: In Erinnerung an NS-Zeit freiheitliche Gesellschaft gestalten," *Der Tagesspiegel*, May 8, 1985: 6.

112. "Parteien ziehen unterschiedliche Schlußfolgerungen aus dem 8. Mai 1945," *Der Tagesspiegel*, May 8, 1985: 6.

113. "Weizsäcker nennt 8. Mai tag der Befreiung und Ende eines Irrweges," *Der Tagesspiegel*, May 9, 1985: 1; "Die Rede Weizsäckers in Wortlautauszügen," *Der Tagesspiegel*, May 9, 1985: 6.

114. "Gottesdienst im Kölner Dom," *Frankfurter Allgemeine*, May 9, 1985: 2; Bishop Lohse, "Gott hat man die Ehre gestohlen und war fremden Göttern nachgelaufen," *Frankfurter Allgemeine*, May 9, 1985: 6; Cardinal Höffner, "Schuld läßt sich nicht durch politische und psychologische Analysen bewältigen," *Frankfurter Allgemeine*, May 9, 1985: 6.

115. Karl-Alfred Odin, "In den Gottesdiensten wird der Blick auf die Schuld gelenkt," *Frankfurter Allgemeine*, May 8, 1985: 7.

116. Achim Forst, "Nach vierzig Jahren," *Der Tagesspiegel*, May 9, 1985: 4.

117. Elie Wiesel, "Gedenken vor der Wannsee-Villa," *Der Tagesspiegel*, May 9, 1990: 8. "Mahnung des Jüdischen Weltkongresses zum 45. Jahrestag des Kriegsendes," *Der Tagesspiegel*, May 9, 1990: 1.

118. " 'Furcht und Beben, Zorn und Schmerz,' " *Frankfurter Allgemeine*, May 9, 1990: 3.

119. "Herzog: Der Tag, an dem ein Tor in die Zukunft aufgestoßen wurde," *Frankfurter Allgemeine*, May 9, 1995: 1–2.

120. Wolfram Werte, " 'Jude gleich Partisan,' " *Die Zeit*, May 5, 1995: 19; Robert Leicht, "Nur im Untergang lag die Befreiung," *Die Zeit*, May 5, 1995: 1; Regina Mönch, "Der Ort, an dem der Krieg zu Ende ging," *Der Tagesspiegel*, May 8, 1995: 9.

121. Gunter Hofmann, "Eine Woche in Deutschland," *Die Zeit*, May 12, 1995: 4.

122. Johann Georg Reißmüller, "Tag des Zwiespalts," *Frankfurter Allgemeine*, May 8, 1995: 1.

123. "Zentrum der Juden in der Mitte Berlins," *Der Tagesspiegel*, May 7, 1995: 1.

124. Malte Lehming, "Unfähig zu trauern, unfähig zu feiern," *Der Tagesspiegel*, May 8, 1995: 6.

125. Stefan Kuschel, "Ein Optimist überlebte—vor 50 Jahren," *Der Tagesspiegel*, May 8, 1995: 9.

126. Thomas Lackmann, "Immer am 29. April," *Der Tagesspiegel*, May 8, 1995: 19.

127. Wolfgang Ebert, "Die Amerikaner!" *Die Zeit*, May 5, 1995: 2.

128. Manfred Sack, "Auf wen wartest du eigentlich?" *Die Zeit*, May 9, 1975: 52; Manfred Sack, "Vollständig irre," *Die Zeit*, May 5, 1995: 2.

129. *Pimpf* was the name given to those who were in the Hitler Youth for ten- to fourteen-years-olds. *Pimpf war jeder*, Dir. Erwin Leiser. ZDF, May 7, 1995.

130. *ZDF Presse Programm* 19/95, May 7, 1995.

131. *Die Befreiung*, Dir. Ekkehard Kuhn and Carl-Ludwig Paeschke. ZDF, May 7, 1995.

132. *ZDF Presse Programm* 19/95, May 7, 1995.

133. *Deutschlandlied*, Dr. Tom Toelle. ZDF, May 8, 10, and 14, 1995.

134. *ZDF Presse Special: Deutschlandlied: Ein Film von Tom Toelle.* ZDF Press Archive.

135. ZDF Telefon-Protokoll File, *Das Deutschlandlied*, part 1, May 8, 1995; part 2, May 10, 1995; part 3, May 14, 1995.

Chapter 7. Conclusion

1. Alexander Mitscherlich and Margarete Mitscherlich, *The Inability to Mourn: Principles of Collective Behavior*, trans. Beverley R. Placzek (New York: Grove Press, 1975), 28.

2. Mark A. Wolfgram, "What Can War Crimes Trials Teach? German Collective Memories of the Nuremberg Trials" (conference paper, annual meeting of the International Studies Association, New York, February 15–18, 2009).

3. Aber Cohen, *Two-Dimensional Man*, 13.

Filmography

German Pre-1945

Triumph des Willens [Triumph of the Will]. Dir. Leni Riefenstahl. Leni Riefenstahl, 1934.

East German

Die Abenteuer der Werner Holt. Dir. Joachim Kunert. DEFA, 1964.
Die Affäre Blum. Dir. Erich Engel. DEFA, 1948.
Berlin—Ecke Schönhauser. Dir. Gerhard Klein. DEFA, 1957.
Eine Berliner Romanze. Dir. Gerhard Klein. DEFA, 1956.
Chronik eines Mordes. Dir. Jo Hasler. DEFA, 1965.
Ehe im Schatten. Dir. Kurt Maetzig. DEFA, 1947.
Der Fall Dr. Wagner. Dir. Harald Mannl. DEFA, 1954.
Die Flucht. Dir. Roland Gräf. DEFA, 1977.
Geschichte Jener Nacht. Dir. Karlheinz Carpentier. DEFA, 1967.
Der geteilte Himmel. Dir. Konrad Wolf. DEFA, 1964.
Ich war neunzehn. Dir. Konrad Wolf. DEFA, 1968.
Im Sonderauftrag. Dir. Heinz Thiel. DEFA, 1959.
Iregendwo in Berlin. Dir. Gerhard Lamprecht. DEFA, 1946.
Jakob der Lügner. Dir. Frank Beyer. DEFA, 1975.
Kinnhaken. Dir. Heinz Thiel. DEFA, 1962.
Das Leben Beginnt. Dir. Heiner Carow. DEFA, 1960.
Lebende Ware. Dir. Wolfgang Luderer. DEFA, 1966.
Die Mörder sind unter uns. Dir. Wolfgang Staudte. DEFA, 1946.
Nackt unter Wölfen. Dir. Frank Beyer. DEFA, 1963.
Professor Mamlock. Dir. Konrad Wolf. DEFA, 1961.
Der Prozeß wird vertagt. Dir. Herbert Ballmann. DEFA, 1958.
Roman einer jüngen Ehe. Dir. Kurt Maetzig. DEFA, 1952.
Rotation. Dir. Wolfgang Staudte. DEFA, 1949.
Die Schauspielerin. Dir. Siegfried Kühn. DEFA, 1988.
Sein grosser Sieg. Dir. Franz Barrenstein. DEFA, 1952.

Sonntagsfahrer. Dir. Gerhard Klein. DEFA, 1963.
Sterne. Dir. Konrad Wolf. DEFA, 1959.
Stielke, Heinz, Fünfzehn. Dir. Michael Kann. DEFA, 1987.
Das Tal der sieben Monde. Dir. Gottfried Kolditz. DEFA, 1967.
. . . und deine Liebe auch. Dir. Frank Vogel. DEFA, 1962.
Unser täglich Brot. Dir. Slatan Dudow. DEFA, 1949.
Zwischenfall in Benderath. Dir. János Veiczi. DEFA, 1956.

West German and Post-1990

Am Galgen hängt die Liebe. Dir. Edwin Zbonek. Rex/Bloemer, 1960.
Aimée & Jaguar. Dir. Max Fäberböck. Senator, 1998.
Anna. Dir. Uschi Reich. WDR, 1975.
Der Arzt von Stalingrad. Dir. Geza von Radvanyi. Divinia, 1958.
Auf Wiedersehen Amerika. Dir. Jan Schütte. Novoscop/Pandora/arte /Casting S.F. / WDR, 1993.
Bittere Ernte. Dir. Agnieszka Holland. CCC Filmkunst/Admiral-Film, 1984.
Blutiger Schnee (Zu Freiwild verdammt). Dir. Jerzy Hoffman. CCC-Filmkunst/SFB / PRF Zespoloy Filmowe Zespol `Zodiak,' 1983.
Das Boot. Dir. Wolfgang Petersen. Bavaria/Radiant/WDR/SDR, 1981.
Canaris. Dir. Alfred Weidenmann. Fama, 1954.
David. Dir. Peter Lilienthal. Von Vietinghoff/Pro-ject/ZDF, 1978.
Des Teufels General. Dir. Helmut Käutner. Real-Film, 1954.
Eisenhans. Dir. Tankred Dorst. Bavaria/WDR, 1982.
Es geschah am 20. Juli. Dir. G.W. Pabst. Ariston/Area, 1955.
Flucht nach Berlin. Dir. Will Tremper. Stun and Tremper, 1960.
Friedericke von Barring. Dir. Rolf Thiele. 1956.
Georg Elser—Einers aus Deutschland. Dir. Klaus Maria Brandauer. Söhnlein/Borman Prod./Mutoskop Film/Saturn, 1989.
Genosse Münchhausen. Dir. Wolfgang Neuss. Satir, 1962.
Grün ist die Heide. Dir. Hans Deppe. Berolina, 1951.
Die grünen Teufel von Monte Cassino. Dir. Harald Reinl. Franz Seitz, 1958.
Haie und kleine Fische. Dir. Frank Wisbar. Zeyn/Seveerin, 1957.
Das Haus in der Karpfengasse. Dir. Kurt Hoffman. Independent Film/German TV, 1964.
Heimat. Dir. Edgar Reitz. SFB/WDR, 1984.
Himmel ohne Sterne. Dir. Helmut Käutner. Neue Deutsche Filmgesellschaft, 1955.
Hunde, wollt ihr ewig leben? Dir. Frank Wisbar. DFH, 1958.
Ich weiß, wofür ich lebe. Dir. Paul Verhoeven. Neubach-Film, 1955.
Lang ist der Weg. Directors Herbert B. Fredersdorf and Marek Goldstein. IFO-Film, 1947.
Leni. Dir. Leo Hiemer. DAZU Film/SDR/arte/WDR, 1994.
Die letzte Nacht. Dir. Eugen York. Real, 1949.

Lieb Vaterland, magst ruhig sein. Dir. Roland Klick. Solaris/Cotta/Filmstudio Havelchaussee, 1975.

Liebling der Götter. Dir. Gottfried Reinhardt. CCC, 1960.

Ein Lied geht um die Welt (Die Joseph-Schmidt-Story). Dir. Geza von Bolvary. Neubach, 1958.

Der Mann auf der Mauer. Dir. Reinhard Hauff. Bioskop/Paramount/ZDF, 1982.

Nacht fiel über Gotenhafen. Dir. Frank Wisbar. DFH, 1959.

Rosen für den Staatsanwalt. Dir. Wolfgang Staudte. Kurt Ulrich, 1959.

Das schreckliche Mädchen. Dir. Michael Verhoeven. Michael Senftleben, 1990.

Solange du lebst. Dir. Harald Reinl. Eva, 1955.

Stalingrad. Dir. Joseph Vilsmaier. Royal/Bavaria/B.A./Pevathon, 1991/92.

Stern ohne Himmel. Dir. Ottokar Runze. Ottokar Runze, 1980.

Strafbataillon 999. Dir. Harald Philipp. Willy Zeyn, 1959.

Tunnel 28. Dir. Robert Siodmak. Hans Albin/Waller Wood, 1962.

. . . und der Himmel steht still. Dir. John Schlesinger. Sievernich Film/Lakehart, 1993.

Unruhige Nacht. Dir. Falk Harnack. Real/Carlton/Filmaufbau, 1958.

U47—Kapitänleutnant Prien. Dir. Harald Reinl. Arca, 1958.

Das Versprechen. Dir. Margarethe von Trotta. Bioskop/J.M.H./Odessa, WDR, 1995.

Versteckt. Dir. Anthony Page. Jodack-Decade/Forstater/Clasart/Anthea/Stella, 1984.

Die Wannseekonferenz. Dir. Heinz Scheik. Manfred Korytowski/Infafilm GmbH Munich/ORF/Bavarian Broadcasting Corporation, 1984.

Weg ohne Umkehr. Dir. Victor Vicas. Occident, 1953.

Westler. Dir. Wieland Speck. Searcher Filmproduction Sunger & Grüttgen/ZDF, 1985.

Wie ein Hirschberger dänisch lenrte. Dir. Rolf Busch. 1968.

Wir Wunderkinder. Dir. Kurt Hoffmann. Filmaufbau, 1958.

Zeugin aus der Hölle. Dir. Zica Mitrovic. CCC/Avala, 1965.

Der 20. Juli. Dir. Falk Harnack. CCC, 1955.

From Other Countries

Apocalypse Now. Dir. Francis Ford Coppola. 1979.

Blokada. Dir. Michail Jerschow. 1974.

Dark Lullabies. Dir. Irene Lilienheim Angelico. National Film Board of Canada, 1993.

Deveti Krug. Dir. France Štiglic. Jadran Film (Yugoslavia), 1960.

East of Eden. Dir. Elia Kazan. 1954.

Lacombe Lucien. Dir. Louis Malle. 1974.

Life Is Beautiful [La Vita è bella]. Dir. Roberto Benigni. 1997.

Night and Fog. Alain Resnais. 1955.

Holocaust. Dir. Marvin Chomsky. Robert Berger, 1978.

On The Waterfront. Dir. Elia Kazan. 1954.

Rebel without a Cause. Dir. Nicholas Ray. 1955.

Schindler's List. Dir. Steven Spielberg. 1993.

Shoah. Dir. Claude Lanzmann. 1985.

Shtetl. Dir. Marian Marzynski. Marz Associates in association with WGBH/Frontline, 1996.

The Sorrow and the Pity. Dir. Marcel Ophuls. 1971.

The Wild One. Dir. Laslo Benedek. 1954.

The Wonderful Horrible Life of Leni Riefenstahl. Dir. Ray Müller. Hans-Jürgen Panitz/ Omega Films/Nomad Films, 1993.

Bibliography

Academic Literature

Aguilar, Paloma. *Memory and Amnesia: The Role of the Spanish Civil War in the Transition to Democracy.* Translated by Mark Oakley. New York: Berghahn Books, 2002.

Ahren, Yizhak et al. *Das Lehrstück "Holocaust": zur Wirkungspsychologie eines Medienereignisses.* Opladen: Westdeutscher Verlag, 1982.

Alexander, Jeffrey C. "Analytic Debates: Understanding the Relative Autonomy of Culture." In *Culture and Society: Contemporary Debates,* edited by Jeffrey C., Alexander and Steven Seidman, 1–27. Cambridge: Cambridge University Press, 1990.

Alexander, Jeffrey C. *The Meanings of Social Life: A Cultural Sociology.* Oxford: Oxford University Press, 2003.

Alexander, Jeffrey C., and Bernhard Giesen. "From Reduction to Linkage: The Long View of the Micro-Macro Debate." In *The Micro-Macro Link,* edited by Jeffrey C. Alexander, Bernhard Giesen, Richard Münch, and Neil J. Smelser, 1–42. Berkeley: University of California Press, 1987.

Alexander, Jeffrey C., and Jason L. Mast. "Introduction: Symbolic Action in Theory and Practice: The Cultural Pragmatics of Symbolic Action." In *Social Performance: Symbolic Action, Cultural Pragmatics, and Ritual,* edited by Jeffrey C. Alexander, Bernhard Giesen, and Jason L. Mast, 1–28. Cambridge: Cambridge University Press, 2006.

Allan, Seán. "DEFA: An Historical Overview." In *DEFA: East German Cinema, 1946–1992,* edited by Seán Allan and John Sandford, 1–21. New York: Berghahn Books, 1999.

Almond, Gabriel A., and Sidney Verba. *The Civic Culture: Political Attitudes and Democracy in Five Nations.* Princeton, NJ: Princeton University Press, 1963.

Anderson, Benedict. *Imagined Communities: Reflections on the Origins and Spread of Nationalisms.* New York: Verso, 1991.

Angress, Ruth Klüger. "A 'Jewish Problem' in German Postwar Fiction." *Modern Judaism* 5 (1985): 215–33.

Ankersmit, F.R. *Narrative Logic: A Semantic Analysis of the Historian's Language.* Boston: Kluwer, 1983.

Archer, Margaret S. *Culture and Agency: The Place of Culture in Social Theory.* Rev. ed. Cambridge: Cambridge University Press, 1996.

Art, David. *The Politics of the Nazi Past in Germany and Austria.* Cambridge: Cambridge University Press, 2006.

Assmann, Aleida. *Der lange Schatten der Vergangenheit: Erinnerungskultur und Geschichtspolitik.* Munich: Beck, 2006.

Barlog-Scholz, Renata. *Historisches Wissen über die national-sozialistischen Konzentrationslager bei deutschen Jugendlichen.* Frankfurt am Main: Peter Lang, 1994.

Bar-On, Dan. *Legacy of Silence: Encounters with Children of the Third Reich.* Cambridge, MA: Harvard University Press, 1989.

Bartov, Omer. *Hitler's Army: Soldiers, Nazis and War in the Third Reich.* New York: Oxford University Press, 1992.

Bartov, Omer. "Professional Soldiers." In *The German Army and Genocide: Crimes Against War Prisoners, Jews, and Other Civilians, 1939–1944*, edited by The Hamburg Institute for Social Research, 10–17. New York: The New Press, 1999.

Becker, Wolfgang, and Norbert Schöll. *In jenen Tagen . . .: Wie der deutsche Nachkriegsfilm die Vergangenheit bewältigte.* Opladen: Leske+Budrich, 1995.

Ben-Gaviel, M.Y. *Das Haus in der Karpfengasse.* Berlin: Colloqium-Verlag, 1957.

Berdahl, Daphne. *Where the World Ended: Re-Unification and Identity in the German Borderland.* Berkeley: University of California Press, 1999.

Berg, Bruce L. *Qualitative Research Methods for the Social Sciences*, 5th ed. Boston: Pearson Education, 2004.

Berger, Peter L., and Thomas Luckmann. *The Social Construction of Reality: A Treatise in the Sociology of Knowledge.* New York: Anchor Books, 1966.

Blum, Heiko R., ed. *30 Jahre danach: Auseinandersetzung mit dem Nationalsozialismus im Film 1945 bis 1975.* Cologne: Horst May Schnelldruck & Verlag, 1975.

Bodemann, Y. Michal. "Reconstructions of History: From Jewish Memory to Nationalized Commemoration of Kristallnacht in Germany." In *Jews, Germans, Memory: Reconstructions of Jewish Life in Germany*, edited by Y. Michal Bodemann, 179–223. Ann Arbor: University of Michigan Press, 1996.

Bodemann, Y. Michal. "The Uncanny Clatter: The Holocaust in Germany before Its Mass Commemoration." In *Remembering the Holocaust in Germany, 1945–2000: German Strategies and Jewish Responses*, edited by Dan Michman, 43–53. New York: Peter Lang, 2002.

Bordwell, David, and Noël Carroll. *Post-Theory: Reconstructing Film Studies.* Madison: University of Wisconsin Press, 1996.

Bourdieu, Pierre. *Language and Symbolic Power/Pierre Bourdieu.* Edited by John B. Thompson. Translated by Gino Raymond and Matthew Adamson. Cambridge, MA: Harvard University Press. 1991.

Brady, Martin. "Discussion with Kurt Maetzig." In *DEFA: East German Cinema, 1946–1992*, edited by Seán Allan and John Sandford, 77–92. New York: Berghahn Books, 1999.

Braumann, Christa. "Fernsehforschung zwischen Parteilichkeit und Objektivität: Zur Zuschauerforschung in der ehemaligen DDR." *Rundfunk und Fernsehen* 42 (1994): 524–41.

Browning, Christopher. *Ordinary Men: Reserve Police Battalion 101 and the Final Solution in Poland.* New York: HarperCollins, 1992.

Buruma, Ian. *The Wages of Guilt: Memories of War in Germany and Japan.* Middlesex, England: Meridian, 1995.

Classen, Christoph. *Bilder der Vergangenheit: Die Zeit des Nationalsozialismus im Fernsehen der Bundesrepublik Deutschland 1955–1965.* Cologne: Böhlau Verlag, 1999.

Cohen, Abner. *Two-Dimensional Man: An Essay on the Anthropology of Power and Symbolism in Complex Society.* Berkeley: University of California Press, 1974.

Cohen, Anthony P. *The Symbolic Construction of Community*. London: Routledge, 1985.

Confino, Alon. *Germany as a Culture of Remembrance: Promises and Limits of Writing History*. Chapel Hill: University of North Carolina Press, 2006.

Davies, Douglas James. *A Brief History of Death*. Malden, MA: Blackwell, 2005.

DEFA-Filme: Ein alphabetisches Titelverzeichnis von Filmen der DEFA nebst Personenregister. Mit einem Bestandnachweis der bei der Universitätsbibliothek Oldenburg vorhandenen Filme. Oldenburg: (BIS) Bibliotheks- und Informationssytem der Universität Oldenburg Verlag, 1993.

Deutsches Rundfunkarchiv. *In geteilter Sicht: Fernsehgeschichte als Zeitgeschichte—Zeitgeschichte als Fernsehgeschichte*. Potsdam: Verlag für Berlin-Brandenberg, 2003.

Deutschkron, Inge. . . . *denn ihrer war die Hölle. Kinder in Gettos und Lagern*. Cologne: Verlag Wissenschaft und Politik, 1965.

Deutschkron, Inge. *Mein Leben nach dem Überleben*. Munich: Deutscher Taschenbuch Verlag, 1995.

Dolan, Anne. *Commemorating the Irish Civil War: History and Memory, 1923–2000*. Cambridge: Cambridge University Press, 2003.

Douglas, Mary. *Purity and Danger: An Analysis of the Concepts of Pollution and Taboo*. London: Routledge & Kegan Paul, 1966.

Douglas, Mary. *Natural Symbols: Explorations in Cosmology*. London: Routledge, 1996. First published 1970 by Barrie & Rockliff.

Dudek, Peter. *"Der Rückblick auf die Vergangenheit wird sich nicht vermeiden lassen": Zur pädagogischen Verarbeitung des Nationalsozialismus in Deutschland (1945–1990)*. Opladen: Westdeutscher Verlag, 1995.

Edel, Peter. "An meine Leser, Hörer und Zuschauer: Zur Wiederaufführung des vierteiligen Fernsehfilms 'Die Bilder des Zeugen Schattmann.'" *FF Dabei* no. 46 (8–14 November 1982): 6–7.

Edel, Peter. *Die Bilder des Zeugen Schattmann: ein Roman über deutsche Vergangenheit und Gegenwart*. Berlin: Verlag der Nation, 1969

Edelman, Murray. *Constructing the Political Spectacle*. Chicago: University of Chicago Press, 1988.

Edelman, Murray. *From Art to Politics: How Artistic Creations Shape Political Conceptions*. Chicago: University of Chicago Press, 1995.

Eley, Geoff, ed. *The "Goldhagen Effect": History, Memory, Nazism—Facing the German Past*. Ann Arbor: University of Michigan Press, 2000.

Elsaesser, Thomas. *New German Cinema: A History*. New Brunswick, NJ: Rutgers University Press, 1989.

Emmerich, Wolfgang. *Kleine Literaturgeschichte der DDR*. Leipzig: Gustav Kiepenhauer, 1996.

Engelhardt, Isabelle. *A Topography of Memory: Representations of the Holocaust at Dachau and Buchenwald in Comparison with Auschwitz, Yad Vashem and Washington, DC*. Bruxelles: P.I.E.-Peter Lang, 2002.

Ensel, Leo. *Warum wir uns nicht leiden mögen. Was Ossis und Wessis voneinander halten*. Münster: agenda, 1993.

Fehrenbach, Heide. *Cinema in Democratizing Germany: Reconstructing National Identity after Hitler*. Chapel Hill: University of North Carolina Press, 1995.

Feinstein, Joshua. *The Triumph of the Ordinary: Depictions of Daily Life in the East German Cinema 1949–1989*. Chapel Hill: University of North Carolina Press, 2002.

Festinger, Leon. *A Theory of Cognitive Dissonance.* Stanford, CA: Stanford University Press, 1957.

Filme, Festivals, Tendenzen—Mit TV und Video Erstaufführungen. Edited by Horst Schäfer and Walter Schobert. Frankfurt am Main: Fischer Taschenbuch Verlag, [various years].

Filmstatistisches Taschenbuch. Edited by Spitzenorganisation der Filmwirtschaft, Wiesbaden, 1952–.

Finkelstein, Norman G., and Ruth Bettina Birn. *A Nation on Trial: The Goldhagen Thesis and Historical Truth.* New York: Henry Holt, 1998.

Fischer Film Almanach. Frankfurt am Main: Fischer Taschenbuch Verlag, [various years].

Foa, Anna. *The Jews of Europe after the Black Death.* Translated by Andrea Grover. Berkeley: University of California Press, 2000.

Fox, Thomas C. *Stated Memory: East Germany and the Holocaust.* Rochester, NY: Camden House, 1999.

Foucault, Michel. *Foucault Live: Collected Interviews, 1961–1984.* Edited by Sylvère Lotringer. Translated by Lysa Hochroth and John Johnston. New York: Semiotext(e), 1989.

Frei, Norbert, ed. *Hitlers Eliten nach 1945.* Munich: Deutscher Taschenbuch Verlag, 2003.

Fulbrook, Mary. *German National Identity after the Holocaust.* Cambridge, UK: Polity Press, 1999.

Gay, Peter. *My German Question: Growing Up in Nazi Berlin.* New Haven, CT: Yale University Press, 1998.

Gay, Ruth. *The Jews of Germany: A Historical Portrait.* New Haven, CT: Yale University Press, 1992.

Geertz, Clifford. *The Interpretation of Cultures.* London: Hutchinson, 1975.

Gellantely, Robert. *Backing Hitler: Consent and Coercion in Nazi Germany.* Oxford: Oxford University Press, 2001.

Giddens, Anthony. *Central Problems in Social Theory: Action, Structure and Contradiction in Social Analysis.* Cambridge: Cambridge University Press, 1979.

Good News Study Bible. Nashville: Thomas Nelson, 1986.

Goldhagen, Daniel Jonah. *Hitler's Willing Executioners: Ordinary Germans and the Holocaust.* New York: Vintage Books, 1997.

Goulding, Daniel J. *Liberated Cinema: The Yugoslav Experience, 1945–2001*, 2nd ed. Bloomington: Indiana University Press, 2002.

Grass, Günter. *Two States—One Nation?* Translated by Krishna Winston and A. S. Wensinger. San Diego: Harcourt Brace Jovanovich, 1990.

Gregor, Erika, Ulrich Gregor, and Helma Schleif, eds. *Jüdische Lebenswelten im Film.* Berlin: Freunde der Deutschen Kinemathek, 1993.

Gregson, Julie. "East or West—a Straight Choice? Representations of Masculinity and Constructions of National Identity in Wolfgang Kohlhaase and Gerhad Kein's *Berlin Ecke Schönhauser.*" In *Millennial Essays on Film and Other German Studies*, edited by Daniela Berghahn and Alan Bruce, 63–77. Oxford: Peter Lang, 2002.

Greiner, Bernd. "Bruch-Stücke." In *Eine Ausstellung und ihre Folgen: Zur Rezeption der Ausstellung "Vernichtungskrieg. Verbrechen der Wehrmacht 1941 bis 1944,"* edited by Hamburger Institut für Sozialforschung, 15–86. Hamburg: Hamburger Edition, 1999.

Grossmann, Atina. "A Question of Silence: The Rape of German Women by Occupation Soldiers." *October* 72 (April 1995): 43–63.

Grunenberg, Antonia. *Antifaschismus—ein deutscher Mythos.* Reinbeck bei Hamburg: Rowohlt, 1993.

Habel, F. B. *Das große Lexikon der DEFA-Spielfilme.* Berlin: Schwarzkopf & Schwarzkopf, 2001.

Hackett, David A. "Buchwenwald: Symbol and Metaphor for the Changing Political Culture of East Germany." In *Changing Identities in East Germany: Selected Papers from the Nineteenth and Twentieth New Hampshire Symposia.* Studies in GDR Culture and Society 14/15, edited by Margy Gerber and Roger Woods, 127–42. Lanham, MD: University Press of America, 1996.

Halbwachs, Maurice. *On Collective Memory.* Edited and translated by Lewis A. Coser. Chicago: University of Chicago Press, 1992.

Hamburg Institute for Social Research, ed. *The German Army and Genocide: Crimes against War Prisoners, Jews, and Other Civilians, 1939–1944.* New York: New Press, 1999.

Hamburger Institut für Sozialforschung, ed. *Eine Ausstellung und ihre Folgen: Zur Rezeption der Ausstellung "Vernichtungskrieg. Verbrechen der Wehrmacht 1941 bis 1944."* Hamburg: Hamburger Edition, 1999.

Hamdorf, W.M. "Der Holocaust im Film." *Filmdienst* 20 (1995): 36–39.

Hardt, Roland. *Der Landser #1122: Der letzte Kampf.* Rastatt: Erich Pabel Verlag, 1979.

Hartmann, Christian, Johannes Hürter, and Ulrike Jureit, eds. *Verbrechen der Wehrmacht: Bilanz einer Debatte.* Munich: Verlag C. H. Beck, 2005.

Heinmann, Thomas. *DEFA, Künstler und SED-Kulturpolitik: Zum Verhältnis von Kulturpolitik und Filmproduktion in der SBZ/DDR 1945 bis 1959.* Beiträge zur Film- und Fernsehwissenschaft BFF, edited by Peter Hoff and Dieter Wiedemann. Potsdam-Babelsberg: Hochschule für Film und Fernsehen Konrad Wolf, 1994.

Heisler, Martin O., ed. "The Politics of History in Comparative Perspective." Special issue, *Annals of the American Academy of Political and Social Science* 617 (May 2008).

Helt, Richard C., and Marie E. Helt. *West German Cinema since 1945: A Reference Handbook.* Metuchen, NJ: Scarecrow Press, 1987.

Helt, Richard C., and Marie E. Helt. *West German Cinema, 1985–1990: A Reference Handbook.* Metuchen, NJ: Scarecrow Press, 1992.

Hembus, Joe, and Christa Bandmann. *Klassiker des deutschen Tonfilms, 1930–1960.* Munich: Goldmann, 1980.

Herf, Jeffrey. *Divided Memory: The Nazi Past in the Two Germanys.* Cambridge, MA: Harvard University Press, 1997.

Herrigel, Gary. *Industrial Constructions: The Sources of German Industrial Power.* Cambridge: Cambridge University Press, 1996.

Hirschmann, Albert. "Exit, Voice and the Fate of the German Democratic Republic," *World Politics* 45, no. 2 (January 1993): 173–202.

Hobsbawm, Eric, and Terence Ranger, eds. *The Invention of Tradition.* New York: Cambridge University Press, 1983.

Holler, Regina. *20 Juli 1944 Vermächtnis oder Alibi? Wie Historiker, Politiker und Journalisten mit dem deutschen Widerstand gegen den Nationalsozialismus umgehen. Eine Untersuchung der wissenschaftlichen Literatur, der offiziellen Reden und der Zeitungsberichterstattung in Nordrhein-Westfalen von 1945–1986.* Munich: K. G. Saur, 1994.

Holzweissig, Gunter. *Massenmedien in der DDR.* Berlin: Verlag Gebr. Holzapfel, 1989.

Housden, Martyn. *Resistance and Conformity in the Third Reich*. London: Routledge, 1997.

Humphreys, Peter J. *Media and Media Policy in Germany: The Press and Broadcasting since 1945*. 2nd ed. Oxford: Berg, 1994.

Inglehart, Ronald. *Culture Shift in Advanced Industrial Societies*. Princeton, NJ: Princeton University Press, 1990.

Insdorf, Annette. "*David:* A German-Jewish Film about the Holocaust." *Martyrdom and Resistance* 8, no. 2 (March–April 1982): 4.

Insdorf, Annette. *Indelible Shadows: Films & the Holocaust*. 2nd ed. Cambridge: Cambridge University Press, 1989.

Insdorf, Annette. "A Passion for Social Justice." *Cineaste* 11, no. 4 (Winter 1982): 36–38.

Johnson, Eric A. *Nazi Terror: The Gestapo, Jews, and Ordinary Germans*. New York: Basic Books, 1999.

Johnson, Eric A., and Karl-Heinz Reuband. *What We Knew: Terror, Mass Murder, and Everyday Life in Nazi Germany*. Cambridge, MA: Basic Books, 2005.

Kaes, Anton. *From Hitler to Heimat: The Return of History as Film*. Cambridge, MA: Harvard University Press, 1989.

Kansteiner, Wulf. "Finding Meaning in Memory: A Methodological Critique of Collective Memory Studies." *History and Theory* 41 (May 2002): 179–97.

Kansteiner, Wulf. *In Pursuit of German Memory: History, Television, and Politics after Auschwitz*. Athens: Ohio University Press, 2006.

Kertzer, David I. *The Popes against the Jews: The Vatican's Role in the Rise of Modern Anti-Semitism*. New York: Knopf, 2001.

Kertzer, David I. *Ritual, Politics, and Power*. New Haven, CT: Yale University Press, 1988.

King, Gary, Robert O. Keohane, and Sidney Verba. *Designing Social Inquiry: Scientific Inference in Qualitative Research*. Princeton, NJ: Princeton University Press, 1994.

Klemperer, Victor. *I Will Bear Witness*. Translated by Martin Chalmers. New York: Random House, 1998.

Knight, Julia. *Women and the New German Cinema*. London: Verso, 1992.

Knilli, Friedrich, and Siegfried Zielinski, eds. *Betrift, "Holocaust": Zuschauer schreiben an den WDR: ein Projektbericht*. Berlin: V. Spiess, 1983.

Kohlhaase, Wolfgang. "DEFA: A Personal View." In *DEFA: East German Cinema, 1946–1992*, edited by Seán Allan and John Sandford, 117–30. New York: Berghahn Books, 1999.

Koshar, Rudy. *From Monuments to Traces: Artifacts of German Memory, 1870–1990*. Berkeley: University of California Press, 2000.

Kött, Martin. *Goldhagen in der Qualitätspresse: eine Debatte über "Kollektivschuld" und "Nationalcharakter" der Deutschen*. Konstanz: UVK Medien, 1999.

Kreuz, Anja, and Susanne Vollberg. *Beiträge zur DDR-Fernseh- und Magazingeschichte: Eine kommentierte Auswahlbibliographie*. Frankfurt am Main: Peter Lang, 1998.

Kumpfmüller, Michael. *Die Schlacht von Stalingrad. Metamorphosen eines deutschen Mythos*. Munich: Fink, 1996.

Ladd, Brian. *The Ghosts of Berlin: Confronting German History in the Urban Landscape*. Chicago: University of Chicago Press, 1997.

Lan, David. *Guns and Rain: Guerrillas and Spirit Mediums in Zimbabwe*. Berkeley: University of California Press, 1985.

Langenbacher, Eric. "The Return of Memory: New Discussions about German Suffering in World War II." *German Politics and Society* 21, no. 3 (Fall 2003): 74–88.

Langguth, Gerd. *In Search of Security: A Socio-Psychological Portrait of Today's Germany.* Translated by Dirk Johnson. Westport, CT: Praeger, 1995.

Lavigne, Marie. "The Economics of the Transition Process: What Have We Learned?" *Problems of Post-Communism* 47, no. 4 (July/August 2000): 16–23.

Lebow, Richard Ned, Wulf Kansteiner, and Claudio Fogu, eds. *The Politics of Memory in Postwar Europe.* Durham, NC: Duke University Press, 2006.

Lévi-Strauss, Claude. *Structural Anthropology.* Translated by Claire Jacobson and Brooke Grundfest Schoepf. New York: Basic Books, 1963.

Liss, Andrea. *Trespassing through Shadows: Memory, Photography, and the Holocaust.* Minneapolis: University of Minnesota Press, 1998.

Lopex, Daniel. *Films by Genre.* Jefferson, NC: MacFarland, 1993.

Lüdtke, Alf. ">Helden der Arbeit<—Mühen beim Arbeiten. Zur mißmutigen Loyalität von Industriearbeitern in der DDR." In *Sozialgeschichte der DDR,* edited by Hartmut Kaelble, 188–213. Stuttgart: Klett-Cotta, 1994.

Lustick, Ian. "History, Historiography, and Political Science: Multiple Historical Records and the Problem of Selection Bias." *American Political Science Review* 90, no. 3 (September 1996): 605–18.

Maier, Charles S. *The Unmasterable Past: History, Holocaust, and German National Identity.* Cambridge, MA: Harvard University Press, 1988.

Markovits, Andrei S., and Philip S. Gorski. *The German Left: Red, Green and Beyond.* New York: Oxford University Press, 1993.

Markovits, Andrei S., and Simon Reich. *The German Predicament: Memory and Power in the New Europe.* Ithaca, NY: Cornell University Press, 1997.

McLellan, Josie. *Antifascism and Memory in East Germany: Remembering the International Brigades.* Oxford: Oxford University Press, 2004.

Merelman, Richard M. "The Mundane Experience of Political Culture." *Political Communication* 15, no. 4 (Octber/December 1998): 515–35.

Merritt, Anna J., and Richard L. Merritt, eds. *Public Opinion in Semisovereign Germany: The HICOG Surveys, 1949–1955.* Urbana: University of Illinois Press, 1980.

Messerschmidt, Manfred. "Zur neueren Diskussion um Opposition und Verweigerung von Soldaten, Deserteure, Zersetzer und Verweigerer." In *Der 20. Juli. 'Das andere Deutschland' in der Vergangenheitspolitik nach 1945,* edited by Gerd R. Ueberschär, 388–424. Berlin: Elefanten Press, 1998.

Meuer, Hans Joachim. *Cinema and National Identity in a Divided Germany, 1979–1989: The Split Screen.* Lewiston, NY: Edwin Mellen Press, 2000.

Meyen, Michael. *Einschalten, Umschalten, Ausschalten? Das Fernsehen im DDR- Alltag.* Leipzig: Leipziger Universitätsverlag, 2003.

Misztal, Barbara A. *Theories of Social Remembering.* Maidenhead, UK: Open University Press, 2003.

Mitchell, W. J. T. *Picture Theory: Essays on Verbal and Visual Representation.* Chicago: University of Chicago Press, 1994.

Mitscherlich, Alexander, and Margarethe Mitscherlich. *The Inability to Mourn: Principles of Collective Behavior.* Translated by Beverley R. Placzek. New York: Grove Press, 1975.

Moeller, Robert G. *War Stories: The Search for a Usable Past in the Federal Republic of Germany.* Berkeley: University of California Press, 2001.

Morsch, Günter, ed. *Von der Erinnerung zum Monument: Die Entstehungsgeschichte der Nationalen Mahn- und Gedenkstätte Sachsenhausen.* Oranienburg: Stiftung Brandenburgische Gedenkstätten, 1996.

Mosse, George L. *The Crisis of German Ideology: Intellectual Origins of the Third Reich.* New York: Universal Library of Grosset & Dunlap, 1964.

Müncheberg, Hans. *Blaues Wunder aus Adlershof: Der Deutsche Fernsehfunk Erlebtes und Gesammeltes.* Berlin: Das Neue Berlin, 2000.

Musial, Bogdan. "Bilder einer Ausstellung: Kritische Anmerkungen zur Wanderausstellung 'Vernichtungskrieg: Verbrechen der Wehrmacht 1941 bis 1944.'" *Vierteljahrshefte für Zeitgeschichte* 47, no. 4 (October 1999): 563–91.

Naimark, Norman M. *The Russians in Germany.* Cambridge, MA: Harvard University Press, 1995.

Nedelmann, Birgitta. "Die Ausstellung 'Vernichtungskrieg. Verbrechen der Wehrmacht 1941 bis 1944,' und die Konstruktion öffentlicher Diskurse." In *Eine Ausstellung und ihre Folgen: Zur Rezeption der Ausstellung "Vernichtungskrieg. Verbrechen der Wehrmacht 1941 bis 1944,"* edited by Hamburger Institut für Sozialforschung, 230–61. Hamburg: Hamburger Edition, 1999.

Neill, Alex. "Empathy and (Film) Fiction." In *Post-Theory: Reconstructing Film Studies,* edited by David Bordwell and Noël Carroll, 175–94. Madison: University of Wisconsin Press, 1996.

Neumann, Erich Peter, and Elisabeth Noelle. *Antworten. Politik im Kraftfeld der öffentlichen Meinung.* Allensbach: Verlag für Demoskopie, 1954.

Neumann, Erich Peter, and Elisabeth Noelle, eds. *The Germans: Public Opinion Polls 1947–1966.* Allensbach: Verlag für Demoskopie, 1967.

Niemann, Heinz. *Meinungsforschung in der DDR. Die geheimen Berichte des Instituts für Meinungsforschung an das Politbüro der SED.* Cologne: Bund-Verlag, 1993.

Niethammer, Lutz. "Juden und Russen im Gedächtnis der Deutschen." In *Der historische Ort des Nationalsozialismus: Annäherungen,* edited by Walter H. Pehle, 114–34. Frankfurt am Main: Fischer Taschenbuch Verlag, 1990.

Niethammer, Lutz, Alexander von Plato, and Dorothee Wierling. *Die volkseigene Erfahrung: Eine Archäologie des Lebens in der Industrieprovinz der DDR.* Berlin: Rowohlt, 1991.

Niethammer, Lutz. "Erfahrungen und Strukturen: Prolegomena zu einer Geschichte der Gesellschaft der DDR." In *Sozialgeschichte der DDR,* edited by Hartmut Kaelble, Jürgen Kocka, and Hartmut Zwahr, 95–115. Stuttgart: Klett-Cotta, 1994.

Niven, Bill. *The Buchenwald Child: Truth, Fiction, and Propaganda.* Rochester, NY: Camden House, 2007.

Niven, Bill. *Facing the Nazi Past: United Germany and the Legacy of the Third Reich.* London: Routledge, 2002.

Noelle-Neumann, Elisabeth. *The Spiral of Silence: Public Opinion, Our Social Skin.* Chicago: University of Chicago Press, 1993.

Noelle-Neumann, Elisabeth, ed. *The Germans: Public Opinion Polls, 1967–1980.* Westport, CT: Greenwood Press, 1981.

Noelle-Neumann, Elisabeth, and Renate Köcher, eds. *Allensbach Jahrbuch der Demoskopie 1993–1997.* Munich: K. G. Saur, 1997.

Norton, Ann. *95 Theses on Politics, Culture, and Method*. New Haven, CT: Yale University Press, 2004.

Novick, Peter. *The Holocaust in American Life*. Boston: Mariner Books, 1999.

Oehme, Christa. "Die Zuschauerforschung als ein Instrument der Leitung, Planung, Programm- und Sendungsgestaltung des Fernsehens der DDR—ihre Möglichkeiten und Grenzen—dargestellt an empirischen Forschungsergebnissen." Diss., Akademie für Gesellschaftswissenschaften beim ZK der SED, Institute für Marxistisch-Leninistische Kultur- und Kunstwissenschaften, Berlin, 1978.

Olick, Jeffrey K., ed. *States of Memory: Continuities, Conflicts and Transformations in National Retrospection*. Durham, NC: Duke University Press, 2003.

Palmer, R. R., and Joel Colton. *A History of the Modern World*. 8th ed. New York: McGraw-Hill, 1995.

Paul, Gerhard, and Klaus-Michael Mallmann, eds. *Die Gestapo: Mythos und Realität*. Darmstadt: Wissenschaftliche Buchgesellschaft, 1995.

Raasch, Dr. Rudolf. *Zeitgeschichte und Nationalbewußtsein*. Berlin—West: Hermann Luchterhand Verlag, 1964.

Reimer, Robert C., and Carl J. Reimer. *Nazi-Retro Film: How German Narrative Cinema Remembers the Past*. New York: Twayne, 1992.

Ricoeur, Paul. *Memory, History, Forgetting*. Translated by Kathleen Blamey and David Pellauer. Chicago: Chicago University Press, 2004.

Rinke, Andrea. "From Motzki to Trotzki: Representations of East and West German Cultural Identities on German Television after Unification." In *The New Germany: Literature and Society after Unification*, edited by Osman Durrani et al., 231–51. Sheffield, England: Sheffield Academic Press, 1995.

Roesler, Jörg. "Privatization by Treuhand and the Restructuring of East German Industry—a Model for Middle Europe?" Paper presented in Prague, 7–9 December 1993.

Rohrlich, Ruby, ed. *Resisting the Holocaust*. Oxford: Berg, 1998.

Ross, Marc Howard. *Cultural Contestation in Ethnic Conflict*. Cambridge: Cambridge University Press, 2007.

Ross, Marc Howard. "Culture and Identity in Comparative Political Analysis." In *Comparative Politics: Rationality, Culture, and Structure*, edited by Mark Irving Lichbach and Alan S. Zuckerman, 42–80. Cambridge: Cambridge University Press, 1997.

Rousso, Henry. *The Vichy Syndrome: History and Memory in France since 1944*. Translated by Arthur Goldhammer. Cambridge, MA: Harvard University Press, 1991.

Rüther, Günther. *"Greif zur Feder, Kumpel": Schriftsteller, Literatur und Politik in der DDR 1949–1990*. Düsseldorf: Droste, 1991.

Sa'adah, Anne. *Germany's Second Chance: Trust, Justice, and Democratization*. Cambridge, MA: Harvard University Press, 1998.

Schacter, Daniel L., ed. *Memory Distortion: How Minds, Brains and Societies Reconstruct the Past*. Cambridge, MA: Harvard University Press, 1997.

Schacter, Daniel L. *Searching for Memory: the Brain, the Mind, and the Past*. New York: Basic Books, 1996.

Schirrmacher, Frank, ed. *Die Walser-Bubis Debatte: eine Dokumentation*. Frankfurt: Suhrkamp, 1999.

Schlant, Ernestine. *The Language of Silence: West German Literature and the Holocaust*. London: Routledge, 1999.

Schmitt-Sasse, Joachim, ed. *Widergänger: Faschismus und Antifaschismus im Film*. Münster: MAkS Publikationen, 1993.

Schmitt, Sigrid. "Konrad Wolf: Assoziationen zur Gegenwart." In *30 Jahre danach: Auseinandersetzung mit dem Nationalsozialismus im Film 1945 bis 1975*, edited by Heiko R. Blum. Cologne: Horst May Schnelldruck & Verlag, 1975.

Schneider, Michael. "Fathers and Son's, Retrospectively: The Damaged Relationship Between Two Generations." *New German Critique* 31 (Winter 1984): 3–51.

Schneider, Peter. "Der Bundestag wolle beschließen: Zur Debatte über die Ausstellung 'Vernichtungskrieg. Verbrechen der Wehrmacht 1941 bis 1944.' " In *Eine Ausstellung und ihre Folgen: Zur Rezeption der Ausstellung "Vernichtungskrieg. Verbrechen der Wehrmacht 1941 bis 1944,"* edited by Hamburger Institut für Sozialforschung, 112–22. Hamburg: Hamburger Edition, 1999.

Schornstheimer, Michael. *Bombenstimmung und Katzenjammer: Vergangenheitsbewältigung—Quick und Stern in den 50er Jahren*. Cologne: Pahl-Rugenstein, 1989.

Schudson, Michael. "How Culture Works: Perspectives from Media Studies on the Efficacy of Symbols." *Theory and Society* 18 (1989): 153–80.

Schwan, Gesine. *Politik und Schuld: Die zerstörische Macht des Schweigens*. Frankfurt am Main: Fischer Taschenbuch Verlag, 1997.

Schwartz, Barry. *Abraham Lincoln and the Forge of National Memory*. Chicago: University of Chicago Press, 2000.

Shandley, Robert R., ed. *Unwilling Germans? The Goldhagen Debate*. Minneapolis: University of Minnesota Press, 1998.

Sigl, Klaus, Werner Schneider, and Ingo Tornow. *Jede Menge Kohle? Kunst und Kommerz auf dem deutschen Filmmarkt der Nachkriegszeit*. Munich: Filmland Presse, 1986.

Silberman, Marc. "Remembering History: The Filmmaker Konrad Wolf." *New German Critique* 49 (Winter 1990): 163–91.

Skirball, Sheba F. *Films of the Holocaust: An Annotated Filmography of Collections in Israel*. New York: Garland, 1990.

Smith, Rogers M. *Stories of Peoplehood: The Politics and Morals of Political Membership*. Cambridge: Cambridge University Press, 2003.

Steven Spielberg Jewish Film Archive, the Hebrew University of Jerusalem—Institute of Contemporary Jewry. On-line archive. URL: http://www.spielbergfilmarchive.org.il

Travis, Carol, and Elliot Aronson. *Mistakes Were Made (but Not by Me): Why We Justify Foolish Beliefs, Bad Decisions, and Hurtful Acts*. Orlando, FL: Harcourt, 2007.

Tschakowski, Alexander. "900 heroische Tage." *Sowjet Film* 1978 (9): 7–9.

Turner, Victor. *The Forest of Symbols: Aspects of Ndembu Ritual*. Ithaca, NY: Cornell University Press, 1967.

van Gennep, Arnold. *The Rites of Passage*. Translated by Monika B. Vizedom and Gabrielle L. Caffee. London: Routledge & Kegan Paul, 1960.

Verdery, Katherine. *National Ideology under Socialism: Identity and Cultural Politics in Ceausescu's Romania*. Berkeley: University of California Press, 1991.

von Plato, Alexander, and Almut Leh. *"Ein unglaublicher Frühling": Erfahrene Geschichte im Nachkriegsdeutschland 1945–1948*. Bonn: Bundeszentrale für politische Bildung, 1997.

Wedel, Mathias. *Einheitsfrust*. Berlin: Rowohlt, 1994.

Welzer, Harald, Sabine Moller, and Karoline Tschuggnall. *"Opa war kein Nazi": Nationalsozialismus und Holocaust im Familiengedächtnis*. Frankfurt am Main: Fischer, 2002.

White, Hayden. *The Content of the Form: Narrative Discourse and Historical Representation.* Baltimore: Johns Hopkins University Press, 1987.

White, Hayden. *Metahistory: The Historical Imagination in Nineteenth Century Europe.* Baltimore: Johns Hopkins University Press, 1973.

Williams, Alan. "Introduction." In *Film and Nationalism*, edited by Alan Williams, 1–22. New Brunswick, NJ: Rutgers University Press, 2002.

Winter, Jay. *Remembering War: The Great War between Memory and History in the Twentieth Century.* New Haven, CT: Yale University Press, 2006.

Winter, Jay, and Emmanuel Sivan. "Setting the Framework." In *War and Remembrance in the Twentieth Century*, edited by Jay Winter and Emmanuel Sivan, 6–39. Cambridge: Cambridge University Press, 1999.

Wistrich, Robert S. *Who's Who in Nazi Germany.* London: Routledge, 1995.

Wojak, Irmtrud, and Susanne Meinl. "Forschungskolloquium: Der erste Frankfurter Auschwitz-Prozeß, Geschichte und Wirkungsgeschichte." *Newsletter: Informationen des Fritz Bauer Instituts*, Fall 1999: 11–18.

Wolf, Dieter. "Gesellschaft mit beschränkter Haftung." In *Babelsberg: Ein Filmstudio 1912–1992*, edited by Wolfgang Jacobsen, 247–70. Berlin: Argon, 1992.

Wolfgram, Mark A. "Blood and Redemption: German Collective Memory of Elite Resistance against the Nazis." *Journal of Political and Military Sociology* 35, no. 1 (Summer 2007): 63–84.

Wolfgram, Mark A. "Gendered Border Crossings: Germany's Films of Division." *Symploke* 15, nos. 1–2 (2007): 152–69.

Wolfgram, Mark A. "The Holocaust through the Prism of East German Television: Collective Memory and Audience Perceptions." *Holocaust and Genocide Studies* 20, no. 1 (Spring 2006): 57–79.

Wolfgram, Mark A. "Das kollektive Gedächtnis als theoretisches Konzept aktueller Forschung." Translated by Cornelia Dörries. *Berliner Journal für Soziologie* 9, no. 4 (1999): 567–75.

Wolfgram, Mark A. "The Legacies of Memory: The Third Reich in Unified Germany." *German Politics & Society* 21, no. 3 (Fall 2003): 89–100.

Wolfgram, Mark A. "Rediscovering Narratives of German Resistance: Opposing the Nazi 'Terror-State.'" *Rethinking History* 10, no. 2 (June 2006): 201–19.

Wolfgram, Mark A. "What Can War Crimes Trials Teach? German Collective Memories of the Nuremberg Trials." Conference paper, annual meeting of the International Studies Association, New York City, 15–18 February 2009.

Wolfsfeld, Gadi. *Media and the Path to Peace.* Cambridge: Cambridge University Press, 2004.

Zerubavel, Yael. *Recovered Roots: Collective Memory and the Making of Israeli National Tradition.* Chicago: University of Chicago Press, 1995.

German and Other Print Media Sources

Frankfurter Allgemeine

"9 November ein 'verfluct deutscher Tag.'" *Frankfurter Allgemeine*, November 9, 1998: 1.

"Adenauer zur 'Kristallnacht.'" *Frankfurter Allgemeine*, November 8, 1958: 1.

"Bilder einer Ausstellung." *Frankfurter Allgemeine*, October 22, 1999: 1.

Busche, Jürgen. "Schwieriger Gedenktag." *Frankfurter Allgemeine*, July 20, 1979: 21.

"Chaoten verwüsten die City und terrorisieren Unbeteiligte." *Frankfurter Allgemeine*, June 19, 1978: 29.

Dombrowski, Erich. "8. Mai 1945." *Frankfurter Allgemeine*, May 7, 1955: 1.

Fest, Joachim. "Gedanken zu Erinnerungen." *Frankfurter Allgemeine*, November 9, 1978: 1.

"Fotos der Wehrmachtausstellung falsch zugeordnet." *Frankfurter Allgemeine*, October 20, 1999: 1.

"'Furcht und Beben, Zorn und *Frankfurter Schmerz*.'" *Frankfurter Allgemeine*, May 9, 1990: 3.

"Gedenkfeiern für Opfer der Juden-Verfolgung." *Frankfurter Allgemeine*, November 11, 1968: 1.

"Gedenkfeiern zum 20. Juli." *Frankfurter Allgemeine*, July 22, 1974: 5.

Gillessen, Günter. "Verwandlungen eines Besuches." *Frankfurter Allgemeine*, May 8, 1985: 1.

"Gottesdienst im Kölner Dom." *Frankfurter Allgemeine*, May 9, 1985: 2.

Graml, Hermann. "Goebbels' Pogrom." *Frankfurter Allgemeine*, November 9, 1963: 'Bild und Zeiten' 3.

"Großer Bußgottesdienst in der Festhalle." *Frankfurter Allgemeine*, November 8, 1978: 41.

"Herzog: Der Tag, an dem ein Tor in die Zukunft aufgestoßen wurde." *Frankfurter Allgemeine*, May 9, 1995: 1–2.

"Historische Unpäßlichkeit." *Frankfurter Allgemeine*, November 9, 1993: 1.

Höffner, Cardinal. "Schuld läßt sich nicht durch politische und psychologische Analysen bewältigen." *Frankfurter Allgemeine*, May 9, 1985: 6.

"Hunderttausende bei den Feiern zum Nationalen Gedenktag." *Frankfurter Allgemeine*, June 19, 1963: 1.

"In Dachau entsteht eine Sühne-Christi-Kirche." *Frankfurter Allgemeine*, November 11, 1963: 3.

"Ein Jahr Grundgesetz." *Frankfurter Allgemeine*, May 8, 1950: 2.

Kaiser-Nebgen, Elfried. "Mut und Tragik um den 20. Juli." *Frankfurter Allgemeine*, July 20, 1954: 2.

Kohl, Chancellor Helmut. "Die Menschen von heute sind nicht besser oder mutiger als damals." *Frankfurter Allgemeine*, November 10, 1988: 5.

"Kohl dankt den Widerstandskämpfern des 20. Juli." *Frankfurter Allgemeine*, July 20, 1989: 1.

Krausnick, Helmut. "Im Zwiespalt von Soldateneid und Gewissen." *Frankfurter Allgemeine*, July 20, 1959: 9.

Lohse, Bishop. "Gott hat man die Ehre gestohlen und war fremden Göttern nachgelaufen." *Frankfurter Allgemeine*, May 9, 1985: 6.

"Löschen nur mit Erlaubnis: Freiwillige Feuerwehren in der Pogromnacht." *Frankfurter Allgemeine*, November 9, 1998: 13.

"Lübke nennt den 20. Juli ein Symbol der Selbstachtung." *Frankfurter Allgemeine*, July 20, 1964: 1.

"Mahnung, nicht Schuld." *Frankfurter Allgemeine*, November 10, 1988: 1.

"Neue Synagoge für Hamburg." *Frankfurter Allgemeine*, November 10, 1958: 4.

Odin, Karl-Alfred. "In den Gottesdiensten wird der Blick auf die Schuld gelenkt." *Frankfurter Allgemeine*, May 8, 1985: 7.

Reißmüller, Johann Georg. "Tag des Zwiespalts." *Frankfurter Allgemeine*, May 8, 1995: 1.

"Ringsum Peinlichkeit." *Frankfurter Allgemeine*, November 11, 1988: 1.

Sethe, Paul. "Für immer gescheitert?" *Frankfurter Allgemeine*, July 20, 1954: 1.

"Scheel: Den November 1938 nicht vergessen." *Frankfurter Allgemeine*, November 9, 1978: 1.

Schuster, Jacques. "Nur eine Generalsrevolute?" *Frankfurter Allgemeine*, July 20, 1994: 10.

"Schweigeminute zum 8. Mai." *Frankfurter Allgemeine*, May 9, 1955: 1.

"Die sowjetische Fahne an Privathäusern." *Frankfurter Allgemeine*, May 8, 1950: 4.

"Sühne-Kirche für Dachau." *Frankfurter Allgemeine*, November 9, 1963: 17.

"Eine Synagoge am alten Ort." *Frankfurter Allgemeine*, November 9, 1998: 4.

"Unsere Wirklichkeit durch Hitlers Niederlage entstanden." *Frankfurter Allgemeine*, May 9, 1970: 7.

" 'Die Wahrheit ist die härteste Anklage.' " *Frankfurter Allgemeine*, May 8, 1965: 17–18.

"Weizsäcker: Der 8. Mai nicht das letzte Datum gemeinsamer Geschichte." *Frankfurter Allgemeine*, May 9, 1970: 7.

Winters, Peter Jochen. "Koalition der Vernunft." *Frankfurter Allgemeine*, July 21, 1984: 25.

"Zehn Prozent der Bilder zeigen eindeutig Taten der Wehrmacht." *Frankfurter Allgemeine*, October 22, 1999: 2.

"Zerstört, entweiht, wiederentdeckt und renoviert." *Frankfurter Allgemeine*, November 9, 1998: 13.

Neues Deutschland

"8. Mai: NS-Opfer warnen vor Alltagsfaschismus." *Neues Deutschland*, May 8, 2000: 1.

Amendt, Jürgen. " 'Verziehen, nicht vergessen.' " *Neues Deutschland*, November 8, 1993: 3.

"Die Arbeiter werden die Maßnahmen voll unterstützen." *Neues Deutschland*, June 16, 1953: 1.

Arnold, Willi, and Gertrud Glondajewski. "Magnus Poser—treuer Sohn der Arbeiterklasse." *Neues Deuschland*, July 21, 1959: 4.

Benz, Professor Dr. Wolfgang. "Der Novemberpogrom." *Neues Deutschland*, November 9, 1993: 9.

"Berlin (West): Ausstellung über Kampf gegen Faschismus." *Neues Deutschland*, July 20, 1989: 7.

"Berliner Synagoge wurde umfassend rekonstruiert." *Neues Deutschland*, November 9, 1978: 8.

Berthold, Dr. Lothar. "Heusingers hündische Heuchelei." *Neues Deutschland*, July 19, 1959: 4.

Brückner, Dieter, Günter Stechow, and Wolfgang Spickermann. "Bewegende Begegnung Erich Honeckers mit jüdishcen Persönlichkeiten im Staatsrat." *Neues Deutschland*, November 9, 1988: 1.

"Bubis: Neue Kultur des Wegschauens." *Neues Deutschland*, November 9, 1998: 4.

Dahlem, Franz. "Tag der Befreiung." *Neues Deutschland,* May 7, 1950: 2.
Fink, Heinrich. "Nachdenken zum 8. Mai." *Neues Deutschland,* May 6/7, 2000: 1.
Finker, Prof. Dr. Kurt. "Am 20. Juli vor 40 Jahren." *Neues Deutschland,* July 20, 1984: 3.
Finker, Dr. Kurt. "Der Versuch einer Wende?" *Neues Deutschland,* July 20, 1994: 3.
"Gedenken zum 60. Jahrestag der Pogrome." *Neues Deutschland,* November 10, 1998: 1.
"Gedenkgottesdienst in den Synagogen." *Neues Deutschland,* November 9, 1948: 6.
"Gedenkstunde im jüdischen Friedenstempel." *Neues Deutschland,* November 10, 1968: 2.
Helig, René. Interview with Uli Faber. "Die, die nicht sehen die Schrift an der Wand . . ." *Neues Deutschland,* November 8, 1993: 3.
Honecker, Erich. "Verpflichtung zu einer Politik des Humanismus, des Friedens und der Völkerverständigung." *Neues Deutschland,* November 9, 1988: 2.
Hübner, Wolfgang. "Sonntagsreden." *Neues Deutschland,* November 10, 1998: 2.
"Jüdischer Friedhof wird würdig ausgestaltet." *Neues Deutschland,* November 10, 1978: 8.
"Der jungen Generation Erfahrungen weitergeben." *Neues Deutschland,* November 10, 1988: 3.
Kant, Hermann. "Hauptsachen." *Neues Deutschland,* November 9, 1993: 3.
Liesch, Helfried. "Auf dem Weg ins 4. Reich?" *Neues Deutschland,* November 9, 1993: 1.
Löwel, Dr. Bruno. "Am 20. Juli vor 20 Jahren." *Neues Deutschland,* July 19, 1964: 3.
Merker, Paul. "Die Hintergründe der Kristallnacht." *Neues Deutschland,* November 10, 1948: 3.
"Nach der Befreiung." *Neues Deutschland,* May 7, 1950: 6.
Pätzold, Professor Kurt. "Der Pogrom, der Profit und der Weg in den Tod." *Neues Deutschland,* November 9, 1978: 4.
Paulus, Günter. "Der 20. Juli 1944—ein Versuch zur Rettung des deutschen Imperialismus vor der Niederlage." *Neues Deutschland,* July 20, 1954: 3.
"Ruhm dem Sowjetvolk, das uns vom Faschismus befreit hat." *Neues Deutschland,* May 8, 1968: 3.
"Ruhm und Ehre den Befreiern!" *Neues Deutschland,* May 7, 1950: 1.
Scharfenort, Lucie. "Berliner erinnern sich an den 8. Mai 1945." *Neues Deutschland,* May 7, 1950: 8.
Steinführ, Margarete. "Ein ganzes Brot." *Neues Deutschland,* March 16/17, 1985: 9.
Vesper, Karlen. " 'Endlich waren wir wieder frei!' " *Neues Deutschland,* May 8, 2000: 3.
Zweig, Arnold. "Enthüllter Rat der Götter." *Neues Deutschland,* May 7, 1950: 3.

Der Tagesspiegel

"Der alltägliche Widerstand." *Der Tagesspiegel,* July 21, 1984: 12.
Bahra, Hanne. " '. . . Synagogen sofort niederbrennen . . .' " *Der Tagesspiegel,* November 10, 1998: 18.
"Berlin gedachte des Volksaufstandes." *Der Tagesspiegel,* June 19, 1963: 5.
Beukert, Günter. "Als Bildjournalist in der 'Reichskristallnacht.' " *Der Tagesspiegel,* section, special, "Vor Aller Augen," 8 November 1988: 4.
Bölke, Joachim. "8. Mai 1945–8. Mai 1955." *Der Tagesspiegel,* May 8, 1955: 3.
Bölke, Joachim. "Dreimal 9. November." *Der Tagesspiegel,* November 9, 1958: 3.
"Bundespräsident Lübke ruft zur Einigkeit auf." *Der Tagesspiegel,* June 19, 1963: 5.

"Bundestag gedachte des 25. Jahrestages der deutschen Kapitulation." *Der Tagesspiegel*, May 9, 1970: 9.

"Demonstranten ketten sich am Eingang der Neuen Wache an." *Der Tagesspiegel*, November 10, 1993: 1.

"Denkmale des Widerstandes." *Der Tagesspiegel*, May 9, 1970: 6.

"Das deutsche kernproblem." *Der Tagesspiegel*, November 9, 1948: 1.

"Ein deutsches Datum." *Der Tagesspiegel*, November 9, 1998: 8.

"Diepgen und Rasch würdigen Rolle des Widerstands gegen die Hitler-Diktatur." *Der Tagesspiegel*, July 19, 1984: 8.

"Erhard: Positive Mitarbeit im Interesse des Friedens." *Der Tagesspiegel*, May 8, 1965: 1.

"Erklärungen zum 8. Mai." *Der Tagesspiegel*, May 7, 1965: 6.

Forst, Achim. "Nach vierzig Jahren." *Der Tagesspiegel*, May 9, 1985: 4.

"Galinski: In Erinnerung an NS-Zeit freiheitliche Gesellschaft gestalten." *Der Tagesspiegel*, May 8, 1985: 6.

"Gedenken an den 9. November 1938." *Der Tagesspiegel*, November 9, 1993: 10.

"Gedenken und Kränze zum 8. Mai." *Der Tagesspiegel*, May 8, 1975: 12.

"Gedenkfeier zum 20. Juli mit Protesten gegen Filbinger." *Der Tagesspiegel*, July 20, 1974: 1.

"Gottesdienste zum 9. November." *Der Tagesspiegel*, November 9, 1978: 11.

Gralla, Peter. "Widerstand gegen den NS-Staat." *Der Tagesspiegel*, July 20, 1984: 10.

Grunert, Brigitte, and Lothar Heinke. "Die späte Ehrung der Helden des 17. Juni." *Der Tagesspiegel*, June 18, 1993: 3.

Heuss, Federal President. "20. Juli 1944—Grenzsitutation der sittlichen Entscheidungen: Aus der Rede des Bundespräsidenten . . ." *Der Tagesspiegel*, July 20, 1954: 3.

Hildebrandt, Rainer. " 'Vom menschenrechtlichen Anliegen ist das politische nicht zu trennen.' " *Der Tagesspiegel*, June 17, 1973: 3.

Hübner, Ralf. "Ausdruck des Neubeginns." *Der Tagesspiegel*, November 10, 1998: 5.

J. B. "Bitburg und Mitterrand." *Der Tagesspiegel*, May 7, 1985: 1.

"Jüdische Gemeinde gedachte des Jahrestages des Kriegsendes." *Der Tagesspiegel*, May 10, 1965: 2.

"Kohl: Attentat vom 20. Juli 1944 Symbol für ein anderes Deutschland." *Der Tagesspiegel*, July 20, 1984: 2.

"Der Krieg als Männerlandverschickung." *Der Tagesspiegel*, May 8, 2000: 7.

"Kritik aus Israel an Besuch Reagans." *Der Tagesspiegel*, May 7, 1985: 7.

"Kranzniederlegungen." *Der Tagesspiegel*, June 19, 1968: 11.

"Kranzniederlegungen am 17. Juni." *Der Tagesspiegel*, June 16, 1978: 10.

"Krawalle nach Gegendemonstration." *Der Tagesspiegel*, June 19, 1983: 15.

Kulke, Heinz. "Auf den Bergen die Burgen." *Der Tagesspiegel*, June 16, 1963: 3.

Kuschel, Stefan. "Ein Optimist überlebte—vor 50 Jahren." *Der Tagesspiegel*, May 8, 1995: 9.

Lackmann, Thomas. "Immer am 29. April." *Der Tagesspiegel*, May 8, 1995: 19.

Lehmann, Wolfgang. "9. November 1938: Vor Aller Augen." *Der Tagesspiegel*, November 8, 1988: 12.

Lehming, Malte. "Unfähig zu trauern, unfähig zu feiern." *Der Tagesspiegel*, May 8, 1995: 6.

"Mahnung des Jüdischen Weltkongresses zum 45. Jahrestag des Kriegsendes," *Der Tagesspiegel*, May 9, 1990: 1.

Mönch, Regina. "Der Ort, an dem der Krieg zu Ende ging." *Der Tagesspiegel*, May 8, 1995: 9.

Mönch, Regina. "Rechzeitig auf der richtigen Seite." *Der Tagesspiegel*, May 7, 1995: Welt Spiegel 11.

"'Moralische Enttrümmerung streckengeblieben.'" *Der Tagesspiegel*, November 9, 1963: 7.

"'Die Mörder von gestern.'" *Der Tagesspiegel*, May 8, 1965: 5.

"Neue Wache 'kein Mahnmal.'" *Der Tagesspiegel*, November 10, 1993: 9.

Pajević, Aleander. "'Sag beim Abschied leise . . . Shalom!'" *Der Tagesspiegel*, November 10, 1998: 16.

"Parteien ziehen unterschiedliche Schlußfolgerungen aus dem 8. Mai 1945." *Der Tagesspiegel*, May 8, 1985: 6.

"Propst Heinrich Grüber wurde Ehrenbürger von Berlin." *Der Tagesspiegel*, May 9, 1970: 5.

"Rede Scheels zum 40. Jahrestag des Pogroms der 'Kristallnacht.'" *Der Tagesspiegel*, November 9, 1978: 1.

"Die Rede Weizsäckers in Wortlautauszügen." *Der Tagesspiegel*, May 9, 1985: 6.

"Reste des Stalinismus Beseitigen." *Der Tagesspiegel*, June 19, 1963: 5.

RM. "Weitab vom Rias." *Der Tagesspiegel*, June 17, 1993: 9.

Rudolph, Hermann. "Was der 9. November uns zu sagen hat." *Der Tagesspiegel*, November 9, 1993: 1.

Sachs, Shimon. "Berliner erinnerungen eines Israeli." *Der Tagesspiegel*, November 10, 1988: 12.

"Scheel warnt die Jugend vor Demagogen." *Der Tagesspiegel*, May 7, 1975: 5.

"Schmidt bittet Juden um Versöhnung." *Der Tagesspiegel*, November 10, 1978: 1.

"Schmidt fordert zu entschlossener Wahrung der Verfassung auf." *Der Tagesspiegel*, May 8, 1975: 1.

Schmidt, Werner. "Den Nazis entgegengestellt." *Der Tagesspiegel*, November 10, 1998: 16.

Schulz, Bernhard. "Grenzen des Darstellbaren." *Der Tagesspiegel*, July 19, 1989: 3.

"Süssmuth: Kein Schlußstrich unter die Vergangenheit." *Der Tagesspiegel*, November 10, 1993: 1.

"Trauer gilt den menschen, nicht den Symbolen: Rabbiner Friedländer zum 20. Juli 1944." *Der Tagesspiegel*, July 20, 1964: 10.

"Verteidigungsminister Leber zum 20. Juli." *Der Tagesspiegel*, July 19, 1974: 2.

"Von der 'Befreiungsfeier' befreit." *Der Tagesspiegel*, May 9, 1950: 3.

"Vor Aller Augen." Special insert to *Der Tagesspiegel*, November 8, 1988: 1–12.

Walden, Matthias. "Spielende Kinder hinter dem Stacheldraht." *Der Tagesspiegel*, June 16, 1963: 3.

"Was SFB und ZDF verschwiegen." *Der Tagesspiegel*, July 20, 1974: 2.

"Der Weg zur Soveränität." *Der Tagesspiegel*, May 8, 1955: 25.

"Weizsäcker nennt 8. Mai tag der Befreiung und Ende eines Irrweges." *Der Tagesspiegel*, May 9, 1985: 1.

Wiesel, Elie. "Gedenken vor der Wannsee-Villa." *Der Tagesspiegel*, May 9, 1990: 8.

Wolle, Stefan. "Lebendiges Bewußtsein gegen paranoide Angst." *Der Tagesspiegel*, June 17, 1993: 6.

"Der Wortlaut der Rede Heinemanns zum 25. Jahrestag des Kriegsendes." *Der Tagesspiegel*, May 7, 1970: 9.
"Zentrum der Juden in der Mitte Berlins." *Der Tagesspiegel*, May 7, 1995: 1.
"Zeugnis der neuen deutschen Demokratie." *Der Tagesspiegel*, November 11, 1958: 9.
"Zum Gedenken an die 'Kristallnacht.'" *Der Tagesspiegel*, November 9, 1948: 6.
"Zum gedenken der Kriegsgefangenen." *Der Tagesspiegel*, May 8, 1955: 2.

Der Spiegel

"Fernsehen: Gaskammern a la Hollywood?" *Der Spiegel*, May 15, 1978: 228–231.
"Fernsehen: Nachwirkungen von 'Holocaust.'" *Der Spiegel*, May 7, 1979: 202, 205.
"'Holocaust': Die Vergangenheit kommt zurück." *Der Spiegel*, January 29, 1979: 17–34.
"Ist die Schuld verjährt?" *Der Spiegel*, November 30, 1998.
Kielar, Wieslaw. "'Niemand kommt hier raus.'" *Der Spiegel*, February 5, 1979: 36–49.
"Kriegsverbrechen." *Der Spiegel*, June 15, 1960: 20–33.

Die Zeit

"Ein Datum." *Die Zeit*, November 12, 1993: 1.
Dönhoff, Marion Gräfin. "Das Gewissen steht auf." *Die Zeit*, July 15, 1954: 17.
Dönhoff, Marion Gräfin. "Heusingers Tagesbefehl." *Die Zeit*, July 17, 1959: 1.
Dönhoff, Marion Gräfin. "25 Jahre nach Hitler." *Die Zeit*, May 8, 1970: 1.
Dönhoff, Marion Gräfin. "Verschwörer gegen das Unrecht." *Die Zeit*, July 20, 1984: 3.
Dönhoff, Marion Gräfin. "Die Last der Kindeskinder." *Die Zeit*, May 10, 1985: 1.
Ebert, Wolfgang. "Die Amerikaner!" *Die Zeit*, May 5, 1995: 2.
Freund, Michael. "Die Wochen, die ein Jahrtausend zerstörten." *Die Zeit*, May 5, 1955: 2.
Hofmann, Gunter. "Eine Woche in Deutschland." *Die Zeit*, May 12, 1995: 4.
Janßen, Karl-Heinz. "Wollen wir noch eine Nation sein?" *Die Zeit*, June 16, 1978: 1.
Janßen, Karl-Heinz. "Die Revolution aus dem Stegreif." *Die Zeit*, June 18, 1993: 13–16.
Kielmansegg, Johann A. Graf. "'An jedem anderen Tag, nur heute nicht . . .'" *Die Zeit*, July 21, 1949: 10.
Koch, Thilo. "Ist Deutschland doch teilbar?" *Die Zeit*, June 12, 1958: 3.
Leicht, Robert. "Im Schatten der Schande." *Die Zeit*, November 11, 1988: 1.
Leicht, Robert. "Nur im Untergang lag die Befreiung." *Die Zeit*, May 5, 1995: 1.
Robinsohn, Hans J. "Ein Versuch, sich zu behaupten." *Die Zeit*, November 7, 1958: 4.
Sack, Manfred. "Auf wen wartest du eigentlich?" *Die Zeit*, May 9, 1975: 52.
Sack, Manfred. "Vollständig irre." *Die Zeit*, May 5, 1995: 2.
Sternburg, Wilhelm von. "Ein Flammenzeichen." *Die Zeit*, July 15, 1994: 16.
Strothmann, Dietrich. "Haltungen—Fehlhaltungen." *Die Zeit*, May 7, 1965: 21.
Völkein, Ulrich. "Nochmal nach Theresienstadt." *Die Zeit*, November 10, 1978: 10.
Werte, Wolfram. "'Jude gleich Partisan.'" *Die Zeit*, May 5, 1995: 19.
Wette, Wolfram. "Als Deutschland sterben sollte." *Die Zeit*, May 4, 2000: 84.
Zundel, Rolf. "Schlußstrich unter die Vergangenheit?" *Die Zeit*, November 10, 1978: 9.

Other Print Media Sources

"Der Arzt von Stalingrad." *Stuttgarter Zeitung*, February 22, 1958. LBS newspaper clippings archive.

Blum, Heiko. "Die Blonden sind blond." *Rheinische Post* (Düsseldorf). LBS newspaper clippings archive.

Cohen, Roger. "Germany Searches For 'Normality.'" *New York Times*, November 29, 1998: 10.

Daniel, Peter. "Kurt Hoffmanns 'Das Haus in der Karpfengasse.'" *Die Andere Zeitung* (Hamburg).

"Des Meeres und des Krieges Wellen." *Stuttgarter Zeitung*, August 30, 1957. LBS newspaper clippings archive.

"Harold Reinl wurde getötet." *Nürenberger Nachrichten*, October 10, 1986. LBS newspaper clippings archive.

Hermann, Hugo. "Ein Film klagt an." *Tägliche Ründschau*, September 5, 1948. LBS newspaper clippings archive.

Kaeppner, Joachim. "Mehr Verbrechen." *Süddeutscher Zeitung*, November 24, 2000: 15.

"*Lang ist der Weg*/zu einer Film-Diskussion." *Der Kurier*, October 11, 1948. LBS newspaper clippings archive.

"Lang ist der Weg." *Westfälishce Rundschau* (Dortmund), January 24, 1955. LBS newspaper clipping archive.

"Lang ist der Weg." *Westfalenpost* (Hagen), September 23, 1952. LBS newspaper clipping archive.

Lange, Rudolf. "Canaris—Verräter oder Held?" *Die Welt*, January 3, 1955. LBS newspaper clippings archive.

"Lob für Stalingrad-Film." *Welt am Sonntag* (Berlin/West), July 27, 1958. LBS newspaper clippings archive.

Miserony, J. Hyzdal von. *Mann ohne Namen* in *Hören und Sehen*. ARD, July 20, 1959.

Prantl, Heribert. "Wie geht Erinnerung?" *Süddeutsche Zeitung*, May 8, 2000: 4.

Stempel, Hans. "Canaris." *Deutsche Volkszeitung* (Düsseldorf), January 22, 1955. LBS newspaper clippings archive.

"Tschechische Hilfe für Kurt Hoffmann." *Neue Zürcher Zeitung*, February 24, 1962.

"Völkerversöhnung muss anders aussehen." *Deutsche Woche* (Munich) August 6, 1958. LBS newspaper clippings archive.

Wichmann, Dominik. "These richtig, Bilder falsch?" *Süddeutscher Zeitung*, October 16, 1999: 17.

Willms, Johannes. "Erdrückende Beweislast." *Süddeutscher Zeitung*, October 21, 1999: 15.

East German—Other

"Die Dulles waren auch dabei." *Die Wahrheit*, June 3/4, 1978. DRA newspaper clippings archive.

"Ein Film—politisch gesehen." *Berliner Zeitung*, September 8, 1948. LBS newspaper clippings archive.

"Mörder, Schläger und Brandstifter." *Die Wahrheit*, June 10/11, 1978. DRA newspaper clippings archive.

"Schildern Sie uns Ihre Erlebnisse." *Berliner Zeitung*, January 14, 1975: 7.

Television Programs

With archival reference information.

East German

Als die Synagogen brannten. Dir. Guenter Wittenbecher. DDR-F, 1988. DRA Lagernr.: AC 0364.

Das Attentat auf Hitler. Dir. Rolf Schnabel. DEFA-Studio Dok.-Filme, 1984. DRA AC 2246.

Die Bilder des Zeugen Schattmann. Dir. Kurt Jung-Alsen. DEFA, 1971. DRA Lagernr.: AC 5040 (Part 1), AC 5041 (Part 2), AC 5042 (Part 3), and AC 5043 (Part 4).

Festveranstaltung des ZK der SED der Regierung der DDR und des Nationalrates zum 15. Jahrestag der Befreiung. DFF, May 7, 1960. DRA Lagernr.: 04429/93561.

Kundgebung anläßlich des Kapitulationsfeiertages. DFF, May 7, 1965. DRA Lagernr.: 05368/94365.

Leutnant Yorck von Wartenberg. Dir. Peter Vogel. DEFA-Studio Spielfilme, 1981. DRA AC 7315.

Manifestation der FDJ und der Pionierorganisation 'Ernst Thälmann' anläßlich des 40. Jahrestages des Sieges über den Hitlerfaschismus und der Befreiung des Deutschen Volkes. DDR-F, May 7, 1985. DRA Lagernr.: FAZ 02634.

Die Nacht der Pogrome. DDR-F, 1982. DRA Lagernr.: FAZ 02198.

Revolution am Telefon. Dir. Günter Stahnke and Karl Gass. DEFA-Studio Dok.-Filme, 1964. (1) "Das Attentat und der Prozeß." DRA Lagernr.: AC 12716.

(2) "Legende und Wirklichkeit." DRA Lagernr.: AC 12717.

Ruhm und Ehre den sowejtischen Helden. DDR-F, May 8, 1960.

Stauffenberg: 13 Bilder über einen Täter. Dir. Erich Thiede. DDR-F, 1989. DRA AC 1685.

Strasse zur Freiheit. Dir. Horst Schubert. DFF, May 8 or 13, 1970. DRA Lagernr.: AC 11659.

Wir haben nichts zu bereuen. Dir. Ulrich Teschner. DDR-F, 1984. DRA AC 1169.

West German

Als die Synagogen brannten . . . ZDF, November 8, 1988.

Als sie in Deutschland mit Steinen nach uns warfen. Dir. Rolf Seelmann-Eggebert. NDR, November 10, 1978. Archive Nr.: 1034282.

Eine Armee wird mißbraucht. Dir. Jürgen Neven-Dumont. NDR, February 1, 1963.

Aufstand des Gewissens. Dir. Hannes Huepper. ARD, July 20, 1954.

Die Befreiung. Dir. Ekkehard Kuhn and Carl-Ludwig Paeschke. ZDF, May 7, 1995.

Bernhard Lichtenberg. By Maria Matray and Answald Krüger. Dir. Peter Beauvais. ZDF, July 20, 1965.

Die Bertinis. ZDF, October 31, 1988 (Part 1); November 1 (Part 2); November 6 (Part 3); November 7 (Part 4); November 8 (Part 5).

Bilanz eines Verlustes: Jüdische Mitbürger in Deutschland—gestern und heute. ZDF, November 8, 1963.

Denn ihrer war die Hölle. Dir. Horst Siebecke. BR Archive Number 8210/42058.

Deutsche gegen Hitler: Ein Rückblick auf den Widerstand im Dritten Reich. From F. A. Krummacher. ZDF, July 20, 1969.

Deutschlandlied. Dir. Tom Toelle. ZDF, May 8, 10, and 14, 1995.

Einer aus Königsbronn: Der Widerstandskämpfer Georg Elser. From Eva Witte. ARD/SDR, November 7, 1998.

Er wollte Hitler töten. By Juergen Engert. ARD/SFB, July 20, 1989.

Der Fall Nebe. Part 1 "Glanz und Elend einer großen Karriere;" Part 2 "Widerstand, Flucht und Ende." Dir. Georg Tressler. ZDF, November 18–19, 1964.

Gespräch des Monats. Discussion leader Fritz Bruehl. ARD, July 20, 1959.

Das Haus in der Karpfengasse. Dir. Kurt Hoffmann. WDR, March 7, 9, and 11, 1965.

Hitler und der Zweite Weltkrieg. ZDF, August 27, 1964.

Hitlerjugend—Mißbrauch einer Generation. Dir. Horst Siebecke. BR, April 13, 1965. BR Production Number 37913.

Im Schatten der Väter. By Walter Leo and Lothar Janßen. ARD, July 20, 1969. NDR Archive 1025003.

Juden in München. BR, April 3, 1972. BR Archive Nr.: 314300 / 14414.

Das letzte Ghetto. Dir. Arno Rattay. ZDF, November 8, 1978.

Das letzte Kapitel. Dir. F. A. Krummacher. ZDF, May 8, 1965.

Mann ohne Namen. Dir. Curt Goetz-Pflug. ARD, July 20, 1959.

Netzwerk—Adam von Trott zu Solz und der 20. Juli 1944. By Henric Wuermeling. ARD, July 20, 1994. BR Archive Production Number 95553.

Pimpf war jeder. Dir. Erwin Leiser. ZDF, May 7, 1995.

Reichskristallnacht: Die November-Pogrome 1938. BR, November 9, 1988. BR Archive Number 80285.

Schicksalstag 9. November. ARD, November 9, 1953.

Schicksalstag des deutshcen Volkes. ARD, November 9, 1958.

Stalingrad. Dir. Gustav Burmester. NDR, January 31, 1963.

Ein Tag. Dir. Egon Monk. NDR, May 6, 1965.

Die verschlossene Tür. Dir. Dieter Lemmels. ZDF, March 10, 1965.

Die Verschwindenen Stetl. Dir. Karl Nikolaus Renner. BR (unknown broadcast date, 1980s). Archive Number 70403.

Waldhausstr. 20. Dir. John Olden. NDR, October 23, 1960. NDR Archive Nr.: 45927/03.

Warum habt ihr Hitler widerstanden? 1. Das andere Deutschland. From Guido Knopp and Ralf Piechowiak. ZDF, July 18, 1984. *Warum habt ihr Hitler widerstanden? 2. Das andere Deutschland im Exil.* From Achim Gerloff. ZDF, July 19, 1984.

Widerstand—Eine Diskussion. ZDF, July 20, 1963.

Widerstand—Kampf gegen Hitler. NDR Archive 1062093 for part 6 and 7.

Other Television Programs:

Lost King of the Maya. Dir. David Stewart. Nova-PBS, April 16, 2002.

Index

Breinigsville, PA USA
03 December 2010
250518BV00005B/1/P